THE WIVES

THE WIVES

THE WOMEN BEHIND RUSSIA'S LITERARY GIANTS

ALEXANDRA POPOFF

PEGASUS BOOKS
NEW YORK LONDON

THE WIVES

Pegasus Books LLC
80 Broad Street, 5th Floor
New York, NY 10004

Copyright © 2012 by Alexandra Popoff

First Pegasus Books cloth edition 2012

Interior design by Maria Fernandez

All rights reserved. No part of this book may be reproduced in whole or in part without written permission from the publisher, except by reviewers who may quote brief excerpts in connection with a review in a newspaper, magazine, or electronic publication; nor may any part of this book be reproduced, stored in a retrieval system, or transmitted in any form or by any means electronic, mechanical, photocopying, recording, or other, without written permission from the publisher.

Library of Congress Cataloging-in-Publication Data is available.

ISBN: 978-1-60598-366-0

10 9 8 7 6 5 4 3 2 1

Printed in the United States of America
Distributed by W. W. Norton & Company

To My Parents

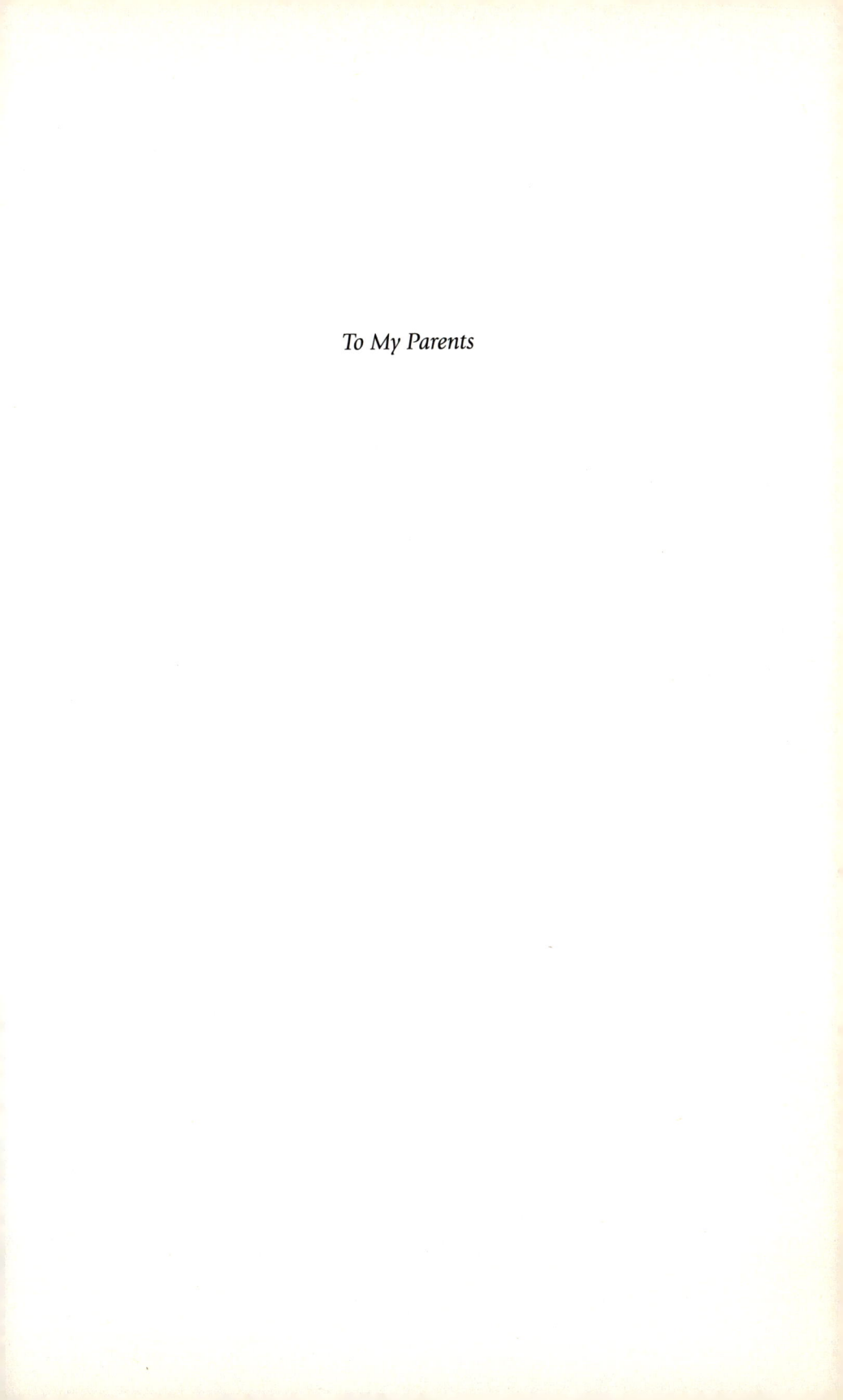

A Note on Russian Names

In the Russian language, a formal address requires the use of first name and patronymic (derived from the father's first name). In the text I use only first names as this is more familiar to a Western reader.

With few exceptions, I use the masculine form of family names (e.g., Anna Dostoevsky, Sophia Tolstoy, Véra Nabokov, Elena Bulgakov, and Natalya Solzhenitsyn). In Russian, these names have feminine endings: Dostoevskaya, Tolstaya, Nabokova, Bulgakova, and Solzhenitsyna. Nadezhda Mandelstam's name has the same ending in both English and Russian.

The names Anna Karenina, Natasha Rostova, Anna Akhmatova, and Marina Tsvetaeva are familiar to the reader and appear unchanged in the text.

Among family and friends, a diminutive of the first name is commonly used; for example, Tanya for Tatyana, Masha for Maria, Sasha for Alexandra, Fedya for Fyodor, and Vanya (or Vanechka) for Ivan.

In this book Lev is used interchangeably with Leo.

Prologue

I grew up in Moscow in the family of a writer and used to believe that every writer's wife was involved in her husband's creative work as much as my mother was. She collaborated with my father from the moment his novel was conceived till its completion. She was a natural storyteller and, at my father's request, talked about her childhood in Kiev during Stalin's mass purges of the 1930s. My grandfather had a job in a ministry as a speechwriter, and his family lived in an apartment house populated with government officials. During the height of the purges, my mother had witnessed the arrests in their building. Every night, she listened to the sound of the "black marias" stopping at their entrance. In the morning, some of their neighbors' doors were sealed; the adults had disappeared in prisons or camps and their children sent to orphanages. My grandmother kept a razor under her pillow to escape such a fate: there was at least personal choice in suicide. Fortunately, my grandfather was transferred to a different bureaucracy in Moscow where, because of the sweeping arrests, Soviet secret police lost track of him; then the war started.

In the fall of 1941, my mother saw gulag inmates at a railway station, a sight she would never forget: men in prison clothes were forced to kneel on the snow-covered platform while guards counted them, like cattle. This was just one of my mother's stories employed in my father's novel *July 1941*, among the first anti-Stalinist works published in the Soviet Union.[1] The railway scene later became a bone of contention between my parents: mother claimed the scene as "hers," while father insisted he had other sources.

My mother was her husband's first reader, editor, and literary adviser. She routinely discussed the scenes from his novels, and when she proofread, she lived his fiction again. In childhood I used to believe that there was nothing unusual about my parents' collaboration and that, in fact, a writer's wife was a profession itself.

This was not incorrect: literary wives in Russia traditionally performed a variety of tasks as stenographers, editors, typists, researchers, translators, and publishers. Russian writers married women with good literary taste who were profoundly absorbed with their art and felt comfortable in secondary roles. Living under restrictive regimes, the women battled censorship and preserved the writers' illicit archives, often putting themselves at risk. They established a tradition of their own, unmatched in the West.

∽

Ithaca, September 1958: An evocative photograph shows Véra Nabokov at her typewriter and a mirror-reflected image of the writer himself, dictating. Throughout their marriage of fifty-two years, Véra was Vladimir Nabokov's assistant and inspiration for his best thoughts, as he said. In 1965, Nabokov described their work together in an interview:

> Well . . . my very kind and patient wife . . . sits down at her typewriter and I, I dictate, I dictate off the cards to her, making some changes and very often, very often discussing this or that.

She might say, 'Oh, you don't say that, you can't say that.'
'Well, let's see, perhaps, I can change it.'²

Nabokov's marriage was central to his writing: Véra contributed ideas, assisted with research, edited manuscripts, read proofs, translated his works, conducted his correspondence, and when he taught at Cornell assisted in preparing his lectures and marked students' papers. As Saul Steinberg remarked, "It would be difficult to write about Véra without mentioning Vladimir. But it would be impossible to write about Vladimir without mentioning Véra."³

Although Véra worked alongside Nabokov, she remained discreet about her involvement and, as she told an interviewer, would even panic when finding her name in his footnotes. Her concern for Nabokov's reputation was paramount and she preferred to remain in his shadow, reluctant to share private information.

The truth is, in their country of origin, the Nabokovs' close literary marriage was not unusual. Véra was simply following in the path of her great predecessors, Sophia Tolstoy and Anna Dostoevsky, their husbands' indispensable aides and collaborators. To use Nabokov's expression, these women formed "a single shadow" with the writers.

When Leo Tolstoy first met Dostoevsky's widow, he exclaimed, "How astonishing that our writers' wives look so much like their husbands!" Tolstoy was referring to a particular bond between the writers and their muses. In her reminiscences, Anna Dostoevsky describes the episode with a mild irony, inherent in her style:

"Do you really think I look like Fyodor Mikhailovich?" I asked happily.
"Extraordinarily like! It was just precisely someone like you that I've been picturing as Dostoevsky's wife!"⁴

Tolstoy's reaction when he saw Anna was both amusing and noteworthy: he had never met Dostoevsky, so it was certainly not a physical resemblance that he had in mind. Upon meeting Anna, Tolstoy sensed an aura, which belonged specifically to Dostoevsky's fictional world and which his widow was now bearing.

Years later, when Tolstoy died, Boris Pasternak observed Sophia at the funeral. He describes his feeling of awe before the woman who had assisted the great novelist and was a model for his heroines; she seemed inseparable from Tolstoy's creations:

> In the room lay a mountain like Elbrus, and she was one of its large, detached crags; the room was filled by a storm cloud the size of half the sky, and she was one of its separate lightnings.[5]

Sophia admired Tolstoy's writing while still a girl, when they first met. Upon marrying him at eighteen, she settled with Tolstoy at Yasnaya Polyana, then an isolated estate and ideally suited for the writer. She was always eager to assist him by copying his works and contributing her diaries and letters, which gave him a deeper insight into the female psyche. Sophia would copy his manuscripts overnight: their growing family demanded her attention during the day. This work was never a burden: she was artistically gifted and Tolstoy's writing fascinated her:

> As I copy I experience a whole new world of emotions, thoughts and impressions. Nothing touches me so deeply as his ideas, his genius . . . I write very quickly, so I can follow the story and catch the mood, but slowly enough to be able to stop, reflect upon each new idea and discuss it with him later. He and I often talk about the novel together, and for some reason he listens to what I have to say (which makes me very proud) and trusts my opinions.[6]

In 1865, during *War and Peace*, a visitor to their estate called Sophia "the perfect wife for a writer" and "the nursemaid" of her husband's talent.[7] Tolstoy's most celebrated novels were created during their first two decades of marriage—and these works draw closely from their family life. During the following decades, Sophia continued to inspire Tolstoy and contribute to him as his publisher, translator, photographer, and biographer.

Although the Tolstoys' marriage has been described many times, it remains little understood. Sophia did not receive credit for her many contributions to the writer. Instead, she became widely criticized for not supporting Tolstoy during his religious phase when he renounced his copyright and property. When Tolstoy fled their estate at the age of eighty-two, the world around Sophia turned into a courtroom where she stood accused. Regardless of the fact that Tolstoy himself chose to flee because he wanted to live out his days as a simple pilgrim and die a simple death, Sophia was blamed for his departure. She was prevented from entering Tolstoy's room in a stationmaster's house at Astapovo where he lay dying, and so the great man died surrounded by his disciples.

The Russian public treated their writers as prophets and gave little personal sympathy to their wives; the latters' dedication was taken for granted. After Fyodor Dostoevsky's death, Anna received delegations from across the country that, to her annoyance, came to speak about her late husband's importance for the national literature, about the "great loss Russia had suffered." When someone finally expressed consideration for her personally, she seized the stranger's hand and kissed it in gratitude.

Anna was a twenty-year-old stenographer when she received an assignment to take dictation from Dostoevsky. The circumstances of their encounter were dramatic: in 1866, the writer was trapped in an impossible contract, which forced him to produce a full-length novel in just four weeks. Should he fail to meet the obligation, he would lose the rights to all his work.

For twenty-six days, Anna took his dictation and transcribed her notes at home; due to her perseverance, Dostoevsky escaped catastrophe. When the novel *The Gambler* was completed, he realized he could no longer write without his collaborator: dictating became his preferred way of composition. He told Anna of an insightful dream, that he found a sparkling diamond among his papers. The writer did indeed find his prize.

Dostoevsky proposed to Anna through a thinly disguised story about an elderly, sick, and debt-ridden artist, in love with an exuberant girl. Would the girl marry the artist, or would that be too much of a sacrifice? For Anna, who had been "enraptured" with Dostoevsky's novels since childhood, the idea of helping him in his work and caring for him was attractive.

> My love was entirely cerebral. . . . It was more like adoration and reverence for a man of such talent and such noble qualities of spirit. . . . The dream of becoming his life companion, of sharing his labors and lightening his existence, of giving him happiness—this was what took hold of my imagination; and Fyodor Mikhailovich[8] became my god, my idol.[9]

Her attitude to Dostoevsky did not change during fourteen years of marriage filled with financial uncertainty; despite privations, she considered her life to "have been one of exceptional happiness."[10] Anna had committed to paper many of his novels, including his most celebrated, *Crime and Punishment* and *The Brothers Karamazov*. Dostoevsky called her his collaborator and guardian angel: she nursed him through his gambling addiction and his epileptic attacks, and helped him return to writing, time and time again. Eventually, Anna paid off Dostoevsky's debts by bringing out his books and managing his business affairs. But as she remarked in her memoir, it was not only for profit that she became a publisher—she found an interesting occupation for herself.

Dostoevsky remained her idol after he died: Anna collaborated with his biographers and established his museums. In the same way, Sophia during her widowhood continued to work for Tolstoy: she prepared his letters for publication, collected everything about him that appeared in print, catalogued his library, and toured visitors around their estate, which she preserved intact.

Both women have meticulously documented their own and their husbands' lives through their diaries, memoirs, and correspondence. But Anna Dostoevsky was far more guarded than Sophia: she kept stenographic records and, in addition, used her own code, inaccessible even to another stenographer. Unlike Tolstoy, Dostoevsky could not read his wife's diaries, a wise arrangement given his suspiciousness and volatility. Anna transcribed her notes thirty years later when preparing her diary for publication. She did not want readers to know her actual experiences and, furthermore, tried to create an improved portrait of Dostoevsky as a private man. To accomplish this, she had to sacrifice accuracy and even rewrite some episodes. None of this was known until the end of the twentieth century, when a Russian expert managed to crack her code and her surviving original notebooks were published.[11] This new biographical material gives insights into her character and the couple's relationship during their first and most trying year together.

Sophia Tolstoy's and Anna Dostoevsky's inspired collaboration with Russia's most prominent writers have undoubtedly influenced literary marriages in the twentieth century. But in the age of Stalin's political dictatorship, free expression ceased to exist and writing could be ruled a crime punishable by death. For these women, assisting genuine writers required extraordinary courage.

When Osip Mandelstam, a major twentieth-century poet, was sent to the gulag in 1938, his wife, Nadezhda, barely escaped the same fate. But she took the risk of concealing his illicit archive: if his poetry were confiscated and destroyed, this would also result in his spiritual demise. For decades, she led a nomadic life, hiding from the authorities and supporting herself with teaching. What kept her alive was her mission to publish Mandelstam's works and tell his story. Nadezhda memorized much of his verse and prose, making her memory an additional storage. After Stalin's death in 1953, she committed to paper Mandelstam's works, along with background information, and began to struggle for posthumous publication.

Some of the best twentieth-century Russian literature survives today only because these women had the courage to preserve it.

Elena Bulgakov married the ingenious and tormented satirical writer to whom Stalin personally denied publication. Mikhail Bulgakov's only play that could be staged in the 1930s was *The Days of the Turbins*, inexplicably Stalin's favorite. The tyrant, however, refused publication of his subsequent plays, and Elena witnessed the continual banning of Bulgakov's productions.

In her diary, which she courageously kept during the purges of the 1930s, Elena chronicled Bulgakov's harassment and the arrests of their friends—actors, writers, directors, and military officers. Through Bulgakov's depression, their penury, and his debilitating kidney disease, she remained a source of hope and strength. Elena was the inspiration for a principal character in *The Master and Margarita*, also a writer's wife, who allies with supernatural forces to save the novel of her beloved master.

In 1940, when dying from the kidney disease and by this time almost blind, Bulgakov dictated to Elena his revisions for *The Master and Margarita*. Now published worldwide, this final masterpiece reached the reader only because she preserved the archive and tenaciously pursued publication, achieving her goal twenty-five years after Bulgakov's death.

Many writers in history relied on their wives for moral and practical support. Nora Joyce was the "rock" of James Joyce's life as well as his model, but although she inspired Molly Bloom in *Ulysses*, she never read the book nor did she take interest in his creativity. Unlike Nora, Russian literary wives actively helped produce literature. These women became so much a part of it that they commonly used the word "we" to describe the progress of their husbands' work.

The writers' dependence on their wives, from inspiration to technical help, is surprising. Tolstoy could have hired a scribe to copy his novels, but he wanted Sophia to do the work because she was his first audience. His literature united them: Sophia would even refer to *War and Peace* as their child. Dostoevsky, Nabokov, Mandelstam, and Bulgakov wanted their wives to take dictation, so they could receive instant responses to their writing. Nadezhda Mandelstam intimated that the poet did not write a single line on his own, because she recorded his verse as she watched him compose. Mandelstam expected her to even hold variations of his poems in her memory—and this "technicality," in Joseph Brodsky's words, strengthened the bond of their marriage.[12] When Mandelstam died in a camp, Nadezhda survived "for the joy breathed by his verse." Theirs was a relationship between two intellectuals and artists (she was a painter), but Nadezhda adapted her intellect to serve her husband.

As Nadezhda remarked, Mandelstam had made her "a complete partner in his life."[13] When her brother remarked that she had become the poet's echo, Mandelstam replied: "That's how *we* like it." Nadezhda's loss of identity resembles Véra Nabokov's: both women were their husbands' invisible creative partners and seemed to prefer it that way.

When, in 2002, I met Natalya Solzhenitsyn in Moscow, I asked her whether she knew of any biographer writing about her life. She replied, in the manner of a Véra Nabokov: "I would never allow that."[14] Natalya did not regret abandoning her own career as a mathematician, since she considered her collaboration with Solzhenitsyn far more important.

Natalya met Solzhenitsyn at twenty-eight, when she was studying for her doctorate in the late 1960s. He needed a reliable helper to type *The First Circle* but keep their collaboration secret. His dissident friends recommended Natalya, who had worked as a literary assistant to none other than Nadezhda Mandelstam. Natalya, of course, knew Solzhenitsyn from his earlier novella, *One Day in the Life of Ivan Denisovich*, which, as the first published account of Stalin's crimes, rocked the entire country. Upon meeting its author, she took up his literary work and his struggle against the Communist state.

In 1974, when Solzhenitsyn was arrested and deported, Natalya masterminded the smuggling of his illicit archive to the West. The writer needed all his material to go on working, and Natalya said she would only join him when all of his papers were saved. By then, the couple had had three small children together, the youngest still a toddler. She risked her own and her children's safety by organizing a secret network of allies. Acting with steely resolve, Natalya connected with foreign correspondents and diplomats who could transport suitcases of Solzhenitsyn's documents. When the archive was safely distributed, Natalya crossed the Soviet border with her children and their bulky luggage, which included Solzhenitsyn's writing desk.

Natalya Solzhenitsyn would surprise visitors in the West with the amount of labor she invested to assist her husband. Aside from handling massive research for his historical novels, Natalya edited and typeset Solzhenitsyn's collected works. In addition, there were secretarial duties because Solzhenitsyn, like Nabokov, rarely picked up the phone. Always keen to give his wife credit, Solzhenitsyn called himself the luckiest among Russian writers to have found such a devoted collaborator.

As Véra Nabokov remarked during the first decade of her marriage, "Someone should write a book on the influence a woman bears on her husband, in other words on stimulation, and inspiration."[15] However, she did not write this book or any other on her own. At the age of eighty-two, still spending full days at her writing desk translating Nabokov's fiction, Véra believed she lacked epistolary gifts. Elena Bulgakov never wrote a book of reminiscences about her husband, although it was something she wanted to accomplish. Anna Dostoevsky penned brilliant memoirs, but insisted that she was "utterly lacking in literary talent."[16] And although Sophia Tolstoy wrote fiction, she did not live to see it published.

The picture was different in the West where women, as early as the eighteenth century, established themselves as successful novelists and competed with male writers. The Fitzgeralds' marriage is a good example of such rivalry. Zelda had no intention of submitting her ideas and themes to her husband or of "being a footnote in someone else's life," to use Martha Gellhorn's famous words.

When Gellhorn visited Nadezhda Mandelstam in Moscow, she spoke casually about her former husband Ernest Hemingway: "Why do they like this chatterbox in your country?"[17] Gellhorn resented her fame as Hemingway's wife, an attitude that surprised Nadezhda, since Russian writers' wives were usually their ambassadors.

There is no simple explanation why in Russia these gifted women did not pursue independent writing careers. One needs to know, however, that until the twentieth century Russian literature was predominantly male. Writing prose was not yet a province of women—the majority found a niche writing memoirs, letters, and diaries. This made an impact on how the women told their stories—they often spoke to the world through their husbands' genius.

CHAPTER ONE

Anna Dostoevsky: Cherishing a Memory

Few writers describe their day of birth as a festive event, but for Anna it portended her later mission of being married to Dostoevsky. She was born in St. Petersburg on August 30, 1846, the feast day of St. Alexander Nevsky,[18] near the monastery built in his name. When a cheerful procession, which included the Emperor himself, began to move out of the monastery gates to the tolling of church bells and holiday music, Anna set out on her life's road. Being born on a feast day was believed a good omen. "The prophecy came true," Anna writes. "Despite all the material misfortunes and moral sufferings it has been my lot to bear, I consider my life to have been one of exceptional happiness, and I would not wish to change anything in it."[19]

She was christened in a parish church of Alexander Nevsky Monastery, the place where her parents had been wed; Dostoevsky would be buried in the monastery cemetery thirty-five years later. In her mind's eye, the two great names were interrelated: Alexander

Nevsky, a national hero and a saint, flared at her dawn and sunset, while Dostoevsky was, in her words, the sun of her life as well as her god.

Anna came from a family whose parents became drawn to each other at first sight. They did not even speak the same language when they met: Anna's mother was Swedish and her father Ukrainian. Maria Anna Miltopeus grew up in a Swedish community in Finland, in the ancient city of Turku (Åbo in Swedish). Some of her prominent ancestors, clerics and scholars (one was a Lutheran bishop), were buried inside the Cathedral of Turku,[20] the Westminster Abbey of Finland. At nineteen, Maria Anna became engaged to a Swedish officer, but he was killed in action in Hungary. For ten years after his death, she did not consider marrying—even though her strikingly good looks and fine soprano voice (she had dreamed of a stage career) had attracted suitors. Later, her relatives in Petersburg, with whom she was staying, hosted a party with several young bachelors. Grigory Ivanovich Snitkin[21], an unimposing civil servant of forty-two, was not considered a possible match (he simply came with one of the guests), but he alone impressed the young Swede. As Maria Anna told her family, "I liked the old fellow better—the one who kept telling stories and laughing." Because their different faiths presented an obstacle to marriage, Maria Anna, a Lutheran, decided to enter the Orthodox Church. (After converting, she took the name Anna Nikolaevna.) Later, she integrated Orthodox rites with her Lutheran prayer book.

Although occupying a modest rank, Snitkin was a well-educated man who had graduated from a Jesuit school and worshiped literature and the arts. A theater connoisseur since youth, he revered a prominent tragic actress, Asenkova. When Anna and her sister were small, he took them to Asenkova's tomb and asked them to kneel and pray "for the repose of the soul of the greatest artist of our time."[22] This incident made a deep impression on Anna, who would revere Dostoevsky's talent as her father had admired the late actress.

Anna's family lived "without quarrels, dramas, and catastrophes." Her parents' characters were well matched: a strong-willed and practical mother and a romantic and timid father. Snitkin accepted his wife's authority, only reserving one liberty for himself—collecting curios and antique porcelains. The family's friendly atmosphere generated Anna's balanced and cheerful character, which would enchant Dostoevsky, who himself was tempestuous and grim. Anna—a middle child with an older sister and a younger brother—was her father's favorite. Like Snitkin, she would live for a month under the spell of the opera and ballet performances the family attended on holidays.

For a girl of her time, Anna received an excellent education. She studied in a primary school where most subjects were taught in German, the language her mother spoke at home. (Anna would become Dostoevsky's translator in Germany and in Switzerland, where they traveled shortly after marrying.) Enrolling in the newly opened Petersburg Mariinskaya Gymnasium,[23] a secondary school for girls, she graduated with a silver medal, a distinction that, in her eyes, would justify her marriage to the brilliant writer.

Dostoevsky's name was familiar to her in childhood: her father called him the greatest among living writers and subscribed to his literary magazine *Time*.[24] Fresh issues of this magazine with installments of Dostoevsky's novel *Insulted and Injured* were fought over in their family; his characters' names became household words. Anna was dubbed Netochka Nezvanova, after the heroine of Dostoevsky's novel of the same title. At fifteen, she cried over *Notes from the House of the Dead*, an account of Dostoevsky's life in the Siberian prison camp he was sent to for dissident activity. In the late 1840s, with European revolutions in the air, Dostoevsky had briefly participated in the Petrashevsky circle[25], an intellectual group that discussed socialist utopian ideas. Anna was three years old when in 1849 Dostoevsky was convicted and sentenced to exile with hard labor.

She belonged to the generation of Russian women who pursued higher education and careers following the Great Reforms of the

1860s under the Tsar Alexander II: "The idea of independence for me, a girl of the sixties, was a very precious idea." In 1864, she entered the recently opened Pedagogical Institute to study natural sciences: "Physics, chemistry, and zoology seemed a revelation to me, and I registered in the school's department of mathematics and physics." But lectures on Russian literature interested her more than science classes, and after her first year she left this school without regret.

It was also a time when her elderly father became ill and she wanted to be with him to care for her "beloved invalid." She read Dickens's novels to him, unaware they were also Dostoevsky's preferred reading. Her father was upset that she left school and, to assuage him, Anna enrolled in an evening course in stenography, then a novelty in Russia. A newspaper announcement said that graduates would be employed in the law courts, at meetings of learned societies, and during congresses; this, Anna felt, would give her the economic independence she yearned.

While the first public lecture was not recorded in Russia by a stenographer until 1860, stenography had long been practiced in Germany and in England: Dickens mastered it as a young reporter covering Parliament. The first course available in 1866, which caught Anna's attention, was taught by Professor Pavel Olkhin, who used the Gabelsberger System. A medical doctor, Olkhin also wrote books on popular subjects; one of them, a book about the final days of suicides, fascinated Dostoevsky because of his long-standing interest in the subject.[26]

Olkhin's stenography course became instantly popular and drew a hundred and fifty students, but the majority soon quit. Like others, Anna was saying that it was "all gibberish" and she would never be able to master it, but her father reproached her for lack of persistence, saying she would become a good stenographer—a prophecy on his part.

When her father died later that year, Anna was so distraught that she could not attend classes. Her professor allowed her to complete the course by correspondence, and after three months of practicing shorthand Anna had mastered the skill. By September 1866, she was the only student Professor Olkhin could recommend for literary work.

The day she received her first assignment—and with her favorite author—was the happiest of her life. Dostoevsky wanted to dictate his new novel, she was told, and would pay fifty rubles for the entire project. The idea that she was becoming independent and was able to earn money delighted her so much that "if I were to inherit 500 rubles I wouldn't be as glad. . . ."[27] Olkhin, however, warned Anna that Dostoevsky was difficult to get on with: "He seemed to me such a surly, gloomy man!" This did not shake her confidence because she needed the job: her family was struggling financially after her father's death, and although they had two rental houses, generating two thousand rubles annually, there were also debts.

Anna spent a sleepless night before her appointment, worrying that Dostoevsky would examine her on his novels. "Never having known any literary celebrities in my social circle, I imagined them as being exceptional creatures who had to be spoken to in a special way." She would discover that she remembered Dostoevsky's works better than the writer did himself: he had only "a vague recollection" of what *The Insulted and Injured* was about, he would tell her during their courtship.

On the fateful day of October 4, she left home early to buy a supply of pencils and a portfolio to make her look more businesslike. The Alonkin house where Dostoevsky lived was a large multistoried apartment building occupied by merchants and artisans, and it instantly reminded her of Raskolnikov's house in *Crime and Punishment*. Anna was entering the world of Dostoevsky's heroes: a maid who opened the door was wearing a checked shawl, as in the novel, where it was a shared property of Mrs. Marmeladov and her children. She was told to wait in the poorly furnished dining room, but within minutes Dostoevsky appeared. He led her to his study, a long room with two windows and a high ceiling, which appeared strangely gloomy and hushed. Perhaps it was the dark wallpaper:

"You felt a kind of depression in that dimness and silence,"[28] Anna would remember.

Dostoevsky, of average height, was dressed in a worn blue jacket. He looked rather weary and old, his face unkind, his reddish-brown hair pomaded and carefully smoothed, resembling a wig. But it was his eyes that most struck her because they were not alike—one was dark brown, while the other had a pupil so dilated that she could not see the iris. "This dissimilarity gave his eyes an enigmatic expression."

This appearance was a result of Dostoevsky's injury: during a recent epileptic attack, he had fallen against a sharp object. Almost at the start of the meeting, he announced that he suffered from epilepsy and had had an attack a few days earlier. As she sat at a small table by the door, Dostoevsky nervously paced the room, smoking incessantly and asking random questions.

He asked Anna why she had become a stenographer, whether it was because her family was poor. Wanting to begin the relationship on an equal footing, she replied in a businesslike way that did not allow for familiarity. Her proper behavior at once appealed to Dostoevsky, who thought his stenographer might be a Nihilist, the new type of young person, already captured in literature. (Turgenev had portrayed Russian Nihilists in *Fathers and Sons*, where he also satirized a smoking and vulgar bluestocking, Kukshina.)[29] Moreover, proper young girls did not come to men's apartments unaccompanied. Still nervous and unable to collect his thoughts, Dostoevsky repeatedly asked Anna her name and repeatedly offered a cigarette, which she declined, saying that she did not even like to watch women smoke.

To test her abilities, Dostoevsky dictated a passage from a literary magazine, beginning extremely fast, so that she had to ask him to slow down. When she transcribed her notes, he quickly read them and sharply reprimanded her for a missed comma. Eventually, he told Anna that he was unable to dictate until later that evening, but did not bother to inquire whether this suited her; she felt that he treated her "as a kind of Remington typewriter."[30] Seeing Anna to the door, Dostoevsky told her he was glad his stenographer was a woman because she was less likely to fall into drinking habits and disrupt his work.

> It is impossible to put in words what a depressing and pitiful impression Fyodor Mikhailovich produced on me during our first meeting. He seemed to me absent-minded, heavily preoccupied, helpless, lonesome, irritated, almost sick. He looked so oppressed by his misfortunes that he did not see one's face and was unable to lead a coherent conversation.[31]

This impression was somewhat mended when she returned in the evening and Dostoevsky began to reminisce about his arrest in 1849. Incarcerated in the Peter and Paul Fortress with other members of the Petrashevsky Circle and sentenced to death, he was awaiting the verdict with the other condemned, when suddenly the drums sounded a retreat. That day, when his death penalty was commuted to hard labor, was the happiest of his life, he told Anna: back in his cell, he was singing out loud. Dostoevsky's frankness both surprised and appealed to her: "This man, to all appearances withdrawn and severe, was telling me of his past life in such detail, so openly and naturally, that I couldn't help feeling amazed. . . . His frankness with me on that day . . . pleased me deeply and left me with a wonderful impression of him."

Sensing that his reminiscences put him in the right mood for work, Anna would herself encourage Dostoevsky to talk about his past. He told a whole sequence of sad stories—his harsh childhood, an unhappy marriage to Marya Isaeva, who died of consumption, and a broken engagement with the writer Anna Korvin-Krukovskaya.[32]

When next day she arrived late for the morning dictation, Anna found Dostoevsky in panic: he imagined she had decided to quit and that the portions he had dictated would be lost. He had to deliver a full-size novel in less than a month or lose the rights to his work for nine years. The enslaving contract had been forced on him when he was completing *Crime and Punishment* and under pressure from creditors for his late brother's debts. Anna took this trouble close to heart, becoming determined to meet the deadline and even working nights to transcribe her notes.

Despite the pressure, they established a good working pattern with interludes to discuss the novel. It told about an obsessive gambler living in the fictional city of Roulettenburg, a story based on Dostoevsky's own gambling escapades. When Anna condemned the gambler for his weakness, Dostoevsky explained to her the nature of the addiction he knew firsthand. She liked their evening chats—about his past and the novel—and was pleased that the brilliant writer heeded her "almost childish remarks." He also told her about his travels abroad, how he lost at roulette in Homburg and had to pawn his suitcase. It flattered her vanity that she sat at Dostoevsky's desk when taking his dictations, the very desk where *Crime and Punishment* was written.

Anxious about his looming deadline, Dostoevsky asked whether they could finish in time, and Anna would count up pages of the manuscript to reassure him. "He would often ask, 'And how many pages did we do yesterday? And how many do we have altogether?'" The growing number of completed pages cheered him tremendously: Dostoevsky no longer paced the room while dictating but sat across the table from Anna reading to her from a draft he had prepared the night before.

When the work on the novel was coming to a close, he told Anna it was terribly sad for him to think he could not see her again, for where could he see her? She invited him to visit her and her mother at home. Dostoevsky asked to fix a date immediately and demanded her address (her mother lived in a desolate neighborhood near the Smolny Institute for Noble Maidens); he wrote it down in his blue notebook.

On October 31, Anna brought the final pages of *The Gambler*: the novel had been completed in twenty-six days, just before the deadline. She wore a lilac dress for the first time (while mourning her father's death, she had dressed in black), and when she came in Dostoevsky blushed. She sensed that he would most likely propose, but did not know whether to accept, having written in her diary, "He pleases me very much, but at the same time frightens me because of his irascibility and illness."[33]

Dostoevsky pinned hopes on her for a better future: "But I haven't had any happiness yet . . . I still go on dreaming that I will begin a new, happy life." He also sought her "advice" on whether he should remarry and, if so, what kind of wife he should choose—a kind or an intelligent one. She suggested an intelligent one, but he argued he needed a kind wife: "She'll take pity on me and love me."

Dostoevsky said that he had escaped a catastrophe thanks to her and was enormously pleased with his new way of working, so he would like to dictate to her the final installment of *Crime and Punishment*. And he wanted to celebrate the completion of *The Gambler* with few friends at a restaurant; would she join? She told him that perhaps she would, knowing in her heart that she would be too shy to come.

Because Dostoevsky's time was consumed with writing and making a living, he could not meet women socially. The women with whom he had been involved in the past—Korvin-Krukovskaya and Apollinaria Suslova[34]—were aspiring writers he met through his literary journal *Time*. (Dostoevsky had published Suslova's first novella and had a stormy relationship with her. Suslova, twenty years his junior, matched Dostoevky's own erratic character. Although she put him through torment, she made an important contribution because he repeatedly used her as a model for his heroines. In turn, Suslova described their relationship in her final novella.[35])

Helpless in business matters, Dostoevsky asked Anna's opinion on what he should do if the publisher went into hiding and refused to accept his manuscript of *The Gambler*. She asked her mother to consult a lawyer who advised that Dostoevsky should obtain an official receipt for his novel from a notary or a police officer. When, as expected, his publisher went into hiding, the receipt proved vital.

Anna was caught by surprise when Dostoevsky asked her if she had been abroad and suggested they go together next summer. Dostoevsky's query may have been inspired by the painful memory of his European travel with Suslova three years earlier. During that disastrous trip the femme fatale fell in love with a Spanish medical student and Dostoevsky became victim to his gambling passion. Anna, who knew none of that at the time, replied diplomatically she was not sure her mother would let her go abroad. Dostoevsky saw her to the door and carefully fastened her hood. She left his apartment feeling "happy, but horribly sad,"[36] likely a premonition of her destiny.

On November 8, Anna arrived to work on the third part of *Crime and Punishment*. Dostoevsky met her with a "heightened, fervid, almost ecstatic" expression, announcing that he had had a wonderful dream. He pointed to his big rosewood trunk, a treasured gift from his Siberian friend where he stored his manuscripts, letters, and things that mattered:

> And so this is my dream: I was sitting in front of that box and rearranging the papers in it. Suddenly something sparkled among them, some kind of bright little star. I was leafing through the papers and the star kept appearing and disappearing. And this was intriguing me. I started slowly putting all the papers to one side. And there among them I found a little diamond, a tiny one, but very sparkling and brilliant.

The dream was a starting point for a further improvisation: he told Anna that he wanted to share with her an idea for a new novel and needed advice on the psychology of a young girl. It was a story about an elderly artist in love with an exuberant girl and hoping to find happiness. His hero was sick, debt-ridden, and gloomy, although he had "a splendid heart." He was an artist, and a talented one, and yet "a failure who had not once in his life succeeded in embodying his ideas in the forms he dreamed of, and who never ceased to torment himself over that fact." The girl, on the other hand, was very nice-looking ("I love her face") and possessed great personal tact. But what could this old artist give a young and vivacious girl? And "wouldn't her love for him involve a terrible sacrifice on her part? . . . That is what I wanted to ask your opinion about, Anna Grigorievna . . . Imagine that this artist is—me; that I have confessed my love to you and asked you to be my wife. Tell me, what would you answer?"

> His face revealed such deep embarrassment, such inner torment, that I understood . . . that if I gave him an evasive answer I would deal a deathblow to his self-esteem and pride. I looked at his troubled face, which had become so dear to me, and said, "I would answer that I love you and will love you all my life."

When Dostoevsky pressed her to tell when she had become fond of him, Anna said that she had fallen in love with the hero of *Insulted and Injured* at fifteen. She had been full of sympathy for Dostoevsky when reading his Siberian account, *Notes from the House of the Dead*, and "it was with those feelings that I came to work for you. I wanted terribly to help you, to lighten in some way the existence of the man whose work I adored." The concept of female sacrifice had a special meaning for Anna's generation, inspired by the example of the Decembrist women who followed their husbands to exile in Siberia after the failed uprising against autocracy in 1825. However, the women in Dostoevsky's life had previously been unwilling to forgo their own interests to serve him. Korvin-Krukovskaya, a talented woman whom Anna would meet and befriend six years into her marriage, felt unsuited for the role. As she remarked, Dostoevsky's wife "must devote herself to him entirely, give all her life to him. . . . And I cannot do that, I want to live myself! Besides, he is so nervous, so demanding!"[37]

Realizing that he had solicited Anna's consent, Dostoevsky nonetheless declared that he was proud of his improvisation and considered it superior to his novels because it "had an instant success and produced the desired effect." When it sunk in that she would marry Dostoevsky, Anna "was stunned, almost crushed by the immensity of my happiness."

The writer's betrothal to a young and attractive stenographer became a news item: *Son of the Fatherland* published an article, "Marriage of a Novelist." In it, Dostoevsky was described walking back and forth when dictating and pulling his long hair during difficult spots, a portrayal which Anna found amusing and accurate.

She had to rescue Dostoevsky yet again when Mikhail Katkov, the editor of *The Russian Herald*, demanded the continuing installments of *Crime and Punishment* for the fall and winter issues. Because of their engagement, Dostoevsky had neglected sending chapters, so he was exasperated when faced with another close deadline and having to complete his novel before Christmas. Because he was now using stenography, which shortened his work time "nearly by half,"[38] he could make such a promise. Dostoevsky took the editor's letter to Anna, who advised him to shut his doors to visitors so he could work; in the evenings, he would come to her mother's apartment to dictate to her from his manuscript. Soon they were back to their routine: they would sit down at a desk together and, after a chat, "the dictation would begin, punctuated with talk, jokes and laughter." Dostoevsky admitted that his writing had never come so painlessly before and attributed this to their collaboration.

Turning forty-five, Dostoevsky was her father's contemporary, and Anna cared for his well-being as she had for her father's. Dostoevsky became more cheerful on her watch and his health improved. "During the entire three-month period before our wedding he suffered no more than three or four epileptic attacks." He had had weekly attacks when they met, some of them so severe that he was unable to speak or regain his memory for hours; they also left him despondent.

Their age difference bothered Dostoevsky because of Anna's youthful appearance: he was embarrassed that she looked like a girl. But Anna reassured him that she would age quickly. "And although this promise was meant as a joke, the circumstances of my life made it come true. . . . The difference in age between my husband and myself soon grew almost imperceptible." A few years into her marriage, Anna would notice from her portrait how her soft features and the expression in her eyes had turned grave.

On top of his illness, Dostoevsky was overloaded with family and debts. He accepted his dead brother's financial obligations and also supported his stepson, his alcoholic brother, his widowed sister-in-law, and her children. His relatives expected this aid, although he often had to pawn his belongings to provide it. Anna cried upon learning Dostoevsky pawned his winter coat five or six times each winter to support his ever-demanding family. His precious Chinese vases also disappeared from his apartment while she was still taking dictation there, and Anna saw that on his dining table wooden spoons had replaced silver. She realized that his debts required Dostoevsky to accept pitiable offers from publishers: he was not in a position to negotiate.

Days before proposing to Anna, Dostoevsky appealed to *The Russian Herald*, desperately asking to advance him 500 hundred rubles: "I have absolutely exhausted all my money . . . and I have nothing to live on."[39] The editor gave him the loan, but it was almost immediately gone to cover some debts, leaving Dostoevsky penniless again. Since there was no money for the wedding, Dostoevsky decided to travel to Moscow and meet his editor to request a bigger loan.

Anna's mother did not dissuade her from marrying Dostoevsky, despite his penury and illness. Anna would gratefully remember this, observing that her mother undoubtedly realized that this marriage had "much torment and grief in store for me" but did not interfere. Decades later, Anna would remark, "And who indeed could have persuaded me to refuse this great imminent happiness which later, despite the many difficult aspects of our life together, proved to be a real and genuine happiness for both of us?"

Dostoevsky's letters to his fiancée from Moscow were affectionate, anxious, and unromantic. "The sleeping cars are the vilest absurdity, hideously damp, cold, smelling of charcoal fumes. I suffered from a tooth ache . . . all day and night until dawn."[40] But Anna read his letters "with great joy" and shared Dostoevsky's fervent hope for their *new happiness* together. "I believe and trust in you, as in my whole future," he wrote her.[41]

When learning about Dostoevsky's marriage, Katkov agreed to a generous loan of 2,000 rubles; it was more than the magazine could pay, so he sent it in installments. Now, they could make wedding arrangements. But as before, Dostoevsky's relatives put forward their demands and he had no strength to refuse his late brother's family and his stepson Paul, who was the same age as Anna but lacked desire to work. They all were exploiting Dostoevsky's sense of guilt: he felt he was not doing enough for his family and so the new loan was melting away quickly. This time, Dostoevsky handed several hundred rubles over to Anna to cover wedding expenses, with the warning that their future depended on it.

The wedding took place on February 15, 1867, at 8 P.M., at the Trinity Izmailov Cathedral. "The cathedral was brilliantly lit, a splendid choir sang, many elegantly dressed guests were there. . . ." The reception was at her mother's apartment, where a beaming Dostoevsky introduced Anna to his friends, telling each: "'Look at that charming girl of mine! She's a marvelous person, that girl of mine! She has a heart of gold!'—and similar phrases that embarrassed me terribly."

In the aftermath of the celebrations, Dostoevsky experienced a double epileptic attack just as they were visiting Anna's sister. This was the first of his attacks that Anna witnessed: he suddenly broke off in the middle of a sentence, giving a horrible, "inhuman" scream.

> In later years there were dozens of occasions when I was to hear that "inhuman" howl, common with epileptics at the onset of the attack; and that howl always shocked and

terrified me. But on this occasion I was not the least bit frightened, to my own surprise, although it was the first time in my life I had ever seen an epileptic fit. . . . I pushed aside a chair with a lighted lamp on it, and let him slide on the floor. I too sat down on the floor and held his head in my lap all through his convulsions. There was no one to help me: my sister was in hysterics, and my brother-in-law and the maid were fussing over her.

A second and more severe attack soon followed, leaving Dostoevsky, when he regained consciousness, screaming in pain for hours. Anna recognized the severity of his illness when she spent the night listening to his cries, groans, and incoherent speech, and it frightened her to see his wild stare and face distorted with convulsions.

It was with "vexation and sorrow" that she would recall her honeymoon: her fervent dream of becoming Dostoevsky's companion and helping him fulfill his destiny collided with harsh reality. Dostoevsky lived with his stepson Paul, who met Anna with hostility, evidently afraid of losing his allowance and privileged position (he called Dostoevsky "papa"). With Paul bickering and complaining about her to Dostoevsky, and with his other relatives perennially present, Anna felt estranged from her husband before their marriage even really began. They were never left alone, and the rift between them grew: Dostoevsky worked nights, and in the daytime she had to entertain his family and guests, a task she disliked immensely because she was used to independence. Raised in a traditional family, she could not refuse hospitality, but was left with no time for her own pursuits—reading, practicing stenography, and helping Dostoevsky. Without their conversations and spiritual intimacy (she was not then physically attracted to Dostoevsky), Anna felt that their relationship could soon end in divorce.

To rescue the marriage, the couple decided to go abroad for a few months, but as soon as they raised the needed money and announced their intentions, Dostoevsky's relatives insisted on receiving cash for several months in advance. His creditors also pressed for payment and threatened Dostoevsky with court action. Crushed by his troubles, he was ready to give up the idea of going away. Anna, however, was determined to free them from their domestic nightmare at any cost and begin a true married life, "to become knit together,"[42] using Dostoevsky's expression. She was prepared to pawn her dowry, although "I was extremely fond of my piano, my charming little tables and whatnots, all my lovely things so newly acquired."

Her mother was in favor of her European trip, upset as she was that her industrious daughter had to amuse visitors instead of working. "She was a Swede, her view of life was Western, more cultured; and she feared that the good habits inculcated by my upbringing would vanish thanks to our Russian style of living with its disorderly hospitality." When her mother helped pawn her piano, furniture, fine clothes, and jewelry, Anna had a premonition she might not see these things again, which indeed happened. Aside from the dowry, there was her inheritance: one of her mother's rental properties would go to Anna within months, when she turned twenty-one. But because they wanted to leave abroad urgently, before new complications arose, Anna would never benefit from this house, which was auctioned off in her absence.

On April 14, 1867, on Good Friday, the couple left Petersburg for a three-month vacation, not to return until four years later. Anna started a shorthand diary of her impressions and conversations with Dostoevsky. These notes interested Dostoevsky "very much, and he would often say to me, 'I'd give a lot, Anechka, to find out what it is you're writing in those little squiggles of yours—you're saying bad things about me, no doubt?'"[43] Recording her thoughts in shorthand allowed her to express them without reservation, vital to her during their foreign travel when she had no one else but her diary to confide in. Besides, she wanted to make a faithful record of their daily life and conversations.

My husband was to me such an interesting and wholly enigmatic being, that it seemed to me as though I should find it easier to understand him if I noted down his every thought and expression. Added to which, there was no single soul abroad to whom I could confide either my doubts or my observations, and I came to regard my diary as the friend to whom I could entrust my hopes, my thoughts, and all my fears.[44]

Their travel began in Vilna,[45] where the couple stayed briefly after crossing the Russian border. It was Easter Sunday and the hotel staff left for morning service. Dostoevsky, mistrustful of Western Europeans, despite having traveled abroad before, feared that they might be robbed, so he not only locked their doors, but barricaded them with tables and trunks. Anna had no time to ponder his eccentricity, having to spend that night caring for him after he suffered a powerful attack lasting fifteen minutes.

She soon discovered this was not the European trip she had been imagining. Dostoevsky may have seemed an "enigmatic being" to her, but in daily life he was irritable and tactless and, upon their arrival in Berlin, "began to curse everything, the Germans, the hotel, and the weather."[46] This bored her, so Anna suggested a walk on Unter den Linden. Having pawned her fine clothes, she was in a winter hat and coat, making her look preposterous on a warm rainy day. In addition, Dostoevsky scolded her for being badly dressed and for her shabby gloves. "I was very hurt, and told him, if he thought me so badly dressed we had better not go about together; after which I turned round, quick sharp, and went off in the opposite direction."[47] (When preparing her diaries for publication she added a sentence to assuage the impression of a quarrel and to assume blame for it: "At last I calmed down and realized that Fyodor never really meant to hurt me by what he said, and that I had had no reason to get so excited."[48])

The abuse continued in Dresden, where Dostoevsky reprimanded his bride for dressing "like a kitchen aid." Because he then managed all their funds, she commented, "He could at least give me 20 francs per month . . . since our arrival abroad he hasn't bought me a single dress, so how can he possibly complain. . . ."[49] In her memoir, written forty-five years later, Anna changed her account dramatically to present Dostoevsky the opposite from what he was in life: "Then . . . the two of us went to buy me some summer outwear, and I marveled at the fact that Fyodor Mikhailovich did not grow bored with choosing and examining fabrics . . . pattern and cut of the article we were buying. Everything he chose for me was of good quality, simple and elegant, and after that I had complete confidence in his taste."[50] In fact, Dostoevsky bought summer clothes for himself alone, while Anna continued to walk around in her tatty black dress among the elegantly clad European ladies. But complaining was not in her nature and she merely wrote in her shorthand diary, "I keep thinking, perhaps he might himself figure out, himself will offer, why, you also need summer dresses, especially that they are so inexpensive here."[51]

Their isolation abroad compelled them to hold on to each other, and so, despite their immense differences and lack of means, the bond created during their travels would strengthen their marriage and make it indestructible. Anna's naïveté and innate cheerfulness helped mend disagreements and avoid bitterness. In Berlin, after she ran away from Dostoevsky on Unter den Linden, she was soon worried that he might divorce her and send her home; telling him of her fears amused and softened him.

In Dresden, the Gallery became the magnet and focus of their spiritual lives: both were passionately interested in art; moreover, they could not afford other distractions. Dostoevsky first ran through the Gallery, bypassing other masterpieces, to his favorite painting, the *Sistine Madonna* by Rafael; Anna saw it for the first time. "No other painting had produced such a strong impression on me before," she wrote. "What beauty, innocence, and sadness in her majestic face, and there is so much submission and so much suffering in her eyes! Fedya thinks her smile is sorrowful."[52] An eccentric Dostoevsky mounted a chair to look closer at the painting (he was near-sighted). When a commissionaire reprimanded him, he got off; but as soon as he left, Dostoevsky resumed his position, remarking he did not care if the guard would throw him out since the man had "nothing but the soul of the lackey." Although shocked, Anna left the room so as not to argue ("why blame the lackey whose job it is to keep order?"), and soon Dostoevsky joined her, satisfied he had seen the painting properly.[53] Because Dostoevsky considered this Rafael painting "the highest manifestation of human genius,"[54] he would stand in front of it for hours, lost in thought. Titian also gave him "intense pleasure: he could not take his eyes of *The Tribute Money*, moved by the image of the Savior. Anna shared his fascination with Biblical themes in the paintings by Murillo, Correggio, and Carracci, but also loved landscapes and Rembrandt's self-portraits, particularly *Rembrandt and His Wife*.

At three o'clock, when the Gallery closed, they would dine at a nearby restaurant aptly named "Italian Village" (Italienisches Dorfchen), with huge windows overlooking both banks of the Elbe and a menu of cheap but enjoyable fare, which always included fish freshly caught in the river. The restaurant subscribed to foreign newspapers, including French, which Dostoevsky liked to read. But his habit of starting quarrels with waiters over tips and service filled Anna with apprehension whenever they went to restaurants, cafés, and shops; Dostoevsky would loudly complain about the quality of pies and other foods. He was obsessive in his dislike of the Germans, whom he abused as "stupid." Although he spoke their language with difficulty, to Anna's surprise he found the right words, and plenty of them when shouting insults. Anna was soon influenced to believe that German waiters were cheats and the passersby they asked for directions were "particularly dense of understanding." But her ability to turn Dostoevsky's quarrels into a joke assuaged him: usually sullen and uncommunicative, he was laughing and joking in Dresden. She learned to cope with his sudden and unpredictable mood changes, his suspicion, and his contempt: when he called her "damn vermin," Anna would laugh spontaneously; her reaction puzzled and disarmed him. (Dostoevsky's past as a convict in Siberia might explain why he used strong language, but mainly it was his hot temper and irascibility: he could praise her one minute and insult her the next.) Occasionally, she would assume the blame to restore peace: "Of course, everything was my fault—but what does that matter, so long as we are no longer cross with one another?"[55]

Evenings were spent walking and drinking beer in Dresden's Grossen Garten, where they liked to listen to the nightly brass band. Once, Dostoevsky started arguing with Anna when the band was playing the overture to Franz von Suppé's operetta *Poet and Peasant*. To divert his thoughts, Anna begged him to listen carefully because of "how this opera was meant to impersonate *us*, that he was the poet, and I the peasant. . . . It really was like our quarrel. Two voices could be distinctly heard—that of the peasant, gentle, pleading, and insistent, and then that of the poet, screaming, refusing to listen to anything, and perpetually contradicting." She then began to hum the peasant's aria, improvising the text, "Fyodor, my darling, my sweetheart, forgive me, I beg you. . . ." Dostoevsky, joining in the fun, responded, "No, no, not for anything. . . ."[56] Anna was a faithful and practical companion to Quixote (Dostoevsky), and he liked the idea.

At night, while Dostoevsky was reading in bed, Anna lay beside him ("it's my favorite spot, as in childhood behind my father's back"[57]). He would stay up until 2 A.M., when Anna would be already fast asleep, but he would wake her up to say good-night and for half an hour they kissed, laughed, and talked—the happiest time of the entire day: "I tell him my dreams and he shares his impressions of the day, and together we are terribly happy."[58]

In June, invited to meet with a group of stenographers who used her method—the Gabelsberger System—Anna became the center of attention as the first Russian female stenographer. Professor Woldemar Zeibig, a librarian at the Royal Stenographic Institute, was a friend of her teacher, Olkhin, who wrote him about Anna, resulting in her cordial reception. She responded to the welcome with a few words of acknowledgement, but later regretted not making a proper speech. When the following day *Dresdner Nachrichten* ran an article about her, Anna noticed "an expression of hostility" on Dostoevsky's face. He made a scene when they happened to meet several stenographers during a walk, which led Anna to promptly distance herself from her professional circle and even from the kindly Zeibig with his Russian wife. (Zeibig would later write an essay "Women and Stenography.") Her concern for Dostoevsky's peace of mind always prevailed, requiring her to make sacrifices "to avoid any such complications in future."[59]

Three weeks into their mostly blissful stay in Dresden, when reminiscing about their work on *The Gambler*, Dostoevsky mentioned trying his luck at roulette in Homburg. As he kept bringing up the idea, Anna felt that since "the thought of this trip fills his mind to the extinction of everything else, why not let him indulge in it?"[60] Sensing that she was powerless to stop him from gambling, she did not oppose the trip. Her recent discovery that Dostoevsky continued to correspond with his old love, Suslova, bothered her more. Finding Suslova's letter in Dostoevsky's pocket, she read it on the sly, while dreading that the femme fatale might turn up in Dresden and his passion for her would return. "Lord, don't send me such misery," Anna wrote.[61] (Suslova was unaware of Dostoevsky's marriage and he eagerly informed her of all the circumstances in his reply, also describing Anna's "extraordinary kind and clear character."[62])

Upon arriving in Homburg, Dostoevsky quickly lost "everything, down to the last kopeck, to the last guilden...."[63] His daily letters to Anna were so muddled and anxious that he begged her, "Give me your word that you'll never show anyone these letters."[64] He attributed his losses to their separation: although Anna wrote regularly, he missed her and dreaded, on those occasions when her letter was delayed in the mail, "that you were sick and dying."[65] Because Anna did not reproach him and only wrote to console, her letters were like "manna from heaven."[66] He instructed her to send more money "right away, the same day, the same minute, if possible."[67] Having just received a check from her mother, Anna was able to cover some of the losses, but felt more funds were needed:

"I wrote Mama, begging her to secretly pawn my fur coat and send some money."[68]

In another letter, Dostoevsky explained his theory of playing roulette: he did not gamble for pleasure, but to pay off his pressing debts, and if he played coolly, with calculation, "THERE'S NO CHANCE of not winning." He had noticed that the first half-hour always brought gain, so the trick was to get away immediately, but he was irresistibly drawn back to the tables and would continue to play, although he knew almost for certain he would lose.[69] Upon reading this, Anna gathered "that Fedya, evidently, wants to stay longer and play. I wrote him at once that he can stay if he wishes. . . . Nothing is to be done and, perhaps, it's necessary in order to get this silly idea about winning out of his head. I felt very sad. . . ."[70]

Dostoevsky played away the amount Anna sent him and was in agony over his losses and his deception: he also gambled away the money he asked her to send for his return. In all, he estimated that he lost more than 1,000 franks (350 rubles), "a crime" in their financial circumstances. Promising to ask for another loan from Katkov and to "triumph through work," Dostoevsky dreaded Anna's judgment. His pleading for another rescue and self-castigation would become a familiar tune:

> Anya, dear, my dear, my friend, my wife, forgive me, don't call me a scoundrel! I have committed a crime, I have lost everything that you sent, everything, everything down to the last kreuzer; I received it yesterday, and yesterday I lost it. Anya, how am I going to look at you now, what will you say about me now?[71]

When Dostoevsky, without his watch, returned to Dresden, the joy of their meeting was immense, despite his losses, of which he had to inform her in detail. The gambling trip only fueled his old passion, and he dreamed of spending several weeks in a roulette town, convinced he could win a fortune if she were with him and he did not have to hurry. He promised to remain "cold and *inhumanly* careful." She was persuaded to travel with him to Baden-Baden, later realizing that his plan had a major flaw: "His success might have been complete—but only on condition that this system was applied by some cool-headed Englishman or German and not by such a nervous and impulsive person as my husband, who went into outermost limits in everything."[72]

In Baden-Baden, a popular gambling spa where the couple spent five weeks, Anna lived the nightmare of Dostoevsky's addiction—"an all-consuming passion, an elemental force against which even a strong character could not struggle."[73] They rented cheap furnished rooms over a blacksmith shop where the racket began at four in the morning. Anna, who at the start of her pregnancy suffered morning sickness, was perennially sleep-deprived, but lack of means prevented them from moving.

Dostoevsky's gambling anxiety in Baden-Baden affected her more than it did in Homburg because she observed it at close quarters. Having to wait for Dostoevsky's return (he insisted that as a respectable woman, she must not enter a casino), Anna trembled that there would not be enough money for meals and to pay the landlady.

Both decided that she should keep their funds so he would not play away everything, but in reality this meant that Dostoevsky would come back again asking for more. His tearful scenes were more traumatic than losing money: he would throw himself on his knees before her, repenting, begging her to forgive him, and pleading for more funds. Anna feared that this would trigger an epileptic attack and would try to cheer him up, presenting their situation as not so hopeless. But eventually she had to give him the sum requested: "If I were to refuse him the money, he would go out of his mind."[74]

When funds ran out, Dostoevsky would pawn their few possessions and his wedding present to Anna. "I took off my ear-rings and my brooch and looked at them a long, long time; to me it seemed as though I were saying good-bye to them. . . . Fyodor says he is ashamed of himself and it breaks his heart to take my things, especially when they are so precious to me, but that there is no help for it."⁷⁵ Her earrings and a diamond and ruby brooch were lost in Baden-Baden to Dostoevsky's compulsive gambling.

However, their misfortunes drew them closer: her unconditional love was the source of hope for Dostoevsky, who now depended on her as a child. "We talked together, and came to the conclusion that our love increased in proportion as our money dwindled, and, after all, that is the chief thing."⁷⁶ He told her she gave him many new feelings and thoughts and was influencing him to become a better man.⁷⁷

When Dostoevsky happened to win at roulette, he came home with a bouquet of white and red roses, his pockets "crammed full" of packages of cheese, caviar, and *ryzhiki*, Anna's favorite salted mushrooms. She was pleased he could remember her craving: "Was there ever such a man! What other husband in the world would have found the Russian *ryzhiki* for his wife in Baden-Baden? . . . Wasn't it sweet of him, and haven't I the dearest husband in the world?" He brought baskets of fruit and they feasted on apricots, cherries, and gooseberries. On such occasions, their wealth seemed fantastic to them, though they could not hold on to it.

In a letter to his friend, the poet Apollon Maikov, Dostoevsky described their tribulations during the four months abroad, adding that Anna "has turned out to be stronger and deeper than I knew her to be and imagined, and in many cases she has simply been a guardian angel for me; but at the same time there is much of the child and the twenty-year-old in her, which is wonderful and naturally *essential*, but to which I doubt that I have the energy and capacity to respond."⁷⁸ They were constantly "alone together," hard enough for a young girl, and on top of it were his illness and growing debts.

The letter to Maikov was written in Geneva, the next stop in Anna and Dostoevsky's travels; tickets were purchased with a check from her mother. Dostoevsky continued to gamble in Baden-Baden right up to the moment of their departure, with money meant for the journey, then pawned his ring for twenty francs. An hour before the train, he came in with a story of his losses. Anna, who had been packing alone, was furious; nonetheless, she told him "not to give up, but help . . . to fasten the trunks."[79]

In Geneva, although their means were scarce, life seemed blissful compared to the calamitous Baden-Baden. Seven months into her marriage, Anna knew how to cut back on every expense and mend her worn dresses. With no money for a decent apartment, they shared a single room, in which they slept, took their meals, read, and wrote. Anna told Dostoevsky that she was prepared to live with him on "a desert island," and he remarked in a letter to Maikov: "Truly, Anna Grigorievna is an angel. . . . She says that she is happy, quite happy, and needs no entertainment . . . and that together with me in one room she is quite content."[80] In this room, she reread *Crime and Punishment*, read Balzac's collected works and Dickens' *Little Dorrit*, after Dostoevsky had read it, took his dictation, and practiced translating from the French. Thinking she would need to earn a living, she had begun translating while in Baden-Baden. She had been also chronicling events of the previous year in her diary: her life before Dostoevsky, their meeting, and their collaboration on *The Gambler*.

In the fall of 1867, Dostoevsky wrote an outline for *The Idiot*, intended for the first 1868 issues of *The Russian Herald*. The idea was "an old and cherished one—to depict a positively good man."[81] Prince Myshkin is a romantic seeker, like Quixote, an "open-hearted childish soul."[82] But portraying a "perfectly beautiful" hero was overwhelmingly difficult, and Dostoevsky was afraid to fail badly, admitting he did not know how to develop such a character.[83] With only months remaining until he had to deliver the first installment of the novel, he "took a risk, as at roulette, 'Maybe it will develop under my pen.'"[84] Continually disappointed with his execution, he told Anna that he was only implementing a tenth of his poetic idea.

In Geneva, Dostoevsky's epilepsy increased: he suffered powerful attacks every ten days, as compared to once a month at better times; after each attack, he needed five days to recuperate. Depressed and anxious because of his illness and looming deadline, he also fretted over his inability to provide for their growing family. They lived by pawning their things (Anna's two spare dresses and her black lace mantilla fetched fifty francs) and on small loans from friends, including Maikov, while waiting for yet another advance from *The Russian Herald* where Dostoevsky was obliged to contribute his new novel in installments. As usual, their relationship was unaffected either by hardships or monotonous routine (both dreamed of going to a theater in Geneva, but because of their penury could not). In the evenings, they were composing a comic poem, "Abracadabra," an activity that kept them amused. "We are very close now and it seems to me that he loves me terribly," Anna wrote on the day she had to pawn her dress.[85]

Their livelihood depended on Dostoevsky's new novel, but he was too nervous and frequently too ill to settle down and work steadily. A desperate remedy was needed to bring him back to writing, and so, three months before the birth of their child, painfully short of money, Anna agreed to Dostoevsky's proposal that he try his luck at roulette again. "What a strange man," she commented in her diary. "It seems fate punished him badly enough and proved to him many times that he will not become rich through roulette; but this man is incorrigible, he is still convinced . . . that he will definitely become rich, will definitely win. . . ."[86]

In October of 1867, Dostoevsky traveled to Saxon les Bains, a few hours from Geneva, returning to Geneva exhausted, without money and having again pawned his wedding ring. He told Anna a tale of his misfortunes, which she barely heard. Dostoevsky now came up with a new plan—to ask Katkov to send them a small monthly stipend, which, he was convinced, the editor would not refuse because Anna was soon to give birth. Ashamed that he had used her pregnancy as an excuse, Anna begged her mother to send money, while she would have given anything not to bother her. (Her mother in Petersburg was paying interest on Anna's furniture while being harassed by Dostoevsky's relatives and creditors.) Despite the loss of money, there was some benefit from Dostoevsky's casino outing: it gave him a flash of inspiration. "When he came back to

Geneva he settled down to his interrupted work with fervor, and wrote about ninety-three pages . . . within twenty-three days."[87]

The winter of 1867–68 passed swiftly "in unremitting mutual work on the writing of the novel."[88] With Anna taking dictation and copying, Dostoevsky barely met his deadline, sending the first installment at the last moment; it appeared in the January issue. Anticipating the birth of their child, the couple moved to a bigger apartment, with two bedrooms, but as their finances were weakened and they saved on fuel, their place remained "awfully cold."[89] In the evenings they talked about books they were reading together, about Christ and the Gospels. "I am always happy when he talks to me not just about ordinary subjects . . . but when he finds me capable of listening and discussing with him more important and abstract issues."[90]

During their walks, Dostoevsky liked to stop at shop windows, pointing to diamond earrings, which he wanted to buy for Anna to replace those he had gambled away. Throughout his life he tried to save enough to buy her jewelry to replace his wedding gift; once he used an entire honorarium to buy her a golden bracelet, but money was always needed for bare necessities, and Anna returned it to the shop.

Their child was expected in March 1868. During the last month of Anna's pregnancy, Dostoevsky walked past the midwife's house daily so as to remember it at the critical moment: his memory, weakened by epilepsy, "has grown completely dim . . . I don't recognize people anymore. I forget what I read the day before."[91] Knowing that his daily walks up the hill were difficult because of his asthma, Anna appreciated the sacrifice. But preparation proved futile: hours before Anna went into labor, Dostoevsky experienced a severe attack and, exhausted, fell asleep. When her pains began, she tried to awaken him, only to find that he was completely incapacitated. She had to wait eleven hours, praying for strength, before Dostoevsky could summon the midwife.

> But what a dreadful night I spent then! The trees around the church were rustling violently; wind and rain rattled at

the windows . . . I have to admit that I was oppressed by the feeling of being completely alone and helpless. How bitter it was for me that during those trying hours of my life there was no close relative near me, and that my only guardian and defender, my husband, was himself in a helpless state. I began to pray with fervor, and prayer sustained my failing strength.[92]

The Swiss midwife told Anna that she had never met a newborn's father in such distress. Banished from the room, Dostoevsky prayed on his knees, his palms covering his face, as the midwife reported in response to Anna's inquiries about his condition: "Remembering my thoughts and feelings then, I have to say that it was not so much myself I pitied as my poor husband, for whom my death might prove catastrophic."[93] When the child was born, Dostoevsky pushed open the door of Anna's bedroom and threw himself on his knees before her, kissing her hands. Later, he described the stormy emotions he experienced at the birth of their daughter Sonya in *The Devils*. He wrote a friend how the experience changed him: "I heard a baby's cry, *my child's*. That's a strange sensation for a father, but of all human sensations it is one of the best. . . ."[94]

Dostoevsky proved to be "the tenderest possible father," cradling their Sonya in his arms and singing to her. He said she had his features and even his facial expression, "including the wrinkles on the brow—she lies there and looks as though she's writing a novel!"[95] But even his love for the newborn could not stop Dostoevsky from playing roulette: in April, one month after Sonya's birth, he was back in Saxon les Bains. This time, he lost all his money, 220 francs, within the first half hour of arriving. By now, he had accumulated a colossal debt to *The Russian Herald* of 5,060 rubles, and, more disastrously, proved to be an unreliable contributor: his recent installments were late and of insufficient length. But as he frantically wrote Anna from Saxon les Bains, their future depended on the success of his novel, which is why she should not regret the money: after his loss an "amazing, superb idea" occurred to him.[96]

"That's exactly how it was in Wiesbaden, when right after a loss, too, I thought up *Crime and Punishment*. . . ."[97]

In May, the couple was struck with grief when Sonya, three months old, caught a cold and developed pneumonia. One of the best children's doctors in the city was summoned and daily examined the child; only hours before Sonya died, he reassured the parents that her condition was improving. "I cannot express the desolation that took hold of us when we saw our lovely daughter lying dead." Shaken as she was, Anna felt even more distressed for her inconsolable husband: "His grief was stormy. He sobbed and wept like a woman, standing in front of the body of his darling . . . and covering her tiny white face and hands with burning kisses. I never again saw such paroxysms of grief."[98]

The medical expenses and funeral, following Dostoevsky's gambling losses, left the couple completely destitute. As usual, Dostoevsky appealed to the sympathetic Katkov, and with his money the couple moved across the lake from Geneva, which had become hateful to them, to the small town of Vevey. Their summer was cheerless: Anna was "horribly sad," her nerves frayed, and spent nights crying. Dostoevsky's emotional state alarmed her as his grief completely absorbed him, and he complained that the passing of time only made his memory of Sonya more painful. In addition, the "rotten little town of 4,000"[99] lacked a good library and Russian newspapers, on which he relied for inspiration. Unable to focus on the novel, which he wrote now with a heavy heart, he decided to move to Italy.

That fall, they journeyed across the Alps, part of the time walking in front of "an enormous mail coach, which was climbing the mountain." They gathered Alpine wildflowers and admired the picturesque mountain route, blue sky, and waterfalls. In Milan, where they stayed for two months, they lived on a narrow street, near the main corso, where neighbors talked back and forth between opposite windows. Strangers in this milieu, the couple felt more isolated, and Anna quickly became homesick. The fall was cold and rainy, confining them to their apartment. They lived peacefully but in complete isolation, "in monastery fashion,"[100] in Dostoevsky's words, with occasional excursions to the Milan Cathedral as their main attraction. Dostoevsky, lacking Russian news and realities for his novel, began to urge Anna to move to Florence, then the capital of Italy, which they hoped would have a superior library. The move would cost them 100 francs, but, as Dostoevsky wrote his niece, Anna was "tolerant, and my interests are dearer to her than anything else. . . ."[101]

In Florence they settled near the Palazzo Pitti, a vast Renaissance palace on the River Arno, which in the sixteenth century belonged to the Medici family and later became a treasure house: future owners amassed paintings, porcelain, and jewelry. The couple frequented its art gallery and afterwards would invariably go to the statue of the Medici Venus, which Dostoevsky considered a work of genius. "To our great joy, the city of Florence had an excellent library and reading room which subscribed to two Russian newspapers, and my husband went there every day. . . ."[102] In Florence, Dostoevsky feverishly worked on the novel, which had to be finished by the year's end. Dictations were rushed: Dostoevsky did not reread the clean copy, which Anna made, but even with this haste he feared he would not meet his deadline. (Despite flaws, *The Idiot* remains one of Dostoevsky's most original novels.) When the novel was near its end, the couple began to fear that its completion would terminate their monthly stipend from *The Russian Herald*.

Having learned some Italian to speak and read newspapers, Anna became Dostoevsky's translator during their excursions in the city and to the shops where, despite lacking funds, he stubbornly looked for jewelry for her. The New Year, 1869, brought welcome news—in January, Anna discovered she was expecting another child. "Our joy was boundless, and my dear husband began showing as much concern for me as he had during my first pregnancy."[103] That year, *War and Peace* appeared in Russia, a major literary event, and the couple was absorbed in it. (Nikolai Strakhov, Dostoevsky's friend and later Tolstoy's editor, sent them the novel, comprising six volumes.) Discovering that the third volume was missing, Anna reproached Dostoevsky for losing this fascinating book, but he told her that it was likely lost in the mail. Later she learned that Dostoevsky had hidden it from her because the volume contained the part describing the death of Andrei Bolkonsky's wife in labor.

Their final three months in Florence were spent in anguish. In May, waiting for a small advance to arrive from *Dawn*, a recently started magazine to which Dostoevsky was contributing his minor fiction, they moved to a tiny apartment, to save rent. The apartment overlooked the marketplace, located in the midst of stone buildings, with arcades and columns. In the summer heat, the area turned into a furnace, heating up their tarantula-ridden apartment to the temperature of a Russian steam bath. To make matters worse, Anna was in the last months of pregnancy, and they shared the little space they had with her mother, who arrived to help with the baby. The advance took several weeks to come and when it did, the money went to rent and to cover some debts, requiring Dostoevsky to plead for further salvation from Katkov. (After submitting the completed novel, Dostoevsky still owed 1,000 rubles to *The Russian Herald*. *The Idiot* was not a success and although Katkov failed to make money from it, he continued to support him. The editor realized the magazine would be remembered in history for publishing Tolstoy and Dostoevsky.)

During 1869, the year *The Idiot* was completed and their second daughter was born, the couple traveled to Prague where both hoped to find a Slavic intellectual milieu and where Dostoevsky had fans. But failing to find affordable housing, they went on to Dresden, a relatively inexpensive city they had "tested" before, where they had some friends and where Dostoevsky resolved to work without raising his head.

The Dostoevskys expected their child in early September, "with excitement, and with fear, and with hope, and timidity."[104] Anna was unwell throughout the year: "I fear terribly for her health," Dostoevsky wrote to his friend Maikov, "she's constantly sick . . . and in addition is seriously afraid that she'll die in childbirth. . . ."[105] Both wanted a girl and, already loving her, decided to name her

Lyubov (Love in Russian) or Lyuba for short. When, on September 14, the happy event took place, Dostoevsky informed Maikov that LYUBOV had been born: "Everything went superbly, and the baby is big, healthy, and a beauty. Anya and I are happy."[106] Maikov was chosen as the girl's godfather and Anna's mother, who stayed in Dresden with the couple, as godmother.

In Dresden, Dostoevsky worked on "The Life of a Great Sinner," which he would later develop into *The Brothers Karamazov*, and *The Devils*, a tendentious novel about revolutionaries and political anarchy in Russia. Meanwhile, his artistic doubts returned: he told Anna of the inevitable "destruction" of his talent, caused by constant pressure of deadlines and the inability to polish his creations. Anna thought his novels could be the equal of Tolstoy's if only there was financial security and time for revision. She witnessed his despair at the sight of mistakes in the dispatched chapters: "If only I could bring it back! If only I could correct it! Now I see . . . why the novel isn't going right."[107] (While abroad, he did not receive the magazine that published his novel.) *Poor Folk*, his early novel, which Anna had read in her teens, was likely the only work that he wrote without pressure and fear of deadlines and which he was able to plan.

The couple's financial circumstances remained dismal and, one month after their daughter was born, Dostoevsky drew a picture of his and Anna's desperation in a letter to Maikov: "How can I write when I'm hungry, when I've pawned my pants in order to raise two talers for a telegram! But never mind me and my hunger! But after all, she is nursing a baby. What if she *herself* goes to pawn her last warm wool skirt!"[108]

Despite hardship, their second stay in Dresden was more comfortable: Anna was no longer isolated as before. In addition to her mother, Anna's brother, Ivan, arrived: "I was surrounded by the creatures most beloved and precious in the world to me—my husband, my child, my mother and brother. . . ."[109] Ivan Snitkin was enrolled at the Moscow Agricultural Academy, which had recently been shaken with a murder of a student who was his classmate; the victim belonged to a conspiratorial organization, People's Reprisal, headed by the revolutionary terrorist Sergei Nechaev. A prominent radical who had plotted to assassinate Alexander II, the fanatical Nechaev was mistrustful of people around him and ordered the student's killing in November 1869.[110] Dostoevsky was following the event in German newspapers, which also reported about a network of revolutionary organizations in Russia. Ivan told him about the mood among the students and described the Agricultural Academy's park, the scene of the crime, which Dostoevsky replicated in *The Devils*, where the murder is a major event.

Dostoevsky began to publish *The Devils* in Katkov's magazine in 1871 when, after four tumultuous years abroad, the couple ended their exile. In spring, on the eve of their return to Russia, Dostoevsky became restless again and left for Wiesbaden to play roulette with money Anna had managed to save up. She was expecting their third child and put aside three hundred talers for the birth, but gave it Dostoevsky: "In order to soothe his anxiety and dispel the somber thoughts which prevented him from concentrating on his work, I resorted to the device which always amused and distracted him."[111] The trip would become the final gambling experience of Dostoevsky's life.

His guilt at losing the money taken from his pregnant wife, their baby daughter, and their unborn child, along with a tormenting dream of his late father (whenever he had dreamed of his father, he considered it a premonition of disaster), and other mystical experiences on that night, all changed him profoundly.[112] He suddenly became cured of his obsession, describing his conversion to Anna: "A great thing has been accomplished over me, a vile fantasy that had *tormented* me for almost ten years has vanished. For ten years . . . I kept dreaming of winning. I dreamed seriously, passionately. Now that's all finished with!"[113] As usual, his gambling losses stimulated his imagination and, upon his return to Dresden, seeking salvation through work, he settled down to write *The Devils*.

Preparing to return to Russia, the couple discussed what should be done with the archive Dostoevsky had accumulated during their travels. Because he was a former political prisoner, officials would inspect his correspondence, as a well-wisher warned. Dostoevsky insisted on burning his drafts, but Anna managed to save the notebooks for *The Idiot* and *The Devils* by leaving them with her mother, who was returning home separately.

Indeed, at the border in Verzhbolovo the couple's possessions and papers were painstakingly searched by Russian customs; they nearly missed their train to Petersburg. The search was terminated when little Lyuba, bored and hungry, began to scream for a roll at the top of her voice: sick of her crying, the officials returned the papers.

Years of hardship had made Anna a decisive woman capable of handling any practical problem. She had aged significantly and, at twenty-four, looked nearly her husband's contemporary. Her friends and family noticed the change and "reproached me for not paying attention to my appearance, for not dressing well and not doing my hair fashionably." Anna could not afford stylish dresses, and, moreover, wore dark colors to appear less attractive. It pained her, though, when people confused her age, but concerns over Dostoevsky's tranquility would prevail:

> I was firmly convinced that Fyodor Mikhailovich loved me not for my appearance only, but also for the good qualities of my mind and character.... And my old-fashioned appearance and obvious avoidance of male society could only act beneficially on my husband, since it gave no occasion for him to display the unfortunate side of his character—his groundless jealousy.[114]

Despite their tribulations abroad, Anna would recall the European period of their marriage "with deepest gratitude to fate." They came to understand and value one another deeply: their hearts had truly "knitted together."[115] Dostoevsky now depended on her emotionally and for all his decisions: "He willingly turned over all his affairs to me, listened to my advice and followed it...."[116] (In 1873, Dostoevsky wrote a will, leaving his literary rights to Anna.)

The Dostoevskys returned to Petersburg on July 8 and, only eight days later, Anna gave birth to their son, Fedya. They lived in furnished rooms until Anna was able to rent a suitable apartment: she negotiated a deal with a merchant, obtaining a few pieces of furniture on installment. This was essential, since in their absence all their possessions in Russia had been lost: Anna's furniture had gone for insurance premiums; the house she had inherited had been lost through machinations by her sister's husband; and Dostoevsky's valuable library had been sold by his stepson Paul.

Like Job, calamities followed them everywhere: less than a year after their arrival, little Lyuba broke her wrist, which was reset under chloroform. Both parents frantically worried that she would not survive the anesthetic, then relatively new.[117] Anna "vividly pictured" the death of their first child and did not expect Lyuba to survive, apprehension Dostoevsky shared. Pale, his hands trembling, he accompanied Anna to a room where they awaited the outcome with dread, and prayed: ". . . we got down on our knees and prayed as fervently during those moments as perhaps we had ever prayed in our lives before."[118] The surgery was successful, but the couple's anxiety over their children's health would only increase.

Their arrival in Russia could not be kept secret from Dostoevsky's creditors for long: learning about his return from a newspaper report, they demanded immediate settlement and threatened him with debtor's prison. Dostoevsky paced his room, pulling his hair at the temples and repeating: "Now what in the world, whatever in the world are we going to do?" To shield him from stress, which interfered with his work on the novel *The Devils*, Anna met with the creditors on her own.

While Dostoevsky's debts totaled twenty-five thousand rubles, Anna estimated that he was personally responsible for about a tenth of the amount. Having rashly assumed responsibility for his dead brother's debts, Dostoevsky signed promissory notes with childlike impracticality: he trusted people's word and was frequently swindled. Because he was easily upset, Anna concealed her negotiations with creditors. These were shady types who had bought up

Dostoevsky's promissory notes for pennies and wanted to redeem them for their original value; they came to Anna with threats. Undaunted, she told them that if Dostoevsky was put in debtor's prison, he would stay there until the term of the debt expired, in which case his creditors would receive nothing. Meantime, she would make his prison stay fully comfortable and visit him daily with the children. Their property could not be attached because she rented their apartment in her name and bought furniture on the installment plan. The creditors accepted her arguments and agreed to spread payments over the years. But this new arrangement was only marginally better, since it required her, without a regular income, to deliver the promised sums on time. And because their income depended on the success of Dostoevsky's work, she lived perennially under pressure and worry: "Where to get such-and-such an amount by such-and-such a date; where and for how much to pawn such-and-such an article; how to manage so that Fyodor Mikhailovich wouldn't find out about some creditor's visit. . . ."[119] (She managed to settle the debts by 1881, the year Dostoevsky died.) Their stepson Paul, now married, continued to press for cash and threatened to complain to Dostoevsky, who felt a sense of moral obligation to care for the young man, having promised this to his dying wife.

Anna sought an independent position as a stenographer, but Dostoevsky thwarted her employment because the thought of her being away from home troubled him more than their financial strain. In 1872 she applied to work at a provincial conference and Dostoevsky consented, later admitting that he counted on her rejection by the chairman of the conference. When Anna was hired, he raised objections to her traveling alone. She declined the job offer, fearing his scenes and also realizing that he was capable of showing up at the conference to fetch her back.

That year, trying to secure an income, the couple launched their own publishing venture, deciding to bring out *The Devils*. It was a bold move: their friends believed the project financially risky. At the time, books were printed and distributed across Russia by several major firms; a novelist publishing his own work and selling it from his home was likely to fail. Although Dostoevsky had successfully produced *Time* and *Epoch* magazines with his brother, he had handled only the literary duties.

Having to gain business experience they both lacked, Anna gathered information: she came to printing houses and bookshops with casual inquiries, learning about methods of dealing with booksellers, such as discounts based on the number of copies. Books were published on a cash basis, but she learned that for a well-known author, like Dostoevsky, any printer would extend six months' credit, to which interest would apply. After estimating that they needed to produce thirty-five hundred copies, she contracted a reputable printing firm and the work began. Anna managed the entire business part, but was also checking first and second proofs, while the final proofreading was left to Dostoevsky. "The end of 1872 and the beginning of the following year passed in work connected with the book."[120] When the novel was bound and delivered to their house, the couple admired its appearance. Impatient to make a first sale, Dostoevsky took a copy to a prominent bookseller, his acquaintance, but returned with a money-losing offer. Anna decided he had failed because he did not take the initiative.

In January 1873, she advertised the novel and anticipated a response. Her calculation proved accurate: that same morning, messengers from several bookshops were at her door. They began bargaining over the discount on the retail price, only to find that Anna knew all about the trade and what terms to accept.

> New buyers came, and the morning buyers returned for a new supply of books. It was evident that the book was having a great success, and I felt a rare sense of triumph. I was happy about the money, of course, but mainly because I had found myself an interesting business—the publication of my dear husband's work. I was pleased also with the fact that the enterprise had come out so well in defiance of the warnings of my literary advisors.[121]

Waking up at noon, after he wrote all night, Dostoevsky learned that Anna had sold a hundred and fifteen copies. The stock was almost sold before the year's end, providing the couple with a profit of four thousand rubles. This success encouraged the Dostoevskys to also publish *The Idiot* and *Notes from the House of the Dead* on their own. In addition, in 1876–77 Anna handled publication of a monthly journal, *Diary of a Writer*, to which Dostoevsky was sole contributor. During her publishing activity of thirty-eight years, she would prove herself an expert manager. A printer, Mikhail Alexandrov, who worked with her, recalls how she handled the business side of publishing the journal:

> . . . All the transactions with the printing plant, with the paper factory, with the binders, with the booksellers and newspaper distributors and also with the packaging and shipping of the publications through the mail, were undertaken by Anna Grigorievna, who had earlier received an excellent preparation for the activity by supervising the publication of individual works of Fyodor Mikhailovich.[122]

In 1873, Dostoevsky became editor-in-chief of a conservative magazine, *The Citizen*, which provided a modest but steady income of three thousand rubles (five thousand with his regular contributions). It was a demanding job requiring him to read piles of manuscripts and galley proofs, which took time from his creative work. But it was even more difficult for Dostoevsky, given his irritability and explosive nature, to maintain good relationships with the staff and authors. He could not avoid conflicts even with some of the most loyal contributors and, by all accounts, was unpopular. Anna managed to save some of his relationships by "forgetting" to dispatch Dostoevsky's angry letters. His editorship led to a major blunder in 1874 when in violation of censorship rules he published a direct quotation from the Emperor's address. He pleaded guilty and was sentenced to forty-eight hours' arrest. While he served this sentence in a guardhouse, Anna came to visit him with his favorite fresh rolls. In excellent spirits after his imprisonment, Dostoevsky joked that it was good they had put him away, for in jail he reread *Les Misérables*.

Although Dostoevsky's editorship lasted just over a year (he resigned his position in April of 1874), his health noticeably declined during this term. He developed a cough, and his breathing problems deteriorated into an early stage of emphysema, which would kill him seven years later. For several years he traveled without his family for rest cures in Ems, Germany.

While apart from Anna, Dostoevsky suffered from anxiety and "from all sorts of doubts" and had difficulty writing.[123] His letters from Ems were filled with requests that she write more often, "even just 12 lines, like a telegram about the children's health and your own. You wouldn't believe how I worry about the children and suffer because of that."[124] If her reply was delayed (Dostoevsky was under surveillance until 1875 and censors still read his correspondence although he was a loyalist), he imagined every conceivable trouble. Dostoevsky would tell Anna, expecting officials to read his letter, that he did not mind if the censors knew how much he loved his wife. "I can hardly wait for a letter from you, my darling. . . . You're a little nasty in that regard, but still you're my only joy, and it's very hard for me alone here without you . . . I have complete loneliness now and in addition nothing but trouble. Write me in detail about the children. . . . Details about their conversations and their gestures."[125] Her stories about the children "revived" Dostoevsky.[126] According to Anna, he had a great capacity for relating to children, entering their world; he played games with them, danced, and carried on "the most animated conversations with them."[127]

While the couple's apprehension over their children's health was shared, Dostoevsky took his to extremes. He could be alarmed by small occurrences at home and scrutinized Anna's letters for any sign of trouble. Once, he wrote her of his exasperating nightmare, that their son, Fedya, climbed onto the windowsill and fell from the fourth floor. Anna replied with irony, which had a sobering effect on Dostoevsky: "Please calm yourself, my darling! The children are in good health and Fedya, from Saturday to Sunday night, was not falling from the fourth floor, but peacefully sleeping in bed."[128]

Anna's cheerful nature had begun to change: she complained of bad nerves and was now prone to anxiety and mood swings. During Dostoevsky's absences, she feared he would have an epileptic attack, leaving him helpless among strangers. In 1873, upon receiving a telegram from him, she screamed and burst into tears in front of the postman, imagining that her husband was ill. Her hands shook so badly that she could not open the telegram, and she continued to scream, drawing a small crowd. "When I finally read it, I became insanely happy, and cried and laughed a long time."[129] At Dostoevsky's remark, Anna "merged" with him "into a single body and single soul."[130] In a photograph taken eleven years into their marriage, she stares unsmilingly, with grave expression: her face and posture betray the tension and stress she has absorbed while handling Dostoevsky's heightened emotional states.

Her happiest memories were of winter 1874–75 in Staraya Russa, a place south of Petersburg, which the family initially chose as their summer retreat. They kept returning over the years, but to Anna, their first trip was the most memorable, when from the boat taking them across Lake Ilmen, she and Dostoevsky admired the white stone walls of ancient Novgorod with its church cupolas. "It was a long time since we had felt so happy and so much at peace!"[131]

At Staraya Russa, Dostoevsky wrote his novel *A Raw Youth*, to be published in *Notes of the Fatherland*, a prominent populist magazine. Katkov was publishing *Anna Karenina* and his magazine was paying top royalties to Tolstoy, so he could not afford advances to Dostoevsky. But in 1874, he received a profitable offer from Nikolai Nekrasov, the editor of *Notes of the Fatherland*, a magazine of the political camp opposite to the extremely conservative *The Citizen*, which Dostoevsky had edited. (The first to recognize Dostoevsky's literary talent, Nekrasov became his friend; later, they were "literary enemies" representing different political camps.) Nekrasov was also a great poet, so when he visited their apartment a curious Anna would stay by the closed door listening to their conversation.

Dostoevsky replied to Nekrasov's offer that he did not make any decisions without his wife and had to consult her. Nekrasov was appalled that he was so much under his wife's heel, to which Dostoevsky responded that he trusted Anna's intelligence and business sense. As Dostoevsky walked out of the room, Anna told him to accept Nekrasov's offer immediately. Nekrasov would pay more than Katkov's magazine, but Dostoevsky doubted whether his novel would fit into the populist magazine and whether he would be required to make changes he could not accept; he would then have to return the advance. His fears were unjustified, but because of financial uncertainty Anna decided to spend the winter in Staraya Russa where life was much cheaper than in Petersburg.

In this retreat, they were just as isolated as during their years abroad, while maintaining an exact schedule to accommodate Dostoevsky's work. "After midday he would call me to his study and dictate what he had written during the night. Working with him was always a joy for me, and I privately took great pride in helping him and in being the first of his readers to hear the author's work from his own lips." He would dictate from two to three in the afternoon and, when finished, would always ask her opinion.

> "I say it's fine," I would reply. But my "fine" meant to Fyodor Mikhailovich that perhaps the just-dictated scene, though successful from his point of view, had not produced any particular effect on me. And my husband placed great importance on my spontaneous reactions. Somehow it always happened that those pages of the novel which had a moving or shattering effect on me had the same effect on most of his readers as well. . . .[132]

When Dostoevsky had doubts about certain chapters, he would read them to Anna and watch her reaction. A chapter describing a young girl's suicide in *A Raw Youth* produced an overwhelming impression on her, as it later would on Nekrasov. When Dostoevsky took the first installment of the novel to his editor, Nekrasov stayed up reading all night; as he remarked, the suicide scene was "the peak of perfection."[133] Upon learning about this observation from Dostoevsky, Anna wrote back to him that she was the first to use those very words.[134] Dostoevsky not only accepted her business advice, but also heeded her suggestions about his work. Back in 1874, she was asking him not to begin writing *A Raw Youth* until he worked out a detailed plan for the novel: "Haste will only spoil it. I remember how it was with *The Idiot* and *The Devils*."[135] Dostoevsky's notebooks for *A Raw Youth* where he detailed a plan for the novel were the most extensive he ever made.

Frequent fires in the community's wooden houses were part of the monotony in Staraya Russa. At the sound of the bell Anna would habitually dress the sleeping children and carry them outside. The bundles with Dostoevsky's notebooks and manuscripts of *A Raw Youth* were prepared every evening, to be rescued next. When the danger passed, Dostoevsky's papers had to be unpacked and returned to where they belonged, since he was fussy about order.

These manuscripts and notebooks nearly perished in 1875, when at the end of summer the family—along with their newly born son, Alyosha, and his nanny—journeyed from Staraya Russa to Petersburg. (After Alyosha was born on August 10, Anna quickly regained her strength and was back taking Dostoevsky's final dictations of the novel.) In Novgorod, after they crossed Lake Ilmen, Anna discovered that a black leather suitcase with Dostoevsky's belongings, notebooks, and the manuscript of *A Raw Youth*, had disappeared. Without the notebooks, it would be impossible for Dostoevsky to reconstruct the final parts of the novel, which he was to take to the magazine the following day. When Anna reported the incident to Dostoevsky, "he turned white and said softly, 'Yes, that is a great loss. What in the world will we do now?'" Without telling him, Anna took a cab to the desolate neighborhood of the steamship dock, assuming correctly that the suitcase had been left there. The office was locked for the night, so she banged on the door, found a guard, and obtained the suitcase, weighing over seventy kilos. The guard vanished into the warehouse and the cabby refused to leave his coachbox out of fear of thugs, so she dragged the suitcase herself, stopping at every step. She rode home sitting on the precious cargo, "resolving not to give it up if we should be attacked by the hoodlums."[136] When she noticed that Dostoevsky had come out on the porch to look for her, she yelled to him from a distance, "Fyodor Mikhailovich, it's me, and I have the suitcase!"

Almost ten years into their marriage, Anna wrote Dostoevsky that they were "one in a thousand families" where husband and wife understood each other "so deeply and lastingly."[137] She revered him as an artist and man, and assured him that "I would not have been so happy with anyone else as I am happy with you . . ."[138] Their love and appreciation of each other was only growing: Dostoevsky told her that after ten years, he was more in love with her than on the eve of their wedding.[139] She kept wondering whether she deserved to be loved by such a brilliant man, writing him with a near-religious ecstasy, that she was just "an ordinary woman, the golden mean. . . . As I've always told you, 'You are my sun, you are up the mountain, and I am lying at its foot, praying.'"[140] Dostoevsky responded in tune with her chanting, "You're my idol, my god . . . I fall to my knees before you and kiss both your feet endlessly."[141] Anna was his "only friend," he wrote her, and he felt grateful to her for many things. He believed she was capable of much more than assisting him and managing their publishing enterprise.

> My dear joy, where did you get the idea that you are "the golden mean"? You are a rare woman. . . . You manage not only the entire household, not only my affairs, but you pilot all of us capricious and bothersome people, beginning with me and ending with Lyosha.[142] But in my affairs you have really just squandered your gifts. You stay up nights managing the sale and "office" of *Diary* [*of a Writer*]. . . . If you were made a queen and given a whole kingdom, I swear to you that you would rule it like no one—so much intelligence, common sense, heart and ability to manage do you have.[143]

The year 1876 brought success for their periodical, *Diary of a Writer*, and overall it was a happy year with no major worries for Anna over the children's and Dostoevsky's health. As her natural high spirits returned, she was even up to a prank. To taunt Dostoevsky, who always told her of his love, she sent him an anonymous, clichéd letter she had copied from a trash novel they had recently read together. She thought he would recognize it but, if not, was prepared to risk his reaction. The letter said that "a certain person close to you is deceiving you basely," and it suggested that Dostoevsky look for the proof in his wife's locket, "which she carries next to her heart."

Anna's prank nearly ended in tragedy: when he read the letter, an enraged Dostoevsky ripped the chain off her neck, injuring her. He did not recall it from the trash novel: anonymous letters are so alike. Anna watched as with trembling hands he unsuccessfully tried to open the locket. When he finally succeeded, he was stunned to discover two portraits—his own and their daughter Lyuba's. It took him a while to understand why Anna herself had sent the anonymous letter; when he came to his senses, Dostoevsky told her, "I might have strangled you in my rage! . . . I beg you, don't ever joke about such things—I can't answer for myself when I'm in a fury!"[144] Learning "what a frenzied, almost irresponsible state" Dostoevsky was capable of reaching, Anna did not tease him again.

She had few amusements (collecting stamps was one[145]) and practically never went out, while Dostoevsky's growing popularity required him to accept invitations. Anna did not accompany him to fashionable salons and literary evenings partly because she could not afford to dress for these occasions: "Our financial affairs were always in such a state that it was impossible to think about fancy clothes."[146] There were three small children, Dostoevsky took annual treatments in Germany, and they had debts, so she gave up entertainment. It was at Dostoevsky's insistence that in 1873 she bought a seasonal pass for herself to the Italian opera, which she loved. (Established by Tsar Nicholas I, the permanent Italian opera in Petersburg was regarded as equal to that in Paris or London.)

But since she wanted to save, she purchased a seat in the gallery, opposite an enormous chandelier that obstructed the stage; still, she was able to enjoy the singing of the great artists of their time, Mme. Patti, Sofia Scalchi, and Camille Everardi.

During their evening conversations, Dostoevsky tried to compensate Anna for her lack of society by telling her what he saw and heard during the day—and "his tales were so enthralling and were told so expressively that they completely replaced social life for me." Fascinated with his talk, losing track of time, she occasionally stayed up with Dostoevsky until five in the morning.

Dostoevsky's "personal periodical" made him a public figure whose political and literary views and opinions were heeded. *Diary of a Writer* revealed some of the best and worst aspects of his talent and personality. In it, he displayed his progressive views on women and showed his compassion for the children of the underprivileged, such as the juvenile criminals of whom he wrote in the very first issue of the *Diary* for 1876. But this periodical also revealed his extreme nationalism, religious intolerance, and, primarily, his hatred of Jews, which exceeded the typical contemporary prejudice of his country. (Anna shared this prejudice, but to a lesser degree.)

The December issue for 1877 reported Nekrasov's death. Anna attended the poet's funeral with Dostoevsky, who was grieving the loss of his old friend and editor; the couple spent the evening reading Nekrasov's poetry, which both admired. Walking in the cortege behind Nekrasov's coffin, Dostoevsky contemplated his own death (with his emphysema progressing, he realized it would not be long). He asked Anna to promise that she would not bury him among his literary "enemies," and, on the spur of the moment, she promised to bury him beside the poet Vasily Zhukovsky, whom he esteemed, in the most important cemetery of Petersburg, the Alexander Nevsky Lavra. When Dostoevsky died three years later, Anna, without expecting to, was actually able to keep her "fantastic" promise.

In May 1878, the Dostoevskys' younger son, Alyosha, died of epilepsy he had inherited. The death of their beloved three-year-old had a shattering effect on both. Anna grew apathetic, "impassive to everything: the management of the household, our business affairs, and even my own children...." Dostoevsky's plea that she submit to God's will and accept their child's death with humility had no effect. Later describing her grief in *The Brothers Karamazov*, Dostoevsky employed Anna's experiences, doubts, and thoughts, which she shared with him, in the chapter "Women of Faith." As he dictated the chapter to her, Anna "wrote with one hand and wiped my tears with the other. Fyodor Mikhailovich saw how excited I was, came over to me, and kissed me on the head without saying a word." *The Brothers Karamazov* was Dostoevsky's last and most important novel, which brought him wide recognition and which he dedicated to Anna.

In January 1879, when the first chapters of this novel appeared in *The Russian Herald*, it was an immediate success. Throughout this year and in the next, Dostoevsky was frequently invited to readings where audiences received him enthusiastically. Because of his fragile health, Anna accompanied him to these literary events, dressed in an elegant gown of black silk made for such occasions. She would be loaded with Dostoevsky's books, cough medicine, extra handkerchiefs, and a plaid to wrap around his throat: he called her his "faithful armor-bearer." Before going onstage, Dostoevsky would invariably ask her to give him her hand for luck; at the lectern he would not begin reading until he spotted her in the audience, so she would take out her white handkerchief to help him find her. When she asked what he would do if she were to leave, Dostoevsky replied that he would stop reading, quit the stage, and follow her.

Their finances improved and he was finally able to buy her expensive diamond earrings to replace his wedding present. (Dostoevsky consulted a connoisseur of precious stones on the purchase. Ever meticulous, Anna recorded, in an index of his gifts, the date of purchase, name of merchant, and price.) When at a literary evening she wore the earrings for the first time, Dostoevsky was jubilant.

While other writers were reading my husband and I were sitting together along a wall decorated with mirrors. I suddenly noticed that he was looking to the side and smiling at somebody. Then he turned to me and whispered blissfully, "They sparkle, they have a gorgeous sparkle!" It turned out that the play of the stones was brilliant under the multiple lights, and my husband was as happy as a child.

A superb reader, Dostoevsky produced an overwhelming effect on his audience. His voice, usually thin and delicate, was penetratingly distinct in moments of excitement. A contemporary recalled that Dostoevsky's audience was gripped by his emotion when he read a chapter from *The Brothers Karamazov*: "And never since have I felt such deathly stillness in an auditorium, such total absorption of the spiritual life of a crowd of a thousand people in the mood of one man.... When Dostoevsky read, the listener ... fell utterly under the hypnotic power of this emaciated, unprepossessing, elderly man...." Like other listeners, Anna often wept during the readings, although she knew these excerpts by heart.

As fans surrounded him afterward, she "used to stand aside, though never far away." When at Easter Dostoevsky read at a benefit for the Bestuzhev Higher Courses for Women, a throng of female students separated the couple in the foyer. Although the crowd pushed her aside, Anna was sure Dostoevsky would not leave without her. Indeed, he soon addressed the girls: "Wherever is my wife? ... Please, find her!"

Unlike Dostoevsky, who was jealous of the slightest attention paid Anna by their male acquaintances, she was relaxed even when female admirers followed him in throngs. Korvin-Krukovskaya, to whom Dostoevsky had briefly been engaged, visited the family in Staraya Russa and was welcome to stay for the summer. (She married a French revolutionary socialist and member of the Paris Commune, Charles Victor Jaclard. In 1887, when the Russian authorities wanted to deport Jaclard, Anna interceded through Dostoevsky's government connection, and deportation was postponed.) Anna rarely accompanied Dostoevsky to fashionable salons hosted by his women friends Elizabeth Naryshkin-Kurakina and Countess Alexandra Tolstoy, both ladies-in-waiting to grand duchesses. (The latter was also Leo Tolstoy's relative and confidante.) Dostoevsky enjoyed conversations with these worldly and intelligent women and preferred their company to male society in which he was quickly exasperated by political arguments.

Although he had few male friends, Dostoevsky acquired a companion in the government official Konstantin Pobedonostsev, having met him during his editorship at *The Citizen*. Back then, Pobedonostsev was a highly placed official and a tutor of the future Alexander III. In 1880, Pobedonostsev became the Ober-Procurator of the Holy Synod and the secular head of the Orthodox Church. Dostoevsky thus maintained a relationship with one of the most influential men in the empire who would symbolize reactionary Russia, and who would become responsible for Tolstoy's excommunication in 1901.

In 1880, Russia celebrated the Pushkin festival with the unveiling of his monument in Moscow. In a rare display of unity, the statue was funded by the public, making it a truly popular event. With political rivalry temporarily abandoned, the liberal Ivan Turgenev would share the podium with the conservative Dostoevsky. Their speeches were greatly anticipated: to rent a window or a balcony overlooking the square for the ceremony cost an exorbitant fifty rubles.

In the eyes of readers, Dostoevsky's recently published *The Brothers Karamazov*, his best creation, made him an equal of Tolstoy. But after his religious conversion, Tolstoy believed such events futile and did not attend, so the festival was remembered for decades because of Dostoevsky's participation. (The two writers never met, but had a high regard for each other's work. *The Brothers Karamazov* was the last book Tolstoy read on the fateful night of his departure from home in 1910.) However, Anna would not witness Dostoevsky's triumph, later considering this the greatest deprivation of her life.

She wanted to go along, but he objected: after Alyosha died of epilepsy, Dostoevsky doubled his anxieties over the children's health and would not leave Lyuba and Fyodor in the care of a nurse, even for a single day. In addition, there was Dostoevsky's pettiness, for which he was well known. They estimated that the family's expenses of living in Moscow for a week would come to around three hundred rubles, and Anna would need to tailor a respectable light-colored dress. After much deliberation, the couple decided they could not afford it, even though their financial circumstances were no longer as shaky as before. By then, most of their debts had been paid, Dostoevsky was receiving higher royalties for his new novel, and in January 1880 Anna had launched a new profitable enterprise: a book service for out-of-town residents. During the very first year her business yielded a profit of eight hundred rubles, far more than what she needed for the trip.

Dostoevsky promised to write daily, describing the festival in the minutest detail, and to obtain signatures from distinguished Russians for Anna's autograph collection. But all this could not replace a chance to be with her husband and see him at the height of his success, for which they both had worked indefatigably for fourteen years. Although he not only kept his word, but on occasions even wrote twice a day, Anna was tempted to attend and even dreamed of coming incognito to witness his speech. Concerned over Dostoevsky's health, she feared the excitement would trigger an epileptic attack: "More than once I decided to make the trip to Moscow and stay there without showing myself to anyone but only watching over Fyodor Mikhailovich." But throughout his exhausting twenty-two-day stay in Moscow, Dostoevsky remained surprisingly cheerful and in good health. (As with other speakers, his expenses were paid by the city government, the Moscow Duma, something neither he nor Anna knew at the start.)

On June 6, the date of the unveiling, public jubilation ran high: as Dostoevsky wrote Anna, "You couldn't describe it even in 20 pages. . . ."[147] During the following days when speeches were presented, Dostoevsky delivered his address to a packed Hall of Moscow Nobility, and was received with a roar of "rapture, enthusiasm (all because of *The Karamazovs*!) . . . I was stopped by thunderous applause on absolutely every page . . . I read loudly, with fire." Dostoevsky expressed his cherished idea that Pushkin gave Russians faith in their individuality and special destiny, "hope in the strength of our people, and with it our faith in our future independent mission in the family of European peoples."[148] He accurately guessed the mood of the crowd that had come to celebrate their national poet, unlike Turgenev, whose attitudes were Western. Dostoevsky stole the event; when he finished, there was a thirty-minute ovation. He described his triumph to Anna, "When I concluded—I won't tell you about the roar, the outcry of rapture: strangers among the audience wept, sobbed, embraced each other. . . . The meeting's order was violated: everyone rushed toward the platform to see me: highborn ladies, female students, state secretaries . . . they all hugged me and kissed me."[149]

Because Dostoevsky praised the spiritual strength of the Russian woman, a delegation of female students crowned him with a laurel wreath, which read, "On behalf of Russian women, about whom you said so many good things." The speech appeared in several periodicals and in *Diary of a Writer*; six thousand copies were sold over a few days, with another press run required.

During his final year, the public treated Dostoevsky as an oracle; young people followed him in throngs, asking questions to which he responded almost in speeches. Anna tried to control the stream of visitors to their apartment, but Dostoevsky insisted it was his duty to see everyone. Often people came to argue over political issues, which exhausted him, and Anna would interrupt the meetings with various excuses, as Dostoevsy's doctors had warned him that physical exertion or excitement could trigger a pulmonary hemorrhage.

Dostoevsky had to send the final installment of *The Brothers Karamazov* to *The Russian Herald* by early October. Some 320 pages remained to be written over the summer months, and Anna was helping him meet this deadline in their Staraya Russa cottage all through the summer and in September; "the autumn was a beautiful one."[150] Following its magazine publication, the couple issued *The Brothers Karamazov* in book form: three thousand copies sold out within a few days. In early 1881, their debts were settled and, for the first time in their marriage, they had a surplus of around five thousand rubles.

Dostoevsky, in high spirits, visited friends and even agreed to participate in a theatrical performance at Countess Tolstoy's home; it was a play about Ivan the Terrible in which he had a role as a reclusive monk. Anna was now accompanying him to all these gatherings, aware that his emphysema was progressing: he was breathing heavily, as if through a cloth folded several times, and their ascent to the third floor (of the Nobility Assembly Hall, for example) could take twenty-five minutes.

Anna tells that on January 26, he moved a heavy bookcase to retrieve his penholder, which he also used for rolling his cigarettes.[151] The strain caused an artery in his lung to burst and he began spitting blood. She immediately called a doctor, who was late to arrive. In the meantime, Dostoevsky had had an exhausting visitor: his sister Vera Mikhailovna visited from Moscow and started a quarrel over some property. When his sister left, Dostoevsky suffered another, more forceful hemorrhage.

The news of his grave illness spread quickly and people, some unknown to the Dostoevskys, came to inquire about his health: "The doorbell kept ringing from two in the afternoon until late at night and had to be tied up." Anna spent the night on a floor mattress next to Dostoevsky's couch. He asked her to read an excerpt from the Gospel, given to him by the Decembrist wives in Siberia. It had helped him through the darkest days of his sentence and was now closing his life, at fifty-nine: "But Jesus said to him in answer, 'Do not hold me back. . . .'" When Anna read this passage from Matthew, Dostoevsky told her, "That means I'm going to die." Dostoevsky took communion and bid farewell to the children and to Anna, telling her that he had always loved her passionately "and was never unfaithful to you even in my thoughts."

During his last day, journalists, relatives, and visitors crowded their home. "My dear husband died in the presence of a multitude, some of them deeply attached to him but others entirely indifferent both to him and to the inconsolable sorrow of our orphaned family."[152] Upon his death, a stream of visitors poured through their apartment for two and a half days, and the rooms were so packed that Anna had a hard time pushing through the crowd to stand near the coffin in Dostoevsky's study. "At times the air grew so thick, there was so little oxygen left, that the icon-lamp and the tall tapers surrounding the catafalque would go out. There were strangers in our house not only during the day but even through the night."

Anna shut herself in a separate room occupied by her mother but would not be left alone: delegations knocked on her door to read addresses about Dostoevsky's importance as a national writer. She heard them in silence, suppressing every show of emotion, "out of fear that some idle reporter would write a preposterous description of my grief the next day."

After three days of listening to the many speeches of condolence, I finally became desperate and said to myself, "My God, how they torture me! What is it to me, 'what Russia has lost'? What do I care about Russia now? Can't you understand what *I've* lost? I've lost the best person in the world, the joy and pride and happiness of my life, my sun, my god! Take pity on me, take pity on me as a person, and don't tell me at this time about Russia's loss!"

A messenger on behalf of the Alexander Nevsky Lavra came to offer a place in one of their cemeteries without charge, an honor to the writer who advocated the Orthodox faith. As she had promised Dostoevsky, Anna inquired about a plot near the poet Zhukovsky's grave and it turned out that the site was available.

Thirty thousand people attended the funeral, but Anna and Lyuba, eleven, left their tickets at home and were stopped at the monastery gate, nearly missing the requiem. They told Anna that there were "plenty of Dostoevsky's widows here who have gone inside already, and some of them are with children, too." There were fifteen hundred mourners in the Church of the Holy Spirit, and Anna and her daughter only managed to get in when an acquaintance confirmed their identity. Walking directly behind the coffin to the cemetery, Anna could not see the huge procession, stretching for almost a mile, with banners and wreaths bearing Dostoevsky's name, titles of his works, and his quotations; she would only later learn this from illustrations and articles. When the procession entered the cemetery, already packed, fans had to climb trees and cling to fences. More than seventy wreaths were brought to Dostoevsky's grave, taken away at the end of the ceremony for souvenirs.

Anna refused the offer from the Ministry of Internal Affairs to pay for the funeral, believing it was her responsibility. Another offer was to educate her children at state expense in the most prestigious institutions. She could enroll Fedya at the Imperial Page Corps, which educated aristocratic elite, being Russia's equivalent of Eton, and send Lyuba to the Smolny Institute, the best school for daughters of the nobility. But she was determined to raise her children on the proceeds from publishing Dostoevsky's works, by the labor of their father and mother, as he himself would have done, so she would send them to other schools.

When the Minister of Finance sent a letter saying that the Emperor had granted her an annual pension of two thousand rubles, Anna rushed to Dostoevsky's study to share the news, which would undoubtedly make him happy,[153] but upon entering his room realized he was no longer in this world. Her forgetfulness lasted several months after Dostoevsky's death: Anna would hurry home so as not to keep him waiting for dinner, bought his favorite sweets, and would want to share some news with him right away.

Although Anna was only thirty-five when Dostoevsky died and survived him by thirty-seven years, she never considered remarrying. "I was clearly aware of one thing only: that from that moment on, my personal life . . . was finished, and that I was orphaned in my heart forever." Later, she would remark with a typical irony, "But whom could one marry after Dostoevsky? Tolstoy only!"[154] During the decades that followed, Anna carried on her mission as before: she felt strongly that her task was to disseminate Dostoevsky's ideas and works.

Contemplating the fourteen years of their marriage, which she said gave her "the greatest happiness possible," she wrote that theirs was a union of two different personalities with "dissimilar views." She didn't echo Dostoevsky's political views, nor did she try to meddle with his soul, and he "prized my non-interference in his spiritual and intellectual life. And therefore he would sometimes say to me, 'You are the only woman who ever understood me!' ... He looked on me as a rock on which he felt he could lean, or rather, rest. 'And it won't let you fall, and it gives warmth.'"[155]

The only person Dostoevsky trusted completely, Anna became his ambassador after his death. This role required her to eventually liquidate her prosperous book business, *F.M. Dostoevsky, Bookseller (To the Provinces Only)*. Offered fifteen hundred rubles to sell it, she refused, feeling responsible for the integrity of the firm, established under her husband's name. It was inexpensive to run and had the potential to develop into a major book firm, which had happened to similar small services she knew about. But she gave up this attractive idea, closed her firm rather than sell it, and undertook publishing Dostoevsky's collected works.

Beginning in 1883, Anna issued seven editions of Dostoevsky's works, with a success she did not anticipate. The first edition in fourteen volumes included, aside from Dostoevsky's fiction, his letters, notebooks, and material for his first biography. These were mostly reminiscences about Dostoevsky, which friends and family contributed at Anna's urging. Later, to satisfy the demand, she also issued separate volumes of Dostoevsky's prose at affordable prices.

Her financial success left her with mixed feelings because Dostoevsky could not enjoy it. He used to worry that after his death his family would become impoverished and there would be no money for his children's education. Anna also witnessed his artistic despair when he wrote hurriedly without time to revise his great novels. He worked under tight deadlines, his memory clouded by epileptic attacks, with no time to recover: he had to rush to dispatch his manuscripts to get paid. Anna would remind Dostoevsky's critics of this when reading their remarks that his prose was less polished than Tolstoy's.

For decades, Anna collected everything associated with Dostoevsky's memory. When the Moscow Historical Museum gave her a separate space for storage, a bright eight-cornered room to keep Dostoevsky's archive, she donated his manuscripts, notebooks, letters, portraits, busts, library, autographs, and numerous other artifacts—4,230 items in all. In addition, Anna produced a detailed four-hundred-page index of these items, including information about books Dostoevsky read, buildings associated with his memory, etc. When her index was published in 1906, it was described as "a unique achievement in Russian literary bibliography."[156]

With proceeds from her publishing she established a parochial boarding school in Dostoevsky's name for peasant children in Staraya Russa, both boys and girls. Becoming the school's administrator, she raised funds at charitable concerts she organized. Before 1917, over a thousand girls graduated from Dostoevsky's school, becoming rural teachers. Her other dream was to establish a Dostoevsky literary museum in their Staraya Russa house, which she purchased after his death. According to her will, the house would go to their son Fyodor, who had to maintain it as a museum.[157]

In her letter to philosopher and Dostoevsky scholar Vasily Rosanov, who left a prominent work about *The Brothers Karamazov*, Anna wrote, "If I did something for the memory of my dear husband, I did it out of gratitude for . . . the hours of highly artistic enjoyment I experienced reading his works."[158] (Rosanov was fascinated with Dostoevsky, whom he never met; this interest led him to marry Dostoevsky's former mistress, Apollinaria Suslova.)

In 1906, Anna sold the copyright to Dostoevsky's collected works to the rich publisher Alfred Marx, who issued them with a circulation of 120,000 copies, exceeding Anna's publications more than twenty times over. Although she shared proceeds with her children, the public speculated about her immense wealth. Anna wrote to Rosanov in October 1907, "I am amused when they call me 'rich.' I have no wealth. I have invested and keep investing my earnings in a school in Staraya Russa, the Museum, and my publications [of Dostoevsky's separate works], and as for myself I live very modestly."[159] Although Anna worked to preserve Russia's cultural heritage, in pre-revolutionary years she was seen as "a tight-fisted and shrewd businesswoman." Dostoevsky's biographer Leonid Grossman, who interviewed her in winter 1916–17, summarizes contemporary criticism of her:

> During her lifetime Anna Grigorievna earned a reputation as a business person, practical, resourceful, but at times going too far in her efficiency. She achieved brilliant results in a complex publishing business, which she learned on her own. . . . Anna Grigorievna's efficiency inspired many accusations and in the end cast a . . . shadow on her reputation, obscuring the true achievements of this remarkably hard-working woman. . . .[160]

In her sixties, Anna was regularly seen in public libraries, where, in Grossman's words, she worked with "all the stamina and verve of a young student."[161] She was working on her *Reminiscences*, she told Grossman, and her mission was far from over. In 1909, she became a member of the newly established Russian Stenographical Society. Anna revisited Europe, the cities where she and Dostoevsky had lived; in the Dresden gallery and in Basel she stood in front of the paintings that had impressed him. She dined in the "Italian Village" overlooking the Elbe, writing her daughter Lyuba, "The memories overwhelmed me."[162]

In 1910, upon learning that a talented director, Vladimir Nemirovich-Danchenko, was staging *The Brothers Karamazov* at the Moscow Art Theater, Anna wrote him saying she wanted to see the play. Two years later, during its premiere in Petersburg, she met with the actor[163] who played the role of Dmitry Karamazov. He would later describe how during an intermission, Anna (then sixty-five) approached him, saying excitedly, "How wonderful, that's precisely what Fyodor Mikhailovich had in mind. Oh, if only he were alive, if only he were alive!" Their ten-minute conversation was more valuable to the actor than "a hundred biographies about Dostoevsky . . . I sensed his breath beside me."[164] Anna too recalled that premiere with elation: "I was sitting in my box-seat and praying to God, so that He would grant me the ultimate happiness by sending me death right here, this very minute. My sacred dream came true—I saw my *Brothers Karamazov*. To die with theater glasses in my hands, which Fyodor Mikhailovich presented to me—what a good death that would be!"[165]

In 1917, Sergei Prokofiev, who had recently composed the opera *The Gambler*, also wanted to meet Anna. He said he was anxious to meet the woman to whom Dostoevsky had dictated this novel. When they parted, the composer asked Anna to make an inscription about the sun in his guest journal. He expected she would write something about slanting rays of the evening sun, since it was Dostoevsky's celebrated imagery, but Anna wrote: "The sun of my life—Fyodor Dostoevsky."[166]

She met the outbreak of the 1917 Revolution in a sanatorium near Petersburg, working on some unfinished projects and annotating Dostoevsky's letters, which she was preparing for publication. As she remarked in 1916, his letters to her were still the source of her greatest joy and pride. In her temporary home she was surrounded, as usual, with Dostoevsky's portraits, manuscripts, and books. Soon after the March uprising in 1917,[167] a crowd of armed workers came to the resort, searching for a tsarist minister. "The crowd moved directly to our hotel, and in a few minutes we heard from downstairs the slamming of doors and tramping of feet . . . I locked myself here, in this room, thinking with horror that these things, so precious to me, all these portraits, piles of manuscripts, letters, and books were doomed to perish."[168] The revolutionaries did not search her room, saying they knew who she was. Their contemporary events did not interest her: as she told Grossman, she remained fully immersed in the past, somewhere around the 1870s, amidst the society of Dostoevsky's friends, the circle that was no more. "I feel that everyone who studies Dostoevsky's life and works becomes my family."[169]

In May 1917, she traveled to the Caucasus, joining her son's family at her dacha near the Black Sea. Part of a small estate, it consisted of a cottage and an apple orchard she herself had planted; she loved the place, naming it "Otrada" (bliss). Dostoevsky felt his family should have an estate, and she wanted their son to inherit it.

That summer, malaria became widespread when construction of a railroad between Adler and Tuapse disturbed swamps. Anna and her family caught the disease and had to urgently leave their place in August. Arriving in Tuapse exhausted, she was unable to continue to Petersburg with the others and stayed to recuperate. Later, she proceeded alone to Yalta in the Crimea and settled in a hotel called "France." In this room, in addition to fighting malaria, she suffered a series of mini-strokes.

She spent days in bed, shivering underneath a heap of blankets and her coat, speaking with occasional visitors about Dostoevsky. A woman physician, Zinaida Kovrigina, who visited Anna recalls that Dostoevsky constituted "the goal of her existence, the air she breathed till her last days."[170] According to her visitors and her grandson Andrei Dostoevsky, Anna had several baskets with Dostoevsky's manuscripts, but the fate of these papers is unknown.[171]

At the start of the Civil War and Allied intervention in 1918, Anna was trapped in the Crimea without resources. At seventy-one, she lived through the nightmare Dostoevsky had envisioned, when a single human life did not matter. After the Revolution, her pension was stopped; she wrote her son that she heard a rumor that all pensions would be abolished. "I have no money at all," she told Fedya on January 8. "I have to pay a doctor, for my hotel, and for expensive medicine."[172] There were food shortages, and bread was rationed. As during the first year with Dostoevsky, Anna worried about her hotel bill. She wrote Fedya that a woman librarian had lent her some money to pay it; there was even credit extended for several weeks. Anna also worried about Lyuba, who had lived abroad since 1913 but now was left without interest from the family bank account; she knew nothing about her daughter because correspondence had been severed in mid-October 1917.

On January 21, she wrote to her son about a recent battle in Yalta: revolutionary sailors fired a bomb at the city from a torpedo-boat. It exploded near her hotel, breaking neighbors' windows. When the Bolsheviks entered the city, they held a solemn funeral in the City Gardens, burying their dead in a shallow common grave, so there was fear of disease spreading in summer. "But summer is far away. Perhaps, we will be all slaughtered by then. I am so used to the thought of dying suddenly that I fear nothing. If I should die remember me well. I always loved you both and . . . I love you now."

In February, there was a week of bombardment followed by several weeks of anarchy. Anna wrote that the Yalta Revolutionary Committee demanded 20 million rubles from the city; when it failed to collect the sum, the committee forced the banks to release deposits from their current accounts. Anna did not receive the money Fedya had managed to send her: the check was held by the post office to be deposited to a bank from where, she assumed, the Bolsheviks would access it. There was a rumor that the entire bourgeoisie would be annihilated as early as mid-March, that a revolutionary committee would run her hotel; meanwhile, proletarian women wore ominous crests on their sleeves, which read: "The bourgeoisie will be ground down." But, as Anna wrote, "I'm already prepared for death and I'm calm."[173]

Her final letter was on March 29: she needed 200–300 rubles to pay for her hotel and worried that she could be evicted. She shared the terrible news that their dacha by the Black Sea had been burned down and the two old women who lived there as guards had perished; "I would meet the same fate if I would move back, as I wanted. . . ." Anna died on June 9, at the height of Civil War, during starvation and epidemics, and was buried in Yalta, inside

Aleutsky Church. Fedya outlived her by only three years: he died in 1921 in Moscow, from typhus. Lyuba, who became a writer and penned reminiscences about her father, died in Italy in 1926 from leukemia.

While Dostoevsky's grave was a place of pilgrimage, Anna's was only saved from oblivion by a handful of volunteers. Anton Chekhov's sister Maria, a director of his museum in Yalta, looked after it in the early 1930s. Andrei Dostoevsky, Anna's grandson, who was devoted to her memory, visited her grave. In 1932, when Aleutsky Church was demolished, along with numerous others, under Stalin, the family excavated the ruins and moved Anna's grave. Soon after, it was damaged by robbers looking for gold. During World War II, an antiaircraft battery was stationed at the cemetery and Anna's grave was lost, but in 1960 a local researcher detected the site.

Anna had asked to be buried next to her husband at the Alexander Nevsky Monastery, without a separate monument. It took many years for Andrei Dostoevsky to persuade the bureaucracy to fulfill her wish. On the fiftieth anniversary of Anna's death, her remains were reburied in Alexander Nevsky Monastery near the place where her life had begun.

People who met Anna during her final years remember her as a woman of great faith who felt she had realized her dreams. As she told Grossman in 1916, fate gave her, "an ordinary woman," the infinite happiness of being married to a great writer. "But sometimes I redeemed my happiness with great suffering."

CHAPTER TWO

Sophia Tolstoy: Nursemaid of Talent

In 1863, the year Tolstoy began *War and Peace* and the couple's first child was born, nineteen-year-old Sophia wrote in her diary: "My life is so mundane, and my death. But he has such a rich internal life, talent and immortality."[174] Critics would compare Tolstoy to Homer, the creator of the *Iliad*, and even to God Almighty who created the universe. Tolstoy produced a universe of his own: there are 559 characters in *War and Peace* alone. His novels, non-fiction, letters, and diaries add up to ninety volumes, an astounding amount of writing to produce in a lifetime.

Few realized what an extraordinary burden Sophia had to carry: for almost fifty years she was married to one of the most complex artists of the nineteenth century, whose name became as familiar to the world as Shakespeare's. Over the decades, she remained the only woman in Tolstoy's life and also the one on whom he relied for his inspiration and in all his practical affairs.

Sophia was eighteen when she married Tolstoy, who at thirty-four was already celebrated for the novels *Childhood* and *Boyhood* and for *Sebastopol Stories*, his realistic accounts from the battlefield of the Crimean War. When, in winter 1854, the twenty-six-year-old Tolstoy was leaving for the war, Sophia was ten. Struck by the news of his departure (Tolstoy was a frequent guest in her parents' house), she had a cry and decided that she would become a nurse and join him at the front to care for him. In a sense, her juvenile fantasy came true: she was destined to take care of Tolstoy as long as he lived.

In the year Tolstoy left for the war, Sophia read his novel *Childhood* and memorized her favorite passages about the boundless need for love and the power of faith. She said that only Dickens's *David Copperfield* had produced such a powerful impression on her. Coincidentally, this was also Tolstoy's favorite book: "If you were to put the whole of world literature through a sieve and keep only the very best, you would be left with Dickens. If you had to do the same with Dickens, you would be left with *David Copperfield*."[175]

Sophia did not remember when Tolstoy entered her life: he was a friend of her mother, Lyubov Alexandrovna Islavin. Their two families were close for generations: Sophia's maternal grandfather, Alexander Islenev[176], was a neighbor and hunting companion of Tolstoy's father Nicholas. Sophia's mother danced with Tolstoy on his birthdays, and he had experienced even something of a first love toward her. At sixteen, she had married a physician, Andrei Behrs, twenty years her senior.

Sophia's ancestors on her father's side were German Lutherans. Her great-grandfather Ivan Behrs (Johann Bärs) was invited to Russia from Austria as a military instructor by Empress Elizabeth I. Sophia's father and her uncle, Alexander Behrs, became medical doctors and made their careers with the government. (At the time, most prominent doctors in Moscow and Petersburg were German.) Both were music connoisseurs: Sophia's uncle played clarinet and gave concerts in Petersburg to full houses.[177] Among Uncle Alexander's admirers was novelist Ivan Turgenev, with whom the family had close ties. Sophia's father had had an affair with the novelist's mother in his youth and sired a daughter by her. Thus, Sophia's family knew the two foremost Russian novelists, Tolstoy and Turgenev, and both writers visited her parents' home when she was growing up.

Born on August 22, 1844, Sophia was the second of thirteen children, five of whom died in infancy. Behrs was a court physician, and the family lived in a Kremlin apartment near the entrance to Red Square. As children of a court official, they did gymnastics in the Great Kremlin Palace and worshiped at the Church of the Virgin Birth, the chapel for the Grand Dukes and Tsaritzas, and the one where Sophia would marry Tolstoy.

Though Sophia and her two sisters received a typical genteel education at home, with marriage being their goal, their Lutheran background made them feel different. The Behrs children were told they would have to earn their own living and, unlike in noble families, were assigned chores. Sophia, the middle sister, tutored her younger brothers and took turns with Liza, the eldest sister, in the kitchen. They knew how to fix simple meals and had to make coffee for their father in the mornings, tasks that in noble families were performed by servants. Liza, serious and unsociable, was a diligent student, nicknamed "professor" in the family, while Sophia, a spirited girl, did not care much for learning and was her mother's right hand. Tanya, the youngest sister and the family's favorite, was Sophia's confidante and would remain her lifetime friend.

Since childhood, Sophia had been interested in art, later believing it was her Uncle Konstantin Islavin, a talented pianist and a friend of both Tolstoy and Nikolai Rubinstein[178], who influenced her most. In childhood, his stays were a delight for Sophia and her siblings: "He introduced us to all the arts and for the rest of my life I maintained . . . a strong desire for learning, eager to understand every type of creativity."[179] The musical evenings in their house when her uncle played Chopin and her mother sang in her high soprano were etched in Sophia's memory.

Turgenev visited her parents whenever in Russia and would amuse them with his hunting tales at dinner, describing masterfully "the beautiful scenery, the setting of the sun, or a wise hunting dog."[180] He was very tall and Sophia, shortsighted, could only see his face when he bent over to pick her up. "He would lift us into the air with his large hands, give us a kiss, and always tell something interesting."[181] When Sophia was seven, Behrs took her and Liza to meet Turgenev's great love, the celebrated mezzo-soprano Mme. Viardot.

Tolstoy treated the Behrs children equally and occasionally participated in their Christmas games. Once, he composed a mini-opera, in which Sophia sang along with her siblings. In summer, when the family retreated to their dacha near Moscow, Tolstoy would call in and here, Sophia tells, something of an early romance began between them:

> I remember we were once feeling very happy and playful, and I kept repeating the same foolish sentence: "When I am Tsarina I'll do such and such," or "When I am Tsarina I'll order such and such." Just beneath the balcony stood my father's cabriolet, from which the horse had been unhitched. I hopped inside and shouted, "When I am Tsarina I'll drive around in a cabriolet like this!" Lev Nikolaevich immediately stepped into the horse's place, seized the shafts and pulled me along at a brisk trot. "And I'm going to take my Tsarina for a drive!" he said. . . . "Do stop, please! It's much too heavy for you!" I cried, but I was loving it, and was delighted to see how strong Lev Nikolaevich was, and to have him pull me around.[182]

She was in her teens when her family staged amateur performances and vaudevilles, which Tolstoy also came to watch. Sophia was a natural actress and, "being the most rambunctious" among her siblings, was even given masculine roles. She easily adjusted to different characters and situations, an ability that earned her a nickname, "weathercock," and which would serve her well later on. Their family frequented the Bolshoi Theater, where Behrs (he was also a supernumerary doctor of Moscow theaters) had seats in the director's box. Tolstoy once joined them at the Bolshoi for his favorite Mozart opera, *Don Giovanni*. During an intermission, he spoke with Sophia and Liza about his favorite themes in the opera and "we had interesting and fun time with him."[183]

At sixteen, Sophia passed her external examinations at Moscow University, receiving a diploma as a home teacher. She had a flair for literature: her essay on music was judged as the best among the girls' compositions that year. Later, when she was already married, her professor recalled her essay and on occasion told Tolstoy he was fortunate to have a wife who possessed literary sensitivity. The exams marked the end of her childhood: she was given a watch, allowed to plan her leisure, tailor a long dress, and put up her braids. During the brief interlude between her childhood and marriage, she read a great deal and tried herself at painting, music, writing, and photography, forms of creativity that fascinated her for the rest of her life.

Around this time, she had written a novella, called *Natasha*, describing her family and her sisters' first loves. Tolstoy read it shortly before their marriage, remarking in his diary, "What force of truth and simplicity!"[184] Sophia burned her novella on the eve of their wedding, later to regret it because Tolstoy was recognizable in it and because he later used the germ of her story in *War and Peace* to depict the Rostov sisters: "When Lev Nikolaevich depicted [Natasha Rostova] in *War and Peace* he drew on my novella and borrowed the name for his heroine. . . ."[185] Watching the three Behrs sisters grow up, Tolstoy once remarked that if he were to get married, he would only marry into this family. He was orphaned early and Sophia's family had replaced his own, as he would explain in *Anna Karenina* when depicting himself in Levin:

> Strange as it may seem, Konstantin Levin was in love precisely with the house, the family, especially the female side

of it. He did not remember his own mother, and his only sister was older than he, so that in the Shcherbatsky's house he saw for the fist time the milieu of an old, noble, educated and honorable family, of which he had been deprived by the death of his father and mother.[186]

In summer 1862, when Tolstoy started visiting the Behrs frequently, the parents expected him to propose to their eldest daughter Liza, as custom required. At nineteen, Liza contributed stories to Tolstoy's educational magazine *Yasnaya Polyana* and led literary discussions with him. Tolstoy's situation in the Behrs' household was becoming entangled, because his real choice was Sophia: he admitted in his diary that she drew him irresistibly.[187]

That same summer, Sophia joined her mother and sisters on a visit to their grandfather's estate, Ivitsy, neighboring Yasnaya Polyana. Liza expected Tolstoy to propose to her, but the trip decided Sophia's fate. "I am a firm believer in destiny," she would write. "It was this same destiny which threw me into the life of Lev Nikolaevich."[188] Their first intimate conversation was at her grandfather's estate where Tolstoy turned up unexpectedly during a dance. When guests were leaving, he asked Sophia to stay with him on the terrace, picked up a piece of chalk, and began writing on a card table. Tolstoy only initialed the words of his long sentences, which she deciphered, on the spur of the moment: "We were both very serious and excited. I followed his big red hand, and could feel all my powers of concentration and feeling focus on that bit of chalk and the hand that held it."[189] He told her that her family was wrong about his intention to marry Liza and although this was not where Tolstoy proposed to her, Sophia felt that something significant had occurred, "something we were unable to stop."[190]

> Those last days of my girlhood were extraordinarily intense, lit by a dazzling brightness and a sudden awakening of the soul.... "Mad nights!" Lev Nikolaevich would say as we sat on the balcony or strolled about the garden. There were no

romantic scenes or confessions. We had known each other for so long. Our friendship was so simple and easy. And I was in a hurry to end my wonderful, free, serene, uncomplicated girlhood.[191]

When Sophia's family returned to Moscow, Tolstoy continued to visit, but now carried a proposal letter in his pocket. He submitted it to her on September 16, the day before Sophia's and her mother's name day, celebrated together. In that letter, he pleaded that if she had even a shadow of doubt, she must not accept. Sophia skimmed his letter to the words, "Tell me *honestly*, do you want to be my wife?" (A more intricate variation of this proposal Tolstoy showed her later contained the words: "I make terrible, impossible demands on marriage. I demand that I be loved the way I am capable of loving. But that is impossible."[192]) Tolstoy nervously awaited her reply in her mother's bedroom. "I went up to him and he seized both my hands. 'Well, what's the answer?' he asked. 'Yes—of course,' I replied."[193] Tolstoy insisted on having the wedding as soon as possible, so the engagement lasted only a week. In *Anna Karenina*, he would change it to a month to make it more credible.

During that frantic week of their betrothal, Tolstoy gave Sophia his bachelor diaries, to inform her of his sexual past and his liaison with the peasant Aksinya Bazykina, by whom he had a son. The first diary opened with an entry at nineteen while he took treatment for gonorrhea, contracted from a prostitute. "I remember how shattered I was by these diaries. . . . I wept when I saw what his past had been."[194] Sophia believed it was wrong of him to give her the diaries, especially on the eve of their wedding. She experienced disillusionment with the man who had inspired her girlhood ideals. Only a few years earlier, Tolstoy read Turgenev's novella *First Love* to their family and she remembered his comment that the feeling of the sixteen-year-old youth was pure and genuine, while his father's physical passion was "an abomination and a perversion."[195] She was appalled by an obvious incongruity between Tolstoy's words and actions.

After the ceremony on September 23, Tolstoy "was impatient to be off" to Yasnaya Polyana, while Sophia now dreaded their intimacy. They drove in a large sleeper carriage Tolstoy had bought especially for the journey, and this is where "the torment began, which every bride must go through."

> How painful, dreadfully humiliating! And what sudden new passion, unconscious, irresistible, was awakened, dormant until then in a young girl. Mercifully, it was dark in the carriage, so that we couldn't see each other's face. . . . Conquered by his power and intensity, I was obedient and loving, although crushed by the agonizing physical pain and unbearable humiliation.[196]

Three decades later, in her novella *Who is to Blame?* she would describe their first night as a rape. "Violence had been committed; this girl was not ready for marriage; female passion, recently awakened, was put back to sleep. . . ."[197] A new diary, begun upon her marriage, shows her confusion and disappointment. "I always dreamed of the man I would love as a complete whole, new, *pure* person."[198] She had worshiped Tolstoy as a writer, but was yet to separate the man from his works.

Despite their differences—in age, intellect, and life experience—Sophia was determined to make her marriage a success. Tolstoy expected her to quickly adapt to his way of life on the estate and to assist him in his projects. He was then passionately interested in farming, and Sophia began to help by managing the office and recording butter production. She soon wrote sister Tanya of her new responsibilities: "We have become quite the farmers: we are buying cattle, fowl, piglets, and calves. We are purchasing bees. . . ."[199] But she was far more interested in his literature and in late October wrote Tanya that she was copying Tolstoy's novella *Polikushka* to send to a literary magazine. Tolstoy welcomed her involvement, allowing her to stay in his study when he wrote; he also encouraged her to read his letters and diaries, leaving them open on his desk.

As a young man outlining his family ideal, Tolstoy wrote that his wife will take interest in his work, as well as his hobbies, and give up her love of entertainment. Upon reading this at nineteen, Sophia remarked, "Poor man, he was still too young to realize that happiness can never be planned in advance, and you will inevitably be unhappy if you try to do so. But what noble splendid dreams these were nevertheless."[200] And yet, she would soon share his family ideal and work hard to achieve it.

In the spring of 1863, Sophia wrote her sister that Tolstoy had settled down to write a new novel; this was the first mention of *War and Peace*. Tolstoy made many drafts of the novel's opening; he wrote slowly, "with difficulty," perfecting his prose, and Sophia had to keep copying his revisions. The novel was a vast world, which she had not had a chance to experience, and she invested her entire soul to understand what she was writing. She loved copying *War and Peace*, work she did for seven years, remarking, "The idea of serving a genius and great man has given me strength to do anything."[201] Used to a more boisterous life, Sophia had to learn to endure solitude: they lived in the country uninterruptedly, only traveling to Moscow when Tolstoy needed to do research.

Their family life supplied "peaceful scenes" for the novel. The couple's first son, Sergei, was born on June 28, 1863, and Tolstoy would describe the event and the commotion that followed and discuss the advantages of breastfeeding and "the unnaturalness and harmfulness of wet nurses."[202] Sophia's nursing did not go well: she developed mastitis, and a wet nurse had to be engaged. Tolstoy could not hide his disappointment and avoided the nursery with an expression of "morose animosity" on his face. Sophia felt that he blamed her for failing to live up to his Rousseauian ideal of a healthy mother and wife. That summer, she noted in her diary, "I am in agonizing pain. Lyova is murderous.... He wants to wipe me from the face of the earth because I am suffering and am not doing my duty, I want not to see him at all because he is not suffering but just goes on writing."[203]

In the fall, the Tula gentry held a ball to honor heir Nikolai Alexandrovich. Sophia dreamed of attending, but it was decided that Tolstoy would escort her younger sister Tanya, then visiting Yasnaya. As Sophia confided to Tanya, she could not go because Tolstoy disapproved of married women wearing low-cut evening dresses and, besides, was jealous of her. "When Lev Nikolaevich put on his dress coat, he and Tanya left for Tula and the ball; I started to cry bitterly and wept all evening. We were living a monotonous, secluded, dull life, and suddenly such an opportunity comes up and I (just nineteen) am deprived of it."[204] His expedition with Tanya would inspire Natasha Rostova's first ball in *War and Peace*.

Tolstoy "mixed" Sophia with her sister to create his Natasha. Tanya was the model for the heroine's youth and Sophia, who never had a chance to be carefree, was used for her motherhood. Tanya went snipe shooting with Tolstoy, trips he would describe in an enchanting chapter about the Rostovs. Sophia accepted his pursuit of inspiration when Tolstoy read the chapter to her, "after he had just written it, and together we laughed and were happy."[205] Sophia was a perceptive listener, and their conversations and readings gave Tolstoy a spark. In the novel, making his Natasha a keen listener, he endowed her with an ability to bring out her husband's best.

Later that year, making progress with the novel, Tolstoy admitted to many people that he considered himself extremely fortunate. As he wrote his relative Alexandrine, "I am a husband and a father, who is fully satisfied with his situation . . . I only *feel* my family circumstances, and don't think about them. This condition gives me an awful lot of intellectual scope."[206] In another letter, he explained that his marriage had transformed him, allowing greater productivity: "I imagine myself an apple tree, which used to grow with watersprouts in every direction, and which became pruned in the course of life; now, that it's trimmed, tied, and supported, its trunk and roots can grow without hindrance. And that's how I grow. . . ."[207] When during *War and Peace* Vladimir Sollogub, a man of letters, visited Yasnaya, he became impressed with Sophia, who arranged Tolstoy's life to the minute and was always ready to assist him. Sollogub remarked that she was "the perfect wife for a writer" and "a nursemaid" of her husband's talent. Pleased with his praise, Sophia vowed in her diary to become "an even better nursemaid of Lyovochka's talent from now on."[208]

In October 1864, days before she gave birth to their first daughter, whom they named Tanya, Tolstoy had an accident while hunting. He broke his arm and dislocated his shoulder. The following month, still unable to use his right arm, Tolstoy went to Moscow to consult doctors whom Sophia's father had engaged. He had asked Sophia to copy the first installment of the novel, which he wanted to offer to *The Russian Herald*. As he was leaving for Moscow, Tolstoy told her: "You are my helper." Sophia responded that she would be happy to help him and copy for him "from morning till night."[209]

In the meantime, he had to undergo surgery on his arm. It was performed at his in-laws' apartment on November 28, with Sophia's mother and sister Tanya present in the operating room. Tolstoy's arm was rebroken and reset under chloroform. After the surgery, he became depressed and, soon after receiving the chapters Sophia sent, he wrote her that his talent "disappointed" him. He continued in another letter that a great misfortune had befallen him and he was "beginning to cool off to his novel."[210] Away from home, he lost his mental balance and confidence: "I lose my *'équilibre'* without you. . . ."[211] The new chapters he had dictated to her sisters in Moscow were flat and unexciting, "and without emotion a writer's work cannot flow."[212] His despair growing, he continued in another letter: "As a good wife, you think about your husband as you do about yourself, and I remember your saying to me that all the military and historical side over which I'm taking such pains will turn out badly, but the rest—the family life, the characters, the psychology—will be good. That couldn't be more true."[213] Sophia knew that he occasionally doubted his powers and denied his talent and wrote to reassure:

> Remember, how many joys your novel gave you, how well you were thinking it over, and now you don't like it! No,

Lyovochka, it's wrong. Just come back and instead of the dirty, stone Kremlin house you will see our Chepyzh[214] shining in the bright sun . . . you will remember our happy life here . . . and again, with a happy face, you will share your writing plans with me. . . . And you will dictate to me. . . .[215]

Sophia's letters raised Tolstoy's spirits. "My dear heart," he replied. "Only love me as I love you, and nothing else counts for me, and everything is fine."[216] Recalling the elation of their reunion in Yasnaya, Sophia would write: "A woman cannot possibly love stronger than I loved Leo Nikolaevich. He was neither handsome nor young, with only four bad teeth in his mouth. But the joy that would rise in me when I met him . . . that joy illuminated my life for a long, long time."[217]

The years when he wrote *War and Peace* and three of their children were born were the happiest in their marriage. Sophia recalls: "I lived with the characters of *War and Peace*, loved them, watched the life of each of them unfold as if they were living beings. Our life was so full and extraordinarily happy with our mutual love, with our children, and, mainly, with the work on a great masterpiece, first loved by me and later by the entire world. . . ."[218] The work on the novel united them: the bond established then would prove enduring. When in 1866 Tolstoy traveled to conduct research in Moscow, he wrote Sophia daily of his progress with the novel and of his love for her: "I am not remembering you, but I am always aware of you. This is not just a phrase. . . ."[219] Sophia was sending him a new installment of the manuscript she had copied to take to the magazine, and, referring to the novel's publication, wrote Tolstoy, "I am beginning to feel that this is your child and so it is mine, and sending this batch of sheets to Moscow I feel like I'm letting the child go out into the world, afraid someone might hurt him. . . ."[220]

Tolstoy worked with great intensity, hoping to complete the novel by the end of 1867. The pressure increased when, on top of the magazine deal, he signed a contract to publish the book.

Rarely pleased with his work, he put in long hours to perfect it. At times when he read chapters to Sophia, his nerves were so strained that he broke into tears. Sophia had to share the tension, remarking, "Lyovochka has been writing all winter, irritable and excited, often with tears in his eyes. I feel this novel of his will be superb. All the parts he has read to me have moved me almost to tears too. . . ."[221] By then, she understood the novel on a new level, admiring both the war and the peace parts.

In winter, Sophia nursed their children through scarlet fever, a bacterial infection for which there was practically no cure. Little Tanya was unconscious for several days and Sophia was afraid of losing her. Although drained by worry and sleeplessness, she continued to copy for Tolstoy. Regardless of how tired or unwell, she never considered this work a burden. Her involvement in Tolstoy's writing was a source of pride; at his request, she also recorded her experiences in a separate diary.

Despite his deadlines, Tolstoy insisted on several sets of proofs and Sophia kept copying his revisions. Only infrequently, when proofs had been dispatched and the children were asleep, would the two have an evening of recreation. They would stay up late, playing duets. "Lev Nikolaevich was particularly fond of Haydn's and Mozart's symphonies. At that time I played rather badly, but I tried very hard to improve."[222]

In February 1868, the first volumes of *War and Peace* came out and were swept from bookshelves despite their steep price—ten silver rubles—and colossal size. The novel enjoyed unprecedented success even before completion: Turgenev foretold that it would live as long as the Russian language. Tolstoy was soon proclaimed "a veritable literary lion" and "a giant among his fellow writers."

When, the following May, Sophia bore their fourth child, named Lev after his father, Tolstoy wrote her from Moscow, "Except for the needs of the mind there is nothing on earth which could interest me even the slightest, or could distract me from the thought of you and of home."[223] Sophia is reflected many times in the novel, especially in its epilogue where she is recognizable in Natasha Rostova and in Princess Marya, both of whom inspire their husbands' best aspirations. The two harmonious marriages project Tolstoy's family ideal, which Sophia helped implement in life.

With the publication of *War and Peace*, Tolstoy established himself as the greatest living writer, but the couple did not enjoy his success. After completing his great epic at forty-one, Tolstoy became severely depressed; he frequently spoke of death. As Sophia remarked in her diary, "Sometimes (but only when he is away from his home and his family) he imagines that he is going mad, and so great is his fear of madness that I am terrified whenever he talks about it."[224] In September of 1869, writing Sophia from Arzamas where he had traveled to buy more land, Tolstoy described a dreadful night in a hotel where he was suddenly overcome "by despair, fear and terror."[225] Tolstoy had suffered bouts of despair since childhood and had to be "constantly busy" to cope with them; without the novel to absorb his energies, he entered a period of mental inactivity and doubt.[226] Lying in bed in Yasnaya and staring emptily at one spot, he would growl at Sophia if she disturbed him: "Leave me alone, you can't let me even die in peace."[227]

During this transitional time, Tolstoy occupied himself with diverse projects, from studying Greek to reforming public education. He wrote his own curriculum and primers, believing that "two generations of *all* Russian children, from tsars' to peasants', will study with the aid of this primer alone. . . ."[228] Sophia contributed her original stories for his *Russian Reader*, and helped Tolstoy to copy and proofread his primers, which he kept revising as many times as he had his great novel.

In the winter of 1872, Tolstoy opened a school for peasant children in their house, engaging the family and even their guests to teach. While he taught a large group of boys in his study, Sophia instructed a group of girls in another room. As she wrote her sister, there was a "crying need" to teach these children who worked "with such enjoyment and enthusiasm."[229] The school lasted until summer; but Tolstoy's interest in public education was enduring, so over the years, Sophia accommodated teachers' conferences in Yasnaya.

As Tolstoy searched for new themes to inspire him, she recorded his pronouncements in her journal. He considered writing a comedy, a new historical novel from the epoch of Peter the Great, and eventually contemplated a contemporary novel "about a married woman of noble birth who ruined herself."[230] The idea for *Anna Karenina* was prompted by a woman's suicide in their neighborhood, an event that deeply impressed Tolstoy. In 1872, a common-law wife of their neighbor, Anna Pirogova, threw herself under a passing train in a fit of jealousy. Tolstoy, who attended the post-mortem and saw her mutilated body, would later revive the tragic incident in *Anna Karenina*.

In 1873, Tolstoy wrote the novel's opening and read to Sophia the celebrated lines about happy and unhappy families and the confusion in the Oblonsky household. She entered the date in her diary: March 19. As soon as he began writing the novel, she resumed her "responsibilities of copying and keenly sympathizing with his work."[231] The novel would take five years to complete, but unlike *War and Peace*, Tolstoy wrote it with long and frequent interruptions.

During his work on *Anna Karenina*, the family was going through "a patch of grief." From June 1873 till November 1875, Sophia gave birth to three more children, all of whom died in early infancy. Tolstoy's two aunts, who lived with the family, also died during this period. The events deepened Tolstoy's depression. As he wrote Sophia, his depression was "the most painful thing,"[232] dulling his senses. To help him cope, Sophia agreed to travel to the Samara prairies, where he bought a farm. For several summers in a row, she would have to move their entire household to the arid steppe, traveling the long distance with their small children. These annual trips to Samara invigorated Tolstoy and provided material for the novel, where several chapters depict grand spectacles of collective work in the field. Sophia was able to quickly adjust to their Spartan life and even to find poetry in it. Writing to her sister from their Samara estate, she described the oxen plowing land, the infinite spaces, and the inescapable sun.

The steppe lost most of its beauty because of drought, but at night there is something lovely and alien in the upturned bowl of the heavens and in the limitless expanse of land; sometimes you hear men playing their pipes in the distance or oxen tinkling their bells. Ten oxen pull a plough here; everything is so unfamiliar and gigantic, with those plowmen, mowers, and other laborers staying in the field for the night with lights you can see here and there. . . .[233]

In summer of 1873, crops at the Tolstoys' farm were meager, but elsewhere fields stood bare because of drought. "Here there was no rain since the Holy week, so we've been living for a month and watching the infinite space gradually wither before our eyes and horror descending on the local people who struggle for the third year in a row to feed themselves and to sow again."[234] The Tolstoys employed several hundred laborers, costing them more than their land yielded, and hired local cooks to bake bread and make porridge to feed this multitude. While everyone talked about crop failure and the looming famine, the authorities refused to recognize the crisis. Sophia wrote an article about the Samara famine, with an appeal for help, and showed it to Tolstoy. He read it: "But who will believe you without facts?"[235] He promptly set out to survey the province and assess one in every ten households and, upon return, wrote a report about the famine, publishing it in *The Moscow Gazette*. As her article remained unpublished, Sophia would refer to "our article."[236] Aid began to pour in and many benefited; as Sophia remarks in her memoir, "It was not in vain that God sent us that year to live in the Samara steppes; our presence may have saved many people from starvation."[237] Two decades later, during a widespread famine in the 1890s, the Tolstoys would organize another relief operation on a much larger scale.

After the summer break, the family returned to Yasnaya, and Tolstoy resumed writing *Anna Karenina*. At this time, the famous painter Ivan Kramskoy arrived: he had been commissioned by the Tretyakov Gallery to paint prominent Russians and persuaded Tolstoy to sit for a portrait. Sophia was able to observe two creative giants at work. "I remember entering the small drawing room, observing both artists: one is painting Tolstoy's portrait, the other writing his novel *Anna Karenina*. Both serious and absorbed, both genuine artists of great magnitude; I felt admiration for them."[238] She asked Kramskoy to make a copy of that portrait, but he replied that it was easier to paint another original, so he painted two portraits simultaneously.

Kramskoy's painting captured the magnetic power of Tolstoy's gaze. In 1904, when Sophia became obsessed with painting, she copied Tolstoy's portraits by various artists, including Kramskoy's. She executed this task with surprising boldness, given that she had never studied art. But Kramskoy's technique was beyond her and she could not capture that all-penetrating gaze. Instead, she depicted the expression in Tolstoy's eyes she knew and loved, "smiling and kind, and excited."[239]

In November of 1873, the couple's youngest son, baby Petya, died of a throat infection. Sophia was devastated: "I had fed him for fourteen and a half months. What a bright, happy little boy—I loved my darling too much and now there is nothing. He was buried yesterday. I cannot reconcile the two Petyas, the living and the dead; they are both precious to me, but what does the living Petya, so bright and affectionate, have in common with the dead one, so cold and still and serious . . . ?"[240] Petya was buried in the Kochaki family cemetery, near the ancient Nikolsky church, behind the tomb of Tolstoy's parents. Sophia was stunned when she saw him exposed to snow and frost, lying in an open coffin in a white dress: "I nursed him . . . I shielded him from drafts, I dressed him warmly . . . now he is frozen solid. . . ."[241] Tolstoy would use her experiences to depict a mother's grief at the loss of her child in *Anna Karenina*:

> And again there came to her imagination the cruel memory, eternally gnawing at her mother's heart, of the death of her last infant boy, who had died of croup, his funeral, the universal indifference before that small, pink coffin, and

her own heart-rending, lonely pain before the pale little forehead with curls at the temples, before the opened, surprised little mouth she had glimpsed in the coffin just as it was covered by the pink lid with the lace cross.[242]

Sophia's way out of grief was getting on with what needs to be done, forgetting herself in work. "I gave lessons to the children in turns. . . . I copied in the evenings for Lev Nikolaevich, cut and sewed the children's clothes before the holidays. . . ."[243] She was already coping with a new, difficult pregnancy, having conceived when she was emotionally unprepared to nurture new life. "People who never experienced this maternal, utterly physiological life, cannot imagine what a difficult, unbearable toil this is. . . ."[244] Tolstoy depicts her incessant motherhood in *Anna Karenina* where he also makes a reference to contraception. While he was the first Russian writer to raise the issue, practicing contraception was against his beliefs. And yet, each new pregnancy postponed Sophia's dream for a more spiritual life embracing art, music, and literature. She would only begin to explore her talents when the children grew up, by then realizing it was too late for achievement.

Having completed the first part of *Anna Karenina*, Tolstoy was preparing it for publication. "You will like Lyovochka's new novel," Sophia reported to Tanya in December, "it will be very good, as to when he finishes it—God knows."[245] Tolstoy was making continual revisions; she was copying with no end in sight. As in the blissful days of *War and Peace*, the couple would occasionally stay up late playing duets. They would sit until one o'clock, talking and reading, and have a late supper, which Sophia warmed up on a spirit-lamp.[246] After that, utterly exhausted, she would read English novels by Henry Wood, falling asleep at three o'clock.

In 1874, having lost interest in the novel, Tolstoy did not resume it after the summer break, as he normally would. Instead, he became preoccupied with elementary education, passionately advocating his particular method of teaching literacy. He opened schools in their district and dreamed of organizing colleges to train peasant teachers. While touring the new schools, he was struck by the sight of "ragged, dirty, skinny children with their bright eyes" whom he wanted to save from drowning in darkness. Real people interested him more than the imaginary ones. He told Sophia that the novel was repulsive to him and he wanted to give it up.

When he put aside *Anna Karenina*, the family was under financial strain. There was another crop failure in Samara where, at Tolstoy's estimate, the family lost 20,000 rubles in two years. In the meantime, they were "swamped with letters from editors offering ten thousand in advances and five hundred silver rubles per printer's page."[247] But Tolstoy refused to even discuss the matter. Sophia, now unable to sympathize with his passion for elementary education, confided her troubles to sister Tanya:

> It's his vocation, writing the novels, that I love, value, and feel so enthusiastic about, while these ABCs, arithmetics, and grammars I despise. . . . What's lacking in my life now is Lyovochka's work, which I always enjoyed and admired. You see, Tanya, I am a true writer's wife, so close to my heart do I keep our creative work.[248]

By the year's end, Tolstoy returned to the novel, although reluctantly and still lacking inspiration. *The Russian Herald*, which had published *War and Peace*, was now producing *Anna Karenina* in installments. In February 1875, at the height of the work on the novel, the couple's youngest son, Nikolai, died from meningitis at ten months. During their grieving, Tolstoy's editor and friend, Nikolai Strakhov, wrote that the reception of a published installment nearly exceeded that of *War and Peace*. The news left Tolstoy almost indifferent. Sophia wrote listlessly, "Lyovochka's novel is being published, people say it's awfully successful, and I feel strange: we have such grief here, and everyone is celebrating us."[249] Tolstoy was revising completed parts for publication and adding new chapters, and she was copying daily. His fiction gave her a sense of purpose and helped fill the void.

Daughter Tanya, then eleven, would recall her mother settling down at her desk in the evenings. Although behind her was a long day, it was clear "from the expression of concentration on her face, that for her the most important time . . . was just beginning. . . ." Occasionally, Tolstoy approached Sophia as she was copying and looked over her shoulder. "Then my mother would take his big hand and kiss it with love and veneration, while he tenderly stroked her dark, shining hair, then bent to kiss the top of her head."[250] The couple's seven-year-old son, Ilya, remembered hearing the name "Anna Karenina" in their house, later realizing it was "a title of a novel on which both *papa* and *maman* were at work."[251]

In early 1876, *The Russian Herald* published an installment, which contained the chapters with Levin's proposal to Kitty, drawn from their own betrothal. It also had a chapter on Anna Karenina's close escape from death when she develops puerperal fever after the birth of her daughter. Tolstoy drew it from Sophia's experiences: she had contracted this infection in 1871 after giving birth to their second daughter, Masha.

At thirty-two, having never traveled, Sophia dreamed of a holiday abroad. Although Tolstoy promised to consider a European vacation, he was clearly reluctant to leave Yasnaya: "It's very likely that we shall go abroad soon, and probably to Italy, which is so repulsive to me, but less so than Germany. In Europe it seems to me that I could only live in England, but people go away from there for their health, and there is no point in going there."[252] The final argument against the trip was the expense, which, apparently was not a problem when in September 1876 Tolstoy purchased purebred English stallions for their Samara estate. Tolstoy then owned three hundred horses and was passionately interested in breeding, having employed a team of keepers and grooms for his stud farm. Several years later, when he cooled off to the project, most of the expensive stallions died of neglect.

In spring of 1877, *Anna Karenina* was making an "astonishing, wild success."[253] The chapters produced an "explosion" in literary circles, and reviews were ecstatic. Every installment was an event anxiously anticipated by the public. Strakhov quipped that each piece was announced in the press with an urgency similar to reporting a war. Publication of *Anna Karenina* made Tolstoy the most celebrated and prosperous Russian novelist. The magazine deal and a separate edition of *Anna Karenina* published in 1878 brought him 20,000 rubles, money he used that same year to buy an additional 10,800 acres in Samara.[254] But already in 1881 (the date Tolstoy considered his spiritual conversion), his views shifted to another extreme, inspiring him to renounce his wealth as futile.

When Tolstoy was finishing *Anna Karenina*, Sophia began to notice a major spiritual change in him: "One could already sense some anxiety rising within Lev Nikolaevich, his dissatisfaction with life, his search for more meaning, and the need of a more spiritual, religious life for himself."[255] The novel's epilogue projects Tolstoy's own doubts and suicidal thoughts. Unlike a decade earlier, after he completed *War and Peace*, his depression was deeper and would change him more profoundly.

In March 1877, Tolstoy told Sophia what was making him happy: "First of all you do, and secondly my religion."[256] Recording a positive change in his mood, she commented in her diary, "After a long struggle between lack of faith and the longing for faith, he has suddenly become much calmer." At first, Tolstoy became devotedly Orthodox, obeying all commands of the Church. To accommodate him, Sophia introduced strict observance of all Orthodox customs in the household, while suspecting that Tolstoy's new enthusiasm would not last. Indeed, the family soon witnessed Tolstoy's period of piety end as abruptly as it had begun.

Strakhov, who had accompanied Tolstoy on a pilgrimage to Optina Pustyn monastery in 1877, was stunned when on his next visit to Yasnaya he found Tolstoy "in a new anti-Church phase."[257] While Tolstoy's spiritual search was complex, his conversions were sudden and astonishing to people around him. A recent devotee of the Orthodox Church, he became its most vocal critic, accusing it of alliance with the state and describing its history as a series of "lies, cruelties, and deceptions."[258] (Tolstoy was ahead of his time by pointing out the major ills that plagued their official Church—its intolerance of people who practiced other religions and its support of government policies, such as capital punishment and war. Tolstoy's insistence that the Church must not submit to political power would make him into an arch-enemy of the government and the Orthodox Church.)

Tolstoy asserted his new beliefs in a series of non-fictional works, beginning with *An Investigation of Dogmatic Theology*, and, in addition, undertook a laborious translation of the four Gospels. In 1879, Sophia reported the new developments to sister Tanya: "Lyovochka is working, or so he says, but alas! He is writing religious tracts, reads and thinks until his head aches and all this to prove how inconsistent the Church is with the teaching of the Gospels. There will be hardly ten people in Russia interested in this. . . . I only wish . . . this passes as a malady."[259] But Tolstoy's religious quest would occupy him for the rest of his life: during the following decades, he would return to literature only sporadically.

Tolstoy's attacks on traditional religion offended Sophia, and his pressure on her to accept his new beliefs created a rift: "No argument would force me to separate from the Church. I could not accept Lev Nikolaevich's view of Christianity and religion in general. . . . I felt that Lev Nikolaevich was right, but only on the matter of his personal self-perfection. . . . His renunciations of the Church and the existing social order I could not accept . . . my soul could not take it."[260] Unable to sympathize with his non-fiction ("it pains me, but I cannot change myself"[261]), she resigned as Tolstoy's copyist.

Around this time, Tolstoy began to criticize his family's lifestyle as not austere enough. By 1879, the couple had six living children. The eldest, Sergei, was expected to enter university and Tanya had to make her society debut. But Tolstoy's ideas about their children's future had changed radically. While in the past he himself had sought the best foreign teachers and governesses for their children, he now disapproved of their education and social success and also objected to the family's move to the city, which had been long decided. (In 1882, with a change of heart, Tolstoy himself bought their house in Moscow.) According to daughter Tanya, it was Tolstoy who took her to the first ball. A short while later, he condemned entertainment, criticizing people of their class and everyone else who was rich.

The change in Tolstoy occurred at the peak of his fame, affecting his views, character, and writing; it also turned Sophia's life upside down. She feared having to raise their children on her own—at a time when the older boys needed their father to guide them. On December 20, 1879, she gave birth to their seventh living child, Misha. Painful nursing and sleepless nights lay ahead and, as she admitted to her sister, she had no more capacity for motherhood.[262] At thirty-five, after almost two decades in the country, Sophia wanted to experience society and travel, and to explore her own talents and needs. But with all this she had no sympathy from Tolstoy, who instead expected her to abide his new ascetic ideals.

Tolstoy was gradually becoming more aloof, his mood darkening. In his major non-fiction work of the time, *A Confession*, he depicted their previous life as a series of mistakes, decrying his literary vocation, fame, wealth, position as a landowner and family man. His literary work was a thing of the past. To an acquaintance who admired *Anna Karenina*, Tolstoy replied, "I assure you that this vile thing no longer exists for me."[263] He referred to himself as a writer in the past tense: "I *was* a writer, and all writers are vain and envious—I at least was that sort of writer."[264] His friends Strakhov and poet Afanasy Fet were appalled to learn that he had left fiction for religious writing, as was Turgenev.

Beginning to assert his religious views with the zeal of a convert, Tolstoy insisted that everybody "can and must" agree with him.[265] In Petersburg he quarreled with his relative Alexandrine, who was stunned by his abuse of Orthodoxy. He called it a bunch of lies; when she protested, he left Petersburg without saying good-bye. Tolstoy would later soften his intolerant ways; but in the late 1870s and early 1880s, he refused to compromise.

Describing how Tolstoy's change of vocation affected her, Sophia would remark: "Certainly, it was impossible not to regret the end of activity by such a great artist, as Lev Nikolaevich, and I could not but regret the end of my happiness."[266] Tolstoy's new tendency to moralize was "insufferably boring"[267] to her, and there was no sense of togetherness after he had left his literature behind.

Tolstoy now visited prisons, courts, and houses of detention, sympathizing only with the oppressed. "His disapproval and condemnation turned also against me, our family, and everyone who was rich and not unhappy."[268] Tolstoy cared for the suffering of humanity but was insensitive to the needs of his own family. For Sophia, the opposite was the case. She did not care for the humanity as an abstraction, but sympathized with people who were close to her, not only her family. Over the years, she had provided free medical help in Yasnaya. Although she was helping the very poor whom he idealized, Tolstoy ignored her efforts: "In all this I was alone because Lev Nikolaevich rejected medicine; not only did he have little sympathy for my work, he mocked it, which upset me terribly."[269] Her knowledge of medicine came from observing her father in childhood; later, she consulted Florensky's *Family Medicine* to treat her family, guests, servants, teachers, etc. As her patients recovered, Sophia's fame grew. With no medical help in the entire district, peasants drove from afar to see her with a variety of ailments. She was often summoned to help with difficult childbirths in nearby villages, saving her patients where a midwife would fail.

In 1883, a peasant looking for medical help came to Yasnaya in Sophia's absence, telling Tolstoy she was a good healer. Coming from a peasant, the praise got Tolstoy's attention, and he wrote Sophia that he "felt flattered."[270] Charity was at the core of her life, and she could not disagree with Tolstoy on Christ's teachings, especially the most important among them: helping one's neighbor. Friction between them arose when Tolstoy insisted that his own interpretation of the Gospels must be followed in daily life.

Having rejected the entire metaphysical side of Christianity, Tolstoy stripped the Gospel down to five moral imperatives, of which the principle of non-resistance was most important. Tolstoy argued that no physical force must be used to compel any human being.[271] His doctrine had far-reaching consequences, requiring him to renounce property, since it had to be protected by the law, and this in turn led to rejection of all government institutions.

Tolstoy's religious maxims generated discord in his own family, not unity and peace. Back in 1881, he began to give away his property and cash. Pilgrims and peasants poured into Yasnaya, asking for, among other things, livestock and seed for planting. When Sophia tried to restrain this distribution, Tolstoy quoted from the Gospel: "Give to him that asketh thee!" Sophia feared Tolstoy had lost his mind, observing in a letter to her sister that this religious-philosophical mood was "most dangerous."[272]

Tolstoy did not care how his money was used: his goal, in fact, was not to help the poor but to feel "less guilty." As daughter Tanya observes, "Giving away everything he possessed meant freeing himself from a sin—the sin of ownership."[273] Sophia, with her middle-class upbringing, did not share his sense of guilt as a noble and believed her God-given responsibility was to provide for her own family rather than strangers.

In his unfinished play *And the Light Shineth in Darkness*, Tolstoy describes the actual drama that took place between him and Sophia when he announced his intention to give their land to the peasants.[274] Like the hero of his play, Tolstoy had several plans for divesting himself of property: he considered giving it up altogether, leaving a plot for himself and family, or transferring everything to his wife. Tolstoy (like the hero of his play) expected his wife's endorsement when declaring that their family should support themselves by physical work. Sophia dismissed Tolstoy's plan as unfeasible, explaining that both of them were not young and strong anymore. Their children, raised as nobles, would be morally confused and unable to lead a life they did not believe in.

> How could Seryozha, in whom we instilled, since his beginning, the idea of . . . university education, suddenly

believe that his efforts were futile, and pick up an axe and a plow? How could Tanya, with her love of art, society, theater, gaiety, and smart dresses, give this up, and stay in the country to farm? And finally, how could I . . . give up my usual life for the sake of an ideal, created not by me but forced upon me? And so, the painful discord has ensued.[275]

When Sophia rejected his plan, Tolstoy proposed turning their estate over to her. She rejected this, too, realizing that because of the stigma Tolstoy attached to ownership, her position would become vulnerable. Since he believed property was evil, she argued, why should he pass this evil thing to her? As his play reveals, Tolstoy wanted to be free from the moral quandary and obligations that come with ownership. The hero of his play puts it plainly: "Take over the estate, then I won't be responsible."[276]

On May 21, 1883, Tolstoy gave Sophia power of attorney, signing the document in her absence at a law office in Tula. He was obviously relieved to sign his property away, attaching this informal note: "To her excellency, kind madam, and dear wife Sophia Andreevna. I entrust you to manage all my affairs. . . ."[277] When Sophia received the power-of-attorney document, she felt that Tolstoy loved her little, having shifted to her shoulders "the responsibility for the family, the management of the estate, the house, his books, etc."[278] In the coming decades, on top of handling these responsibilities, she would also face disapprobation from Tolstoy and his followers.

In October of 1883, Tolstoy met his first serious follower in a young aristocrat, Vladimir Chertkov. Although twenty-five years Tolstoy's junior and from a family close to court, Chertkov instantly won his trust. He expressed keen interest in Tolstoy's interpretation of the Gospels. Their first meeting lasted past midnight: Tolstoy read chapters from *What I Believe*, his recent work where he formulated his doctrine of non-resistance. Chertkov was the first to accept these views as infallible, which mattered to Tolstoy because his friends and family were at best indifferent to his new writings. At fifty-five, Tolstoy soon addressed his 29-year-old disciple "my dear, close friend." The relationship with Chertkov would become detrimental to Tolstoy's marriage.

Sophia's first impression of the young man who would become her rival was favorable: she described him as "tall, handsome, manly, and a true aristocrat."[279] During his prolonged stays with the Tolstoys, Chertkov often enjoyed Sophia's hospitality. Her attitude would change, however, as Chertkov's influence increased and the disciple worked to further alienate Tolstoy from the family.

On June 18, 1884, Sophia bore their twelfth child, Sasha. Earlier that day, the couple had quarreled after she mentioned Tolstoy's expensive stallions, which had died in Samara of neglect. For Tolstoy, his property was now only a painful reminder of the past, which he had renounced. He stormed out of the house, saying that he was leaving forever, but returned the same night while Sophia was giving birth. Chertkov was invisibly present in this quarrel, having become Tolstoy's confidant and, as such, informed about the developments in the family.

That summer, in a letter to Chertkov, Tolstoy called Sophia's decision to engage a wet nurse for their baby "the most inhumane . . . and unchristian act."[280] Chertkov would seize on their disagreement, pointing out Sophia's further "violations" of her husband's rules and beliefs, and would soon refer to Sophia as "a cross to bear," words that would travel to Tolstoy's diaries.

Sophia had nursed almost all their children herself, but now could not afford sleepless nights with the baby. She had to secure the family's income: within months of giving birth, she was to launch a publishing business. According to her memoir, it was Tolstoy himself who proposed that she publish a new edition of his works: his contract with the Salaev Brothers who had previously produced his collected works was about to expire. The family spent winters in Moscow, so their expenses had increased, while profits from both estates dwindled. Yasnaya now produced negligible revenue, and there was another bad year in Samara.

To start her publishing enterprise, Sophia borrowed ten thousand rubles from her mother and fifteen thousand from a family friend. She promptly turned the annex of their Moscow residence into her office and warehouse. At first, she was frightened by the complexities of the new undertaking. But she gradually began to invest her heart in this activity, which allowed her to explore her talents and to work independently.

In February 1885, at Strakhov's advice, Sophia traveled to Petersburg to meet Dostoevsky's widow, who had been producing her husband's works for years. Anna Dostoevsky willingly shared her methods of dealing with booksellers, advertising, and subscription, and cautioned Sophia against mistakes. But in addition to publishing practicalities, there was much that Sophia had to learn on her own. Tolstoy's controversial non-fiction was banned, unlike Dostoevsky's works, and she had to deal with censors. And this was not all. While Dostoevsky had wholeheartedly approved of Anna's publishing activity, Sophia would meet with resistance from Tolstoy.

Her publishing would conflict with Tolstoy's intention to renounce his copyright. At the start, he took interest in her publishing, helped with proofreading, and himself suggested an introduction to the new edition. But soon after, he began to distance himself from the money-making operation. One example of his changing views on copyright was with *The Death of Ivan Ilyich*. That year, Tolstoy gave Sophia the novella for her name day, allowing her to produce it exclusively in the collected works. In a few years, he would release this same story to the public domain.

In April 1885, Sophia launched a new edition in twelve volumes. She was pressed for time: the family had only enough money in their bank account to last a few months. Tolstoy no longer produced novels, and his non-fictional works, critical of the government and the Church, were banned. To speed up publication, she engaged two printing shops simultaneously and was swamped with proofs, writing sister Tanya, "To save 800 rubles of a proofreader's fee, I boldly decided to undertake this work myself, and now I'm harnessed for five months ahead...."[281] Despite the pressure, she enjoyed rereading Tolstoy's prose, telling him that his novel *Childhood* moved her to tears again. She discovered new horizons in *War and Peace*, "surprised, enchanted, and puzzled" by the novel. "How silly I was when you wrote *War and Peace*, and how ingenious you were! . . ."[282]

By then, the family lived separately: Tolstoy wrote in Yasnaya, while Sophia looked after practical affairs and the children in Moscow. She had written him a year earlier, "I'm determined to *fulfill my duty* towards you as a writer and a man who needs his freedom above all; so, I'm not asking anything at all from you. And I am guided by the same sense of duty towards the children...."[283] During the years when Tolstoy produced religious, philosophical, and social works, Sophia gave him the freedom to create by shielding him from all practical concerns. Despite renouncing property, he remained at the estate, which Sophia had to manage as long as he continued to work there. The couple corresponded almost daily, and Tolstoy confided his writing plans to her. In 1882, when he mentioned an idea for a fictional story, Sophia lit up:

> I was seized with joy when I read you wanted to write in the *poetic genre* again. It was as if you felt what I've been longing for. That's where . . . you and I will unite again, what will comfort you and will illuminate our lives. This work is genuine, you're made for it, and outside this sphere there is no peace for your soul. I know you can't force yourself but I hope God helps you to retain this spark and grow it. I'm thrilled by the idea.[284]

Sophia's publishing mattered not only as the source of income for the family. She also wanted to push Tolstoy's banned works through religious censorship. In November, attempting to publish

Confession and *What I Believe* in her collected edition, Sophia traveled to Petersburg to meet with Konstantin Pobedonostsev, Ober-Procurator of the Holy Synod, the only official who could lift the ban. Sophia's argument was that since these works circulated illegally, the ban only generated additional interest and, therefore, it was sensible to allow publication in her limited subscription.

Upon her return to Moscow, Sophia received Pobedonostsev's reply that the volume of her edition where she included Tolstoy's non-fiction was banned irrevocably. In a defiant letter to the Ober-Procurator she called the ban Russia's shame. She had to quickly replace the banned portions with fiction and reprint the final volume, and, while dealing with her publishing crisis, worked long hours in her office.

Tolstoy, staying in Moscow at the time, suffered from the incongruity of his own position: Sophia was about to make a large profit from his works, in which he had renounced money and property. In an unsent letter to Chertkov, he accused her of compromising his teachings by selling his books: "I would go downstairs and meet a customer who would look at me as though I were a fraud, writing against property and then, under my wife's name, squeezing as much money as possible out of people for my writings."[285]

But while Tolstoy agonized over the contradiction between his ideals and their family's practical life, Sophia's position was no easier. That fall, she described her situation to her sister: "Our entire life is in conflict with Lyovochka's convictions and to concur with them . . . in our daily life is impossible. . . . It's painful to me that I have inadvertently become the means to all of this. These persistent demands of life, from which Lyovochka ran away, have besieged me with greater force."[286] When, days before Christmas of 1885, Tolstoy walked into Sophia's publishing office, his anger came like a bolt from the blue. She described the events next in a dramatic letter to sister Tanya:

> As it happened so many times before, Lyovochka became extremely gloomy and nervous. One day, I am sitting and

writing; he walks in, I look up—his face is dreadful. Until then, we lived splendidly, *not a single* unpleasant word was exchanged between us, just nothing at all. "I've come to say that I want to divorce you, I can't live like this, I am leaving for Paris, or America." You know, Tanya, if the house had collapsed on top of me I couldn't have been more surprised. I asked him, "What happened?" "Nothing. But you can only go on loading things onto a cart for so long. When the horse can't pull it any more, the cart stops." What exactly it is I've been loading onto the cart, is unknown. But then the shouting, the reproaches, and insults began to pour. . . . And when he said: "Wherever you are the air is poisoned," I went for a trunk and began packing. I wanted to get away and stay with you for awhile. But the children ran in, sobbing. . . . He pleaded: "Stay!" So I stayed. . . .[287]

Daughter Tanya, then twenty-one, remembered that "terrible winter night" when she and her siblings sat in the hall, listening to their parents argue upstairs. "Both were defending something more important to them than their lives: she, the well-being of her children . . . he, his very soul."[288] In the morning it was decided that Tolstoy, in Tanya's company, should spend Christmas at the Olsufievs, their old friends who owned a large estate thirty-five miles outside Moscow. The Olsufievs' estate was far more luxurious than Yasnaya, but this escaped Tolstoy's criticism, a contradiction Sophia pointed out: "But why is he not bellowing at the Olsufievs?"[289] Unlike Tolstoy, who was resting, playing cards, and enjoying masquerades in good company, Sophia's holiday was spent alone, working on the edition. She wrote Tolstoy, "We have no guests, and there's no *Christmas tree and no merriment* . . . I'm sitting at the desk with my envelopes."[290] To stop subscription to the collected works was impossible: she had obligations to readers.

After working into the night, she would wake up late, to find their youngest children, Sasha, Alyosha, and Misha, waiting for her.

She was raising their youngest children alone, and the profit from selling Tolstoy's books went to support *his* children, she wrote him: "You are always carefully avoiding the question of family responsibilities; if I did not have these responsibilities . . . I would dedicate myself to serving the public good. . . . But I cannot, for the benefit of strangers, let my children, given to me by God, grow up uneducated scoundrels."[291] Returning to Moscow after the holidays, Tolstoy made peace with her, "on a condition never to bring up the past."[292] She promised to forget but could not let go of her pain: "I have never been so unfairly and cruelly insulted as this time."[293]

The new edition sold out quickly, and Sophia followed up with a cheap edition in small print. Tolstoy wished to reduce the price even further to avoid making profit altogether. As he guiltily mentioned to Strakhov, Sophia's second edition "should cost only 8 rubles" and, after all, "there would be a profit of 25–30 thousand. This year, the estates produced only 1.5 thousand [rubles]."[294] Sophia suggested donating part of her publishing profit to charity, writing Tolstoy she could generate enough money to feed a multitude of hungry people.[295] But he believed charity "self-defeating" and rejected her offer: what they could give was but a drop in the ocean.[296]

In two years, Sophia made sixty-four thousand rubles, almost outshining Anna Dostoevsky's publishing success. But her gain only led to more conflict with Tolstoy. When, in February 1887, the inexpensive edition was released, she remarked that she had "completely lost interest in it. The money brought me no joy—I never thought it would."[297] Tolstoy's criticism of her publishing activity was undeserved, because Sophia's collected works were the cheapest and also the most satisfying to readers, according to his follower and biographer Aylmer Maude.[298] Striving for higher standards, Sophia would publish the first illustrated edition of Tolstoy's works in 1892, documenting his life through photographs she had taken herself.

In the summer of 1886, while carting hay for a peasant widow, Tolstoy had injured his leg and developed an infection. Because he refused medical help, Sophia nursed him in Yasnaya with home remedies. When his temperature rose to 40° C, she took the night train to Moscow, returning the following day with a medical celebrity. The doctor told her that had she not acted quickly, Tolstoy would most certainly have died of blood poisoning. For two months, putting aside her other duties, Sophia nursed Tolstoy back to health.

At this time, Tolstoy resumed his creative work, writing a play, *The Realm of Darkness*, a psychological drama from peasant life. Sophia, taking his dictation and copying the play, was moved by its artistic power and humbled by Tolstoy's talent: "I must be careful and considerate with him, and save him for his work, which is so dear to my heart."[299] The couple enjoyed "a peaceful and happy winter" in Yasnaya, united by their collaboration.[300] On her trips to Moscow, Sophia gave readings, inviting acquaintances, and reporting to Tolstoy that the play was making a "powerful impression." Alexander III liked *The Realm of Darkness* and allowed the Imperial theaters to produce it. Rehearsals had just begun when, on instructions from the Holy Synod, the play was banned. (The premiere took place only in 1895 at Petersburg's Alexandrinsky Theater.)

On March 31, 1888, the couple's thirteenth child and their last, Vanechka, was born. A fortnight after, leaving Sophia to care for their sickly and delicate boy, Tolstoy headed for Yasnaya on foot, accompanied with his young follower, Nikolai Gay Jr. At Yasnaya Tolstoy and Gay plowed the land for a peasant widow, pursuing an activity that corresponded with their convictions. Sophia, in Moscow, juggled her responsibilities as a new mother and publisher: "Vanechka's birth and nursing was the last drop which filled the vessel of my life to the brim. . . . Now it's time to publish the edition, and so I move from one task to another, like a machine. . . ."[301]

That same year, Tolstoy wrote *The Kreutzer Sonata*, his most controversial work, in which, much to his readers' surprise, he repudiated sexual love, proclaiming absolute chastity his ideal. Sophia felt that Tolstoy's abstract idea of spiritual love was destroying their genuine bond. It was better, she told him, not to have high moral principles, but to have a sense of right and wrong. Tolstoy argued it was important to strive for an ideal.[302] Tolstoy now viewed her as a source of temptation and, when he succumbed, hated her for the passion she inspired. After insisting they should have sex, he would denounce it in his diary: "It was so disgusting, I felt I'd committed a crime."[303] Sophia found herself trapped by his contradictions, unable to absorb his absurd rules: "He wrote *The Kreutzer Sonata*, rejected sexual love, while in his diary in August 1889, noted: 'Thought: what if there should be another child? How ashamed I should be, especially before the children. They will reckon up when it was, and will read what I'm writing.'"[304]

Readers were struck by Tolstoy's message, finding it unfathomable that "a man who had fathered thirteen children could rise up against conjugal love and even against the continuation of the human race itself." The only explanation they could find was that Tolstoy was old and hated his wife.[305] The banned novella circulated in numerous illegal copies, read widely by educated Russians. Strakhov wrote Tolstoy that instead of saying, "How are you?" people would ask, "Have you read *The Kreutzer Sonata*?"[306] The public interpreted it as a story of Tolstoy's marriage. Once again, he used the material of his betrothal with Sophia, but unlike in *Anna Karenina*, maintained that happy marriages did not exist. Sophia commented in her diary that the story humiliated her in the eyes of the world. Told that Alexander III remarked he was sorry for Tolstoy's poor wife, she decided to prove that she was not a victim at all. In 1890, she included the novella in the final volume of the collected works, becoming determined to achieve its publication.

Arriving in Petersburg, Sophia attained an audience with Alexander III on April 13, 1891. The Tsar allowed her to produce the novella in her limited subscription, which she recalled with a sense of achievement: "I cannot help secretly exulting in my success in overcoming all the obstacles, that I managed to obtain an interview with the Tsar, and that I, a woman, have achieved something that nobody else could have done! It was undoubtedly my own personal influence that played a major part in this business."³⁰⁷ Sophia made "an *excellent* impression" at court, but in Yasnaya the reception was cold.

Sophia's success did not matter to Tolstoy, because he had decided to publicly renounce his copyright. When he informed her, she argued that, coming at this time, such an announcement would hinder her sales. Moreover, permission to publish his censored works had been given to her exclusively and for limited subscription; releasing them to the public would violate the agreement with the Tsar.

But Tolstoy was undaunted: on September 17, 1891, her name day, Sophia was in Moscow where she received the text of his copyright statement with instructions to publish it in the newspapers *Russian Gazette* and *New Time*. Tolstoy released his works written after 1881 to the public domain: anyone in Russia and abroad could now publish them free of royalty. In addition, he renounced copyright on the two final volumes of his collected works, which included the novellas *The Kreutzer Sonata* and *Ivan Ilyich*. Sophia sent his statement to the newspapers; but in her heart, she never believed that renouncing copyright was the right thing. She remarked it was "unfair" to deprive their large family of income. "I knew that rich publishers, like Sytin, would profit from my husband's work. . . . And it seemed to me that for God, in whom I believed, it did not matter whether it was I who sold Tolstoy's works or it was Sytin and Suvorin."³⁰⁸

After Tolstoy renounced his copyright and *The Kreutzer Sonata* was brought out by underground publishers, the Tsar said Sophia had broken his trust. Sophia was still not forgiven at court in 1911: the Empress would refuse her an audience. According to Maude, Tolstoy came to regret renouncing his copyright and "often mentioned the trouble and annoyance over publication of each new book after adopting his self-denying ordinance."³⁰⁹ Unlike in the past, when publishing his new works was a joy, after his repudiation it became a torment: competing publishers approached Tolstoy personally to obtain permission to be the first to produce his new works. Actually, it was Chertkov who had pressed Tolstoy to renounce his copyright, as their exchange reveals. Later, it was also Chertkov who benefited from this decision, having prevailed on the writer, in the name of their cause and friendship, to give him exclusive right to publish his most profitable first editions. Tolstoy made other exceptions for his friend and allowed him to be unaccountable for the proceeds. But this special arrangement led to conflict with Sophia, who was quick to point out Tolstoy's double standard.

The public also did not benefit from his repudiation, because Tolstoy abandoned even an author's control over the published texts. During his lifetime, this led to a flurry of "inadequate and misleading versions of his works in all languages."[310] As competing publishers strove to produce his works first, quality was disregarded, to the disappointment of booksellers and public.

The copyright drama moved into the background when Tolstoy became occupied with a new cause—famine relief. In 1891, newspapers were filled with reports of looming famine. In June, half the Russian provinces were devastated by scorching heat and massive crop failure was predicted. That same summer, Sophia pledged 2,000 rubles for the starving. "I wanted to choose one district and give every starving family there so many *poods*[311] of flour, bread or potatoes per month."[312] This did not stop Tolstoy from renouncing the copyright. Now, when he asked her to donate money from publishing to the relief effort, she was annoyed, having to find the funds from her strained budget.

But when Tolstoy and their older daughters left to organize relief, Sophia urgently sent them 900 rubles. Their sons were also working on the famine: Sergei and Ilya became involved with the local Red Cross, and Lev left to organize relief in Samara. From her family's letters, Sophia realized that the money she could send was indeed a drop in the ocean and that more funds were needed to satisfy the demand. During a sleepless night on November 1, 1891, she wrote an appeal for donations, which appeared two days later in the *Russian Gazette*:

> My entire family has left to help the needy.... Having to stay in Moscow with our four young children, I can only help by supporting my family materially. But the need is so immense! On their own, people are powerless to satisfy such great demand.... We all, living here in luxury, cannot bear the sight of even the slightest pain inflicted on our own children; so, how can we bear the sight of exhausted mothers, whose children are dying of cold and hunger, or of old people with nothing to eat?... If each of us will feed one, two, ten, a hundred people—as many as we can, our consciences will be eased. God willing, we will never have to live through another such year! And so, I want to ask all of you who can and are willing to help, to support my family's undertaking. Your donations will go directly to feed the children and old people in the canteens, which my husband and children are organizing....

Her letter was reprinted by newspapers across Russia and in the West, and soon Sophia found herself in the middle of a huge undertaking: donations were coming from Russia, Europe, and the United States. According to her estimate, in two years their family collected 200,000 rubles (some 30,000 rubles were sent directly to her). What mattered was that the aid was distributed directly to the starving.

To make best use of the public money, Sophia asked Tolstoy what exactly was needed and in what quantities. She met shopkeepers and merchants, to tell them their produce would go to the hungry. They responded with good prices on rye, corn, barley, peas, and flour. Describing the mood of the day, Sophia remarked, "We all had but one thing in our mind: to help the starving people."[313]

In November and December, Sophia dispatched carloads of grain and vegetables to Tolstoy; to son Lev, who had opened soup kitchens in Samara; and to the artist Nikolai Gay and his son, who dispensed relief near Petersburg. Tolstoy reported that all of her donations were very much needed. The cause had united them, and for the first time in years he wrote to her from the heart. When she told him how she had tended to their small children with flu, while herself struggling with asthma and neuralgia, Tolstoy replied with emotion, "Every night, I dream about you, my dear friend. May God keep you healthy and calm."[314] He suggested that the daughters should return to help her, but Sophia declined. Their undertaking was "wonderful and useful," and she was glad the girls were well occupied.[315]

Tolstoy also had doubts about his role in organizing such relief. Some of his followers disapproved of his involvement, pointing out that distributing aid contradicted his idea that money was evil. In November, at the height of the campaign, Tolstoy wrote apologetically to one of his followers, "My wife wrote a letter asking for donations, and without my noticing it I've become a distributor of other people's vomit. . . ."[316] While some disciples participated in the relief, others took a cautious stand. During the famine, Chertkov lived at his mother's estate in Voronezh province, copying Tolstoy's work, *The Kingdom of God Is Within Us*.

Sophia believed that work on the famine was beneficial for Tolstoy, since he was surrounded by "ordinary people," not his fanatical followers.[317] During the famine, she and Tolstoy had no disagreements on the copyright issue: he himself instructed her to accept the royalties for his article "A Terrible Question," published by *The Russian Gazette*. On her own initiative, Sophia obtained royalties from the Imperial Theater in Petersburg, which staged his play *The Fruits of Enlightenment*, and sent money to the relief. That winter, she joined Tolstoy to inspect the canteens in several villages between Tula and Ryazan to see what they were accomplishing. Tolstoy participated in the relief until midsummer 1892, opening more shelters and canteens.

Sophia possessed the capacity for hard work, which women of her class could not match. She managed literary and business affairs and was adept at housework, sewing, and cooking. When in Moscow on publishing business, she lived alone, without servants, writing Tolstoy, "I clean dresses, coats, and shoes, tidy the rooms, repair things, do the laundry, make beds, and carry water."[318] The life of luxury, of which Tolstoy accused her in his diaries, was but a myth.

She had made many attempts to understand Tolstoy's philosophy. Upset with his non-fiction at the start, she later took pride in his religious works, remarking in 1883, "But he must do it, it's God's will; and they may even serve His great purpose."[319] In 1887, she translated her favorite among his philosophical works, *On Life*, into French. Later, she translated into Russian a biography of St. Francis of Assisi by Paul Sabatier, which Tolstoy regarded as an important book for his following. The story of the medieval Italian saint who established a religious order, Friars Minor, had parallels with Tolstoy's life. St. Francis's desire to be loved by the entire world resonated with Tolstoy's aspiration to establish himself as a leader of his own religion. Sophia's translation of Sabatier's biography was produced by Intermediary, Tolstoy's publishing venture with Chertkov, in 1895. However, Tolstoy expected her to accept all of his philosophy, having written to her, "I would give away . . . my fame, if only you could reconcile your soul with mine during my life, as you will reconcile it after my death."[320]

In February 1895, the couple's youngest son, Vanechka, died at seven from scarlet fever. Sophia had invested all her love in this boy and would never recover from the blow. Vanechka's death brought the family together. Tolstoy wrote Alexandrine, "We have none of us felt as close to each other as we do now. . . ."[321] Although Tolstoy was pained by the loss, his philosophy enabled him to see the event as coming from God and therefore "merciful." But Sophia could find no peace as weeks and months went by. She spent hours beside Vanechka's portrait, which she had enlarged, and stood long services in churches and cathedrals. It was music, she would say, that saved her from despair.

That summer, their acquaintance, composer and pianist Sergei Taneev, was looking for a dacha, and Sophia offered him a vacant wing in Yasnaya, which was empty that summer. He taught her to understand music as she had not before. (Taneev was at the center of the Moscow music world, having succeeded Tchaikovsky as head of the Moscow Conservatory. Rachmaninov and Scriabin were among Taneev's students.) During Taneev's stay she became mesmerized with his performances of Chopin and Beethoven, and of his own compositions. In Moscow, Sophia attended all of Taneev's concerts and even began to take piano lessons: "Intoxicated by music, having learned to understand it, I could no longer live without it. . . ."[322] But her sudden onset of musical interest, which she experienced during bereavement, was viewed by her family as an obsession with the musician. Tolstoy pressed her to give up her friendship with Taneev and made scenes in front of guests, eventually driving the musician out of Yasnaya. (The situation seemed to have been scripted in *The Kreutzer Sonata*, written almost a decade earlier. In Tolstoy's novella, Mrs. Pozdnyshev becomes attracted to a musician friend, provoking her husband's jealous rages.) In a letter to a friend Sophia described Tolstoy's jealousy as an egotistical demand to be loved exclusively.[323]

As is apparent from Sophia's novella *Song Without Words*, Taneev was homosexual. He is immediately recognizable in her story as a composer and professor at the conservatory who is intimate with his young pupil. Taneev's lack of interest in women was widely known: at thirty-nine, he still lived with his old nanny, Pelageya Vasilievna. Tolstoy, of course, was aware of this, but remained unappeased, soon writing in his diary that Sophia had become "only more frivolous" after Vanechka's death, a remark she read. His words not only offended her: she realized that Tolstoy's diaries would be published along with everything he wrote. Over the years, she asked Tolstoy to remove the many disparaging entries he had made about her, but he refused. So she wrote him a letter:

> Why do you always in your diaries, when you mention my name, treat me so spitefully? Why do you want future generations and our grandchildren to know me as your *frivolous, evil* wife, who makes you unhappy? Perhaps, it would add fame to you that you were *a martyr*, but how much it would

damage me! . . . Are you really afraid that your posthumous glory would be diminished if you did not present me as your tormentor and yourself as martyr, bearing a cross personified by your wife?. . . . Please delete the spiteful words about me from your diaries. After all, this is only a *Christian* thing to do. . . . Please spare my name. . . .[324]

Upon reading her letter, Tolstoy remarked: "Never before have I felt so guilty and so full of emotion." He deleted some of the most hurtful entries about Sophia and made a note for his biographers: *"I repudiate those angry words which I wrote about her. These words were written at moments of exasperation. I now repeat this once more for the sake of everybody who should come across these diaries. . . .* She was—and I can see now in what way—the wife I needed."[325] But Tolstoy never purged all criticism, so this notation had no influence on biographers. Ever contradictory, he continued to complain to Chertkov (his future biographer) and to other disciples about his marriage. After Tolstoy's death, Chertkov would use his letters and diaries to harass Sophia.

In May 1897, Sophia visited Tolstoy in Yasnaya. When she left, he wrote that her brief stay was "one of the strongest, most joyful impressions I have ever experienced: and that at the age of 69, from a woman of 53."[326] She replied that the rise and fall of their relationship was like the tide: now on the rise.[327] Tolstoy's fiction continued to unite them. Earlier, when he had shared his idea for the story *The Master and Man*, she responded, "I cannot surrender my love of your artistic work; today I realized that's because I had experienced it with you during my best years, my youth. . . ."[328]

Tolstoy's last major novel, *Resurrection*, completed in 1899, two decades after *Anna Karenina*, did not measure up to his earlier fiction. Sophia believed it was a tendentious work, permeated with defiance against their social order and the Orthodox Church. She wrote Tolstoy that he was "inventing" this novel, not living it.[329] Unlike before, she was excluded from Tolstoy's creative work. When she asked Tolstoy to allow her to copy his revisions, he growled that her copying had "always caused trouble." She left his study in tears: "How could he forget the past?"[330] Tolstoy did not need her help because his follower, Paul Biryukov, and daughter Tanya were now copying for him. Nonetheless, Sophia read the manuscript and pointed out a flaw. In the draft she read, the nobleman Dmitry Nekhlyudov atones for his sin by marrying Katyusha Maslova, a convicted prostitute in whom he recognizes the woman he has seduced. Sophia had called this denouement improbable, and Tolstoy eventually agreed and altered the ending.

Tolstoy's ridicule of the Orthodox services and clergy in *Resurrection* antagonized the Church, already irritated by *The Kreutzer Sonata*. When in 1899 he became ill, the Holy Synod secretly instructed priests to refuse him a funeral service. The subsequent decision to excommunicate Tolstoy was designed to undermine public support for him and strengthen the prestige of the Orthodox Church. Instead, the verdict only added to Tolstoy's fame.

The excommunication edict was published on February 24, 1901, by the *Church News*, the official organ of the Holy Synod; the following day, it appeared on the front pages of every newspaper. Sophia immediately protested the decision in an open letter to the Holy Synod and the three Metropolitans. She wrote that the Synod's instructions were utterly incomprehensible to her, since "the religious life of a human soul is known to none but God, and mercifully it is not answerable to anyone." Excommunication would fail to achieve its goal and instead would only inspire "great love and compassion for Lev Nikolaevich. We are already receiving expressions of this—and there will be no end to them—from all over the world."[331] Published by the *Church News* along with a reply from Metropolitan Antony, Sophia's letter received public acclaim as an unprecedented challenge by a woman to the heads of the Orthodox Church.

On the Sunday the excommunication proclamation was published, it was read by everyone, and support for Tolstoy immediately began to pour in. He received baskets of flowers, telegrams, and letters from home and abroad. At the Wanderers' Exhibition,

Tolstoy's portrait by Repin, showing him at prayer in the woods, was garlanded with flowers as an icon. The portrait created so much commotion that it had to be removed.

Tolstoy's excommunication did not affect Sophia's faith, because it was initiated by the Holy Synod, a government institution. As Tolstoy's publisher, she had met the head of the Holy Synod, Pobedonostsev, over censorship, and despised this official. It was unlike her attitude to the Church, which remained reverent: "I have lived amongst these things since I was a child, when my soul was first drawn to God, and I love attending mass and fasting. . . ."[332]

That summer, Tolstoy became dangerously ill with malaria, and when Countess Sophia Panina offered her estate in Gaspra on the Black Sea, it was decided to go to the Crimea to help him recuperate. Panina's gothic palace with two towers and a view of the sea had once belonged to Prince Golitsyn, minister of education for Alexander I. Although Tolstoy's principles stipulated austerity, he would spend almost a year at this estate, joined by the entire family and some friends.

In Gaspra, Sophia nursed Tolstoy for nine months, her husband now becoming her child. She slept next door to Tolstoy, who rang a bell when he wanted her to adjust his pillow, cover up his legs, massage his back, or simply sit beside him and hold his hand. This inspired Sophia's remark, "Lev Nikolaevich is first and foremost a writer and expounder of ideas; in reality and in his life he is a weak man, much weaker than us simple mortals."[333] Three doctors attended Tolstoy almost daily, even refusing compensation: there was something about the genius that inspired everyone to toil for him and consider it rewarding in itself. "Nursing him is extremely hard work, there are a lot of us here, we all are tired and overworked. . . ."[334]

In Gaspra Sophia resumed photography, painted landscapes, studied Italian, and read; among the books was Giuseppe Mazzini's *On Human Duty*. Tolstoy considered it excellent and she was also impressed: "What marvelous ideas and language—simple, concise, full of power and conviction."[335] She read in five European languages, discovering other cultures through such books as Fielding's *The Soul of a People*, which told about Burmese traditions and religion. She now shared Tolstoy's fascination with Buddhism, even remarking that it was "much better . . . than our Orthodoxy."[336]

During the hours she sat beside Tolstoy, Sophia reviewed her life: she had a "sudden vivid memory of the distant past," of skating with her children on their pond in Yasnaya and walking home from the rink, while carrying a baby and pulling a sled with another child. "And behind us and before us were happy, laughing, red-cheeked children, and life was so full and I loved them so passionately. . . ."[337] Three years later, she began her memoir, the work that would take years to research and write. It was time for wisdom, insights, and drawing a line:

> I have served a *genius* for almost forty years. Hundreds of times I have felt my intellectual energy stir within me, and all sorts of desires—a longing for education, a love of music and the arts. . . . And time and again I have crushed and smothered all these longings. . . . Everyone asks: "But why should a worthless woman like you need an intellectual or artistic life?" To this question I can only reply: "I don't know, but eternally suppressing it to serve a genius is a great misfortune."[338]

Sophia still yearned for a spiritual life of her own: there were many things she wanted to try and projects she had been putting off over the years. To her surprise, nothing could extinguish her "desires and aspirations for something loftier, for a more spiritual, more significant life."[339] In 1902, the family returned to Yasnaya, where Tolstoy would now live indefinitely and she would explore her intellectual and artistic interests during the sunset of her marriage.

Sophia had a great desire to study art: back in 1864–65, when Tolstoy wrote *War and Peace*, she had made two splendid drawings. These early pictures, little dogs and a family scene, display her natural artistic talent and good eye for detail. Tolstoy sympathized with her desire to take up art and even promised to engage a teacher, but nothing was done. In 1866, when he became interested in sculpting and took art instruction in Moscow, she had observed him shape a statuette of a horse from red clay. Tolstoy also tried and failed to sculpt her bust. At fifty-eight, Sophia made her own and Tolstoy's profiles out of plaster and sculpted his bust in red clay.

Having observed the famous portraitists Kramskoy and Repin, she was curious about painting in oils and worked to exhaustion trying to figure out the technique. She made a decent copy of Ilya Repin's portrait of Tolstoy reading a booklet at his desk.[340] And she photographed herself at work: brush in hand, she stands near both portraits, smiling. Then she moved on to copy Kramskoy's famous painting of Tolstoy during his work on *Anna Karenina*.

In 1904, *Journal for All* published Sophia's collection of prose poems, submitted under the pen name "A Tired Woman." By then, she was indeed "a tired woman," having lived through many crises: sixteen pregnancies, miscarriages, the deaths of five children, and Tolstoy's difficult moods. That same year, she began her memoir *My Life* and read a few chapters to the family. Tolstoy, present during the reading, praised her work. Based on her correspondence with Tolstoy and family documents, it was a chronicle of their marriage, which provided insights into Tolstoy's character and creativity. She would see only several chapters of her memoir published, as there would be no time and no opportunity to edit or to complete it. (This sizable and informative work remains unpublished in Russia, reflecting widespread prejudice against Sophia.[341])

She now lived mostly in the country, except for business trips to Moscow. In 1903, Sophia launched a new edition of *War and Peace* and began reprinting Tolstoy's collected works in 15,000 copies, the largest circulation ever. The family still depended on her publishing income, now essential to support an ailing Tolstoy, to pay for his doctors and special diet. In 1904, Tolstoy's Slovak follower, Dushan Makovitsky, became his personal physician and settled with the family in Yasnaya.

For a while, Sophia was unwell: pains in her uterus occasionally kept her in bed. She took her illness calmly and told Tolstoy that her condition was not likely to improve. In August 1906, at sixty-two, Sophia was "overcome by excruciating pains." Gynecologist Vladimir Snegirev was summoned to Yasnaya, concluding that her pain was related to a fibroid tumor in her uterus and urgent surgery was required to save her life. He had to perform a rare procedure outside the clinic, on the wife of a celebrity, and was understandably nervous. Snegirev would later publish a paper describing laparotomy, which involved an incision through the abdominal wall.

Tolstoy, who was initially against the surgery, dropped his objections when it was explained that Sophia would die without it. He was crying when he left Sophia's bedroom where she confessed, took communion, and bid her farewells. On September 2, he noted in his diary, "They operated today. They say it's been successful. But it was very hard for her."[342] The tumor in Sophia's uterus was the size of a child's head and it ruptured while being removed. Sophia suffered "endless pain" and was given morphine injections to assuage it.

As in the past, her health and vitality pulled her through: four weeks later, she was able to walk with a cane and, by the end of October, resumed her activities: she practiced the piano, painted landscapes, sewed, and played with her beloved granddaughter, Tanechka. In November, there was yet another blow: daughter Masha came down with pneumonia and developed pleurisy. Tolstoy was at Masha's bedside when she died on November 27 at thirty-six. On the day of the funeral, Sophia followed Masha's coffin to the Yasnaya Polyana stone gate. "Did I survive to bury my children?"[343]

As usual, she drowned her depression in work, running the household and teaching herself to type on a Remington. In the New Year, she worked energetically on her memoir and traveled to Moscow to research it at the Historical Museum, where she had deposited Tolstoy's archive. It included Tolstoy's manuscripts of the literary period, the priceless drafts to *War and Peace* and *Anna Karenina*, which Sophia had collected and preserved. Tolstoy did not care what would become of his papers, nor did the children at the time. Daughter Sasha recalls her mother's story of how she saved a portion of Tolstoy's manuscripts from destruction. When someone tidied up their storage room in Yasnaya, a bundle of papers was discarded. Sophia went to check what it was: "I couldn't believe my eyes—these were drafts for *War and Peace*. They would have perished without me."[344]

Sophia's most daunting task was managing Yasnaya. During pre-revolutionary years, estate affairs had become entangled and chaotic, reflecting growing tensions between peasants and landowners—a small minority, which possessed most of the land. Even Yasnaya, where peasants had always been treated well, was not exempt. Tolstoy admitted that he sensed the peasant hostility directed at him personally.[345] The estate's orchard was raided at night; crops were collected and carted away. Burglars broke into the guest wing and stole property. Peasants raided the woods: 133 oaks were felled and sold in Tula. Sophia hired armed Cossacks to guard their estate, for which she was criticized by Tolstoy and his followers. In September of 1907, after a shooting incident in the woods, she asked the authorities to send armed guards, realizing this would put her in serious conflict with Tolstoy, as police presence could not but upset the man who preached non-violence. But as long as he remained in Yasnaya, she felt she had to ensure his safety. They lived in a time of unparalleled hostility: beginning in 1905, hundreds of police and officials were killed by revolutionary terrorists and estates were robbed and set afire.

A new trial for Sophia began in 1908, with Chertkov's return from England, to where, a decade earlier, he had been exiled for his participation in Tolstoy's causes. On a previous visit to Russia, Chertkov had bought land in Telyatinki, within walking distance of Yasnaya, and built a two-story mansion, along with workshops and stables. By winter, it housed a colony of Tolstoyans to whom Chertkov paid salaries for listening to him preach about the evils of money and property. Sophia, hearing some of his sermons, was struck with his hypocrisy, knowing that Chertkov owned luxurious properties in Russia and in England. But she was more troubled with Chertkov's influence over Tolstoy. The disciple visited Yasnaya daily, arriving with a throng of secretaries and an English photographer, who took portraits of Tolstoy and of Chertkov in Tolstoy's study.

By then, Tolstoy had made Chertkov his sole representative abroad. Chertkov handled Tolstoy's negotiations with foreign publishers and eventually alone decided who should translate and publish his work, even disregarding the writer's wishes. Mikhail Sukhotin, daughter Tanya's husband, was appalled that Chertkov treated Tolstoy's writings as his own. Later, describing the relationship between the two men, Sukhotin wrote that Tolstoy loved Chertkov "with special tenderness . . . blindly; this love drove L.N. to become completely subordinated to Chertkov's will."[346]

Sophia felt that Chertkov was angling for Tolstoy's literary estate. Back in 1904, while still in England, he had sent Tolstoy a questionnaire, to probe whom he wanted to appoint as his literary heir. The questions suggested he should name none other than Chertkov, to which Tolstoy at first responded by accusing his friend of coercion and entrapment. Chertkov demanded an apology, which he received. Over the years, the disciple continued to pursue this goal with his usual tenacity and, upon his return to Russia, doubled his pressure on Tolstoy. Eventually he persuaded the ailing Tolstoy to make a secret will and appoint him executor. With Tolstoy's fame, it was enough to make a statement in his diary, which he had already done, having written in 1908, "I would be glad if my heirs would make all my writings public property. . . ."[347] Because Tolstoy did not recognize government institutions, he did not want a formal will. To persuade him to make it, Chertkov maligned Sophia and the children. He persuaded Tolstoy that his family had "mercenary intentions" and could not be trusted to carry out his requests. Chertkov would later write his own account of these events, making it appear as if he had merely executed Tolstoy's wishes.

Beginning in 1909, Tolstoy signed several redactions of the secret will, which Chertkov and his Moscow attorney had drafted. Daughter Sasha, then twenty-five, was drawn into the conspiracy, believing that Chertkov was her father's genuine friend who wanted to deliver the posthumous copyright to the people. In reality, Chertkov struggled to establish his own authority over Tolstoy's legacy and needed Sasha to cover up his intentions. She was designated as a nominal heiress in the will, with the understanding that this formality would be later dropped.

On July 22, 1910, in a forest near the village of Grumont, Tolstoy signed a final redaction of the secret will. Days later, he regretted the conspiracy, writing in his diary: "Chertkov has involved me in a struggle, and this struggle is both very depressing and very repugnant to me."[348] The will stripped from Sophia the posthumous copyright to Tolstoy's literary works, which she had helped him produce and which he had handed over to her for publication.

Tolstoy's biographer and disciple Paul Biryukov disapproved of the secret will: when he found out, he told Tolstoy it would be better if he announced his wishes openly. Immediately after, Tolstoy wrote Chertkov: "It was bad that I acted secretly, assuming bad things about my heirs. . . ."[349] But as Tolstoy's exchange with Chertkov reveals, the disciple was in full control of the situation.

Chertkov's private meetings with Tolstoy and secret correspondence led Sophia to suspect that the two men had a liaison. When she discussed the matter with Tolstoy, he denied it and "flew into a terrible rage such as I have not seen for a long, long time."[350] As if to confirm Sophia's suspicions, Tolstoy told her in 1910, "Chertkov is the person who is closest to me. . . ."[351] Tolstoy's words and his relationship with the man of deeply flawed character, devious, despotic, and self-righteous, mystified his contemporaries and remain unexplained to this day.

During Tolstoy's final months, Chertkov collided with Sophia over her husband's diaries. He taunted her by saying that he could publish Tolstoy's negative entries and drag her "through mud." At the end of her marriage with the genius, Sophia was nervously ill and suffering: she would become hysterical at the mere mention of Chertkov's name. Alienated from her husband, to whom she had dedicated her life, and betrayed by her daughter, she was driven to despair and made suicidal threats. When, on September

23, the couple's forty-eighth wedding anniversary, Tolstoy posed for a photograph with Sophia, he received an admonishing letter from Chertkov. In his *Diary for Myself Alone*, Tolstoy wrote: "A letter from Chertkov with accusations. They are tearing me to pieces. I sometimes think that I should go away from them all."[352] In that last picture of Tolstoy, taken one month before he fled the estate, Sophia is holding on to his arm, turned toward him with a pleading smile; he looks ahead morosely. During these final months, she lived in fear that Tolstoy would make good on his threat to leave home.

Tolstoy's departure was not as spontaneous as it is believed: he had discussed it with Chertkov and Sasha days earlier. It seems that even the date, October 28, had been decided: Tolstoy believed this number providential for him. And yet, describing the events in his diary, he held Sophia responsible. He accused her of spying on him, searching his papers the night before, which prompted his decision to flee.

In his farewell letter to her, Tolstoy stated that he was fleeing the "conditions of luxury" to spend his remaining days in solitude. His flight would give rise to numerous speculations and legends. Sophia made her own interpretation of his leaving, in a note to Tolstoy's biographers: "The most probable version is that he became ill, sensed intuitively he was dying, and fled to die.... Accusations to his wife, his words about luxury, and his wish to stay alone, all this was false, invented."[353] At eighty-two, after several strokes and suffering from heart and lung problems, Tolstoy was in a fragile state. His life could be only prolonged at the estate, in his habitual environment. It was obvious that his flight would only hasten his death.

And yet, upon learning about Tolstoy's departure, Chertkov congratulated him in a telegram: "I cannot express in words the joy I felt in hearing that you have gone away." Within days of his leaving home, Tolstoy was dying of pneumonia in a small railway station at Astapovo. Fans and reporters from all over the world, filming and photographing, besieged the place. Sophia was photographed on the platform as she peeked at her husband through a shuttered window. Tolstoy died in the presence of his disciples and daughter Sasha, while Sophia was not allowed to bid farewell. It was decided that seeing her would devastate Tolstoy, but nobody even told him that she was in Astapovo. Sophia was finally admitted when he had slipped into a coma. For the rest of her life she suffered from the agonizing thought that Tolstoy had died in her absence and the two of them had not made peace.

The events in Astapovo shocked many. Anna Dostoevsky was among the first to express sympathy to Sophia and write of her outrage that strangers had separated her from her dying husband. "How much grief you endured during these mournful final days! I cried when I read how you were unable to attend to Lev Nikolaevich, to whom you have been a good genius throughout his life."[354] On November 9, 1910, the prominent lawyer and family friend Anatoly Koni expressed condolences and his deep gratitude to Sophia for having nursed Tolstoy's artistic talent. A week later, she received a letter signed by twelve academicians of fine arts who recognized her contribution to Tolstoy and her importance to Russian culture. Sophia would only read these letters to her visitors. She was not able to publish them because Chertkov soon started a defamation campaign against her in the press, accusing her, among other things, of driving Tolstoy out of their home. Chertkov and people close to him would now control everything written about Tolstoy in Russia, so positive information about Sophia could not come out until the end of the twentieth century.

As a widow, Sophia remained in Yasnaya, preserving the estate and Tolstoy's study the way he had left it in 1910. The candles on his desk were never lit after he extinguished them on the fateful night of his departure. The book he read that night was Dostoevsky's *The Brothers Karamazov*, and it would remain opened on his desk. As she wrote in her autobiography, "I live in Yasnaya Polyana and preserve the house with the furnishings just as they were during Lev Nikolaevich's time, and care for his grave."[355] Sophia did not allow Yasnaya to be sold into private hands, as her sons had wanted, and prevented them from challenging Tolstoy's will.

In 1912, the wealthy publisher Sytin bought first rights to three volumes of Tolstoy's unpublished works from daughter Sasha. The money helped resolve the question of how to dispose of Yasnaya. Sasha purchased two thirds of the land from her brothers and transferred it to the peasants to fulfill Tolstoy's wish. Sophia bought the remaining land from her sons to establish the museum. From the land distribution, she reserved 170 acres with the house, grounds, orchard, and forest, which she and Tolstoy had planted "with so much love to improve our estate."

In summer 1918, writer Tikhon Polner visited Sophia in Yasnaya. In his book *Lev Tolstoy and His Wife*, he describes their meeting: "Calm and weary, she met me with dignity. She was then seventy-four. Tall, slightly stooped, very thin, she moved through the rooms like a shadow; it seemed that a gust of wind could take her away.... Sophia Andreevna talked willingly but without a smile.... With obvious pleasure, she read her memoir of the happy days in Yasnaya Polyana.... Of Chertkov she spoke without anger but with cold animosity. Her remarks about the last ten years of her life with her genius husband were not always kind. After falling silent for a moment, she would say, 'Yes, I lived with Lev Nikolaevich for forty-eight years but I never really learned what kind of a man he was.'"[356]

She lived through the First World War, the Revolution, and the Civil War, events that entirely transformed her country. Preserving the isle of culture, she catalogued Tolstoy's library in Yasnaya, copied his fiction, notebooks, and letters, and toured hundreds of visitors through the estate. Her final letters were to Tolstoy's biographers. To one, she gave information about his early story *Polikushka*, the one she had copied out at eighteen. To another, she explained his attitude to the law. Sophia died on November 4, 1919, at seventy-five, three days before the anniversary of Tolstoy's death, also from pneumonia, and was buried in the family cemetery Kochety, next to her children.

Aware of her contribution, Tolstoy had written to her thirty-five years into their marriage: "You gave me and the world what you were able to give; you gave much maternal love and self-sacrifice, and it's impossible not to appreciate you for it."[357]

CHAPTER THREE

Nadezhda Mandelstam: Witness to Poetry

A survivor of Stalin's Terror, which sent millions to death camps, Nadezhda wrote one of the best known accounts about her generation, beginning with her revelatory memoir, *Hope Against Hope*. After her husband Osip Mandelstam perished in the gulag, she made it her mission to preserve his poetry and tell his story.

She could not understand people's obsession with their childhood, saying that her life began when she met Mandelstam on May 1, 1919. Her pampered girlhood with an English governess did not prepare her for life as a poet's helpmate and homeless wanderer in one of the most violent eras in Russian history. And it was not until her late seventies that she began to reminisce. "Why, at the dawn of the new era, at the very beginning of the fratricidal twentieth century, was I given the name Nadezhda [Hope]?"[358]

Nadezhda Yakovlevna Khazina was born on October 31, 1899, in Saratov, a port city on the Volga in southern Russia. Saratov was a multicultural city populated by Germans, Russians, Ukrainians, Tartars, and Jews. Her family had Jewish origins, but the children absorbed little Jewish culture. Nadezhda's grandfather, on her father's side, was forcefully converted to Orthodoxy under Nicholas I. For her father, Yakov Arkadievich, embracing Christianity and forsaking their Jewish roots was a requisite step to university education and entrance to the Bar.

A graduate of the Department of Mathematics, her father possessed "a very orderly mind" and brilliant memory, which allowed him to pass the Bar exams without attending Law School. He further proved himself by making a fortune with his very first case.[359] Yakov Arkadievich read Goethe's *Faust* in German and loved classical languages and literature: he savored Greek tragedies in the original for relaxation. The system of education, which produced such men as her father, was a measure by which Nadezhda would later assess "the gradual fall" of the state of education after the Revolution.

Nadezhda's mother, Vera Yakovlevna, also came from a Jewish family but, unlike her husband, remained Jewish. Educated in Europe and becoming a medical doctor, she was in a vanguard of Russia's professional women pursuing education and careers since the 1860s. Nadezhda's parents were married in France, and their first son, Alexander, was born in 1891. Nadezhda describes her mother as "a student radical" of the pre-Revolutionary days, critical of the tsarist government. She supported the 1917 Revolution, but became disillusioned with the Bolsheviks in power. During the Civil War that followed, the state seized grain and supplies from the peasants, leaving nothing in exchange. With the economy in shambles, Lenin was desperate to feed the major cities, where he was losing control. Lenin's disastrous policy became responsible for the severe famine of 1921–22 that killed around ten million people, to become Russia's greatest calamity since the Middle Ages. Mobilized to work in the Volga region, the most afflicted by the famine and epidemics, Vera Yakovlevna saw devastation unknown under the tsars. (She worked in the same region where Tolstoy had organized his first relief in the 1870s.)

Nadezhda was the youngest in a family of two boys and two girls, all educated by English governesses. Anna, eleven years older, became a specialist in medieval French literature. After the Revolution, unemployed, she lived in her uncle's house, occupying a dark storeroom, a place for servants in the past. Alexander, the older brother, was a gold-medal graduate of Law School with a brilliant career ahead of him. However, his career was halted before it began: during the Civil War, he joined the White Army, fled to the Don region to fight the Bolsheviks, and was never heard of again. Nadezhda was not able to even mention Alexander under Stalin and only told his story in old age when she no longer had anything to fear. Her younger brother Evgeny, who managed to conceal that he also had enlisted in the White Army, made his living as a writer; he and Nadezhda would remain close over the years.

Before the Revolution, their parents took them to France, Germany, Switzerland, Italy, and Sweden. By the age of nine, Nadezhda spoke English, German, and some Italian. In Switzerland, where they lived for two years, she picked up French, later complaining to a friend about the inconvenience of living in the trilingual country, "You go outside to play hopscotch and it turns out that again you have to switch to another language."[360]

Nadezhda was a third-generation Christian Orthodox and had attended church since childhood, despite her Jewish roots. In 1910, when the family moved to Kiev from Switzerland, her Russian nanny often took her to services at the ancient Cathedral of St. Sophia, which she quite liked. (Mandelstam converted in Finland in 1911, which Nadezhda believed was not only for practical reasons but because he was drawn to Christianity.) In Kiev she studied in a gymnasium, which followed a more thorough boys' curriculum and, unlike the easier fare for girls, embraced Latin, Greek, mathematics, and sciences. In 1917, pushed by her father to excel academically, she entered Kiev University to study law. Anna Akhmatova, who would become Nadezhda's close friend, also took law at the Kiev College for Women.[361] Nadezhda stayed at university for about a year, leaving when the country plunged into Civil War.

In Soviet times, one could not pursue a genuine career in law. When the Bolsheviks expropriated the family's possessions, Yakov Arkadievich wanted to launch a court action but returned home, describing the new court as a joke. He said he had fathomed Roman law in two weeks but could not figure out Soviet decrees. Yakov Arkadievich did not complain about the family's impoverishment during the ensuing economic collapse, declaring with typical irony that he was only sorry for their cook, who lost her savings. Nadezhda, with her leftist views, despised property, but only in theory, as it turned out. She remembers "the sharp stab of astonishment" when her father broke the news that their money had come to an end.[362] Yakov Arkadievich did not consider emigration, refusing to abandon his homeland in its misfortune; later, people closest to Nadezhda, Mandelstam, and Akhmatova, held similar views.

After leaving university, Nadezhda joined the studio of Alexandra Exter in Kiev. A prominent avant-garde artist and designer, Exter worked at Alexander Tairov's Chamber Theater. Nadezhda's first assignment as assistant decorator was painting "a huge garland of artificial fruits, vegetables, fish, and birds, all suspiciously phallic in appearance."[363] Nadezhda was "not proud" of her early youth, describing her bohemian milieu and their artistic pursuits with self-deprecating irony: "In those days I ran around as one of a small herd of painters. . . . We were kept busy all the time making stage decorations or painting posters, and we had the feeling that life was a hectic round of pleasure."[364]

Like many of her crowd, she frequented a café popular among artists, writers, and musicians called Khlam[365] (Trash) in the cellar of the Hotel Continental. There Nadezhda met future celebrities, including journalist Ilya Erenburg, artist Alexander Tyshler, and poet Vladimir Narbut. Mandelstam also came to the café when in Kiev. His first collection, *Stone*, published in 1913 at his own expense and only in 600 copies, made an impact beyond his immediate milieu. The book established Mandelstam as a principal poet of a new movement, Acmeism, which he defined as "a yearning for world culture." Nikolai Gumilev, one of the founders of this movement, was a major Petersburg poet, then married to Akhmatova, who would surpass him in fame. Gumilev's life was cut short in 1921 at the age of thirty-five when he was arrested and shot without trial on false charges of belonging to a monarchist conspiracy.

Mandelstam was sometimes seen writing at a table in the café, rocking on his chair while composing. He was nearing thirty, although his thinning reddish hair made him look older. On May 1, 1919, he came down from his room and headed toward Nadezhda's table. He introduced himself: "Osip Mandelstam greets the beautiful Kievan women," bowing toward Nadezhda, and "handsome Kievan men," bowing to everyone else. Asked to recite his poems, Mandelstam readily agreed: "He read with his eyes closed, swimming in the rhythms. . . ." He gazed straight at Nadezhda when he opened his eyes.[366]

Born in 1891, Mandelstam was raised in a prosperous Jewish family, whose children received excellent education. His mother was a music teacher, his father a cultured leather merchant interested in German philosophy. Raised in Petersburg, Mandelstam had traveled abroad as a young man and studied Old French literature at the University of Heidelberg.

Mandelstam and Nadezhda at once took up with each other "as though it were the most natural thing in the world."[367] Nadezhda's "free and easy generation" embraced the concept of woman as girlfriend and companion, rather than wife. "I did not understand the difference between a husband and a lover, and I must confess that I still don't."[368] A few days later, the couple was seen in the café, clearly in love: Nadezhda had a bouquet of water lilies, collected from the Dnieper.[369] Mandelstam had told her that their meeting "was no mere chance"[370] and, indeed, the relationship that began as a casual affair would prove unbreakable.

But their characters were not well-matched, making it difficult to get along. Ten years her senior, Mandelstam bossed her around, and Nadezhda was ill suited for this treatment: "Neither meekness nor forbearance was in my character, and we were constantly colliding head on. . . ."[371] Having obtained employment in a Bolshevik government agency (the Continental housed government offices), Mandelstam hired Nadezhda as his secretary. Earlier, he had worked in the People's Commissariat for Education and had been terrified of his secretary there, he told her. Nadezhda was to remain his private secretary, for he did not allow her to assist others, even their friend Erenburg, who became their coworker.

Although Mandelstam could be despotic in private life, he had an aversion to political tyranny, rejecting capital punishment and the Bolsheviks' use of violence. He had known several revolutionaries, including the notorious Yakov Bliumkin, head of the Cheka's counter-espionage department, who worked under Felix Dzerzhinsky. Bliumkin had become known for murdering the German ambassador Count Mirbach, a crime for which he received a nominal prison sentence.[372] Mandelstam heard Bliumkin boast that he had "powers of life and death in his hands." According to one version, Bliumkin showed Mandelstam a blank death warrant, already signed, and which, while drunk, he was filling with names. Whether Mandelstam grabbed the blank and tore it up, as his biographer Clarence Brown tells, or complained to Dzerzhinsky, Bliumkin became his sworn enemy. In 1919, Nadezhda witnessed Mandelstam's brief encounter with this man, which nearly cost him his life. As she and Mandelstam stood on the balcony of the Hotel Continental, Bliumkin with a mounted escort rode onto the street. The next thing she saw was Bliumkin's revolver aimed at Mandelstam. Instead of ducking, Mandelstam waved to the horseman and the shot was not fired. Mandelstam believed the Bolsheviks had broken a major commandment, "Thou Shalt Not Kill," and foresaw greater suppression of individual rights and tyranny.[373] In 1919, he shared little of his thoughts with Nadezhda: "He always talked to me very cautiously, opening up a chink into his inner world, only to shut it again at once, as though protecting it from me, yet wanting me to have a glimpse at the same time."[374]

They lived through several changes of power in Kiev. When the White Army forced the Bolsheviks out, Mandelstam went into hiding. He quit his hotel room and moved in with Nadezhda's family. From the windows of her father's study, they saw a cart piled with naked corpses: before fleeing Kiev, the Cheka executed their prisoners. During the Civil War, atrocities were committed by both sides: "Blood flowed in every street, outside every home. Bullet-ridden corpses lying in the roads and on the pavements were a familiar sight...."[375] But this was only the prelude to Stalin's terror.

When Mandelstam suggested that they flee the city and go south, she refused, believing travel was risky. They separated, and she thought that in this chaos people were better off forgetting each other. Communication between the cities was severed and, besides, she could not expect Mandelstam to find her, because her family had been evicted from their house. But in December of 1920, she unexpectedly received his letter, carried to Kiev by an acquaintance: Mandelstam had located her through Erenburg's wife, Lyuba. His letter defied time, distance, and war:

> My darling child! You have become so dear to me that I constantly talk to you, call you, complain to you. It is only to you that I can tell everything.... With you nothing will be frightening, nothing will be difficult.... My daughter, my sister, I smile with your smile and hear your voice in the silence.... Nadyusha, we shall be together at any cost. I shall find you and live for you because you give me life....[376]

Mandelstam arrived in Kiev in March 1921; when they met, he ran his fingers over her face: "He always closed his eyes and passed his hand over my face, like a blind man, lightly brushing it with his fingertips. 'So, you don't trust your eyes then?' I would tease him. He said nothing, but the next time he would do the same thing again." In fact, Mandelstam had a highly developed sense of touch and perceived the world more acutely than most people with this additional "window on the world."[377]

By then, Nadezhda's family had been evicted for the second time, their apartment assigned to a high-ranked Bolshevik, but the couple wanted to make use of it. Just as they shut themselves in Nadezhda's former room, a crowd of female prisoners was brought in by soldiers to scrub floors. Unperturbed by what was going on, Mandelstam and Nadezhda spent two hours in the room while soldiers banged on the door. "But we just stayed put. M. read me a lot of poems. . . ." Then the two went to the apartment building where Nadezhda's parents had rooms.

A few weeks later, the couple left the city to seek refuge in relatively peaceful Georgia. It was "destiny, rather than love"[378] that bound them together, Nadezhda remarked. They never separated again until the night of May 2, 1938, nineteen years later, when Mandelstam was taken away under guard.

Soon after the Revolution, many intellectuals fled to Georgia, which remained independent of the Bolsheviks for several years. Their journey to Georgia began in safety and comfort on a special train of a Bolshevik commissar who was Mandelstam's acquaintance. But upon arrival, they found the small independent republic overwhelmed by Civil War refugees. The couple stayed in the Caucasus for about six months, traveling through Georgia "as free as birds." Earning bread by occasional translations, they were homeless and hungry migrants in a land famous for magnificent food and wine. "I know from my own experience how bitter the émigré's bread can be in foreign parts. I discovered this in Georgia."[379] In December 1921, on New Year's Eve, the couple boarded a steamer for the Russian port of Novorossiisk. The ship was so packed that the Mandelstams considered themselves lucky to get sleeping space on the floor of a cabin belonging to a woman commissar who took them in.

In early March 1922, in Kiev, the couple registered their marriage in a civil ceremony, which Nadezhda felt was "a totally meaningless formality."[380] They had believed themselves married back in 1919 when they bought a couple of cheap wedding rings at a market. Mandelstam kept his ring in a pocket and Nadezhda attached hers to her pearl necklace, a present from her father. But now they needed a marriage certificate to share a compartment, a requirement of train commandants. Upon arriving in Moscow, they lost their marriage certificate.

In 1922, they roamed through many cities in search of a home and stability. At thirty-two, Mandelstam was tired of a nomadic existence, but could find only occasional freelance work, publishing articles in local newspapers. In April 1922, they had something of a home in Moscow, a room in the writers' dormitory in the wing of Herzen House on 25 Tverskoi Boulevard. The Empire-style house with columns later became the prestigious Gorky Literary Institute, but then it housed several writers' organizations and lodged impoverished writers.

The Mandelstams lived in a single room, next to the communal kitchen, and their quarters were exceptionally noisy because of the never-ending squabbles of other tenants. For Mandelstam, with his exceptionally good hearing, the noise was sheer torture. The couple's furniture consisted of two spring mattresses and a kitchen table, which someone donated. But since they received food rations, they believed themselves fortunate and even fed a destitute poet, Velimir Khlebnikov, to whom the writers' organization arbitrarily refused rations. Although the couple was hard up, Mandelstam objected to Nadezhda's employment. He wanted her to be "entirely dependent on his will."[381] So she would spend most of her day sitting on her mattress, taking his dictations. During this period she disliked her duties as Mandelstam's secretary and stenographer. "At that time he treated me like a piece of booty he had seized and brought back by force to his lair. All his efforts were directed to isolating me from other people, making me his own, breaking me in and adapting me to himself."[382]

Mandelstam's new collection of poems, *The Second Book*, with dedication to Nadezhda, came out in May 1923. He dictated this book to her and, according to Nadezhda, even stopped making notes beforehand. She had "a good ear for poetry,"[383] so their dictations did not go smoothly: when she made suggestions, "he hissed at me: '. . . You don't understand, so keep quiet.'"³⁸⁴ She would retort that he should hire a stenographer who would "write it all down without batting an eyelid."³⁸⁵ Mandelstam treated her "as a puppy" and even stuck a pacifier in her mouth so she would not interrupt him; he insisted she wear one on her neck, and it was attached to her pearl necklace.³⁸⁶ Nadezhda put up with this abuse because, in fact, he did value her opinion: "Tired, tear-stained, and at the end of my tether, I would doze off on his shoulder, and then, at night, I would wake up to see him standing by the table, crossing out and making changes. Seeing me awake, he would show me a new bit he had just written. . . ."³⁸⁷

Despite their arguments and her lack of secretarial skills, Mandelstam continued to dictate all his compositions to her. Even Nadezhda's faulty grammar (she was influenced by the Ukrainian language) and disorderliness did not relieve her of these duties. Mandelstam was trying to mold her character: "From me he wanted only one thing: that I should give up my life to him, renounce my own self, and become a part of him. . . . He was telling me that I not only belonged to him but was a part of his own being. . . ."³⁸⁸

With the honorarium for *The Second Book*, Mandelstam bought her a blue fox fur; however, "it turned out to be not a real pelt," but tufts of fur cleverly sewn onto cloth.³⁸⁹ Both of them were impractical, but Nadezhda's lack of domesticity became proverbial. Elena Galperina-Osmerkina, who visited the Mandelstams in their dormitory, recalled Nadezhda squatting in a corridor, cooking supper on two Primus stoves. "I wondered why she had to cook in such an uncomfortable pose."³⁹⁰ Nadezhda's privileged upbringing was responsible for her ineptitude: her family had a cook. In addition, as a true Bohemian, she despised domestic duties. Mandelstam, in contrast, liked order and kept his things tidy.

Their hideous room became filled with "gorgeous colors" when the couple acquired a marvelous tapestry of a hunting scene. It had probably been stolen from a palace or a museum, and they bought it for a song at a market. But they could not hold on to their only treasure because they soon lost their room. In fall 1923, Mandelstam got into a conflict with some other tenants who were making noise in the communal kitchen and rashly renounced his room. This led to the couple's "fantastic homelessness"[391] lasting ten years.

The winter of 1924 was spent in a rented room in the Yakimanka, one of the oldest Moscow districts, where both were freezing: their iron stove consumed loads of fuel, but was cold by morning. In fact, most of their earnings from translations went on firewood. They translated Western authors who were approved by the authorities, such as the novelist Henri Barbusse, a French Communist Party member. "What *didn't* we translate?"[392] Both starved and, in addition, lost their sexual drive, depriving them from indulging "in the kind of frivolous things which . . . always cheered us up a little."[393]

Mandelstam, who had learned from a friend in the Party that he would not be allowed to publish his verse, only translations, tried to establish himself as a prose writer. In 1924, he began dictating an autobiographical work, *The Noise of Time*, commissioned by a Moscow literary journal. Before each dictation session, Mandelstam would take a long walk, returning "tense and bad-tempered." Then he would tell Nadezhda to sharpen her pencils and get to work. The first sentences, likely memorized, were dictated quickly, and she could barely keep up. Later he would slow down and even neglect to complete sentences, leaving it to Nadezhda to fill in the blanks. Upon finishing a chapter, he asked her to read it back. If she recorded his sentences unpolished, as he had dictated them, he would be upset, as though he expected her to "hear" words going through his head.[394] When his book of prose was published, Mandelstam received rare praise in the Soviet press and was described as "a master of the refined, rich, and accurate style."[395] The most precious comment came from Boris Pasternak, who wrote in August 1925 that he experienced a rare pleasure from the book, savoring it at his dacha; he also suggested that Mandelstam write a novel.[396]

Although not close friends, Mandelstam and Pasternak had many things in common. Both were genuine poets and intellectuals who wrote prose rich in metaphor but weak in story line. Both men were musically sensitive (their mothers were pianists), and both particularly valued Scriabin's compositions. In addition, Pasternak's first wife, Evgeniya Lurie, was an artist, like Nadezhda, although Nadezhda's work did not survive.

On January 21, 1924, Lenin died—an event that would change their country's destiny. For the next several days and nights, while his body lay in state, lines of people stretched through Moscow. The Mandelstams stood in the same line as Pasternak. There were bonfires on the streets to prevent frostbite; life in the capital had stopped. Mandelstam remarked, "This was the Moscow of ancient days burying one of her tsars."[397] Lenin's funeral, Nadezhda observed, was "the last flicker of the Revolution as a genuine popular movement" when veneration for the leader was not inspired by terror.[398]

Remembering Pasternak's visits, Nadezhda would write that Mandelstam expected her to keep her intelligence to herself, so she "never butted in masculine conversation."[399] She was mostly silent with other friends as well: Mandelstam would inevitably put her down. Vasilisa Shklovsky, the wife of the literary scholar Victor Shklovsky, remembers Nadezhda "sitting with a book in a corner and glancing at us with her dark-blue, sarcastic and sad eyes."[400] The wives often had to take a second role to let their husbands shine. As Akhmatova remarked during her relationship with the art scholar Nikolai Punin, "With our men around we sat in the kitchen cleaning herring."[401]

Nadezhda Volpin, a poet, describes the Mandelstams shortly after they had moved to Leningrad. Mandelstam was briskly walking down the street, holding his head high, as was his habit; Nadezhda followed with a heavy case, an arrangement similar to the Nabokovs' decades later. Vladimir would get out of a car with just a chess set and his butterfly collection while Véra would follow, lugging two suitcases.

The Mandelstams left Moscow in summer 1924. Housing shortages in Leningrad were less severe: the capital had moved to Moscow and, besides, luxurious apartments and palaces of the aristocracy stood empty after their inhabitants had fled abroad. After the Revolution, some scholars and writers were housed in the servants' quarters of the Marble Palace, former residence of Prince Konstantin Romanov. Akhmatova lived there with her second husband, the distinguished scholar Vladimir Shileiko. They froze in winter because heating high-ceiling rooms was unaffordable.

The Mandelstams took two rooms in a private apartment on the Great Morskaya Street, not far from the Winter Palace. Their quarters were impressive even without an entrance door, stolen for firewood. In Leningrad, Nadezhda met Akhmatova for the first time, and the two women became friends for life. Akhmatova, who had known Mandelstam since 1911 and had seen him with other women, describes his affection for Nadezhda as "extraordinary and unbelievable." He was at once possessive of her and dependent on her: "He wouldn't let her out of his sight, didn't let her work, was insanely jealous, and asked her advice on every word in his poems. In general, I have never seen anything like it in my life."[402]

However, Mandelstam soon became involved with a younger woman named Olga Vaksel and, in January 1925, brought her to their apartment. Olga at one time had belonged to a circle of novice poets around Gumilev and had also tried acting. Akhmatova thought she was "a dazzling beauty."[403] Nadezhda realized he had another woman when Mandelstam stopped reading his poetry to her; in fact, his poems were now dedicated to Olga. The three had a turbulent relationship, but according to Nadezhda's version, "It was Olga, not I, who played the part of the demanding, reproachful, weeping woman—something that generally falls to the wife rather than the mistress."[404] In the early 1970s, Nadezhda told Carl Proffer, the American scholar, that the "three of them lived together for six weeks and it was the most shameful memory of her life."[405] Possibly they had a *ménage à trios*, as Emma Gershtein, a friend, implies in her memoir.[406] The affair brought the couple to the brink of divorce: "M's head had really been turned. . . . This was his only affair during the whole of our life together, but it was enough for me to learn what it was like to have a marriage break up."[407] Nadezhda soon decided to leave Mandelstam for Vladimir Tatlin, a prominent painter and architect who wanted to take her in. Upon learning this, Mandelstam severed his relationship with Olga, even though he was still attracted to her. Later trying to understand why Mandelstam made this choice, Nadezhda thought their collaboration was a major factor: "I still suspect . . . that if none of his poetry had yet been written, he might well have decided to let me leave him. . . ."[408]

That spring, Nadezhda, who had been suffering from tuberculosis, went to a sanatorium in Tsarskoe Selo, outside Leningrad. Akhmatova was also there to treat her chronic tuberculosis, and the two spent many hours lying on the verandah, wrapped in coats, taking temperatures, and breathing salubrious air. As Nadezhda's illness continued to progress, she was advised to change climate and take a rest cure in Yalta. When in September she left for the Crimea, Mandelstam wrote almost daily: "My beloved, you're thousands of versts away from me in a big empty room with your thermometer! My life, you must understand that you are my life! What is your temperature? Are you happy? Do you laugh?"[409]

During this turning point of their relationship Mandelstam stopped treating Nadezhda as a "prize" and became her protector and friend. They became a real couple and "from then on, our dialogue never ceased and I always knew what was in his mind."[410] To support her in the Crimea for a year, he sought hackwork and worked at a furious pace to send her money for treatment and nutritious food. Throughout that year, Mandelstam wrote eighteen reviews, published translations in ten anthologies, and produced two books for children. In February 1926, planning to visit Nadezhda in Yalta, he wrote splendid poetic letters: "Nadik, we call to one another like birds—I can't live, I can't live without you! Without you my whole life is dreary—I'm a useless stranger to myself. The day before yesterday I put your telegram under my pillow. . . ."[411] (Frail and elegant, Mandelstam resembled a small bird, many observed, particularly when he read poetry—he was almost singing it, his head thrown back.)

Upon Nadezhda's return to Leningrad in 1926, the couple settled in Tsarskoe Selo, where they lived in abject poverty. Akhmatova describes their apartment: "There was absolutely no furniture in their rooms and there were gaping holes in the rotted floors."[412] Mandelstam was overwhelmed with translations and Nadezhda handled editing jobs for a publishing house. Their hackwork paid little and gave no satisfaction: Mandelstam "translated absolute rubbish"[413] to help make ends meet. Such a life, of course, did not agree with either of them: Mandelstam was by nature an epicurean. He "loved large rooms with plenty of light, a bottle of dry wine for dinner, a well-made suit . . . and most of all, he loved well-baked rolls, something we always particularly longed for. . . ."[414] Nadezhda, spoiled by comfort in her youth, was surprised at how calmly she accepted her fate:

> We were not ascetics by nature, and neither of us practiced self-denial for its own sake; we were simply forced into it by circumstances, because the price demanded in return for an increase of one's rations was just too high. But we did not want to be poor any more than M. wanted to die in a camp.[415]

Their generation of genuine writers and poets, Mandelstam, Akhmatova, Pasternak, Marina Tsvetaeva, Andrei Bely, and Mikhail Bulgakov, succeeded to the mantle occupied by Tolstoy and Dostoevsky in the previous century. But they were outside the mainstream of Soviet literature and found themselves isolated, whereas their predecessors were worshiped like near-deities. Mandelstam was unwilling and unable to adjust his talents to the new demands set forth by the party requiring writers to glorify socialist construction. At best, his books were produced with a circulation of 2,000 copies, but even getting published was becoming increasingly difficult. Describing their circle of writers who embraced artistic integrity, Nadezhda remarked, "Everybody here is a beggar, apart from our rulers and their lackeys, and I prefer to be with the majority, rather than pick up crumbs from the master's table."[416] In contrast, writers subservient to the ruling party and the state were widely published and well paid, but their literary output survived only to the end of the Soviet era.

As ideological control tightened, Mandelstam found himself more isolated and "constantly relegated to a lower and lower category."[417] Among the best poets before the Revolution, he was now treated as a second-class writer and a second-class citizen. His intellectual themes were irrelevant to the new state and, unlike Mayakovsky, the poet of Revolution, he did not write in the brave language of the time. Mandelstam was told he must wake up and realize where and when he was living. Approximately at this time, Nadezhda tells, Mandelstam underwent a medical checkup and was sent to a psychiatrist. "His diagnosis was that M. had the illusion of being a poet and of writing verse." When Nadezhda came to explain that her husband *was* a poet, the psychiatrist advised her not to succumb to the same psychosis.[418] Under such circumstances, when his vocation appeared nonexistent to others, it was Nadezhda's understanding of his role and his talent that became the chief thing the poet himself could rely on.

In 1927, Mandelstam started a new book of prose, *Egyptian Stamp*, which became a complex literary text. And yet it was published in a literary magazine and also appeared as a separate volume, which would not have happened without the support of an influential and intelligent friend, Nikolai Bukharin. A prominent theoretician of Bolshevism and an economist, Bukharin was a member of the Party Central Committee and the editor-in-chief of *Pravda*. He often used his influence in the Party to help Mandelstam. They first had met in 1922 when Mandelstam's brother, Evgeny, was arrested and Mandelstam came to Bukharin to ask for help. He promptly arranged for Mandelstam to meet the head of the Cheka, Felix Dzerzhinsky. After Lenin's death, Bukharin became a full member of the Politburo, a position he still held in 1928, the most successful year for Mandelstam, who published a volume of poems, a collection of criticism, and a book of prose. When helping place one of his books with Gosizdat, the State Publishing House, Bukharin assured the editorial board that Mandelstam was the best of contemporary writers and "should have his own significant place in our literature."[419]

The atmosphere in the country became more frightening with the beginning of Stalin's mass trials. But while others were trying to ignore this reality, Mandelstam, who read accounts of all the trials, refused to remain silent. Once, he overheard a conversation about five elderly bank clerks, sentenced to be shot, and, without knowing these people, rushed to Bukharin to intercede on their behalf. As a final argument, he sent Bukharin a copy of his poems with an inscription that every line in the book argued against what they were planning to do. Bukharin was apparently able to influence the case and informed Mandelstam in a telegram that the sentences had been commuted.

The year also brought trouble for Mandelstam. In 1928, he was accused of plagiarism after his name appeared exclusively on a title page of a book translated by someone else and which Mandelstam had only edited. Although he immediately protested the mistake, demanding that the publisher print a correction, the press attacked him, denouncing him as a petty thief. He was subjected to interrogations and, in addition, his foes strangled him financially, withholding payments for various small jobs. Because of anti-Semitic undertones, the Mandelstams referred to this affair as their "Dreyfus Case." The campaign dragged on for over a year until Bukharin ordered the press to stop the harassment.

In summer, the couple was in Kiev, where Nadezhda underwent an appendectomy while still suffering from her tuberculosis. Mandelstam visited her daily in hospital, tending to her, like a nurse. The couple's desperation was complete when they lost their apartment in Tsarskoe Selo. They moved to Moscow, where Mandelstam's brother was living and where Mandelstam found employment editing the poetry section in the Komsomol newspaper. He was paid so little that his monthly salary went in a few days. While most Soviet employees then received meager wages, the state had other means for compensation, such as special food rations, to which the Mandelstams were not entitled. The following year, Mandelstam quit this job, after the editorial board gave him a humiliating performance review implying political untrustworthiness: "Can be used as a specialist, but under supervision."[420]

By 1930, Bukharin had been stripped of his leadership positions for proposing liberal economic policies, although remaining a nominal member of the Central Committee with a shadow of his former influence. He used his connections to dispatch the Mandelstams on a much-needed vacation to Armenia. In addition, he arranged a stipend for Mandelstam through Vyacheslav Molotov, Stalin's protégé and former secretary who rose to some of the highest government positions. The stipend was allotted to Mandelstam "for services to Russian literature and in view of the impossibility of finding employment for the writer in Soviet literature."[421] The phrasing, which likely came from Bukharin, accurately described Mandelstam's situation.

Their trip to the Caucasus gave them breathing space and restored Mandelstam's ability to write poetry. The couple first celebrated their eleventh anniversary on May 1 in the beautiful Georgian countryside, then traveled on to Armenia, where they would remain until November.

For Mandelstam, Armenia and the Caucasus represented the historical world, the birthplace of European civilization and Christianity. Mount Ararat, where Noah's Ark is believed to have landed, symbolized the Bible and old culture, rejected by the new Soviet state. The Bible connected Mandelstam with the culture of his Jewish ancestors, and so he called Armenia his "Sabbath Land."[422] Soon after arriving, he began to study the Armenian language, telling Nadezhda that he was turning in his mouth the ancient Indo-European roots. Both felt they were more than tourists. Experiencing Armenia's old culture was liberating for both: they enjoyed conversations with Armenian artists, architects, writers, and scholars. While intellectual and artistic freedom was being asphyxiated in Moscow, in Armenia it was still possible to see new and interesting exhibitions and have those genuine arguments that perennially concern artists. For decades to come, Nadezhda fondly remembered the paintings of the blue period by Armenian artist Martiros Saryan, such as *Fairy Tale: Love*, which they saw in his studio where they visited him.

They spent a month by Lake Sevan and on the Island, famed for its 9th century monastery. (The largest lake in Armenia, Sevan is situated four thousand feet above sea level, making it one of the largest high-altitude lakes in the world.) For Mandelstam, seeing the monuments was particularly meaningful because of his love of fixed forms, sculpture, and architecture, revealed in his first collection, *Stone*. Absorbed with Armenian culture, he relished its architecture, literature, and choral music; his spiritual life was so intense that Nadezhda had a hard time keeping up. In Armenia, she began to see the world through Mandelstam's eyes "and hence saw things that others did not see."[423] She had a key to all his poetic metaphors, which he discussed with her while composing, before his poems were ready to be committed to paper. She felt their vacation in Armenia gave Mandelstam a "second breath," a supply of creative energy to last until the end of his life.[424]

It was during this excursion that Mandelstam at last made her "a complete partner in his life." [425] She felt that their bond, strengthened by his poetry and their dialog, became unbreakable.[426] Their communication was so complete that it felt like "a prayer . . . said by two people together." From then on, Mandelstam's sense of "we" included Nadezhda.[427] When on their return from Armenia her brother Evgeny remarked that Nadezhda no longer existed, that she had become her husband's echo, Mandelstam replied: "That's how *we* like it."[428]

They could not dream of stability and children: being homeless, they could not have either. Mandelstam did not expect happiness in a traditional sense and taught Nadezhda not to expect it. But both adored children and enjoyed the company of the local dark-eyed Armenian children during their stay.

Three years later, the couple met starving Ukrainian children when staying in the writers' sanatorium in the Crimea. Mandelstam brought to their room a boy who had been begging for food nearby. They gave him some milk, and next day the boy returned with his siblings and their father, a young Ukrainian, who told them they fled from famine in their native village. By 1933, this part of the Crimea had become crowded with people fleeing the Ukraine and the North Caucasus, areas most afflicted by the famine during Stalin's forced collectivization. The grain seized from the peasants was sold to Western Europe to buy machinery.

The Soviet press was forbidden to report the consequences—the starvation of several million people.[429] But the Mandelstams traveled through the Ukraine and the Kuban, near the Black Sea, and saw "wraith-like peasants,"[430] swollen by starvation and dying in the train stations and by the roadsides. Although the couple did not know the scale of the disaster, they had a surprisingly clear picture of the price paid for Stalin's policies. Nadezhda writes, "I cannot believe that even Tamerlane and the Tartar invasion had an aftermath anything like that of collectivization."[431]

Mandelstam made his first critique of socialism in *Fourth Prose*, dictating it to Nadezhda in winter 1929–30. He described the kind of socialism that required sacrifice on the part of a family where a son denounces his father to help the authorities. The dictations took place at night and lasted into the morning hours. Out of precaution, Nadezhda carried the manuscript of *Fourth Prose* in her handbag, even though the authorities were then unlikely to search their apartment.

In 1931, Nadezhda received her first job in the newspaper *For a Communist Education*. Though her salary was small, the couple had a stable income and vouchers to buy books. In the morning, when Nadezhda left for work, Mandelstam called on their acquaintances. Nadezhda forbade him to visit her at the newspaper. She enjoyed her short-lived employment, a welcome change in their isolation.

That same year, Mandelstam began to write his "dangerous poems" filled with images of chain locks rattling on the doors, suggesting nightly arrests; images of executions and death around them. "Living in Petersburg is like sleeping in a coffin." His own isolation was expressed in "The Wolf" cycle of poems, which suggest his place as an outcast of Soviet literature, rejected by the tribe of his fellow writers. He wrote these poems with a sense of doom, realizing he was taking a path to self-destruction. "We are ruined," he would tell Nadezhda in the 1930s, while throwing his newly written poem into a suitcase, which served as his archive.[432] In winter 1932–33, when Mandelstam read his poems in Moscow, in the building of the *Literary Gazette*, an acquaintance told him, "You are taking yourself by the hand and leading yourself to your execution."[433]

Mandelstam recited some of these incendiary poems in his usual manner, eyes closed, singing his verse. He gave readings in Leningrad, where audiences sat breathless and mesmerized. Vladimir Admoni, a scholar of German literature and a friend of Akhmatova, remembers:

> We were shaken by the poems that Mandelstam read—those we already knew and those we heard for the first time. But we were most struck by Mandelstam's image, a combination of pride and doom, strength and fragility. . . . He behaved with such natural assurance, as if there was room within him for the tremendous power of the human spirit, the inexhaustible and deep source of poetry. And yet, in spite of this, his small figure seemed—and was—extremely vulnerable and unprotected.[434]

But the most unnerving readings took place in their new Moscow apartment, which Bukharin had helped secure in the fall of 1933. The grim-looking apartment house belonged to the Writers' Union and was inhabited by toadies of official literature—and these people filled the Mandelstams' apartment during the readings.

> I can remember nothing more terrible than the winter of 1933–34, which we spent in our new apartment—the only

one I ever had in my life.... We had no money and nothing to eat, and every evening there were hordes of visitors—half of them police spies. Death might come to M. either quickly or in the form of a slow process of attrition. M., an impatient man, hoped it would come quickly.[435]

Mandelstam "steered his life with a strong hand towards the doom,"[436] and she had to share his destiny. During sleepless nights, Nadezhda was beginning to feel she was "the older of the two." Mandelstam, immersed in work, was "becoming younger... while I turned to stone and aged from fear."[437] By then, Mandelstam's *Journey to Armenia* had been attacked in an unsigned article in *Pravda* and condemned as "prose of a lackey." Criticism in the major Party newspaper was more than a condemnation: it suggested the start of an official campaign to eliminate Mandelstam for good.

It was with a sense that his fate was sealed that in November 1933 Mandelstam composed a poem in which he made his indictment of the regime, referring to Stalin as "the Kremlin mountaineer, the murderer and peasant-slayer."[438] He read it in their apartment, exposing himself and his listeners to danger. Mandelstam's friends begged him to forget the poem, realizing that the reading was an act of suicide. "I asked," recalled Vasilisa Shklovsky, "'What are you doing?! Why? You are putting your neck into a noose.' And he: 'I can't do otherwise... I wrote it and I must recite it.'"[439]

Mandelstam wrote his satire on Stalin in an unusually straightforward, uncomplicated style, to make it widely accessible and to exclude misinterpretation. When he recited it to Pasternak during their walk in the city, the latter was terrified: "I didn't hear this, you didn't recite it to me."[440] With mass arrests beginning in 1934, people were afraid of any political conversations. Mandelstam understood what awaited him: when in February he and Nadezhda were in Leningrad, he told Akhmatova that he was "ready for death."[441] Yet he was full of creative ideas, studied Italian, and wrote about Dante, apparently perceiving parallels between the *Inferno* and contemporary events.

The couple was still in Leningrad when Mandelstam assaulted Alexei Tolstoy, one of the most influential writers and Stalin's favorite. (He was not related to Leo Tolstoy.) Mandelstam publicly slapped him in the face and called him "an executioner." Although he was settling his personal scores with this writer, Mandelstam chose accurate words to describe him. Tolstoy was a talented but unscrupulous man, eventually a recipient of three Stalin Prizes for literature. At the height of the terror, from 1936 till 1938, he was the head of the Writers' Union, clamoring for execution of innocent people.

Mandelstam's act of courage and folly took place in early May 1934, in Nadezhda's presence. She remembers that Tolstoy "had shouted at the top of his voice, in front of witnesses, that he would make sure M. was never published again, and that he would have him expelled from Moscow."[442] After Stalin's death, Akhmatova would tell Isaiah Berlin that she believed Tolstoy became "the cause of the death of the best poet of our time."[443] But Mandelstam's arrest cannot be attributed to this incident alone; more likely, it brought on the event.

Immediately after, the couple went to Moscow. Mandelstam began to phone and send frantic telegrams to Akhmatova begging her to come for what could be their last meeting. She arrived, soon to witness Mandelstam's arrest on May 13. At one o'clock in the morning, there was "a sharp, unbearably explicit knock on the door." Nadezhda, who had anticipated the arrest for months now, said simply, "They've come for Osip."[444] She opened the door to the uninvited guests: three secret police agents.

> Without a word or a moment's hesitation, but with consummate skill and speed, they came in past me (not pushing, however) and the apartment was suddenly full of people already checking our identity papers, running their hands over our hips with a precise, well-practiced movement, and feeling our pockets to make sure we had no concealed weapons.[445]

The secret police were then working thoroughly, so the search lasted six hours. (When Mandelstam was re-arrested four years later, the same procedure took only half an hour.) The police rummaged through Mandelstam's manuscripts, confiscating his poems and trampling his other papers. At seven in the morning, when they took Mandelstam away, Nadezhda and Akhmatova stayed in the ransacked apartment, guessing what the indictment would be.

Nadezhda never committed Mandelstam's most dangerous poem about Stalin to paper. But an informer was able to memorize it and report it to the police. As for other Mandelstam's works, Nadezhda had made duplicates while anticipating the arrest. She gave some copies to their friends and hid others at home. The police failed to find the papers she had sewn into her cushions or stuck inside saucepans and shoes. Mandelstam, who believed his poetry was enduring and that his audience would remember it, was then unconcerned for his archive. But Nadezhda realized that his writings could be irretrievably lost.

> On that May night I became aware of yet another task, the one for which I have lived ever since. There was nothing I could do to alter M.'s fate, but some of his manuscripts had survived and much more was preserved in my memory. Only I could save it all, and this was why I had to keep up my strength.[446]

That day, fearing that the police would return for another search, Nadezhda and Akhmatova smuggled Mandelstam's most valuable papers out of the apartment in shopping baskets. Nadezhda's next move was to see Bukharin, who still had some influence as editor of *Izvestiya*. When he asked her whether Mandelstam had written "anything rash," Nadezhda denied it and was later ashamed that she had lied and put their protector Bukharin at risk. The government already knew about Mandelstam's poem. Genrikh Yagoda, the future head of the NKVD, the secret police, who had signed the order for Mandelstam's arrest, recited the poem to Bukharin when he tried to interfere. On her next visit to Bukharin, he refused to admit her. Nadezhda would never see him again: Stalin would destroy Bukharin in a spectacular show trial in 1938, the year Mandelstam died in a camp.

Akhmatova managed to arrange a meeting in the Kremlin with Avel Enukidze, Stalin's old friend.[447] Enukidze knew that Mandelstam had written some poems against the regime. But the very fact that Akhmatova and Pasternak interceded on Mandelstam's behalf influenced Stalin, and he commuted the sentence. Initially sent to the forced-labor camp building the White Sea Canal, Mandelstam had stood no chance of survival. Stalin changed his sentence to three years in exile, a surprisingly mild punishment for offending "the most awesome person in the land."

Another act of clemency confirmed Stalin's personal involvement. Two weeks after the arrest, Nadezhda received a call from Mandelstam's interrogator summoning her to the Lubyanka, headquarters of the secret police. Allowed to meet Mandelstam in his interrogator's presence, she considered it a miracle since other families were denied all information of the arrested: "We lived on rumors and trembled."

The massive building that had housed the central insurance company before the Revolution became a dreaded place of interrogation and imprisonment. The brightest politicians, military officers, scientists, artists, and diplomats would disappear inside the Lubyanka. Mandelstam's protector, Bukharin, wrote several works in the Lubyanka prison before his own execution. Alexander Solzhenitsyn, one of Lubyanka's famous inmates, describes in the *Gulag Archipelago* how the prisoners' spirit and body were broken there.

Although Mandelstam admitted to writing poems against the regime, he was still subjected to intimidation and torture. He was deprived of sleep, refused water, and led to believe that Nadezhda had also been arrested. At night, when interrogations took place, he heard prisoners' screams. Mandelstam had a mental breakdown and slashed both of his wrists with a razor, which he had smuggled in a sole of his shoe.

Nadezhda did not know this when meeting Mandelstam in the Lubyanka, but she saw his "fear-crazed" eyes. The interrogator constantly interrupted their conversation, his language peppered with the words "crime" or "punishment." Nadezhda was reprimanded for failing to report her husband to the authorities:

> The interrogator described M.'s poem as a "counter-revolutionary document without precedent," and referred to me as an accessory after the fact. "How should a real Soviet citizen have acted in your place?" he asked. It appeared that in my place any real Soviet person would immediately have informed the police. . . .

When offered permission to follow Mandelstam into exile, Nadezhda agreed at once. Mandelstam was banished to Cherdyn, a small town in the Urals and a historical place where Russian aristocracy had been exiled since the seventeenth century. An uncle to the first Romanov Tsar was sent there by Boris Godunov, who viewed him as a potential rival. Romanov was held in an earthen pit, dying within a year.

But the Mandelstams were not afraid of exile. "Let them send us away," Mandelstam used to tell Nadezhda. "Others may be frightened, but what do we care?" When the news of their banishment spread through their apartment house, friends, mostly women, began to visit Nadezhda, bringing money for the journey. Elena Bulgakov, who lived in the same building, burst into tears and turned out her pockets when Akhmatova told her the news.

The exiles boarded the train separately. Mandelstam was already in his compartment, guarded by three armed soldiers, when the train pulled up to the platform where Nadezhda was waiting. Her brother, Evgeny, and Mandelstam's older brother, Alexander, came to see them off. Mandelstam was not allowed to open the window and say good-bye to them, he just gazed at their two brothers through the glass: "A barrier had been raised between us and the world outside."

Although Nadezhda was not formally under arrest, she was treated as a prisoner once she joined Mandelstam. At a change in Sverdlovsk, the couple was forced to sit on a wooden bench under guard from morning till night, with no permission to eat, drink, or even stir: "At our least move . . . the guards at once sprang to the alert and reached for their pistols. . . . They had put us on a seat right opposite the station entrance, so we faced the endless stream of people coming in. The first thing they saw was us, but they looked away immediately." Mandelstam whispered in Nadezhda's ear that they could be murdered in front of these passersby and no one would interfere.

> We traveled in crowded cars and on river steamers, we sat in busy stations swarming with people, but nowhere did anybody pay any attention to the outlandish spectacle of two people, a man and a woman, guarded by three armed soldiers. Nobody gave us as much as a backward glance. Were they just used to sights like this in the Urals, or were they afraid of getting infected?

Mandelstam was agitated and refused to sleep during their journey. By then, Nadezhda had learned of his suicide attempt and stayed awake too, watching over him. In early June, when they arrived in Cherdyn, she insisted on being lodged at a local hospital and on the first night there dropped her guard from fatigue. When she dozed off, Mandelstam jumped out of a second-floor window. The immediate consequences were dislocation and a fracture of his right shoulder. Because hospital staff failed to detect the fracture, Mandelstam would have limited use of his right arm ever after. But his jump also helped cure his mental condition, as he describes in a poem: "A leap—and my mind is whole."

Mandelstam developed paranoia in prison, expecting execution at a certain hour each day, so Nadezhda would advance the hands of the clock to help him overcome his bouts of terror. This worked, but Mandelstam continued to have strange fantasies: he believed

Akhmatova was dead and looked for her corpse in the ravines around Cherdyn.

With no psychiatrist in their small town, Nadezhda pleaded to transfer Mandelstam elsewhere. Bukharin, who received her telegram, wrote a long letter to Stalin describing Mandelstam's attempted suicide. He added in a postscript that Pasternak was upset with Mandelstam's arrest. Stalin inscribed on Bukharin's letter, "Who gave them the right to arrest Mandelstam?"[448] With such a remark, however hypocritical, Mandelstam's sentence was reviewed with extraordinary speed. On June 10, he was allowed to settle anywhere except in twelve major cities.

On June 13, Stalin made a phone call to Pasternak, whom he respected. He inquired about the reaction in the literary community to Mandelstam's arrest and asked what Pasternak thought of Mandelstam's poetry: "But he is a genius, he's a genius, isn't he?" Pasternak replied that this was not the point. "What is it, then?" Stalin asked. Pasternak said he would like to meet Stalin and have a talk—"about life and death." Stalin did not reply to this and hung up. Perhaps the most incredible part of this conversation was that Stalin chided Pasternak for failing to stick up for his friend. Nadezhda heard the story from Pasternak himself during her visit to Moscow. When she reported it to Mandelstam, he was pleased with how Pasternak handled it and concurred with his observation that "whether I'm a genius or not is beside the point. . . . Why is Stalin so afraid of genius? It's like a superstition with him. He thinks we might put a spell on him, like shamans."

The Mandelstams chose to settle in Voronezh, an ancient town on the Russian borderlands. They journeyed unaccompanied for the first time since the arrest: Mandelstam could not run away, since the only document he had was a travel warrant. So, the couple did not feel like exiles; moreover, they were privileged: because Mandelstam's papers were stamped by the local intelligence agency, they were entitled to purchase their railway tickets in a military booking office. Travel was restricted, and the crowd

TOP: Anna in 1871, four years into her marriage with Dostoevsky. BOTTOM: Anna with her grandsons, Fyodor's boys. She did not like her photographs, except this one, made in 1912, at age sixty-six. "I consider my life to have been one of exceptional happiness, and I would not wish to change anything in it." *Photos courtesy the Russian State Archive of Literature and Art.*

The Tolstoys in 1884, the year Sophia bore their twelfth child, Alexandra. Tolstoy has already made his material renunciations, leaving her responsible for the family's well-being. *Photo courtesy the L.N. Tolstoy State Museum.*

The Tolstoys in 1908, when the writer's 80th birthday was widely celebrated. "I cannot surrender my love of your artistic work," Sophia wrote him earlier. *Photo courtesy the L.N. Tolstoy State Museum.*

Nadezhda in the 1920s, soon after meeting Mandelstam. Both were penniless and "free as birds." *Photo courtesy the Russian State Archive of Literature and Art.*

Nadezhda in the 1960s, when Mandelstam's poetry was finally printed. "Now it is indestructible, and therefore I feel totally and absolutely free . . ." *Photo courtesy the Russian State Archive of Literature and Art.*

The Nabokovs in 1967, in Switzerland. Véra was Nabokov's ideal listener: "I start to talk—you answer, as if rounding off a line of verse." *Photo: Horst Tappe/ Getty images.*

TOP: Elena in 1928, one year before meeting Bulgakov. BOTTOM: The Bulgakovs in the late 1930s, during *The Master and Margarita*. "To me, when he is not . . . writing his own work, life loses all meaning." *Photos courtesy the Russian State Library.*

The Solzhenitsyns in 2000. Solzhenitsyn, who found a devoted collaborator in Natalya, believed himself the luckiest among Russian writers. *Photo Pavel Kasin/Kommersant.*

in the station, mostly peasants uprooted by collectivization, envied the convict and his wife.

In Voronezh, Mandelstam lucidly described his illness to a psychiatrist who had seen numerous cases of psychological trauma from imprisonment; he even took Mandelstam on a tour of his hospital. Thus reassured, Nadezhda asked to be admitted to the hospital on her own account: she caught spotted typhus on the journey and concealed her fever from Mandelstam. Aside from this incident, the couple enjoyed almost untroubled existence during the first two years of their exile. Nadezhda even remarked that their life in Voronezh "was happier than any we had ever known." Importantly for both, Mandelstam returned to writing poetry.

Despite social isolation, cramped rooms, and the usual lack of funds (they lived mostly on cabbage soup and eggs), Mandelstam worked with great productivity. Sensing that he had little time left, he hurried to write, asking Nadezhda to take down several poems in succession. "The poems poured out of him," she remarked.

In Voronezh, where they shared a single room and were constantly together, Nadezhda witnessed how poetry is made. Mandelstam worked from his voice, as he used to say. His poetry originated in the sounds buzzing in his head, which he "converted" into words. When Mandelstam was restless, Nadezhda knew he was at work: he moved around a lot when he composed. But during the freezing winters in Voronezh, there was nowhere to go and Mandelstam, pacing their small room, looked "like a caged animal." To accommodate him, Nadezhda pretended to sleep. There were other times when they sat across the table from each other, and she knew, from watching him, that he was completing a poem and was about to dictate. In the first stage of composition his lips moved soundlessly, then he began to whisper, "and at last the inner music resolves itself into units of meaning. . . ." Writing poetry was hard work, she realized when watching Mandelstam compose for long hours. At forty-three, he had a weak heart but refused to rest: "'You must understand that I shan't have time otherwise. . . .' He drove himself so hard . . . that he became even more painfully short of breath: his pulse was irregular and his lips blue. He generally had his attacks of angina on the street, and in our last year in Voronezh he could no longer go out alone." But none of this was reflected in his poetry: his unbound verse pulsated with music and joy.

Mandelstam was fond of Voronezh, the town where Peter the Great had built his Azov flotilla. He sensed the free spirit of the borderlands: outcasts and religious sectarians had settled here over the centuries to hide from the law. The Mandelstams, also outcasts, felt more at ease here than in Moscow.

After dictating his new poem, Mandelstam would count up the lines, estimating how much money he had earned. At the end of the day, just before Nadezhda would put his new poems in the suitcase, he added up all the "earnings." Unrealistic in his expectations, Mandelstam sent his poems to literary magazines and to *The Literary Gazette*, controlled by the Writers' Union. Only once did the couple receive a "stilted reply," but in their isolation even a refusal was a welcome event, an acknowledgement of their existence.

In the past, Mandelstam's attitude to getting published had been philosophical. When a young poet complained to Mandelstam that he could not get published, he was thrown out: "Did they publish André Chénier? Or Sappho? Or Jesus Christ?"[449] But in exile, he yearned for publication, since this was the only way he could communicate with the world.

The year 1935 was "prosperous" for the couple: they collaborated on several broadcasts for local radio, producing scripts on such innocuous topics as "Goethe's Youth" and "Gulliver for Children." A local newspaper assigned book reviews; in addition, Mandelstam was asked to write a feature article about a local collective farm. The couple set out together, since Mandelstam now did not go anywhere without Nadezhda, but nothing was written. He was not a feature writer and besides, could not produce a phony story about successes on a state farm after seeing the horrors of collectivization. Their "joint efforts" secured another job: with Nadezhda acting as Mandelstam's agent, he was given a position as literary adviser to a local theater. His salary covered their rent, paid for groceries and cigarettes, and gave the couple a sense of stability. In addition, Nadezhda obtained translating work while visiting Moscow: the State Publishing House gave her a novel by Guy de Maupassant.

Trying to persuade each other to smoke less, the couple invented a game. As soon as Nadezhda would pick up a cigarette, Mandelstam reminded her to put it down. She would let the cigarette rest in the ashtray for a minute and then light it. In her turn, she would pull a cigarette from Mandelstam's lips: "Osya, don't smoke!" When an acquaintance asked what the point of this exercise was, Mandelstam replied, with a smile, that smoking was bad for one's health: "Nadya will argue and rest her cigarette, and this takes time. This means she will smoke six to seven cigarettes less."[450]

The day Mandelstam had his identity papers returned was "an enormous event" for the couple. His passport had been taken away during his arrest, requiring him to renew his residence permit every month. To do this, he had to collect papers from various institutions, standing in long lines each time. Soviet bureaucracy was as bewildering, inefficient, and absurd as in Kafka's *The Trial*. In addition, Mandelstam needed a reference from the local branch of the writers' union, confirming that he was "really engaged in literary work."

Police informers would pay regular visits. Posing as the poet's admirers, they interrogated Mandelstam about his work. Eventually Mandelstam, escorted by Nadezhda, went to the headquarters of the local secret police and suggested that he mail his poems directly to them to spare everyone's time.

In 1936, when loudspeakers began to broadcast news of the show trials, the exiles were refused even basic literary hackwork, since vigilance became the order of the day. Mandelstam was promptly discharged by the theater, the local radio station was abolished as all broadcasting became centralized, and newspaper work also dried up. All doors became closed for Nadezhda as well: she was refused further translating work. They lived on the generosity of their two brothers and several friends: Akhmatova, herself just making ends meet, and Pasternak sent them money. In winter 1936, Akhmatova journeyed to Voronezh, later describing in a poem the town "encased in ice" and "the disgraced poet's room." Mandelstam read his verse to her from his new collection. Akhmatova would convey her impressions in an essay dedicated to him: it struck her "that space, breadth, and a deep breathing appeared in Mandelstam's verse precisely in Voronezh, when he was not free at all."[451] Mandelstam believed his *Voronezh Notebooks* to be his main achievement, but publication would not be attained until decades after his death. During Akhmatova's stay, Nadezhda watched two great poets, both "banished, sick, penniless and hounded" and yet possessing great spiritual power, the only thing that could not be taken away by the regime. As Mandelstam had observed, "Poetry is power."

With repression on the rise across the country, Mandelstam's mental and physical condition deteriorated. His anxiety and fear of having a heart attack made him dependent on Nadezhda. In late summer, to help him recuperate, the couple traveled to the small ancient town of Zadonsk on the Don River. Built in the seventeenth century, the town was famed for its monastery and other holy sites. Tolstoy and Dostoevsky mention it because of their interest in the elder, Tikhon of Zadonsk, canonized by the Orthodox Church. (Dostoevsky refers to St. Tikhon in *The Brothers Karamazov* and Tolstoy compares him with St. Francis of Assisi.) Although churches and cathedrals were not functioning under Stalin, the couple was drawn to the picturesque old town for its history. The place inspired Nadezhda to resume painting: her watercolors captured the golden domes of the cathedrals, the monastery, and the Don. She spread her paintings on the floor of their room, inviting a few writer friends to see her "improvised gallery."[452]

Writer Yuri Slezkin, who helped the couple rent a place in Zadonsk, was surprised with Mandelstam's overwhelming dependency on Nadezhda: she had to be near him all the time. The couple gave his illness a name, "being without You."[453] In Nadezhda's absence, Mandelstam would develop psychosomatic symptoms —attacks of dread and breathlessness. "When I'm with Nadya I breathe normally," he explained, "but when she has to leave I literally begin to suffocate."[454] He could not compose without her either, reporting to her while she was in Moscow, "I find it bitter and empty to write without you."[455]

In September, writers in Voronezh decided to excommunicate Mandelstam from Soviet literature. During their disgraceful meeting, Mandelstam was proclaimed a class enemy and a Trotskyite. Writer Olga Kretova, who held an official position in the Voronezh writers' union, elaborated on their resolution in an article in the local newspaper. (Later, she would remember that article with shame.) Mandelstam and Nadezhda didn't read it until spring 1937, shortly before the end of their exile, when they were destitute and applied everywhere for financial aid, even to the local writers' union. The response was predictable and always the same: "Refused."

During this time, the couple lived on small donations from the local printers and actors who would secretly share a few rubles with them. In the atmosphere of political paranoia, it became dangerous to be seen near the exiles: "We generally arranged to meet them in some deserted side street, where, like conspirators, we walked slowly past each other while they slipped us an envelope with their offering of money."

In early 1937 Mandelstam sent frantic letters to the successful children's writer, Korney Chukovsky, asking for money and explaining that the right to work had been taken away from him: "I have only the right to die."[456] Nadezhda looked for work and money in Moscow. When, in January 1937, she was planning to go there for over a month, Mandelstam pleaded with his mother-in-law, who stayed in their Moscow apartment, to come and be with him in Nadezhda's place. His letter was filled with medical detail to convince Vera Yakovlevna, a doctor, that her presence was essential. She set out at once to look after her son-in-law and give Nadezhda a respite.

Mandelstam wrote childish letters to Nadezhda, refusing to understand the matter-of-fact problems that kept her in Moscow and insisting she return immediately to Voronezh: "I'm counting the days and minutes until Your return."[457] Although not alone, he could not stand their separation, writing to her, "We are together eternally, and that fact is growing to such a degree and growing so formidably, that there is *nothing* to fear."[458]

But fear was a prominent feature of their day and both were afraid of the future. Crushed by dire circumstances, reduced to being a "shadow," as he called himself, Mandelstam was prepared to compromise. In winter of 1936–37, Nadezhda watched him write an "Ode to Stalin." He had an illusion that there was "only one person in the whole world" to whom he could turn for help: Stalin himself.[459] It was the only time when he did not dictate a poem to her, apparently deciding it should come from his hand. "Every morning he seated himself at the table and picked up the pencil, as a writer is supposed to. . . ." After sitting for some time, he would jump up, curse himself, and wonder why others could produce such poems and he couldn't. "This was a sign that he had not been able to stifle the real poetry inside him. . . ." When thinking of Stalin, Mandelstam would see "mounds of heads," he told her. In the end, he did compose the eulogy to the tyrant, something Akhmatova would also do to save her son, Lev Gumilev. Acquaintances later advised Nadezhda to destroy Mandelstam's "Ode," but she preserved it, thinking that "the truth would be . . . incomplete" without it.

The exile term expired in mid-May, but it was understood that the length of a sentence depended not on law, but chance: with civil rights nonexistent, the authorities could always add another term on a whim. When, on May 16, Nadezhda and Mandelstam stood in line at the local office of the secret police, they did not know what fate had in store for them. A clerk from behind a small window gave Mandelstam a paper. He gasped when he read it and asked whether he was free to leave Voronezh. The clerk simply snapped back at him to step out of the line. This was the customary way the state communicated with exiles and the families of the arrested.

Assuming they were free to go, the couple returned to Moscow two days later. It was a great moment when they first opened the door to their flat: it felt like "a real home to which we had returned." But they were not alone anymore in their two-bedroom apartment:

during their exile, the Writers' Union had given one of their rooms to a police informer with a typewriter. Nadezhda had met this man, a party writer, on her previous visits to Moscow. Soon after, without unpacking, the couple went to a downtown gallery to see French art, which Mandelstam had badly missed in exile.

Their stay in Moscow was brief: the authorities refused Mandelstam a living permit and canceled Nadezhda's registration. Soviet "law" could not be fathomed by logic: after serving his sentence, Mandelstam discovered he had fewer rights than before. While in 1934 he was barred from twelve major cities for three years, now he was banished from seventy cities for life and could not even return to Voronezh. Upon learning this, Mandelstam told Nadezhda they should act "as separate persons," a suggestion he made to her this one and only time in their marriage. She tried her luck separately, going to see a high-ranking police official. But in the eyes of the state, her subsequent fate was forever bound with Mandelstam's.

> "I have no conviction," I said indignantly. "What do you mean," the man said, and started looking through my papers. "Here we are: 'Osip Mandelstam, convicted person. . . .'" "That's a man," I interrupted, "but I am a woman—Nadezhda." He conceded this point, but then flew into a fury: "He's your husband, though, isn't he?" He got up and banged his fist on the table: "Have you ever heard of Article 58?" He shouted something else as well, but I fled in terror. . . . I knew that the State was speaking out of his mouth.

In early June, less than a month after their arrival, the couple was ordered to clear out of Moscow. They were given only twenty-four hours. The apartment was eventually granted to their "neighbor" who had written denunciations of Mandelstam. During their last night at home, Nadezhda woke up to see Mandelstam standing by an open window, about to make another leap, as in Cherdyn. Seeing her awake, he suggested committing suicide together, but Nadezhda told him it was not yet time. In the morning, they left for the village of Savelovo, beyond the one-hundred-kilometer radius from Moscow where people of their status had to reside.

Facing their reality, Mandelstam told Nadezhda, "We must change our profession—we are beggars now." No matter how poor, he had always worn his suit and a tie in the past, but was now an old tramp, "haggard, with sunken cheeks and bloodless lips." That summer, life was still good and they lived in the village "like vacationers," making occasional trips to Moscow to ask for money. As Nadezhda observed, unlike "ordinary beggars," they collected their alms wholesale. In the fall, they made an expedition to Leningrad, where Mikhail Lozinsky, the famous translator of Dante and Shakespeare, gave them enough money for three months. Akhmatova would describe her meeting with the Mandelstams that fall as a "terrible dream": it was 1937, the "apocalyptic time" when repressions peaked. Her son Lev, first arrested in 1935 (his only fault being Nikolai Gumilev's and Akhmatova's son), was still in the gulag. Every family had someone arrested or exiled: "Misfortune was at all our heels." Mandelstam was very ill and "gasped at the air with his lips," and both he and Nadezhda were still homeless.[460]

In the fall and winter they lived in the town of Kalinin, or Tver, as it was called originally, some hundred and fifty kilometers north of Moscow. Founded in the twelfth century, it was renamed after a Soviet leader. The town had witnessed the Invasion of the Golden Horde and Ivan the Terrible's mass executions. Under Stalin, it lost its major architectural monument: the Savior Cathedral was blown up in 1936.

While living in Kalinin, the couple continued to make occasional trips to Moscow in search of money or food. The purges had reached their peak, and friends were afraid to meet them: even Pasternak, on behalf of his wife, asked them not to come anymore to their country house at Peredelkino. In Moscow, there was only one house left where an outcast could go: the apartment of literary scholar Victor Shklovsky and his wife, Vasilisa. The Mandelstams spent a night with them and left with money, food, and some old clothing.

Mandelstam and Nadezhda were later remembered by other members of the writers' community as resembling the two inseparable and sad lovers from Marc Chagall's paintings. The Mandelstams looked doomed, their fate written on their faces; people who met them wondered which would be the first to go.

After begging from friends who were also poor, the Mandelstams would be depressed and unable to have a coherent conversation between themselves. Their diet consisted of tea and dried peas, which Nadezhda tried to stretch as long as possible. When, at the railway station in Kalinin, Mandelstam would ask her to hire a horse-cab, she replied they could not afford the ride to their house on the outskirts. Making his way home on foot, he would stop for breath on the bridge over the Volga. "It was particularly hard for him on the bridge where a keen wind was blowing. He said nothing, but I could sense how ill he felt...."[461] A few years later when Nadezhda settled alone in Kalinin and crossed this bridge, she had a vision of Mandelstam stumbling along beside her.

Nadezhda's survival instinct told her they must live unobtrusively and be constantly on the move. Mandelstam, however, wanted to be back in the spotlight: he believed that a poetry reading, organized by the Moscow Writers' Union, could alter his fate. Of course, nothing but trouble came from the idea.

Mandelstam met with writer Alexander Fadeev, influential in the Party and in the Writers' Union, who was moved by his poetry and promised to put in a word for him "at the very top."[462] There was another "unexpected stroke of luck,"[463] or so they thought. The acting head of the Writers' Union, Vladimir Stavsky, arranged a three-month stay for the couple in a rest home at the expense of the Literary Fund. By then, however, Stavsky had already sent a letter denouncing Mandelstam to the Commissar of Internal Affairs, Nikolai Ezhov. The Party provided employment to literary functionaries, like Stavsky, so they willingly collaborated with the security police. As Stavsky wrote in his denunciation, Mandelstam had violated the one-hundred-kilometer zone, where he had to reside, visited friends in Moscow, and continued to write poetry.

Around this time, Fadeev gave a lift to the couple in his government car. He was surprised to learn that the Mandelstams were going to Samatikha, a rest home that did not belong to the Writers' Union. In fact, the place belonged to the Party. When the car stopped, Fadeev got out to give Mandelstam an unexpectedly warm farewell embrace.

In Samatikha, where they arrived in March, they were treated as important people. The resident doctor announced that he had been instructed to create the best conditions for Mandelstam's work. However, when Mandelstam wanted to go to town and asked for transportation, he was refused. He asked Nadezhda, "You don't think we've fallen into a trap . . . ?"[464] But the relaxing environment of the sanatorium, with its regular meals and freedom from financial worries, soon caused them to drop their guard. Later, Nadezhda thought that they probably had been dispatched here because the secret police were overworked and Mandelstam had to wait his turn. The police came to pick him up on May 2, 1938, at dawn. "That night I dreamed of icons—this is always regarded as a bad omen. I started out of my sleep in tears and woke M. as well. 'What have we got to be afraid of now?' he asked. 'The worst is over.' And we went back to sleep. . . . In the morning we were wakened by somebody knocking quietly on the door."[465] There was no time for a search: the police simply emptied the couple's suitcase, where Mandelstam's papers were kept, into a sack.

Nadezhda was still sitting on the bed in a torpor when the military led Mandelstam away and put him in a truck. She and Mandelstam had met on May Day in 1919. They parted on May 2, 1938, "when he was led away, pushed from behind by two soldiers. We had no time to say anything to each other—we were interrupted when we tried to say goodbye."[466]

While the police were still in the room, Nadezhda told them that Mandelstam's archive was in their Moscow apartment. It was a clever ruse: the manuscripts were actually in Kalinin. The deception allowed her to buy time. That same day, as soon as she could leave the sanatorium, Nadezhda rushed to Kalinin to fetch the archive, just one step ahead of the police. They came to her landlady shortly after with a warrant for Nadezhda's arrest, and turned the house upside down.

After Mandelstam's incarceration, Nadezhda moved to the village of Strunino, outside Moscow, finding a job at a textile factory. Wives of convicted men were now allowed to work, since there were so many of them: "I was like a needle in a haystack . . . one of tens of millions of wives of men sent to the camps or killed in the prisons."[467] During her eight-hour night shift at the spinning shop, she walked from one machine to another, repeating Mandelstam's verse. If his manuscripts were lost, they would survive in her memory. In the daytime she traveled to Moscow to stand in line at Lubyanka Prison. A little window with a wooden shutter was now the only place where she could inquire about Mandelstam and pass a parcel for him. Akhmatova spent seventeen months in such prison lines sending parcels to her son and to her husband, Nikolai Punin, experiences she described in the poem *Requiem*.

Once, during a night shift at the factory, two young men walked into the spinning shop, switched off Nadezhda's machines, and led her to the personnel section. Other women workers, knowing that in such cases people were taken straight to the secret police, turned off their machines and followed in silence. A crowd standing outside the personnel doors made it awkward for the police to finish their business, and so Nadezhda was dismissed with a written promise to return for questioning next day. At night, some of her fellow workers stopped by the house where she lived and silently left money on the windowsill so she could flee. Her landlords drove her to the station for the early-morning train.

In late fall 1938, Nadezhda went to Leningrad to see her sister, Anna, who was dying of cancer. She also met Akhmatova, to whom she confided her fear that prisoners were tortured during interrogation. Akmatova remembers, "You could see the fear in her eyes. She said, 'I won't rest until I know that he's dead.'"[468]

In November, Mandelstam's brother Alexander received a letter from a transit camp in Vladivostok. Mandelstam said he was freezing without warm clothes and was "utterly exhausted, emaciated, and almost beyond recognition." Thinking that Nadezhda was also in a camp, he asked to write about her, and sent her this note: "Darling Nadenka, are you alive, my precious?"[469] It was his only letter. (According to a gulag survivor, permission to write home was an act of mercy, given during an anniversary of the October Revolution.[470])

On January 19, 1939, in a desperate move to save Mandelstam, Nadezhda wrote a letter to Lavrenty Beria, newly appointed commissar for Internal Affairs and head of State Security. Beria was in charge of the vast gulag. Nadezhda wrote him, with surprising boldness, that Mandelstam had been taken away at the time when he should have expected publication, not arrest. Mandelstam was a sick man and she, his caretaker, had never left his side. Because he was charged with counter-revolutionary activity, she had to be called as a witness or an accomplice, but the investigation had failed to take this into account. She asked Beria to oversee a review of the case and to determine whether Mandelstam's physical and mental condition made him fit to serve his sentence.[471]

But by the time she wrote this letter, Mandelstam was already no more: in February, a parcel she had sent him was returned with a note that the addressee was dead. She refused to believe this, requesting the Administration of Corrective Labor Camps to send her Mandelstam's death certificate. Meanwhile, thinking that Mandelstam might be released while they took her away, Nadezhda wrote him a farewell letter. She found it among other papers years later:

> Osia, my beloved, faraway sweetheart! I have no words, my darling, to write this letter that you may never read, perhaps. I am writing it into empty space.... Osia, what a joy it was living together like children—all our squabbles and arguments, the games we played, and our love. Now I do not even look at the sky. If I see a cloud, who can I show it to? Remember the way we brought provisions to make

our poor feasts in all the places where we pitched our tent like nomads? Remember the good taste of bread when we got it by a miracle and ate it together? And our last winter in Voronezh. Our happy poverty, and the poetry you wrote . . . I bless every day and every hour of our bitter life together, my companion, my blind guide in life.[472]

In June 1940, Alexander received his brother's death certificate, with instructions to forward it to Nadezhda. The paper said that Mandelstam died on December 27, 1938, of heart failure, which made it sound as though he had died of natural causes. Nadezhda would spend years trying to verify whether the date was accurate.

After his death, Nadezhda went to live with her friend Galina von Meck in Maloyaroslavets, a town southeast of Moscow. Galina, who had just returned from her imprisonment to find that her husband had been re-arrested, did not allow Nadezhda to slip into depression. She told her, referring to Nadezhda's Jewish roots, "I thought the people of your race were tougher. . . ."[473] Galina kept her on the move, sending her to run errands and purchase groceries. When in her "dazed state" Nadezhda forgot what she had to buy, Galina would send her right back to stand in line. This merciless therapy saved Nadezhda from "the inertia of silence." She was then able to think of nothing else but Mandelstam's final hours, visualizing his body thrown into a mass grave: "Sometimes I saw in my mind's eye, with all the clarity of a hallucination, a heap of bodies dressed in the gray rags of camp prisoners, and strained to make out the dying M. among them."[474] (Galina emigrated to the West at the end of the war: like many ethnic Germans in Russia, she escaped with retreating German troops. When in the 1970s Nadezhda's memoirs were published in the West, Galina was living in London; the two women exchanged letters, carried by travelers.)

When Mandelstam died, Akhmatova told her, "Now you are all that remains of Osip." Nadezhda's goal was to preserve his poetry: "When he went out of my life I would have died too but for the joy breathed by his verse."[475] In spring 1939, she joined her close friend

Elena Arens in Kalinin. Elena was the wife of a Soviet envoy who worked in embassies in Paris and New York. In 1937, her husband was abruptly recalled to Moscow, where he was arrested on false charges and shot. Elena, who had recently given birth to their younger son, was tortured in Lubyanka and forced to stand for twenty-four hours in cold water up to her ankles while her breasts were bursting with milk. It was demanded of her that she renounce her husband, but she refused, despite the torture. Miraculously, Elena was only sentenced to exile and moved to Kalinin with her two boys. There she found a job teaching French in a local school and invited Nadezhda to join her. For a while, Nadezhda stayed with Elena's family, becoming particularly attached to her younger boy, Alyosha.

Soon Nadezhda became employed in the same school, teaching English. She made extra money by painting toys for an artisans' cooperative, which allowed her to settle separately and invite her mother to Kalinin. In addition, she enrolled at the Moscow Institute of Foreign Languages, taking classes by correspondence, but her studies were disrupted by the war.

In summer 1941, during the first horrendous months of the war, the German army made a rapid advance and civilians were fleeing in panic. The two barges available in Kalinin could take them down the Volga to Gorky (Nizhny Novgorod), but getting space was extremely difficult, especially for Nadezhda, who had to evacuate her mother and Mandelstam's archive. She would not have made it without her high school students, who came to see her off. As the crowd charged across the gangplank to the barge, the boys passed Nadezhda's mother aboard and then the suitcase with Mandelstam's manuscripts.

Their party of refugees was headed to Central Asia. Nadezhda and her mother traveled in converted freight cars, then sailed on a steamer on the Amu-Darya River. Upon reaching Uzbekistan, they were detained in a refugee camp on the Muynak peninsula in the Aral Sea. Living there in devastating heat and without sanitation, Nadezhda's mother fell ill; visiting her in a local hospital, Nadezhda saw even leprosy cases.

To escape from Muynak, Nadezhda befriended the head of the port, drinking vodka with him for a whole month. One night, when a steamer stopped in the harbor, the man asked the captain to take Nadezhda and her mother. Later, they traveled in freight cars and were prevented from leaving the train at large stations, which were already crammed with refugees. The entire time, Nadezhda guarded the suitcase with Mandelstam's manuscripts: at night, she used it as a pillow. At a small station in Kazakhstan, near Dzhambul, their freight car was detached and the occupants were sent to collective farms to plant beets and clean canals. During the terrible winter in Dzhambul, Nadezhda earned her living "by carrying heavy loads like a camel, and felling trees."[476] It was no better than a labor camp, and Nadezhda had no way of escaping. To move elsewhere, one needed a living permit. She was rescued from this living hell in spring 1942: her brother, evacuated with the writers' colony to Tashkent, managed to locate Nadezhda. With Akhmatova's help, he obtained a permit for his mother and sister to live in Tashkent with him. Vera Yakovlevna died in Tashkent in September 1943, an event Nadezhda never discusses in her memoirs, where she writes little about her own family.

She collected accounts of Mandelstam's final days. In 1944, a gulag survivor, Kazarnovsky, told her he had been in a transit camp with Mandelstam. Completely emaciated, Mandelstam refused to eat his rations for fear they were poisoned. He lived on lumps of sugar obtained in exchange for clothing. Over the years, Nadezhda heard many accounts, some of them improbable. As she observed, the gulag legends depicted Mandelstam as an insane old man of seventy who had written verse before his imprisonment and was called "a Poet." A factual account of Mandelstam's final days was published only during Gorbachev's glasnost, a time Nadezhda did not live to see. This version would add only a few details. Before the New Year, prisoners were taken to a bathhouse. It had no water and they stood undressed and freezing until Mandelstam and another man fell unconscious. Mandelstam's body, along with a tag specifying his name and prison term, was thrown into a pile. From there, it was taken for burial in a shallow common grave dug in the permafrost, just as Nadezhda had visualized it: "Osip was thrown into a common burial pit. . . ."[477] He was forty-seven.

During the first years of the war, the secret police showed no interest in Mandelstam's archive, so Nadezhda made copies of his verse and prose and distributed them among acquaintances for safekeeping. (She had made so many duplicates that eventually she memorized both Mandelstam's prose and verse.) But most people were afraid to keep these papers and destroyed them. In 1944, when Nadezhda briefly shared accommodation with Akhmatova, they began to notice traces of police searches of their belongings. In May, when Akhmatova was leaving for Leningrad, Nadezhda gave her a folder with Mandelstam's most valuable papers, so as not to keep all his archive in one place.

Eduard Babaev, a teenager who was a fan of Akhmatova, was trusted to keep the precious suitcase with Mandelstam's remaining papers. He later remembered that Nadezhda would despair at the mere thought of losing that suitcase. Babaev preserved it intact. In 1959, Nadezhda made a will leaving all her possessions and the copyright to Mandelstam's work to Babaev and his family.[478]

As a widow, Nadezhda revealed a strong "masculine" temperament and an ability to adapt, which Mandelstam lacked. In 1944, she was accepted as a senior lecturer at the Department of Philology in Tashkent, while still studying for her degree. She completed her undergraduate and graduate requirements by taking external exams. Despite being overworked, she refused to take shortcuts. Her professor was impressed that she read *Das Kapital* unabridged, unlike all other students.

In August 1946, Nadezhda used her vacation to go to Moscow and Leningrad, meeting Akhmatova at the worst possible time, when persecution of intellectuals had intensified. On August 14, a Party resolution condemned the journals *Leningrad* and *Zvezda* for publishing apolitical works by Akhmatova and Mikhail Zoshchenko, a popular satirical writer. Shortly after, both were expelled from the Writers' Union. The press denounced Akhmatova's poetry as "harmful and alien to the people." Nadezhda saw Pasternak crying at the entrance to Akhmatova's apartment house in Leningrad. He told Nadezhda of his fear that Akhmatova could be annihilated next, after Osip. The Party's resolution made Akhmatova unpublishable, thus cutting off her income, so Pasternak had gone to Leningrad to give her 1,000 rubles.

Nadezhda's immediate concern was to find a new hiding place for the folder with Mandelstam's papers. Akhmatova, whose position was precarious, passed it to their mutual friend in Moscow, Emma Gershtein. That folder contained Mandelstam's "dangerous" poems of "The Wolf" cycle and his Voronezh poems. Nadezhda was staying with her brother in Moscow when Gershtein returned the folder, which she was afraid to keep. With only hours remaining before her train to Tashkent, Nadezhda had to find another reliable keeper. She knocked on the door of Sergei Bernstein, a university professor of philology who lived within walking distance of her brother's apartment, and asked whether he would hide Mandelstam's papers. He accepted the folder.

The most prominent feature in Bernstein's apartment was his enormous library: bookshelves covered the walls in every room. He kept illicit literature on these shelves, disguising samizdat volumes as Marxist literature. Bernstein and his brother Alexander Ivich-Bernstein, a children's writer, kept Mandelstam's illicit papers for eleven years, until Khrushchev's Thaw. Both risked their own and their families' safety, keeping the folder even when both were harassed and Alexander was labeled "the enemy number one in children's literature."[479]

That same summer, Nadezhda was nearly arrested. Her dean in Tashkent had asked her to bring back copies of archival documents from the Literary Institute in Moscow, and Nadezhda had to reveal her name to receive them. Learning she was Mandelstam's widow, a library assistant gave her a sealed package. It was a plant: in Tashkent, her dean opened the package and was shaken to discover that it contained copies of documents with the names of Stalin's personal foes. The incident was covered up thanks to the dean's connections to the secret police. If Nadezhda had traveled by plane, as she had intended, her package would have been opened in the airport. She managed to get only a train ticket, and although travel to Tashkent by rail was then unreasonably slow and took five days, it saved her life.

Beginning in 1947, Nadezhda spent summers with Sergei Bernstein and the Ivich-Bernstein family at their country house. During these visits, illicit manuscripts were brought out and work began on Mandelstam's future collection. (The Bernsteins had made a typewritten copy of the poems, leaving fragile originals in their hiding place.) The brothers and Nadezhda were preparing Mandelstam's works while it was still impossible to dream of seeing his poetry published. They committed to paper the poems and their variants that Nadezhda had memorized. To check her memory, the brothers would read a line, or even a word, from a random poem, and she would go on reciting it correctly. "Until 1956 I could remember everything by heart—both prose and verse. In order not to forget it, I had to repeat a little to myself every day."[480] They also recorded background information for each poem and supplemented the text with commentaries. Nadezhda's memory was a resource center where different redactions of Mandelstam's works could be found. She compared the variants and selected the final text.

It was without sentiment that Nadezhda told the Bernstein brothers that they would not live to see Mandelstam's publication and that she had to write a will. Nadezhda announced it during a working session on August 9, 1954, when the entire Bernstein family was present. She appointed Ivich-Bernstein's teenaged daughter Sophia as keeper and heiress of the only verified copy of Mandelstam's works. Sophia remembers her astonishment when Nadezhda produced the paper with her "will" and gave it to her: "She said . . . that I should accept it as her daughter would, for she never had children of her own and therefore Mandelstam's legacy would be in my hands. . . ."[481] (Nadezhda's "will" could not be notarized, of course.) Sophia had the impression that Nadezhda believed it was her duty to place Mandelstam's legacy in good hands although in her heart she never gave up hope of living to see his poetry published.

In 1957, during Khrushchev's Thaw, a committee was formed to publish Mandelstam's works, two decades after his death. Abandoning her former loyalties to the Bernsteins, Nadezhda told Sophia's father abruptly on the phone to pass the archive to the future editor of the volume, Nikolai Khardzhiev. Perhaps she believed preserving Mandelstam's poetry the responsibility of any decent person. Perhaps harsh times had taught her to abandon civilities. Whatever the case, her loyalty was to Mandelstam.

Back in 1949, Nadezhda had received a teaching appointment in Ulyanovsk, a city on the Volga some two hundred miles from her native Saratov. (Founded in the seventeenth century as Simbirsk, this city was renamed after Vladimir Ulyanov [Lenin], who was born here.) Each time Nadezhda applied for jobs, she had to fill out dreaded questionnaires. These were composed by the security bureaucracies to expose people with a politically untrustworthy background, which meant that families of those arrested would be "marked for life." Evicted from their homes and banished from major cities, they were also denied work. To survive, one had to be creative: "I have often had to fill in forms with a question about whether I or any close relative has ever been convicted for an offense. To cover up such unpleasant facts, people were always inventing new life stories for themselves. Whether children should mention that their father had died in prison or in a camp was a constant theme of a family discussion."[482] Everyone had something to hide. Solzhenitsyn concealed that his father had been an officer in the Imperial Army, writing instead that he had been a clerk.

While teaching, Nadezhda felt under constant surveillance, having to hide her actual thoughts "every day and every hour: in the classroom, in the lecture hall. . . ." With spying and denunciations still widespread, one careless word could get her ten years in a labor camp. She addressed her students only "in prescribed official jargon" instead of her normal language, sensing that they would report her to the secret police, to ensure she spent "the rest of my life felling timber."[483]

In 1953, "the ultimate purge" was being prepared on a grand scale: institutions across Russia were ordered to expel Jews and everyone else with politically suspect backgrounds. "By April all institutions were supposed to be 'cleaned up' in such a way that it would never again be necessary."[484] Stalin's final terror campaign, known as the "Doctors' Plot," had anti-Semitic undertones. Most of the Kremlin doctors, accused of deliberately mishandling the treatment of highly placed officials, were Jewish. Beginning in 1949, Jews and other "rootless cosmopolitans" lost their jobs across the country. Rumors of more people thrown into prisons filled everyone's heart with fear.

One night there was a knock on her door: Nadezhda was summoned to a late meeting. When she arrived, it was announced that the gathering was actually to discuss her "case." Her legs gave way under her: she was invited to be present at her own denunciation. The accusations were ridiculous, of course, since a semiliterate Komsomol activist was analyzing her lectures on linguistics: "In my lectures on the theory of grammar I had said that the young English gerund was ousting the old infinitive. This statement of mine was seen as a hint of some kind of struggle between fathers and sons. . . ."[485] She was expelled from her position as a senior lecturer on charges of "hostility to youth," with more severe measures to follow. As she packed her suitcase, a colleague burst into her room:

> "Stalin is dead!" she shouted now, from my doorway. I went cold all over and pulled her into the room. As long as a dictator lives he is immortal. I decided my colleague must finally have taken leave of her senses: for such words you could easily be accused of plotting to kill the Leader and be packed off to rot in a camp to the end of your days. I switched on the radio and was overcome by a joy such as I had never known before in my whole life. It was true: the Immortal One was dead. I now rejoiced as I went on packing

my wretched rags and tatters, and for the first time in many years I looked at the world with new eyes.[486]

Soon after Stalin's death, an amnesty was announced and over a million prisoners released, most of them common criminals. Political prisoners, accused on false charges, had to wait their turn in the camps. Only a small fraction of these were freed, including Kremlin doctors accused of the "plot" during Stalin's final campaign. Newspapers revealed that the "Doctors' Plot" had been fabricated. Each day brought new developments. Lavrenty Beria, head of Soviet security and secret police who controlled the gulag empire, was arrested in June and executed in December. Courts were flooded with appeals to review political cases from prisoners and families pursuing posthumous rehabilitation of relatives. Although the "collective leadership" of the country consisted of the same people responsible for the purges, the general mood was changing: "We were no longer paralyzed by fear, but there was still uncertainty how things would go in the new era."[487]

In summer 1953, Nadezhda arrived at the Ministry of Education in Moscow where teachers from across the country received their appointments. They would crowd the corridors, standing along the walls for days. Nadezhda's new appointment was in Chita, a city in the Far East, near the Mongolian and Chinese borders. At fifty-four, she had to travel to one of the remotest places in the Soviet Union, some six thousand kilometers from Moscow. Known as the birthplace of Genghis Khan, Chita was also where the Decembrists had been exiled after their ill-fated 1825 uprising against autocracy and where they worked the silver mines.

Impressed by Lake Baikal and the mountains she saw from the plane, Nadezhda wrote her Moscow friend, Vasilisa Shklovsky, that she liked Chita. She liked the place for its distinct architecture exhibiting a clash of styles and cultures: the city of exiles where people of all nationalities lived, it had a wooden mosque and the eighteenth-century Michael the Archangel Church where a few Decembrists had been married.

To help her prepare for Siberian winters, with temperatures below −40°C, her friends sent warm clothes and a Primus stove from Moscow, for such essential consumer goods were hard to get elsewhere.

Within months at her new job, Nadezhda's erudition won her respect, but it also created problems. In January 1954, she wrote a friend that she was "the smartest" in her department and likely would not be left in peace. Administration would soon begin making inquiries into her background: "It's the usual thing. . . . I am afraid I will have to leave Chita . . . although there are few places on earth I like so much."[488] Constant stress, poor diet, and incessant smoking led to an ulcer, from which Nadezhda would suffer as long as she lived. Ironically, during a medical exam she was diagnosed with arteriosclerosis, with loss of memory one of the symptoms.

In 1953, her dissertation on old Germanic languages was "blocked" in the Institute of Linguistics in Moscow. Before her defense, one of the opponents informed the committee that Nadezhda "had been married to a scoundrel."[489] She wrote a second dissertation, on the functions of the Accusative Case in Anglo-Saxon Poetic Monuments. This defense took place in 1956, during the Khrushchev era, under the tutelage of the renowned scholar Victor Zhirmunsky, Mandelstam's former classmate. Nadezhda's degree, an equivalent of a doctorate, entitled her to a higher salary and made her comparatively well-off. She could finally repay her brother's family and the families of friends who had supported her and Mandelstam in the 1930s.

Despite moving from place to place for two decades after Mandelstam's death, Nadezhda maintained friendships. Her closest friend, Elena Arens, whom she joined in Kalinin before the war, was still in exile with her two boys. At the start of the war, they were dispatched to a village in Udmurtiya, in the Upper Volga—and this is where Nadezhda would visit them. Elena's younger boy, Alyosha, associated her visits with food. They were starving in exile, and their mother's salary as a schoolteacher of French only paid for a small room in a communal apartment. The family survived on cabbage soup, eating it for breakfast, lunch, and dinner. Alyosha remembers playing chess and cards with Nadezhda (they always played for money). After losing a game, she would give him cash, with which he could buy ice-cream or pastries. "I still remember the taste.... Nadezhda Yakovlevna once brought us a huge piece of halva.... She never visited without gifts."[490] Nadezhda was affectionate with all her friends' children; Alyosha remembers her eyes—"attentive, gentle, and remarkably intelligent."[491]

During her vacation in 1955, Nadezhda met Akhmatova, then living in Moscow, and the two went for a stroll, discussing recent developments. Akhmatova had made many unsuccessful attempts to free her son. (Lev was finally freed the following year and, soon after, exonerated by the Supreme Soviet.) Nadezhda was pursuing Mandelstam's posthumous rehabilitation. Akmatova suggested meeting Alexei Surkov, the new head of Writers' Union who, unlike other functionaries, recognized Mandelstam's talent.

The two writers belonged to different worlds: Surkov's patriotic verse won him two Stalin Prizes for poetry; his songs were broadcast across the Soviet Union. But times were different: the Party was rehabilitating victims of Stalin's regime. And so Nadezhda was welcomed at the Writers' Union, the very organization that had helped destroy her husband. Surkov's first question concerned Mandelstam's legacy: "He could hardly believe his ears when I said I had preserved it all—a small part he could have understood, but *all* of it!"[492] They discussed plans for Mandelstam's rehabilitation and publishing his works. On the spur of the moment, Surkov promised to help Nadezhda obtain permission to live in Moscow. In addition, he phoned the Ministry of Education to say that the Writers' Union was handling Mandelstam's rehabilitation. This phone call had a magic effect: Nadezhda, who had unsuccessfully applied for jobs that year, was promptly received by the Minister himself. She was offered a position as acting department head of English at the university in Cheboksary, a port city on the Volga. "I set off ... with the feeling that a new era had begun, and with a promise from Surkov that he would get a room for me in Moscow in a year's time and make arrangements for the publication of Mandelstam."[493] But seven years later, only a few of Mandelstam's poems had been published in his homeland. And she would wait a decade to have the police reissue her Moscow residency permit.

Mandelstam's rehabilitation took place in August of 1956, six months after Khrushchev's secret speech to the Twentieth Party Congress denouncing Stalin's crimes. Nadezhda received a document clearing Mandelstam of the charges of "counter-revolutionary activities," brought against him in 1938. However, the court did not absolve him of the charges made in 1934 for a poem critical of Stalin. Nadezhda's appeal for a review of this earlier case was rejected. She blamed it on timing, coinciding as it did with the Hungarian uprising of 1956. But in fact, such partial rehabilitations were issued frequently in those days. Mandelstam received full rehabilitation only in October 1987, when Nadezhda could no longer bear witness.

When, in 1957, the Writers' Union approved a proposal to publish Mandelstam's works, a committee was appointed. Aside from Akhmatova, Nadezhda, and her brother, it included the influential writer Ilya Erenburg, who had been Nadezhda and Mandelstam's friend for almost forty years. For several decades Mandelstam's name had been taboo, but his resurrection was coming slowly. That year, Nadezhda read his name in a marginal literary publication in a report on the decision to publish his works. The first account of Mandelstam's life appeared in 1961 when the prominent literary magazine *Novy Mir* published a chapter from Erenburg's memoir. Three years later, a small collection of Mandelstam's poems appeared in *Moskva* literary magazine, which inspired Nadezhda's remark that Mandelstam "has at last returned to Moscow."

> Twenty years went by between the time of M.'s death and the moment when I was able to take from their hiding place all the poems I had managed to save and put them openly on the table (or, rather, the suitcase which served me as a table). During all those years I had to pretend to be

someone else, wearing, as it were, an iron mask. I could not tell a soul that I was only waiting secretly for the moment when I could again become myself and say openly what I had been waiting for, and what I had been keeping all these years.[494]

Mandelstam's collection would take many more years to produce. A volume of his poetry was scheduled to appear in 1956, in the Poet's Library, but publication was repeatedly postponed. Ten years later, the collection was still being delayed: it could not appear before or during the fortieth anniversary of the 1917 Revolution. Thinking she would not live to see Mandelstam's poetry published in their homeland, Nadezhda remarked, "I am consoled only by the words of Akhmatova, who says that M. does not need Gutenberg's invention."[495] In the late 1950s his poems had begun to circulate in samizdat, which came into being during the Thaw.

While Mandelstam was returning to Moscow, Nadezhda was still prohibited from living in the capital and had to continue her wanderings. The authorities refused to acknowledge that her apartment had been taken away, maintaining she had left Moscow of her own free will. The bureaucratic formula made her situation unsolvable. In 1958, she left her position in Cheboksary and settled in Tarusa, a town 140 kilometers south of Moscow, where, taking a break from teaching, she supported herself translating from English and French. Living close to Moscow allowed her to meet people who could press for Mandelstam's publication.

At sixty-three, still homeless, she accepted her final teaching appointment in Pskov, an ancient city near the border with Estonia. By 1962, she did not have to hide that she was Mandelstam's widow. Although her colleagues and students now appreciated her, she was too exhausted to keep working and would teach only two more years. In spring 1964, she wrote Elena Arens that she did not want to waste her final years teaching linguistics.[496] She wanted to write a memoir and to devote herself entirely to the project.

Most gulag survivors Nadezhda had met were broken physically and emotionally and afraid to record their accounts; others confused names and events. Her retentive memory made her a valuable witness who could accurately tell what it was like to live under Stalin's dictatorship. "In these later years I have managed to summon up both strength and fury; others—the majority—simply wasted away without saying anything."[497] But first, she had to rise above her fear of speaking up; she managed to overcome it in a dream:

> For twenty or even thirty years I always listened intently as cars went by, straining my ears in case they stopped outside. At the beginning of the sixties, in Pskov, I dreamt I heard a truck come rattling into the courtyard, and then M.'s voice saying: "Get up, they've come for you this time.... I am no longer here." And I answered him, still in my dream: "You are no longer here, so I do not care." After that I turned over and went into a deep sleep without dreams.... By the time I had that dream, M.'s poetry was already printed. Now it is indestructible, and therefore I feel totally and absolutely free.... How many people will understand what joy it is to breathe freely just once before you die?[498]

With Mandelstam's poems now more widely circulating in samizdat, Nadezhda was becoming a legend, since she preserved his verse. Brodsky and Solzhenitsyn were among the intellectuals who came to see her in Pskov. She read chapters from her memoir to her visitors, saying that her only wish was to finish her testimony.

Meanwhile, a respected and well-connected journalist, Frida Vigdorova, organized a group of influential writers to lobby the government for Nadezhda's living permit in Moscow. In 1964, the new Soviet leader, Leonid Brezhnev, gave his personal permission. The following year, writer Konstantin Simonov helped purchase a small cooperative apartment for her, paying one thousand rubles of his own money. Nadezhda returned the sum at the first opportunity.

Located in the outskirts, on the ground floor of a faceless building, her flat consisted of a single room and a kitchen. Her visitors thought the location undesirable, since her windows faced a noisy trolley track, but Nadezhda was delighted: she had a place of her own—for the first time since leaving her parents' house at nineteen. As she wrote in *Hope Abandoned*, "I only hope to die in my own precious little cooperative apartment."[499] The remark also reflected her fear of being arrested; even in old age, she could not completely part with the fear that plagued her entire generation.

On May 1, 1965, Mandelstam's first memorial literary evening was held at the Moscow University. This day was chosen because Nadezhda had met Mandelstam on May 1 and he was arrested in the morning of May 2. Erenburg, who had been present at their 1919 meeting, made a tribute to Nadezhda in his opening remarks: "She lived through all the difficult years with Mandelstam, went into exile with him, saved all his poems. I cannot imagine his life without her." Learning that she was present, the audience gave her a standing ovation. Nadezhda responded by quoting Mandelstam, "'I'm not accustomed yet to panegyrics. . . .' Forget that I'm here. Thank you."[500]

In the West, interest in Mandelstam had been on the rise since 1955, when his collection was published in New York in Russian. It included his pre-Revolutionary poetry and some of the later verse smuggled from the Soviet Union by travelers. Two émigré scholars, Gleb Struve and Boris Filippov, were the first to seek out and compile Mandelstam's texts abroad. At this time, they did not have accurate versions, which Nadezhda alone could provide. As soon as they established contact with her through covert means (Soviet authorities prohibited communication with foreigners), Nadezhda sent them accurate texts. At long last, Mandelstam's comprehensive edition was published in 1967, in three volumes. By this time, Nadezhda was actively helping several scholars in Europe and America to access Mandelstam's texts and background information.

Mandelstam's biographer and translator Clarence Brown describes Nadezhda as "a steel-hard woman of great intelligence, limitless courage, no illusions, permanent convictions and a wild sense of the absurdity of life."[501] They first met in 1966, at the apartment of Akhmatova's friends in Moscow. Brown had come to tape-record his conversation with Nadezhda, but the prospect frightened her so much that she shut herself in a separate room, refusing to go out. Brown's interest in Mandelstam eventually won Nadezhda's trust and they became friends. She had a permanent apprehension of strangers interested in Mandelstam, at first suspecting that they were informers. Back in the 1930s, police informers, posing as Mandelstam's fans, had questioned her about his work and demanded his manuscripts; she would expose them by asking them to recite his poetry.

Carl and Ellendea Proffer, whose publishing house, Ardis, in Ann Arbor, Michigan, was dedicated to Russian literature, met Nadezhda in 1969. Like other foreign guests, they had Nadezhda's instructions not to visit her in the daytime and not to phone from a hotel. If coming by cab, they had to get out several blocks from her house. When the Proffers asked what she was afraid of, given her age, Nadezhda replied that there were things they simply "didn't understand." This was not all paranoia, since phones were still tapped and receiving foreigners at home was still prohibited. She had lived much of her life under surveillance and in fear of arrest, hard to fathom for people from the free world.

Nadezhda's flat lacked comfort—bare light bulbs, bare wooden floors, and wobbly furniture from a thrift shop. What she treasured were her books, the icons above her bed, and paintings by Moscow artists. With a smile, she "pointed out a blackened pot on her shelves—this pot was the 'historical archive' in which many of Mandelstam's poems had been saved from confiscation."[502] Scholars and publishers from Europe and America came to see her because her memory for people and events was unmatched. As Carl Proffer writes, her memory was "one of the primary sources for anyone doing serious research not only on Mandelstam but on the whole period." She not only had met the poets Mayakovsky and Pasternak, but could provide insights into their character and creativity. In addition, she was independent-minded, unlike most people of her generation, and gave her forthright view of the past. Her intellect and boldness made a striking contrast with her perennial fear of arrest: "She seemed so extraordinary, so independent, it was hard to believe her fears."

At home she wore a housecoat pocked by cigarette burns—and met her guests in it. (But at an exhibition, she was stylishly dressed: long woolen skirt, elegant sweater, and colorful scarf.) A chain smoker, she smoked only Belomor cigarettes, a domestic brand named after the White Sea Canal built by slave labor, one of Stalin's construction sites where Mandelstam nearly ended up working. In the 1930s, a score of official writers readily praised the project, although tens of thousands perished on its construction.

Nadezhda stubbornly contradicted her image as a devoted poet's widow. One could recognize the young Bohemian artist in her when she unreservedly discussed sex, taboo in Soviet culture. Her free-spirited language was meant to shock: she would say that she studied Russian poetry in bed. She asked the Proffers to bring her an erotic magazine. At seventy, she was "a very clever woman, and a very silly little girl," as someone had described her long ago.[503] The Proffers thought she was "bright and touching, good-humored and bitter at the same time."

Deprived of society for two decades after Mandelstam's arrest, she relished the freedom of having friends over: in a normal day five or six visited. During "receptions," her flat was crowded with ten to fifteen people—scientists, artists, writers, and famous dissidents. There would be a translator of Robert Frost and poet and writer Varlam Shalamov, a survivor of the notorious Kolyma camp. Pasternak had praised his poetry, which he composed in Kolyma, the place commonly known as "the land of white death." Harsh-looking and reticent, Shalamov had spent a decade and a half in labor camps for such offences as "Trotskyist activities" and referring to the émigré writer Ivan Bunin as a "classic Russian writer." Shalamov's *Kolyma Tales*, which he then was writing, would become his best-known work. Solicitous of him, Nadezhda would make sure someone would give him a ride; but they had a serious falling out over Solzhenitsyn, whom she defended. Nadezhda, like Solzhenitsyn, was deeply religious, while Shalamov, who grew up in the family of a priest, had become an atheist in the gulag. In the 1960s, when Solzhenitsyn visited Nadezhda, he was working on his gulag cycle: he said he had three questions and only half an hour. Nadezhda would laughingly tell her friends that she answered only two because time ran out.[504]

In 1970, Nadezhda's first memoir, *Hope Against Hope*, came out in New York, producing an explosion of interest in Mandelstam. She told the story of his arrest and provided clues to his poetry and prose, which she discussed with great sensitivity. As biographer Brown wrote in the introduction, her memoir was "very much the book of her husband, to whom as man and poet she was utterly devoted."[505]

At home, her book circulated in samizdat, creating a sensation among intellectuals. Beginning in the late 1960s, Stalin's repressions again became a prohibited topic, while a new generation of dissidents wanted guarantees that there would be no return of terror. Nadezhda became their champion: they brought flowers to her doorstep and were eager to help with chores. She lived in a new district without stores nearby and practically did not go out, so her fans would also deliver groceries. Among them was Natalya Svetlova, Solzhenitsyn's future wife, who helped Nadezhda with secretarial work.

When foreign travelers brought royalties from her memoir, Nadezhda distributed the money among her needy friends. She bought a small cooperative apartment for a young woman in Leningrad who had nowhere to live and whom she barely knew. In addition, she established an unofficial fund, collecting cash for political inmates and their families. Those she helped included the prominent dissident writer, Andrei Sinyavsky, and his wife Maria Rozanova. (In 1966, during a show trial that marked the end of Khrushchev's Thaw, Sinyavsky was sentenced to seven years in prison for satirizing the Soviet regime. Allowed to emigrate in 1973, he became a professor at the Sorbonne.) There were also royalties from Mandelstam's works, which Nadezhda also used to feed and clothe many people. Everything from delicacies to fashionable clothes, unavailable elsewhere, could be found in "Beryozka" hard currency stores, which catered mostly to foreigners and Soviet elite. Nadezhda's friends would buy specialty food and gin for her "feasts."

Interested in Mandelstam's success in the world, she was delighted when foreign visitors brought his new editions. In 1971, she received his three-volume collection published in the United States. The books were delivered by an Italian woman who had smuggled them through the border in the lining of her fabulous muskrat coat. At Nadezhda's apartment, she cut the lining with scissors, producing the volumes like a magician.

Contemporary Russian literature barely interested her, if at all. She read the Bible, which also had to be smuggled through the border, and asked foreign visitors to bring additional copies for her friends. Nabokov's works, prohibited at home, were delivered from abroad; in addition, she requested English books and magazines. With no escapist literature in the Soviet Union, she enjoyed Agatha Christie. And to engage her mind she was learning Spanish, one of the languages Mandelstam had studied.

Other gifts brought by foreign visitors would go to friends, with the exception of a colorful throw, which the Nabokovs had sent after they read her memoir. The Proffers delivered this present along with Nabokov's essay about Mandelstam published in 1969 in *The New York Review of Books,* which emphasizes the poet's importance.

Her second memoir, *Hope Abandoned,* which appeared in New York in 1974, angered many at home. Her book told the story of cultural survival under Stalin; it also revealed there was a privileged caste of writers who supported the regime and were treated like Party elite. Numerous writers were offended by this exposure. Veniamin Kaverin, who was awarded the Stalin Prize for his novels for young adults, chastised Nadezhda in a letter released in samizdat, "Who gave you the right to judge artists who gifted their country and the whole world with their brilliant works?" Nadezhda was Mandelstam's shadow, he bellowed, and a shadow should know its place.[506] Joseph Brodsky, enthusiastic about her memoirs, would declare them to be "more than a testimony to her times; they are a view of history in the light of conscience and culture."[507]

By then, Nadezhda was famous, and many people regarded it a privilege to visit her. There was no need for her to go to a hospital after a heart attack in 1977, since some of the best doctors, Vita and Gdal Gelshtein, attended her at home. They came on weekends, when Father Alexander Men also visited. Before she fell ill, Nadezhda visited his parish church in Novaya Derevnya, outside Moscow.

A prominent intellectual and religious writer, Father Men was popular in Nadezhda's milieu. Born to a Moscow Jewish family and baptized as a Christian, he was instrumental in reviving the Orthodox Church and other religions in the Soviet Union. Father Men wrote books on the history of Christianity, which influenced many, including those in Nadezhda's circle. The KGB harassed him for his refusal to collaborate with the authorities, which was demanded of all priests. Father Men received anonymous death threats and, in 1990, was murdered outside his home in Sergiev Posad; his assassin was never found.

Nadezhda was getting weaker; her visitors noticed that even her famous memory had begun to fail. She had completed her tasks—Mandelstam was published, his archive was safely abroad, and her own memoirs completed. Nadezhda's remaining wish was to meet Mandelstam, beyond the grave. He also had believed in their eventual meeting, having written in 1937, "We are together eternally, and that fact is growing to such a degree and growing so formidably, that there is *nothing* to fear."[508] Nadezhda had composed a "Prayer of the Two," repeating it daily, "We pray to Thee, our Lord, to grant us, Osip and Nadezhda, asking Thee in agreement of the Meeting."[509] She talked casually how she would scold Mandelstam there for making her suffer alone all these years.

Designer Tatyana Osmerkina felt there was something maternal in Nadezhda's attitude to Mandelstam. "Whether she remembered him with laughter or with sadness, she always spoke about him as the closest person, her alter ego. She lived without him for so long, but remained conscious of his presence as if they never parted."[510] Human rights activist Vera Lashkova, who knew Nadezhda during her final fifteen years, also sensed this: "It was as though she continued to live with him. . . . He was constantly present in her life. . . ."[511] Lashkova had been arrested for dissident activities and Nadezhda wanted to know everything about her imprisonment. This helped her to imagine what it was like for Mandelstam.

At eighty, also suffering from bronchitis, Nadezhda gasped for air as Mandelstam had during his final years. She died on December 29, 1980, almost the same day as Mandelstam. Lashkova, who was with her, remembers, "And I thought: Lord, now her spirit is rising, now she is meeting Osip Emilievich."[512]

When plainclothes policemen attempted to remove Nadezhda's body before final respects were paid, the dissidents formed a live chain in the corridor, while others read Orthodox prayers in her bedroom. Before leaving Nadezhda's home, friends took some of her things as keepsakes; Lashkova appropriated the Bible, wrestling it from a KGB agent's hands. They closely followed the police vehicle when Nadezhda's body was taken to the morgue. Friends demanded she be buried in downtown Moscow near her brother, but were refused. To avoid commotion in the city center, the authorities allotted a place at Kuntsevo Cemetery, which was on the outskirts of the city.

On New Year's Day, 1981, a crowd of five hundred came to Nadezhda's funeral in the Church of the Assumption of the Virgin Mother. It could not contain everyone, and many waited outside during the requiem. In her coffin Nadezhda was covered with a piece of the throw, which Mandelstam had handled, his only belonging that survived. It came to pass, as Mandelstam wrote in a poem *Midnight in Moscow*: "We have a spiderwork of honest old plaid—drape it over me like a flag, when I die."[513] Believing the poet and his wife were inseparable in spirit, mourners were paying tribute to both. On Nadezhda's grave they erected a cross with her name and, beside it, a separate headstone for the poet, giving him a symbolic resting place.

In 1979, in a letter to Princeton University, where Mandelstam's archive had been transferred from Paris, Nadezhda wrote of her wish to create a center for studying Mandelstam: "Perhaps, many years after his death, the homeless, destitute and little published poet will finally receive a home, with his books, his papers, his archive, and his own press."[514] Princeton became a place for international scholars to study and popularize Mandelstam's legacy. During the poet's centennial in 1991, readings were held across Russia and plaques unveiled in several cities; a Mandelstam society was also formed. In 1998, the Russian State University for the Humanities in Moscow designated a separate room, called Mandelstam's Study, and several years later a cast-iron monument to the poet was erected in Vladivostok, where Mandelstam had perished. Russia has finally paid tribute to the great poet, whose legacy Nadezhda preserved.

CHAPTER FOUR

Véra Nabokov: Making a Single Shadow

After a half century together, the Nabokovs still wondered why they hadn't met earlier. They could have met in Petersburg as children: born only three years apart, they might have walked the same parks with their governesses. As a teenager, Véra belonged to the dance group in which Nabokov's classmates participated and knew boys from the private Tenishev School, his alma mater.

Despite their closeness, the couple came from strikingly different backgrounds: Nabokov was born into a family of Russian aristocracy, though with a tradition of liberalism, while Véra grew up in a family of Jewish immigrants from the Mogilev area, the Belarusian Pale of Settlement, a region of Imperial Russia along the Lithuanian and Polish borders where Jews were allotted permanent residence.

Véra's father, Evsey Lazarevich Slonim, had a law degree (he passed his bar exams with distinction); however, government restrictions to the bar for Jews stymied his career. Though not a practicing Jew, he believed changing his religion would be dishonorable and instead switched his career, becoming a successful businessman. At thirty-four, he owned a tile business and started a family, marrying twenty-eight-year-old Slava Borisovna Feigin in 1899. Of her mother Véra gives scarce information, mentioning that she came from a Jewish merchant family in Minsk. Proud of her father, Véra called him a pioneer: he taught himself forestry, became a timber exporter, and built a railway to bring timber to the bank of the Western Dvina River. Evsey Slonim's wealth before the Revolution allowed him to buy part of a town in Southern Russia. Véra was excited by his plan to modernize its infrastructure, hoping to participate in the grandiose project. In her teens she wanted to be an engineer and was interested in physics.[515]

Born on January 5, 1902, Véra was the second of three Slonim daughters growing up in Petersburg's predominantly Jewish neighborhood. Though their parents' first language was Yiddish, the daughters were taught French as their first tongue. Like noble children, Véra was brought up at home by governesses; she learned English as her second language, while Russian became her third. German was part of the curriculum at the Princess Obolensky School, an expensive private institution where she took her annual exams. A sickly child, often ill with bronchitis, a condition for which the damp Petersburg climate was responsible, Véra was believed too fragile to attend the school regularly. Her parents underestimated her vitality: she lived to be eighty-nine.

Nabokov's parents did not spare funds in educating their oldest son. Family chauffeurs drove Nabokov to Tenishev School, to the disdain of his classmates, which he took unconcernedly. Aside from the gymnasium, Nabokov received instruction from outstanding tutors: the famous painter and designer Mstislav Dobuzhinsky gave him drawing lessons at thirteen.[516] Dobuzhinsky was a great teacher—Marc Chagall was one of his students.

Véra's family made summer trips to Europe, visiting Finland and Switzerland. Once, they stopped a few miles away from the

Montreux Palace Hotel, where Véra was to live her final years with Nabokov. Her husband-to-be frequently traveled to Europe with his parents and, at eleven, while visiting Germany, had an early taste of living in exile.

Although they were growing up during a turbulent decade, it was still possible for their propertied families to lead normal lives, even through the start of the First World War. The 1917 Revolution changed everything: the Bolsheviks overthrew the Provisional Government, of which Nabokov's father was a member. (A professor of criminology and a famous liberal, he was executive secretary of the Provisional Government.) Lenin promptly established a Bolshevik dictatorship and outlawed rival political parties. The Constitutional Assembly, Russia's first Parliament, was also liquidated. Lenin proposed arresting the leadership of the Kadets, or Constitutional Democrats. As one of the Kadet leaders, Nabokov's father went into hiding and escaped with his family to the Crimea in December 1917.

Véra's family also faced gloomy prospects. The newly formed Cheka, the Bolshevik secret police, had extraordinary power to arrest, investigate, and carry out sentences; tens of thousands were executed without trial in the first years after the Revolution.[517] Véra's family, however, managed to survive and keep their fortune. Véra remembered "a long nocturnal search by a band of soldiers" coming to arrest her father, who wisely did not sleep at home.[518] After the incident, the family decided to flee. Slonim went alone to Kiev, apparently unaware that the city was becoming a battleground between the Reds and the Whites in the Civil War. In addition, during 1918–19, the Ukraine was ravaged by Jewish pogroms on a scale unseen before. The rest of the family took a train to Belarus to stay with relatives. Because the railways were practically paralyzed, their travel would take many days, and in the end they were rerouted south to Odessa.

On the train to Odessa, Véra had an encounter with the Petliura militia, Ukrainian nationalists responsible for some of the pogroms. When the Petliura men entered their car and began to terrorize a

Jew, Véra, just seventeen, came to his defense: "He has a right to be here. There's no need to throw him out or threaten him."[519] Véra claimed that her conduct inspired the respect of several Petliurovets, who even escorted the family to Odessa. Whether these men knew Véra was also Jewish is unknown; nonetheless, they delivered the message to Slonim about the family's reroute.

The Slonims managed to reunite despite the chaos of the Civil War. From Odessa, where their father found them, they headed to the Crimea, the final stronghold of the White Army. Arriving in Yalta at the end of 1919, they lived there for six months in a villa. The Crimea was another place where Véra and Nabokov could have met: he was in Livadia, a suburb of Yalta.

In March 1920, the Slonims boarded a Canadian ship to cross the Black Sea. The center of emigration was Berlin, with its low cost of living; in the early twenties it attracted half a million people from Russia. In 1921, when Véra's family arrived in Berlin, the Nabokovs had moved there from London. Their flight from the Bolsheviks a year earlier was more dramatic: their Greek vessel *Nadezhda*, which they boarded during the retaking of the Crimea, was fired at from shore. Sitting on deck with his composed father, Nabokov played chess, a game he would later share with his wife.

Unlike many emigrants who lost their fortunes in Russia, Véra's father had connections and recovered his wealth by selling his Russian assets to a German businessman who was betting against the permanence of the Bolsheviks. Slonim also acted as a broker for his acquaintances, helping them with similar "phantom sales."[520] Thanks to his resourcefulness, the three Slonim sisters completed their education in the finest schools in Europe. Lena, the eldest, obtained a degree in modern languages from the Sorbonne; Sonia went to a boarding school in France and later studied in Germany. Véra wanted to enter Berlin's Technische Hochschule but was stopped by an admission requirement to take additional courses. Her father thought it was too much of a strain for the sickly Véra, despite the fact that she was strong enough to take riding lessons.

Slonim invested his capital in an import-export business, specializing in agricultural machinery; further, in 1923 he became a partner in Orbis, a publishing house, set up to produce literary classics in translation. Nabokov's father was also a publisher in Berlin, where 150 newspapers and journals (and eighty-six publishing enterprises) were started to satisfy the demand of the cultured Russian immigrants. Véra began to work for her father's ventures, learned to type, and was entrusted with foreign correspondence. She nearly met Nabokov when he came to Orbis to negotiate with her father a fee for translating Dostoevsky's work. But soon the publishing house went out of business without producing a single book. In 1924, Slonim's enterprises were ruined by the severe inflation that devastated the German economy after the Versailles Treaty, which imposed huge war reparations.

By 1923 Nabokov had attained some recognition for his poetry, which he published under a pseudonym, Sirin. Russian Berlin was a fairly small community, and the circle of intellectuals attending Nabokov's poetry evenings even smaller. Nabokov later told his biographer that as a young man he possessed *"tremendous* charm." Véra amended this description: "And humor. Charm and humor."[521] She had begun to esteem him as a poet even before they were acquainted, attended his readings, and clipped his publications from the liberal émigré newspaper *Rul*, which Nabokov's father helped set up in 1920.

On May 8, 1923, Véra finally met Nabokov at a charity ball for Russian émigrés. She was wearing a black mask with a "wolf-like profile," as he describes it in a poem, *The Encounter*. Decades later, questioned by biographers, Véra denied meeting her husband at a ball.[522] It seems that she was guarding her past from becoming, in Akhmatova's words, "a fragrant legend." Interestingly, she does not reveal where she did meet Nabokov. Nora Joyce, on the other hand, liked to change her story of how she met her husband.[523]

Véra's companionship helped fill the void that Nabokov experienced with his father's loss. (In March 1922, Vladimir Nabokov senior was shot during an assassination attempt on the leader of his Kadet party, Paul Milyukov, whom Nabokov shielded with his body.)

Nabokov's letters reveal that a spiritual bond between him and Véra was formed in a matter of months: "You came into my life and not the way a casual visitor might . . . but as one enters a kingdom, where all the rivers have waited for your reflection, all the roads for your footfall."[524] She was his ideal listener, as he implied in a poem of the time: "I start to talk—you answer, as if rounding off a line of verse."[525] Her translation of the parable *Silence* by Edgar Allan Poe appeared in the same issue of *Rul* as his poem. In addition, Poe enthralled Nabokov over the years.

Although the couple lived in Berlin, their values and mentality remained Russian. Like Tolstoy, who gave Sophia his intimate diary before marriage, revealing his sexual past (a story told in *Anna Karenina*), Nabokov gave Véra his private journal, expecting her understanding. Véra, for whom the fictional episode, along with its connotations, had been known since childhood, "passed" his test. Nabokov also gave her his Don Juan list, drafted in imitation of Pushkin and containing twenty-eight real "victories." It was his rite of entry to the world of classical literature. His contemporary émigré poets also compiled such rosters. Vladislav Khodasevich made a Don Juan list for his wife Nina Berberova, while Bunin wanted to enumerate "lost opportunities."[526]

Véra's future role became apparent to Nabokov in 1924: he dreamed that he was playing the piano while she turned the pages. It was an incredible dream, since Nabokov was musically deaf and bored by Tchaikovsky's operas, but it augured a perfect marriage. He wrote Véra, "You and I are entirely special; such wonders as we know, no one else knows, and nobody loves the *way* we love."[527] By then, Véra was typing his short stories and, after publishing a few more translations, had ended her independent literary activity.

On April 15, 1925, after two years of courtship, the couple registered their marriage in a civil ceremony at the Berlin town hall. Theirs was a discreet wedding: Véra chose two distant acquaintances as witnesses. The same day, while they were dining at her parents' place, she casually told her mother, "By the way, we got married this morning."[528] The couple could not afford a celebration: Véra's father was bankrupt and Nabokov's widowed mother lived on a pension in Prague. Nabokov himself had only enough money to pay for the ceremony and could not even tip the doorman who congratulated the newlyweds as they were leaving the town hall.

Over the next decade they struggled with poverty, living in cheap apartments. An insomniac, Nabokov wrote at night; during the day, he taught languages, boxing, tennis, and fencing. Véra gave English lessons, collaborated with her husband in translating, and assisted with his other projects taken on for the money. She contributed, for example, to a Russian textbook for Germans and collaborated with him on a Russian-French and a Russian-German dictionary. They were resourceful, as she pointed out: "We always had the possibility of earning more money, had we wanted to put more of our time into earning it."[529] They actually dreamed of a time when their independence could be sustained through Nabokov's literary work.

Despite privation, Véra was supportive of Nabokov's writing, as were her parents. Nabokov was delighted to earn his father-in-law's acceptance when he revealed, over chess, that writing was most important to him. Understanding that writing was worth the shared sacrifice was typically Russian. In a letter to his sister Elena the year he married, Nabokov revealed he expected his beloved to merge with him into a single entity: "In love you must be Siamese twins, where one sneezes when the other sniffs tobacco."[530]

Véra watched Nabokov grow into a prose writer: in winter 1925, she typed his first novel *Mary*, along with revisions. Like Tolstoy, Nabokov was an ardent reviser, having remarked that he was prepared "to undergo Chinese torture for the discovery of a single epithet."[531] He took Véra's technical help for granted: his mother had copied everything he wrote in his youth.

Yuli Aikhenvald, a friend of Nabokov and a reputable literary scholar, was quick to certify Véra as the perfect guide on her husband's "poetic path."[532] Aikhenvald was already an expert on Russian literary wives: in 1925, he had edited and introduced a famous compilation, *The Two Wives*, with excerpts from Sophia Tolstoy's and Anna Dostoevsky's autobiographies. Whether Véra read it at the time, she undoubtedly knew about these women's contributions and was herself beginning to play an important role in Nabokov's career. Decades later, he admitted that she "presided as adviser and judge" over his early fiction. "I have read to her all my stories and novels at least once; and she has reread them all when typing them."[533] Previously, only two people had occupied such a prominent place in Nabokov's writing career—his parents. Five years into their marriage, while writing *Glory*, he read his chapters to Véra every night. During the day, she worked at a law firm, handling correspondence and stenographic assignments in English, French, and German.

In 1928, both her parents died from unrelated causes: her father from pneumonia and her mother from a heart attack. Véra, who had dutifully tended to her father while he was in the hospital, was also taking a course in German stenography. Her new skills proved invaluable: in Germany, with five million unemployed by 1930, she produced a solid second income, even with occasional jobs. With growing inflation, the majority of immigrants in Berlin became impoverished, allowing a local comedian to quip, "I'm a Russian emigrant, and so I live on air."[534]

Despite their dependence on Véra's salary, Nabokov was unhappy that she had jobs aside from being his literary helpmeet: "The typewriter does not function without Véra."[535] In 1928 she accepted a full-time position in the office of the commercial attaché at the French embassy, an envious job in the days of growing unemployment and economic instability. However, her prestigious position mattered only as a source of income and a means to finance Nabokov's forthcoming butterfly expedition. His first butterfly trip to Greece in 1919 had left him with debts, which took a decade to pay off. In 1929, Nabokov's second novel, *King, Queen, Knave*, came out; he profitably sold the German rights and settled his debts. With little thought for tomorrow, Véra quit her well-paid job at the embassy to join her husband for a butterfly hunt in the Eastern Pyrénées.

Like Tolstoy, Nabokov wanted his wife to take interest in both his writing and his hobbies. But unlike Tolstoy, he was committed to his pursuits. Nabokov began to study butterflies in early childhood (a passion he shared with his father, along with chess and boxing) and by the age of nine had mastered all the European species. Véra was assistant lepidopterist to the man who would make drawings of butterflies in his letters, discover new species in France and in America, and still dream of another butterfly hunt almost on his deathbed. On her first major expedition, she was learning about the most efficient and humane way of catching them.

In February 1929, while traveling with her in the Pyrénées, Nabokov began to write his first masterpiece, *The Defense*. He was fully immersed in it when they returned that summer to Berlin with a splendid collection of butterflies. To allow her husband to write without distractions, Véra took him out to Kolberg, renting a humble cottage by the lake. Nabokov worked ten to twelve hours a day and Véra was prepared to buy land and settle in this isolated place. The couple paid a deposit, hoping to build a summer house in the near future, but two years later, they returned the lot to the vendor after discovering they could not keep up the payments. Véra took the episode lightly: she shared Nabokov's disdain for things material. All her ambitions were invested in his writing career, for she believed he had more talent than any other writer of his generation. In August, when Nabokov completed *The Defense*, she proudly wrote her mother-in-law, "Russian literature has not seen its like."[536]

The publication of *The Defense* in the October *Contemporary Annals*, a prominent Paris-based journal, enabled the Russian émigré community to celebrate the birth of a great writer who had emerged "from the fire and ashes of revolution and exile."[537] The majority of his readers had already fled Germany to France; literary cafés and publishing houses in Berlin were closed. In the fall of 1932, during highly successful public readings in Paris, Nabokov reported to Véra that they too must consider moving. She, however, was opposed to leaving Germany, mainly because she was able to find employment in Berlin and doubted they could survive on Nabokov's literary income. When a female fan offered Nabokov rooms in her chateau in the south of France, he wrote Véra that their move was "automatically" decided. Typically, he was more preoccupied with monitoring the butterfly season in spring 1933 than with the advance of fascism in Europe, writing his wife, "Just between us, for your ears only. . . . It's important . . . for me to compare by the day the appearance of this or that butterfly in the eastern and the western Pyrénées."[538] He knew Véra would understand.

When in 1933 Hitler seized power and assaults on Jews, Communists, and intellectuals spilled onto the streets of Berlin, it was no longer possible to remain blind: the threat of ethnic cleansing had become real. Véra carried a handgun in her purse, which nearly got her in trouble when restrictions on personal firearms were introduced: she was on her way to the French Embassy to dispatch the pistol to Paris when her taxi was stopped by a Nazi procession.[539]

In March, Véra lost her secretarial position at the Jewish law firm Weil, Ganz and Dieckmann and feared that she was no longer employable. Blond, with flawless German, she, however, continued to find jobs. She was unexpectedly offered a position as a stenographer during the International Congress of Wool Producers. When she told her German employer that she was Jewish, he surprised her with, "Oh, but it does not make any difference to us. We pay no attention to such things." Véra would laugh as she related the episode.[540] Before her interview in May, she witnessed a book-burning accompanied by slogans, "German students march against the un-German spirit."

On May 10, 1934, Véra gave birth to their only son Dmitry in a private Berlin clinic. She continued to make money almost until her delivery; her pregnancy was kept secret from most friends and even from her mother-in-law. Nabokov visited her and Dmitry in the maternity clinic near the Bayerischer Platz, where they remained for two weeks, and each time he had to walk past the portraits of Hindenburg and Hitler adorned with spring flowers.[541]

Upon Vera's return from the hospital, Nabokov began a new novel, *Invitation to a Beheading*. He wrote it in "one fortnight of wonderful excitement and sustained inspiration."[542] The novel was prompted by the onset of dictatorships in Hitler's Germany and in Stalin's Russia. From their third-floor apartment, the couple could hear Hitler's harangues resounding through loudspeakers: "We heard his voice."[543] True to his conviction that artistry came first, Nabokov had made little application of political content in the past. But this novel, which would become one of his best in the Russian language, was an allegory on a dictatorial state destroying an intellectual. Revising the novel, unlike writing the first draft, took months. Nabokov dictated his revisions to Véra, who resumed her responsibility as his typist and secretary one month after returning from the hospital; the couple was still working on the manuscript in December. That year brought a major development in Nabokov's career: his London agent sold the rights to *Camera Obscura* and *Despair* to the British publisher Hutchinson.

Nabokov's virtuoso style created serious difficulty for his translators. The German and French versions of *The Defense* did not satisfy the couple, while the English translation of *Camera Obscura* frustrated them. Nabokov translated his latest novel *Despair* into English himself, although unsure of his skills. In 1935, in search of a translator who could help with the final draft, Véra phoned the British embassy, asking whether they knew of "an experienced man of letters with a fine style." The embassy employee quizzed her: "Would you like H. G. Wells?" Véra dismissed the irony, replying, "I might."[544] Actually, such an arrangement would have perfectly suited Nabokov, who had met Wells during his visit to Russia and admired his works at age fourteen.

Nabokov worked with great productivity, completing seven novels, short fiction, and a play in less than a decade. During these years, along with financial support, Véra assisted him in every way possible. While she stayed at home with the baby, their debts accumulated. But in 1936, she managed to find a position at the engineering firm Ruths-Speicher, where she handled foreign correspondence. Inevitably she soon lost her job, along with other Jewish employees. The risks Véra was facing as a Jew sped up Nabokov's search for teaching positions and contacts outside Germany. In his letters to European friends, he described his situation as desperate and was ready to grasp at a slightest prospect of work.

That year, Sergei Taboritsky, the man who had assassinated Nabokov's father, was appointed as second in command in Hitler's department for émigré affairs. Véra insisted that Nabokov leave Berlin immediately, and early in 1937 he left on a reading tour of Europe. While visiting Belgium, France, and England he looked for an academic job, which would help secure his family's move.

But in Paris, Nabokov had an affair with the beautiful and divorced Irina Guadanini, a fan of his. Guilt-ridden and worried about his family in Berlin, he developed a bad case of psoriasis. In anxious letters to Véra, he asked her to speed up her departure from Berlin. On April 15, he reminded her that it was their twelfth anniversary. "*My love, my love,* how long it's been since you've stood before me, and God. . . . And somehow one visualizes the Siamese twins being separated."[545] Véra procrastinated as though unaware of the danger she and Dmitry faced in Nazi Germany.

During the couple's longest separation, lasting four months, they painstakingly discussed the time and place of their reunion. Véra wanted to meet in Prague on May 8, the day of their first encounter, and applied for a Czech visa. She had promised to visit her mother-in-law with the grandson. Nabokov, reluctant to leave Irina, was hoping for a reunion in France. The exchange continued until Véra prevailed; Nabokov went to Prague, unaware that he was to meet his mother for the last time.

Véra and Dmitry, three, crossed the German border on May 6, 1937, the year the segregation of Germany's Jews began. However, the Nabokovs were more occupied with private matters than with world events: a cooling off of their relationship made them miserable. In July, the couple moved to Cannes, where Nabokov confessed his love affair. Véra already knew about it from an anonymous letter; she coldly encouraged her husband "to join the lady if he was in love."[546] Nabokov replied, "Not now." He later acknowledged that his uneasy conversation with Véra made him feel as depressed as the evening his father died. In summer, the couple resumed their intimacy, and Véra began to translate *Invitation to a Beheading* into English. When Irina turned up in Cannes in September, Nabokov asked her to leave. As he had written to Véra that year, "My dear love, all the Irinas in the world are powerless." Years later, when preparing his letters for publication, Véra added her editorial comment: "Various ladies by that name who flirted with or had designs on VN."[547]

During their three years in France, the couple survived on occasional royalties from the émigré press.[548] They could not get jobs without the required permanent passports. But while the Nabokovs were hard up, they escaped the fate of the majority of Russian émigrés in France, who were starving. In Paris, where the couple moved in the fall 1938, they were still quite impoverished. According to émigré writer Nina Berberova, their apartment was bare, with the exception of Dmitry's room, which displayed an abundance of toys and a silver-painted Mercedes pedal car, which someone had given him for his second birthday.

> On the floor lay toys, and a child of exceptional beauty and refinement crawled among them. Nabokov took a huge boxing glove and gave it to the boy, telling him to show me his art, and Mitya[549], having put on the glove, began with all his child's strength to beat Nabokov about the face. I saw this was painful to Nabokov but he smiled and endured it. With a feeling of relief I left the room when this was over.[550]

In their small apartment, Dmitry occupied the biggest room: there he drove his Mercedes and slept, while Nabokov would write in the bathroom, placing a suitcase across the bidet. There was no money for a decent flat. Nabokov appealed to the Russian Literary Fund in the United States for financial help, describing his situation as desperate. The Fund could only send $20, but Nabokov's other pleas reached Sergei Rachmaninov in America. Although the two of them never met, the composer admired Nabokov's prose and cabled him twenty-five hundred francs. In addition, Rachmaninov gave Nabokov a box of his old clothing and a suit, which the writer would wear at Stanford in 1941. The money allowed the couple to rent a larger place, where, in December 1938, Nabokov began his first novel in English, *The Real Life of Sebastian Knight*.

Nabokov decided to switch to English for practical reasons: he was trying to reach out to a wider audience. This inspired Véra's remark that while Nabokov's relationship with English had started as a marriage of convenience, it grew into "a tender love affair." For the benefit of future biographers, she added that her remark did *not* apply to their marriage.[551]

His first writing attempt in English had been a biographical sketch in 1935. The *New York Times Book Review* noticed the piece and praised it generously: "Our age has been enriched by the appearance of a great writer."[552] The sketch was later reworked into his recollections *Speak, Memory*, where Nabokov employs Véra's description of their son's early childhood, written at his request. He weaved her account into his story and wrote it from their joint perspective:

> We shall never forget, you and I, we shall forever defend, on this or some other battleground, the bridges on which we spent hours waiting with our little son (aged anything from two to six) for a train to pass below. . . . On cold days he wore a lambskin coat, with a similar cap, both a brownish color mottled with rime-like gray, and these, and mittens, and the fervency of his faith kept him glowing, and kept *you* warm too, since all you had to do to prevent your delicate fingers from freezing was to hold one of his hands alternately in your right and left, switching every minute or so, and marveling at the incredible amount of heat generated by a big baby's body.[553]

With the onset of the Second World War in the fall of 1939, the couple began to plan yet another flight. Fortune smiled on them when the émigré writer Mark Aldanov gave up an offer to teach a summer course in Russian literature at Stanford; he passed it to Nabokov, who seized the opportunity and wrote to accept. Alexandra Tolstoy, the writer's youngest daughter and head of the Foundation in her father's name (it aided Russian refugees in America), helped Nabokov secure entry visas for his family. Ivan Bunin, the first Russian writer awarded the Nobel Prize in 1933, recommended Nabokov in a letter to universities, praising him as a writer of "exceptional talent" and "a profound student of Russian language and literature."[554]

Meanwhile, Véra queried French officials about their exit permits and, to speed the process, resorted to a bribe. Having placed 200 francs in front of an official, she spent two months fearing that they would arrest her for bribery before Nabokov received the passports. But as Nabokov remarks in *Speak, Memory*, the bribe was administered "to the right rat at the right office." He remained detached from world politics and newspaper headlines, writing his lectures on Russian literature and solving chess problems at night, while separated from blacked-out Paris by opaque curtains: "Everything around was very quiet; faintly dimpled. . . . Sleeping in the next room were you and our child. . . ."[555]

In addition, the Nabokovs were aided by the New York-based Jewish rescue organization, which sold them tickets to cross the Atlantic at half price and helped raise the remaining half. The organization was managed by a friend of Nabokov's father who remembered his efforts fighting official anti-Semitism in Russia. In May 1940, when antiaircraft guns could already be heard outside Paris, the family boarded *Champlain*, the last boat to leave France before the occupation. Theirs was a comfortable escape in a first-class cabin. Nabokov took a valuable part of his butterfly collection and entrusted the balance along with his archive to a friend, the writer Ilya Fondaminsky, who was determined to stay in Paris. Arrested as a Jew (even though he had adopted

Christianity), Fondaminsky would perish in Auschwitz in 1942. Nabokov's brother Sergei, a homosexual, would also die in a concentration camp.

On May 28, their boat arrived in New York, and Nabokov cheerfully informed an acquaintance, "A miracle has occurred: My wife, my son and I have managed to repeat Columbus's feat."[556] Their first cab ride in Manhattan became one of those humorous stories Véra liked to tell. She misread the meter and gave a driver one hundred dollars, instead of ninety cents. The honest New Yorker said he wouldn't be driving cabs if he had that amount of change. Eight years later, fully assimilated to America, Véra drove her husband across the continent in their Oldsmobile and could even change a tire on the roadside.

The Nabokovs were remarkably adaptable: in a few months, they felt that America had become their home and praised their new country. In the summer, they were invited to stay in Vermont at the country house of Mikhail Karpovich, a friend and a Russian history professor at Harvard. The place, surrounded by birch trees, reminded them of Russia (the Solzhenitsyns later bought an estate in Vermont for the same reason). The serenity of the New England countryside soon helped erase the painful memories of Europe. Hunting butterflies with her husband, Véra sounded enthusiastic: "I've had wonderful luck. I've gotten many things he didn't get. . . . Once I saw a butterfly that he wanted very much, and he wouldn't believe me that I had seen it."[557] America realized Nabokov's dreams as a writer and as a scientist, who relished an opportunity to study butterflies on a new continent: that fall, he began lepidoptera research at the American Museum of Natural History.

In 1941, Nabokov received an appointment as a lecturer in comparative literature at Wellesley College for women, where he would be the first to teach Russian language and literature. In the spring, they traveled across America with former student Dorothy Leuthold, making stops along the highway to pursue butterflies. At the Grand Canyon National Park, Nabokov discovered an unidentified brown-colored specimen, which he called *Neonympha dorothea*, after the student; Véra caught two more on the roadside with just her hands.

While Nabokov divided his time between entomology, writing, and teaching, Véra assisted him in all these pursuits. To a university colleague who asked how he had time to write, Nabokov replied, "In the morning I peer at the genitalia of butterflies; in the afternoon, I teach Russian grammar to students at Wellesley; in the evening I get into bed with a mug of hot milk and write."[558] This intense schedule could be maintained because Véra occasionally substituted for him at lectern and microscope. Nabokov spent so much time at his microscope that Véra had to waken him, "not from sleeping but from butterflies."[559] In 1942, when he went on a lecture tour to South Carolina, Georgia, and Tennessee, she replaced him at the Museum of Comparative Zoology at Cambridge, where he had been appointed a Research Fellow. He would write her to ask how many trays of butterflies she had filled, and Véra reported her progress.

Véra's influence increased progressively with her involvement in her husband's work. She could tell Nabokov what he should write and publish next and, apparently, this delighted him. In January 1944 Nabokov wrote Edmund Wilson how she had persuaded him to complete his novel *Bend Sinister* and that he had "sulkily pulled it out" from underneath his lepidoptera papers to discover it was worth doing.[560] "My wife, of course, is a wonderful adviser. She's my first and best reader," he told a reporter several years later, upon this novel's publication.[561]

Edmund Wilson was at once impressed and surprised by the amount of work Véra did for her husband. In 1946, he wrote Elena Thornton, his future wife, who would also become the central figure in his life, "Véra is wonderful with Volodya: she writes all his lectures, types his manuscripts, and handles all his publishing arrangements. She also echoes all his opinions—something which would end by making me rather uncomfortable but which seems to suit Nabokov perfectly."[562] Around this time, Nabokov had a poetry reading, attended by his students. Véra was in the front row, and

Nabokov had brief discussions with her during the reading. One of his students found it fascinating that Nabokov consulted his muse as to which of his love poems he should read next.

When in 1948, at the end of his term at Wellesley, Nabokov fell ill with bronchitis, Véra took over his elementary and intermediate language classes. Students found that she had more discipline as an instructor and was a better teacher. Some colleagues shared this view: when Nabokov's application was being considered by another university, one of them told his potential employer, "Don't bother hiring him; *she* does all the work."[563]

At Wellesley, Nabokov was passed over for promotion because of his anti-Communist views and opposition to teaching Soviet literature. Interest in it had increased when America became a Soviet ally in the Second World War. The Nabokovs despised liberals who sympathized with Soviet Russia; they supported McCarthy even after his downfall.

That same year, Nabokov received a long-sought appointment as professor of Russian at Cornell, where his literature classes would become legendary. Véra helped develop a new Russian literature course meant to accommodate more students, and she even wrote some lectures, employing his style. She would, however, downplay her involvement, telling a biographer that Nabokov revised her text until not a word of the original remained. During his lectures, he liked to grade famous writers' works: he gave Dostoevsky a C minus. Véra would launch her attacks on writers during faculty parties: she condemned Jane Austen and told a specialist in Goethe that *Faust* was "one of the shallowest plays ever written."[564] Since Nabokov also liked to provoke people, he would find nothing wrong with what she had to say.

A narcissist, Nabokov divided literature into books he wished he had written and books he had written. His students heard him say he surpassed Joseph Conrad, for whom English was a second tongue. Véra's endorsement nurtured his ego; so when a student praised his lectures in European literature, Nabokov, with childlike vanity, asked him to repeat his remark to his wife.

THE WIVES

Both cared little for people outside their marriage, which inspired a student's reflection: "Inseparable, self-sufficient, they form a multitude of two."[565] As Nabokov's chauffeur, Véra drove him to campus; there she prompted him when they met faculty and staff. Like Dostoevsky, whom he disliked, Nabokov had trouble remembering faces and names and needed his wife to remind him who was who. The couple would enter the lecture hall together: Véra carried Nabokov's briefcase, opened the door for him, put his notes on the lectern, and occasionally rushed to fetch his glasses from the car. Nabokov introduced her to the students as his assistant. She would sit in the front row or near the lectern, and Nabokov seemed to address her alone. Occasionally, she would prompt Nabokov or signal him to stop laughing at some passages in Gogol because nobody could understand what he was saying. She found quotations for him and spelled difficult words on the board since he was allergic to chalk dust. Grading exams was also her responsibility, and she made comments for both of them. When a former student sent a letter remembering Véra's assistantship, she readily signed her reply, "Mrs. Nabokov, still V.N.'s 'assistant.'"[566]

In Ithaca, they led a nomadic existence, occupying vacated homes during owners' sabbaticals. Having to pay for Dmitry's private schools, the couple could not afford other arrangements. Nabokov's salary as a lecturer was then between $5,000 and $6,000. Having to move once or twice a year, with Véra doing all the driving, packing, and housekeeping, they kept possessions to a minimum. Nabokov did not own even a desk, writing in the car, in the bathroom, in bed, or at someone else's desk in the houses they occupied.

In 1950, when Nabokov was hospitalized with neuralgia, Véra took his place at the lectern, reading his notes. Always eager to praise his wife, Nabokov remarked she was "doing an amazing job" at university.[567] In her turn, Véra admired his performance, telling a friend that he was reading *"grandiose* lectures, in an enormous auditorium."[568] Nabokov carefully staged his presentations. In 1952, during a popular class in European literature taught in a planetarium to some four hundred students, he played with a switch, sending beams of light to constellations while announcing, "In the firmament of Russian literature ... this is Pushkin. ... This is Gogol! This is Chekhov!" Then raising a window blind, he would let sunlight flood the room: "And that is Tolstoy!"[569] Describing her husband's lectures to an acquaintance, Véra wrote with exaggeration that five hundred and forty registered students "intently listen and applaud" after each lecture.[570] While Nabokov's lectures were inspiring, his teaching methods did not appeal to everyone. He could give a bad grade to a student for challenging his view on Dostoevsky. A student walked out of his class when he called Freud a "Viennese quack."[571]

Véra described Nabokov as the greatest living writer long before *Lolita* was published. Writing Nabokov's letters, both business and private, she promoted him—in the third person—though the words were often his. When her correspondents protested that she exceeded her authority, Nabokov would stand up for her: "My wife does not make herself the 'echo' of anything; she merely is kind enough to jot down my queries and apprehensions."[572] Some correspondents were further annoyed when she replied on Nabokov's behalf. Professor William Lamont asked Nabokov to supplement his list of under-appreciated masterpieces of European literature, but it was Véra who responded. She suggested Lamont add Nabokov's novel *The Defense* to his list, describing it as "one of the best novels ever written in Russian." Lamont promised to include her "talented boy friend's novel" on his list, an ironic remark that provoked Véra's infuriated response. She retorted that she recommended Nabokov's novel as a connoisseur of Russian literature, not as his loyal and devoted *wife*.[573]

Nabokov began writing *Lolita* in 1950, although the idea was conceived earlier while he was still working at Wellesley College for Women. It was a daring story about a middle-aged man obsessed with a twelve-year-old girl whom he sexually exploits. The topic was taboo and Nabokov even attempted to burn his drafts, but Véra stopped him in front of an incinerator. She saved *Lolita* and later insisted on its publication. Both realized that

Nabokov could lose his professorship if the novel was interpreted as pornography: promoting it in America was illegal. But the couple could also remember how Tolstoy's unpublishable novella, *The Kreutzer Sonata*, succeeded beyond expectations.

Tolstoy's contentious novella, the story of a man who kills his wife, was the first fictional work in Russia exploring a crime of passion. It generated unprecedented interest, becoming the most read and discussed fictional work in late nineteenth-century Russia. Tolstoy increased its emotional intensity by making his provocative work the first-person account of a criminal. The government ban only helped promote it: the novella circulated in numerous underground copies, creating a sensation.

Lolita, also a passionate and psychologically correct account of a criminal, explores his sexual obsession with a prepubescent girl. Nabokov studied newspaper reports on sex crimes, read monographs on girls' sexual maturation, and traveled on buses to hear schoolgirl talk. His knowledge of the subject would deceive even his sophisticated readers. They would think that Nabokov and his notorious hero, Humbert, were the same man. Nadezhda Mandelstam told Carl Proffer that Nabokov could not have written *Lolita* unless he had the "same disgraceful feelings for little girls."[574] Christopher Hitchens felt that Nabokov had invested his personal fascination with the topic and that he "had thought about it a lot."[575]

While Nabokov's passion in this work was real, it could have had a different source of inspiration. In 1951, making progress with the novel, he was also pursuing and studying new species of butterflies and moths. That summer, Véra drove him through butterfly-hunting grounds in Colorado, Wyoming, and Montana. Describing their expedition to his sister Elena, Nabokov told her how Véra navigated their Oldsmobile through poor mountain roads in Colorado in pursuit of a rare species of butterfly. He had found this nameless butterfly among museum samples, but "unbearably wanted to see it live and discover it." They rented a lodge and he hiked with his net every morning to Telluride Mountain where, at 4,000 meters, plant food for this butterfly was found, "on an almost vertical slope . . . in the snow-smelling silence." After days of hunting among rocks and lavender, he caught the first female *Lycaeides sublivens*, "this extremely rare goddaughter of mine."[576] He would describe his triumph in a poem, "A Discovery": "I found it and I named it, being versed in taxonomic Latin; thus became godfather to an insect and its first describer—and I want no other fame."[577] Nabokov's butterfly passion seems related to Humbert's desire to possess Lolita, a nymphet with a sensual Spanish name.

Their drive through the Rockies supplied scenery and inspiration and helped with the plot: the couple lived in the motels where Humbert keeps Lolita prisoner. In the passenger seat, Nabokov recorded Véra's imaginative phrases on index cards: "My Oldsmobile gulps down the miles like a magician swallowing fire."[578]

Nabokov once said he would be remembered for *Lolita* and his translation of Pushkin's *Eugene Onegin*, projects to which Véra contributed. Translating the poem was her idea: she told Nabokov that if the existing English versions did not satisfy him, he should try making his own. The project would become their most consuming joint undertaking, but Pushkin's poetry proved untranslatable and the result also dissatisfied Nabokov, as he admits in his famous humorous lines "On Translating *Eugene Onegin*": "What is translation? On a platter a poet's pale and glaring head, a parrot's screech, a monkey's chatter, and profanation of the dead."[579]

In 1951, Dmitry began his undergraduate studies at Harvard. Coincidentally, that year Nabokov was invited to teach at Harvard the following spring. He and Véra could not pass up an opportunity to live close to their son. Now, they would move twice a year: in the fall, Nabokov taught at Cornell, and in the spring they left Ithaca for Cambridge.

Nabokov was now working on two writing projects simultaneously, and Véra had to switch from taking dictation on the novel to researching the history of nineteenth-century firearms for *Eugene Onegin*. Nabokov literally worked day and night: his insomniac mind refused to slow down. While he thus "tortured" himself, Véra looked forward to the end of the book. "Although I do know that having finished one thing he immediately grasps for the next."[580]

In February 1953, in Cambridge, the couple worked on commentaries to *Eugene Onegin*, which would far exceed the poem's length. Toiling with the zeal of a student, Véra filled hundreds of index cards with her research notes. Later that spring, when Nabokov's obsession with butterflies "turned into a true mania,"[581] at his expression, she drove him to Arizona. Summer was spent in Oregon, where Nabokov hunted butterflies and wrote *Lolita*; in addition, he began a new novel, *Pnin*.

In the fall, as Nabokov worked feverishly to complete *Lolita*, Véra, on top of taking his dictation, graded hundreds of students' papers. Recognizing her separate contribution, Cornell paid her for 130 hours of assistantship. On December 6, after four years of research and writing, Nabokov completed *Lolita*, and the couple began to worry about its publication.

Both believed *Lolita* his greatest artistic achievement, but the subject matter required them to keep it secret. Afraid to put it in the mail, Véra took the manuscript to Nabokov's editor at *The New Yorker*, Katherine White, for her opinion, but months later the editor was still silent. In summer 1954, Nabokov asked his friend Edmund Wilson to read *Lolita*, describing it as "my best thing in English, and though the theme and situation are decidedly sensuous, its art is pure and its fun riotous."[582] Nabokov urged Wilson to keep everything he told him about the novel confidential. The couple was hoping Wilson would help advocate it, but the novel mortified him; he wrote Nabokov that "the characters and the situations are repulsive."[583] Nabokov tried to convince Wilson that *Lolita* was "a highly moral affair,"[584] the notion Véra would later use to promote the work.

By then, the couple had received refusals from major American publishers: Simon & Schuster rejected it as "sheer pornography." At Doubleday, an internal reviewer called the author "a remarkably perverse man."[585] Two years later, these same publishers would compete to produce the American edition. After three decades,

Lolita would be a reading assignment for American schoolgirls and in the 1990s would be read by young women in Tehran.

But in summer 1954, the couple feared prosecution unless a publisher was quickly found. Having exhausted opportunities in America, they decided to pursue European publication. In August, from New Mexico, where Nabokov hunted new butterfly territories, Véra contacted his literary agent in Paris, Doussia Ergaz. "My husband has written a novel of extreme originality, which—because of straitlaced morality—could not be published here."[586] Nabokov was predicting that instead of a serious publisher, his novel would be purchased "by some shady firm," which indeed happened.[587]

In June 1955, Maurice Girodias of the Olympia Press was the first to send Nabokov a contract; his publishing list included pornography. Nabokov's agent would claim she did not realize this, although not only Girodias but his father, Jack Kahane, had published pornography. Nabokov made a costly blunder by accepting instantly and without making sure that the copyright was in his name. The couple paid for it with legal troubles when Girodias demanded fifty percent of royalties for American publication. Véra fittingly would nickname their publisher Girodias the Gangster.

Girodias immediately launched *Lolita*, producing it in September. Nabokov had wanted to publish it anonymously, but was told that the author's name would be uncovered. He advised Girodias that *Lolita* was "a serious book with a serious purpose" and success through scandal would devastate him.[588] However, the man who published pornography welcomed scandal; what he did not anticipate was *Lolita's* astonishing success.

At Christmas, Graham Greene named *Lolita* one of the three best books of the year in London's *Sunday Times*. Simultaneously, the editor-in-chief of *The Sunday Express*, John Gordon, attacked the novel as "sheer unrestrained pornography."[589] Diverse opinions put the book at the center of attention, and a serious publisher, Gallimard, wanted to produce a French edition. More controversy was created when copies of *Lolita*, smuggled across the Channel, were seized in London. But this only encouraged German and Scandinavian publishers to buy rights. In December, Lolita was banned in France, but when Girodias sued the French government the ban was lifted; the case became known as "l'affaire Lolita."[590]

Success through scandal did not devastate Nabokov: to the contrary, it made him a celebrity. Véra was now handling a flurry of letters from American publishers who wanted to produce the novel. Girodia's unrealistic demands discouraged many, however, until Putnam managed to overcome legal obstacles and took it on. In August 1958, Lolita was published in America, and at once began to climb the bestseller list. Within three weeks, a hundred thousand copies were sold, making it the most successful novel since Gone With the Wind. In September, Harris-Kubrick Pictures purchased the Lolita rights for $150,000, a sale negotiated with Véra on the phone while Nabokov, who refused to take the call, stood nearby. As Lolita became a number-one bestseller, Véra observed in her diary that Nabokov was "serenely indifferent" to his fame, occupied with regular work: he had just finished a new story and was spreading two thousand butterflies. When the Times Literary Supplement praised Nabokov as unequaled among contemporary English writers, Véra remarked that "without Lolita this would have taken another fifty years to happen."[591]

The couple's success was soured when a novel by another Russian writer began to compete. Pasternak's *Doctor Zhivago*, released in America in September 1958, four weeks after *Lolita*, was soon outselling it. Clearly jealous, the Nabokovs referred to Pasternak's novel as "trash" and portrayed the author as "a Bolshevik."[592] They claimed that Pasternak's abuse at home was fabricated and that *Zhivago* was a Soviet plant. Véra complained to a friend that *Lolita* was "squeezed out by that pitiful and miserable 'book' by the lowly Pasternak, whom V. is reluctant to badmouth. . . ."[593] Meanwhile, Nabokov wrote to Dwight Macdonald at *The New Yorker*, "Had not *Zhivago* and I been on the same ladder . . . I would have been glad to demolish that trashy, melodramatic, false, and inept book." He was also trying to influence Jason Epstein at *The New York Review of*

Books, writing him that *Zhivago* was "dreary conventional stuff."[594] Wilson thought Nabokov was behaving badly toward Pasternak and wrote a magnificent review of *Zhivago*, distinguishing it as "one of the great events in man's literary and moral history." Pasternak had to possess "the courage of genius" to create this novel in a totalitarian state.[595] That fall, Pasternak was nominated for the Nobel Prize, but had to renounce it under pressure from Soviet authorities. He died of a heart attack two years later.

Like most émigrés, the Nabokovs were unforgiving of the Communist state and showed no sympathy for people who lived there. With the exception of Mandelstam's poetry, they rejected literature of the entire Soviet period. They would also dismiss Solzhenitsyn's novels as third-rate journalism.[596]

Now that they were free from financial constraints, the couple planned their retirement. Nabokov's last lecture at Cornell was to be in January 1959. Before Christmas break, students lined up at their professor's office with copies of *Lolita*, only to learn that Nabokov did not sign his books. When a desperate student asked Véra whether she could sign his copy, she gave him a note as proof that Nabokov gave no autographs.

Writing to publishers before *Lolita*, Véra compared Nabokov with Tolstoy and Proust. After *Lolita's* publication, she objected to any comparison, describing Nabokov as "a completely individual writer.... If you want to compare, please compare the present work to his other publications ... recommend his books as just that: his books."[597] As Nabokov's fame grew, so did Véra's responsibilities: she was handling a flood of correspondence, telephone queries, and contracts. She wrote Filippa Rolf, Nabokov's Swedish female fan and poet:

> I have to carry on the whole business side—not only the enormous correspondence with publishers and agent (we only have one agent, in Paris, and I handle most of the other rights myself), but also investments, banks, planning future moves, etc. etc. And since I have had very little experience in

business matters before, everything is far from smooth. But my husband has neither experience nor time for all this, so there is no choice for me but try to do my best, on a general "hit-and-miss" basis.[598]

In September 1959, the couple journeyed to launch *Lolita* in Europe. Having come to America as refugees, they were returning as guests of honor: in two decades, Nabokov had become an American writer and a celebrity. There was a display of his editions on the ship, and Véra was confronted with the question of where her husband had met the *real* Lolita. She still anticipated such questions in 1981, when Martin Amis visited her in Switzerland: "These *questions* you will ask. Where are these *questions?*"[599]

During their European tour, the British, French, and Italian editions of *Lolita* were launched. Because of the French ban and threat of prosecution by the British, interest in the novel soared. George Wiedenfeld wrote Nabokov that *Lolita* was the most discussed book in Britain before publication. On November 5, the publication eve, Wiedenfeld and his business partner Nigel Nicholson hosted a party for three hundred guests at the Ritz Hotel in London. While everyone anticipated news from the government, Nabokov alone looked unperturbed: according to a correspondent from *Time & Tide*, he seemed not to know "what the party was all about." Emotions ran high when Nicholson announced that the British government had decided against prosecution. Véra, usually composed, was wiping tears from her eyes.

In France, a newspaper headline read, "Madame Nabokov is 38 Years Older than the Nymphet Lolita."[600] At fifty-seven, Véra could take this for a compliment. During the French publisher's reception, reporters separated Véra from Nabokov and discovered that without her he was disoriented. Earlier, he had made a serious blunder by failing to recognize James Harris, producer of the *Lolita* film, who introduced himself as "the man who just bought Lolita." Nabokov took him for a fan and muttered, "I hope you will enjoy reading it."[601] In Rome, Véra made the news by telling the press how she had saved *Lolita* from the fire. In his turn, Nabokov asked the reporter: "Hasn't this been a pleasant conversation? Isn't it true that my wife is a marvelous person?"[602]

In 1960, recovering from another promotional trip to Europe, Véra admitted to a friend, "Nomadic life is a wonderful thing—for a time. Then it becomes something of a strain. I am well qualified to say so after some forty-five years of it. However, we still remain 'homeless.'"[603] When Nabokov began to yearn for an opportunity to write in peace, Véra left society without regret. In 1961 the couple decided to choose "fruitful isolation in Switzerland,"[604] where Nabokov's sister Elena lived. Dmitry, who wanted to become an opera singer, was studying voice in Milan, across the Alps.

The town of Montreux, with its gorgeous view of the mountains and Lake Geneva, offered numerous butterfly expeditions and was perfect for Nabokov's writing. Having no heart for housekeeping and owning things, the couple settled in the Hotel Montreux Palace. In this earthly paradise, the Nabokovs' routine included work, meals, baths, games, and walks by the lake. They were immersed in their private business of creating, printing, correcting, translating, and admiring the works produced by "V&V, Inc.," as Véra jokingly referred to their business.

She remarked that her husband "had the good taste" to keep her out of his books. Both defended their marriage from onlookers. Nabokov was annoyed when critics speculated about autobiography in his works. In 1969, when his new novel, *Ada*, created a stir, Nabokov demanded an apology from a reviewer who implied that Véra was his lewd heroine: "What the hell, Sir, do you know about my married life?"[605] Véra was known to be more private than Nabokov. She disliked even innocuous questions about her life. When publishers Carl and Ellendea Proffer asked her where she had met Nabokov, Véra quipped, "Are you from the KGB?"[606]

In the 1960s, the stream of interviewers, photographers, and reporters to Montreux turned their retreat into "some miserable Yasnaya Polyana" of Tolstoy's final years when his estate was besieged by followers. But the Nabokovs lived and worked in perfect harmony, as the writer himself described it, "in the warmest and most candid friendship."[607] Impressed with their relationship, Nabokov's editor, Bart Winer, remarked, "When you were in their presence the love flowing from one to another was the most extraordinary thing. I've never seen love like that before."[608]

Véra's contribution to Nabokov's career was inestimable and he described it in a metaphor: "Most of my works have been dedicated to my wife and her picture has often been reproduced by some mysterious means of reflected color in the inner mirrors of my books."[609] Nabokov praised her sense of humor and perfect pitch for his ideas: "She and I are my best audience . . . I should say my main audience."[610]

Filippa Rolf, who had become friends with the Nabokovs and was now studying at Cambridge, visited the couple, providing another metaphor for their marriage: "They are mating like butterflies behind any bush right in the middle of the conversation, and they separate so quickly that one doesn't notice until later."[611] When Rolf talked about her favorite scenes in *Lolita*, Véra proceeded to quote them from memory, revealing that she knew her husband's works by heart.

In 1964, launching four volumes of translation and commentaries for *Eugene Onegin* on which they had collaborated for over a decade, the couple traveled to America. Véra suffered severe abdominal pain throughout the trip but stoically concealed it during the publisher's reception; she underwent an appendectomy after the festivities. Three years later, she traveled alone to New York when McGraw-Hill offered Nabokov a contract for $250,000 to produce all his books. She traveled by air, an additional worry for Nabokov, who wrote her, "I was dealt a hellish blow by your departure."[612] In her absence, Nabokov's sister, Elena, a librarian in Geneva, came to keep him company.

The couple rarely parted even for a day and had matching dreams. In November 1964, Nabokov wrote in his journal that they had both dreamed of revolutionary turmoil in Russia on the same night. Nonetheless, Véra told biographer Andrew Field, who had begun collecting information in the 1960s, "We are very different, you know. Very different." When Field reminded her that she had previously told him they were "exactly alike," Véra turned to Nabokov: "Is he a behaviorist, darling?" They were "exactly alike in one or two respects," she clarified.[613] An interviewer from an Israeli magazine thought the Nabokovs talked like "two famous mature actors, aware of their own importance." Véra's beauty also caught his eye:

> Véra is one of the most impressive women I've ever seen. Her black suit shows a nice and well-proportioned figure. She certainly has a "Jewish look." She talks softly and quietly. Her laughter is restrained, while his is rolling. Tears come down his cheeks, and he continually takes off his glasses as the laughter proceeds.[614]

Véra surprised Field by telling him there was "no reason why she should be present in her husband's biography." Nabokov found it amusing: "You can't help being represented! We're too far gone! It's too late!"[615] Eventually, she submitted "a little bit of her story," along with a warning: "I am terribly concerned about accuracy...."[616] But it was Nabokov's depiction that she jealously scrutinized, checking certain passages with him, in the biographer's presence: "Darling, he has something there which he put very cautiously and cleverly. There is something about the way you speak which is, well, there is certain unusual refinement."[617] At the final stage, Field received corrections from the couple: Véra's amendments alone took six pages.

After half a century at a desk, her eyesight was going, her wrists hurt, and she was hospitalized with two slipped discs. This separation in 1973 overwhelmed Nabokov, who wrote in his diary, "The feeling of distress, désarroi [disarray], utter panic and dreadful presentiment every time that Véra is away in the hospital, is one of the greatest torments of my life."[618] She was number one on his list of precious possessions rescued in his dream of a hotel fire: "I saved Véra, my glasses, the Ada typescript, my dentures, my passport—in that order!"[619]

After *Lolita*, Nabokov continued to work at a steady pace: in all, his writings comprised twenty-nine volumes. The interest in his novels, however, was fading away. In 1976, during his final year, Nabokov still worked long hours, getting up at six. He was bound by a contract with McGraw Hill, which required him to deliver six more books over four years. Véra, still proofreading translations (she helped translate *Lolita* into Russian), handled his correspondence and accompanied him on his butterfly expeditions. She was now unable to type, and a secretary, Jaqueline Callier, came to help three afternoons a week.

"Here we are at last, my darling," wrote Nabokov to Véra on their fiftieth wedding anniversary, decorating his card with a butterfly drawing.[620] His butterfly inscriptions were expressions of love. These were resting and feeding butterflies, with rainbow-colored wings spread. Véra had a key to all the meanings of these love notes, as she alone could fully decipher the web of his poetic and fictional works.

After a bad fall on a mountain slope in Davos at seventy-six, Nabokov was repeatedly unwell. He refused to slow down, working on a new novel despite a litany of health troubles. On July 2, 1977, after contracting a cold, Nabokov died in the hospital of bronchial congestion. Véra told Dmitry: "Let's rent an airplane and crash." During the private funeral at Clarens Cemetery, she was composed and asked that there be "no tears, no wails, none of that."[621] She continued to live and work as if the two of them had never parted.

In her late seventies and into her eighties, she still toiled six hours a day, kept the same dictating hours for business correspondence, and continued to live in the same hotel. When in 1990 the Montreux Palace was being renovated, she moved to new rented quarters closer to Clarens Cemetery.

She helped prepare collections of Nabokov's works and letters, worked on the Russian translation of *Pale Fire*, and filed every article about him. Critics and biographers sent their manuscripts for her endorsement. When John Updike sent an introduction to a collection of Nabokov's lectures, Véra returned it with several pages of notes. "What an impressively clear mind and style she has," noted Updike. She made a personal request: "Could you please take me out of the article?"[622] Véra asked other biographers to do the same: she trusted Nabokov alone to represent her.

In 1981, Martin Amis interviewed Véra for an article in *The Observer*. When he asked why Nabokov had dedicated most of his novels to her, she replied that they had had "a very unusual relationship." She continued to believe he was the greatest writer after his fame in the West faded. Suspecting Amis did not admire Nabokov's recently published lectures, she flew into a rage: "Mrs. Nabokov misheard a remark I made about the *first* volume of the *Lectures*, mistaking praise for dispraise. 'What?' she said. And, until I made myself clear, every atom in her body seemed to tremble with indignation. . . .

> She has thick white hair and expressive, ironical eyes. She has been rather ill recently—her hearing is a little weak and she uses a stick; but even now, in her seventies, the deeply responsive face is still suffused with feminine light. It is above all a humourous face.[623]

When nearly blind and writing over her lines, Véra translated an unpublished story by Nabokov and was planning to translate *Ada* into Italian. She died on April 7, 1991. The headline for her obituary in *The New York Times* read, "Véra Nabokov, 89, Wife, Muse, and Agent." Her ashes joined Nabokov's in one urn, and a line was added to his tombstone under his name.

CHAPTER FIVE

Elena Bulgakov: Mysterious Margarita

E lena met Mikhail Bulgakov when both were in their midthirties and in their second marriages. They were instantly attracted to each other: it was love that "lasted for the rest of my life."[624] Elena left her husband, a high-ranked military officer, to join the penniless and harassed writer, whose talent she admired, embracing "poverty, risk, and uncertainty." Her devotion to Bulgakov, who was almost unpublished during his lifetime, inspired the love story of the Master and Margarita in his best novel of the same title. The novel survives only because Elena preserved it and tirelessly pursued its publication.

Born on October 21, 1893, Elena grew up in a cultured family of mixed origins. Her father, Sergei Markovich Nurenberg, was long believed to be a Baltic German. However, biographer Lydia Yanovskaya provides convincing evidence that his origins were different.[625] Born Shmul-Yankel Nirenberg, Elena's father came from the city of Berdichev in the northern Ukraine, the second-largest Jewish community in the Russian Empire. Orphaned early, he pursued a university education in Tartu, an Estonian city under Russian control. Baptized a Lutheran, he adopted a Christian name to overcome restrictions for Jews on education and the professions.

Elena's mother, née Alexandra Alexandrovna Gorskaya, was an ethnic Russian from the family of a defrocked Orthodox priest. (The disciplinary matter which led to his dismissal is unknown.) Nurenberg, who fell in love with this Russian girl, converted from Lutheranism to Orthodoxy to marry her. After the wedding in 1889, the couple lived in several Baltic cities before moving to Riga. Elena was born there, the third child in a family of two girls and two boys. Her early years were spent in the culturally vibrant city by the Baltic Sea where German, Yiddish, Latvian, and Russian were spoken on the streets and one could attend the Russian Theater and the Deutsches Theater. The city was home to Isaiah Berlin, Sergei Eisenstein, and Mikhail Baryshnikov.

German was the language of commerce and culture, while Russian was the language of administration, to which Elena's father belonged: he worked as a teacher and later as a tax inspector. Nurenberg was well read and published articles on education, finance, and theater. His passion for the theater influenced Elena and her older sister Olga to dream of stage careers. Decades later, remembering her anticipation of a new performance, Elena wrote her older brother Alexander, "How splendid was our childhood, how much did we experience, while listening to music or sitting at the Russian theater . . . how rich was our life." Elena and Olga were drawn to artistic milieus as long as they lived, although they did not pursue acting. Olga was employed for decades at the Moscow Arts Theater as secretary to Vladimir Nemirovich-Danchenko, associate of the legendary director Konstantin Stanislavsky. This was where Elena came to see Bulgakov's popular play *The Days of the Turbins*.

Bulgakov liked Elena's stories about her childhood, which resonated with his early memories. He had been raised in Kiev, another multicultural city, in a close-knit and cordial family. Bulgakov's father was a professor of comparative religion at the Kiev

Theological Academy. His mother, like Elena's, was a daughter of a priest, but of an archpriest of the Orthodox Church, to be precise. The children received an excellent education, were widely read and musical; Bulgakov's love of theater and the opera began in childhood. Like Elena, he maintained strong ties to his family, grateful for the upbringing he received; he portrays his mother and siblings in his first novel *The White Guard*.

The women's gymnasium in Riga gave Elena a solid knowledge of French and German. Later, she would translate French literature and also help Bulgakov with research. When her family moved to Moscow during the First World War, Elena learned to type and, like her sister, became a secretary, but at the *Izvestiya* newspaper. At twenty-five, she married Yuri Neelov, son of the famous tragic actor and political anarchist, Mamont Dalsky. (He gave Fyodor Shalyapin his first acting lessons for the opera stage.) Her first marriage was interrupted by the Civil War. In 1920, her husband was dispatched to the Western front as an adjutant to the 16th Red Army commander, Evgeny Shilovsky. When Elena came to see her husband, Shilovsky fell in love with her and promptly dispatched his adjutant to the Southern front. Her marriage was soon terminated and Elena was free to remarry.

Shilovsky, a First World War veteran, was among few officers with a noble background in the Red Army. He was thirty-one, charismatic, educated, and talented; "a wonderful man," according to Elena. Bulgakov describes him in *The Master and Margarita*: "Her husband was young, handsome, kind, honest. . . ."[626] Highly regarded in the army, Shilovsky was invited to teach at the Military Academy in 1921. That year, with Elena expecting a child, the couple decided to marry; she, however, insisted on a church wedding. This presented a major obstacle, since the Bolsheviks were hostile to the Orthodox Church. Elena, who had divorced her first husband in a Soviet registry office, needed the permission of Patriarch Tikhon for a religious wedding.

In summer 1921, the couple secretly arrived at the patriarch's residence, meeting in his reception room with none other than the prominent proletarian writer Maxim Gorky. Having recently launched an international campaign for famine relief, Gorky was there to discuss issuing a joint international appeal.⁶²⁷ After the Civil War, with the economy in ruins, the Bolsheviks seized grain in many regions, resulting in unprecedented famine, afflicting over forty million people. That year, a large-scale relief operation began, in which America played a key role.⁶²⁸ Despite the patriarch's willingness to participate in this relief, the Bolsheviks would accuse him of sabotage in 1922 and incarcerate him as a pretext for their imminent reprisals against the Church and the clergy. Compared to the problems the Church was facing, Elena's and Shilovsky's business was easy to solve: the patriarch heard it with a smile and gave Elena permission to remarry. Later that year, the couple's first son, Evgeny, was born.

Shilovsky was a good husband, but their marriage was, perhaps, too blissful for Elena. Two years later she wrote her sister, who was on a foreign tour with the Moscow Arts Theater, that nothing interested her at home and that she felt like running away. Shilovsky worked long hours, the nanny looked after the baby, and she was left with unspent energies. She needed her own pursuits to satisfy her love of life, gaiety, and fascination with the artistic realm.

In 1926, the couple had a second son, named Sergei after Elena's father. The family's fortune grew: two years later, Shilovsky was promoted to Chief of Staff for the Moscow Military District under the brilliant young Commander-in-Chief Ieronim Uborevich. They received a new apartment in a former noble mansion with white columns, located on a quiet downtown street near the seventeenth-century Rzhevskaya Church of the Virgin Mother.⁶²⁹ Coming to see their recently renovated quarters, Elena chose the best apartment, intended for the Commander-in-Chief, and insisted on having it; Uborevich and his wife Nina, an actress, were won over by her persuasiveness and charisma. In winter 1929, Elena moved into her spacious apartment, adorned with fireplaces and round windows, with her family plus her sister, along with a maid and a German governess. A few years later, she would walk away from this luxury without regret.

In February 1929, when Shilovsky was on a business trip, Elena met Bulgakov at a party of mutual acquaintances. Told that the famous Bulgakov would be there, she at once decided to go: she admired him as a writer, having read his imaginative novel *The White Guard* and his satirical tales, and watched *Days of the Turbins*. On February 28, Elena was sitting next to Bulgakov, who amused the guests with a fantastic tale he was improvising; she hung on to his every word: "Having realized he had such an appreciative listener, he let himself go and put on such a performance that people were moaning with laughter. He jumped free of the table, played the piano, sang, danced; in a word, put on quite a show. He had dark-blue eyes but when he was so animated they sparkled like diamonds." Bulgakov was a master storyteller and talented actor who could create characters and act out their roles on the spot; he transformed the evening into a fiesta. Few friends were surprised that Bulgakov, whom some believed to be a flirt, became captivated by the attractive Elena. The next day, they went skiing together; the day after that, he invited her to a dress rehearsal, then to *Aida* at the Bolshoi, and afterwards to an actors' club where he played a game of pool with Mayakovsky. "In a word, we met every day and, finally, I pleaded with him, saying that I won't go anywhere, I want to get some sleep, so that he wouldn't call me...."

But Shilovsky still had not returned from his trip and Bulgakov phoned her at three in the morning, asking her to come out. He brought Elena to Patriarch's Pond, the place where his characters in *The Master and Margarita* would encounter the Devil, and, pointing to a bench, said: "Here they saw him for the first time." Preserving a mysterious air, Bulgakov took her to the apartment of a strange old man, where they had an elaborate meal by a fireplace.

> We enter a dining room. The fireplace is burning and on the table—fish soup, caviar, appetizers, wine. We are having a lovely supper; everything is fascinating, cheerful.... We

stay until morning. As I sit on a carpet by the fireplace, the old man loses his head: "May I kiss you?"—"Yes," I said, "kiss me on the cheek." And he: "A witch! A witch! She bewitched me!"

That night, Elena also "bewitched" Bulgakov, who would use her as a model for his mystical heroine in *The Master and Margarita*. His prodigious imagination helped him escape the grave realities of his own life and career. A few weeks earlier, Stalin had called his new play, *Flight*, "an anti-Soviet phenomenon," leaving Bulgakov's career in shambles.[630] Although Stalin had made his remark in a private letter to a Soviet dramatist,[631] his opinion became widely known, with disastrous consequences. *Flight* was banned before its premiere and Bulgakov's other plays dropped from the repertoire. Even *The Days of the Turbins*, inexplicably Stalin's favorite—he saw the production fifteen times—was no longer performed.

Flight was Bulgakov's most accomplished play. Structured as a sequence of dreams, it portrays the exodus of the Russian intelligentsia and the White Army officers after the Revolution and their lives as refugees abroad. Stalin, who followed Bulgakov's career with interest, remarked that he did not mind having *Flight* staged if the writer "were to add to the eight dreams one or two more" reflecting the triumph of the Bolsheviks.[632] When advised to write a Communist play, Bulgakov replied he could not succeed writing about things he did not know.

Stalin's negative evaluation of his play left Bulgakov unpublishable and unemployable. The author of a popular novel and four plays, he found himself without means of survival as theaters turned down his applications to work as an actor or even as a stagehand. Despite pressure, he refused to compromise his artistic talent and become subservient to the state.

Bulgakov was still married to Lyubov Belozerskaya, a former émigré who had returned to Soviet Russia in 1923. She became one of his sources for his play *Flight*, where he used her stories about Russian refugees in Constantinople and Paris. This play and

Bulgakov's novel *The White Guard* were dedicated to Lyubov, who was then his muse and assistant.

Elena and Bulgakov kept their affair secret, and neither of them seriously considered divorce. When, in summer, Elena took a vacation with her family in the North Caucasus, Bulgakov wrote her frequently, and she destroyed his letters, in which he had sentimentally inserted red rose petals. He begged her to speed up her return to Moscow, for he had prepared a gift for her. When Elena returned, he gave her his new satirical piece, "To a Secret Friend." It was a story of how he had left the medical profession to become a writer, and all the vicissitudes of his literary career; he addressed it to his most trusted friend, confidante, and new muse—Elena.

In the fall, still hoping to prevail over censorship, Bulgakov wrote a biographical play about Molière titled *Molière, The Cabal of Hypocrites*. He considered Molière the greatest comic dramatist and could also relate to the tragic circumstances of his career. Molière had been under attack for satirizing religious hypocrisy, and was harassed by religious zealots and the Catholic Church, which had condemned *Tartuffe* and banned *Dom Juan*. This evoked Bulgakov's own harassment by Soviet critics and censors. Although the play told about the seventeenth-century dramatist, it sounded modern and the title was a veiled reference to Stalin's regime.

While writing the play, Bulgakov had two enthusiastic assistants: his wife and Elena took his dictation in turns. Elena brought her Underwood to the Bulgakovs' apartment and typed the play. She and Lyubov were on friendly terms, and so Elena would also visit the Bulgakovs with Shilovsky.

Upon completing *The Cabal of Hypocrites* in December, Bulgakov gave it to the Arts Theater. In March 1930, the Repertory Committee censors banned it for performance, another blow to Bulgakov who now viewed his situation as hopeless. Ever after, he would struggle with attacks of anxiety and fear. He was continually refused employment: "They would not hire him as a reporter or even as a printer," Elena recalls. "In a word, there was only one way out—to end his life." She watched Bulgakov burn the drafts for several of his works and the novel about the Devil, the future *Master and Margarita*. In this despondent mood he felt his works had no future.

But later that month, having recovered from the trauma of *Flight*'s rejection, Bulgakov wrote a forceful letter to Stalin and members of his government, defending his right to free speech. He described the harassment campaign against him in the Soviet press and the banning of his plays, which had received high public acclaim. Even *The Turbins*, despite its popular success, was relentlessly attacked by official critics who abused him because of his topic, Russian intelligentsia; for this reason, of 301 reviews of this play, 298 were hostile.[633] Being "condemned to lifelong silence in the USSR," he was asking the government to allow him to leave "for freedom." And if he were not allowed to emigrate, the government should secure his right to find work. At present, strangled financially, he was facing "destitution, the street and death."[634] Elena typed this letter and on March 28, despite strong objections from Shilovsky, helped Bulgakov deliver copies to Stalin, Molotov, and other prominent addressees.

The prompt response surpassed their expectations. Within a week, delegates from the Young Workers' Theater were in Bulgakov's apartment, asking him to accept a position as director. While they discussed the contract, Elena sat in a separate bedroom. Bulgakov kept running from his study to her room for advice, so Elena had to emerge from her hiding place, help finalize details, and type the contract.

Just a few weeks earlier, on April 14, the country was stunned with the news of Mayakovsky's suicide. By taking his life, the revolutionary poet sent a powerful message to the regime, so in this context, Bulgakov's letter had an even stronger impact on its most prominent reader. On April 18, Bulgakov received a phone call from Stalin himself. Elena was at her place that evening when Bulgakov rushed over to see her to report his conversation with Stalin. (It was then unprecedented: four years later, Stalin would phone Pasternak after becoming involved in Mandelstam's fate.) Stalin spoke in his habitually punctuated style, referring to himself in the plural, and Bulgakov perfectly replicated his Georgian accent and intonations: "We received your letter. We read it with the comrades. You will have a favorable reply. . . . Perhaps, you need permission to leave abroad. Are you so tired of us?" Bulgakov, caught off guard, retreated from his decision to emigrate, saying that a duty of a Russian writer was to live and work in his homeland. (He would regret these words many times in the years to come.) "You are right. I also think so," Stalin replied. As for getting a job, he said that Bulgakov should send another application to the Arts Theater. "I think they will accept." Concluding, Stalin proposed to meet Bulgakov and have a talk. Bulgakov enthusiastically accepted, but Stalin never made an appointment and, moreover, no longer showed an interest in Bulgakov's fate.

Over the years, Bulgakov would ask Elena the same question, why did Stalin change his mind about the meeting? "And I would always reply the same: 'What could he possibly discuss with you? He knew, after reading your letter, that you would not ask for money or an apartment; you would talk about freedom of speech, censorship, and the need for an artist to write about the issues that matter. And how could he respond to that?'" When, shortly after, Bulgakov went to the Arts Theater, he was immediately hired as assistant director. After being unemployable for so long, he was now juggling two jobs in addition to his writing.

In the summer of 1930, while touring the Crimea with the Young Workers' Theater, Bulgakov sent telegrams to Elena asking her to join him. When she did not reply, he wrote his wife, asking after Elena's health. For Lyubov, Bulgakov's intimacy with Elena apparently was not a secret by then. But Elena's husband only learned about the affair in February 1931. He demanded that she end all meetings and sever her communication with Bulgakov. When Elena promised this, Shilovsky met Bulgakov privately and, having lost his temper during their conversation, threatened him with a gun. "But you would not shoot an unarmed man?" Bulgakov quipped, adding that he was available for a duel.[635] Elena kept her promise to Shilovsky, and when they stopped seeing each other, Bulgakov noted, on a page of his published novel (it served as a diary), "The misfortune struck on 25.02.1931." They did not meet again for eighteen months.

During this time, Bulgakov's play *The Days of the Turbins* was brought back on stage. This happened after Stalin came to the Arts Theater to see another play and inquired about his favorite *The Turbins*. He was surprised it was no longer performed and had to be reminded of his own negative comment, three years earlier, about Bulgakov's play *Flight*. Stalin wanted *The Turbins* back, and after his visit in January 1932, the theater received a phone call from the Party Central Committee requesting that it revive the production. Although sets had been dismantled long ago and actors were busy, the theater hastily staged the play. Told the news, Bulgakov was overwhelmed with conflicting emotions: there was "a flood of joy," then anguish. Stalin could ban or permit his works on whim, so there was no certainty whatsoever. When actors came to congratulate him, they found Bulgakov in bed with cold compresses over his heart and head. Over the years, it turned out that *The Turbins* would remain the only play Bulgakov could rely on for steady income.

The Molière play was licensed for performance after Gorky commended it to Stalin. But despite Gorky's backing, theaters in Moscow and Leningrad were afraid to make "a political mistake"; and although they rehearsed the play, it was not included in their repertoires. In Leningrad, production of *Molière* was canceled after a communist playwright complained that Bulgakov's topic was inappropriate for the masses. Elena learned these developments from her sister, who was first to know about theatrical productions and enjoyed sharing gossip from the artistic world.

Living apart from Bulgakov, Elena only more acutely realized how her life was devoid of meaning. Her position in the Soviet elite, to which her marriage entitled her, and her freedom from material concerns did not matter so much. What she feared losing was her close family: "We had two wonderful sons; it was a blissful life. But when I met Bulgakov . . . I realized it was fated."[636] She phoned Bulgakov and thus ended their long separation. They met on September 1, 1932, and "the first thing he said was, 'I cannot live without you.'

And I replied: 'I also cannot.'" Bulgakov would depict the meeting of two lovers in *The Master and Margarita*, where his heroine's story is drawn from Elena's: "Obviously she was right when she said she needed him, the master, instead of the Gothic house, instead of a private garden, instead of money. She was right—she loved him."[637] During their meeting, the couple decided they must get married.

Elena took her boys for a short vacation in the country and from there wrote to Shilovsky, asking for a divorce. He gave his consent, admitting that he had treated her as a child and now realized he had been wrong. On September 11, Elena wrote her parents in Riga that she was divorcing her husband to marry Bulgakov. In his letter, Shilovsky wrote his in-laws that he did not blame Elena for her decision, which he believed was an honest one: "She is deeply and seriously in love with another man. . . ."[638] However, it would take Elena an hour to explain to an acquaintance what bound her to Bulgakov and why she left Shilovsky. In the end, her friend admitted: "Now I understand why you have left. Shilovsky is the earth and Bulgakov—the spirit. . . ." There were other friends who predicted that Elena's marriage with Bulgakov would not last.

On October 4, the day after Bulgakov and Lyubov divorced, the couple married in a Registry Office. Soon after, Bulgakov told Elena, "The whole world was against me, and I was alone. Now we are together, and nothing frightens me."[639] For the honeymoon, the couple went to Leningrad, where a theater invited Bulgakov on business, reserving for him a stay at the Astoria Hotel. There he resumed the novel about the Devil (*The Master and Margarita*) that he had burned three years earlier; he dictated new chapters to Elena.

When at the end of October they returned to Moscow, Elena moved into Bulgakov's apartment. She arrived with her six-year-old son Sergei and without luggage; as Bulgakov would like to tell, "She got out of the car. A Primus stove in one hand and Sergei in another."[640] The older boy, Evgeny, stayed with Shilovsky for a few more years until he too joined his mother and Bulgakov. (Shilovsky was among few officers to be spared during the Great Purge. In

1936, he had married a daughter of Alexei Tolstoy, a prominent Soviet writer and Stalin's favorite, which probably saved him.)

Later that fall, Bulgakov began Molière's biography, which a publisher commissioned him to write. Elena accompanied him to the Lenin Library, where the two researched accounts in Russian and French. In addition, she became Bulgakov's business manager, a role she enjoyed because it enabled her to conduct tough financial negotiations with theaters, editors, and publishers. Early in their marriage, Bulgakov authorized Elena to sign contracts with theaters and publishing houses and receive royalties at home and abroad where his plays were staged and his novel *The White Guard* was published. But of course, *The Turbins* was his only play performed at home; foreign royalties could not be collected, because Bulgakov was not permitted to travel. But Elena's duties were important, nonetheless, since she handled the tasks Bulgakov found frustrating, giving him peace of mind to work.

Becoming fully engaged in his literary and artistic life, Elena accompanied Bulgakov to the theater and stayed for rehearsals of his adaptation of Gogol's novel *The Dead Souls*, occasionally bringing little Sergei, who became infected with her love of the stage. Evenings were spent at home with friends, whom Bulgakov entertained with readings and stories. At night, when he would settle down to write Molière's biography, she took his dictation. Bulgakov established a cordial relationship with Elena's son, telling his fellow writer Evgeny Zamyatin, who had been allowed to emigrate and was living in Paris, how they spent the winter "telling fascinating tales of the North Pole and of elephant-hunting; we shot at one another with a toy pistol and were continually ill with flu. During that time I wrote a biography of your fellow Parisian Jean-Baptiste Molière for the series 'Lives of the Great.'"[641]

While working on this biography, the couple was "living in the unreal, fairy-tale Paris of the seventeenth century."[642] Bulgakov, who had never traveled abroad, was trying to visualize the monument to Molière in Paris from published accounts. At his request, his brother Nikolai, who had managed to emigrate and was living in

France, described the materials and the color of the statue. Written in a light and witty prose, Bulgakov's book stood out among the dreary, politically sound Soviet biographies—and this alone made it unacceptable. The editor became alarmed with Bulgakov's unconventional style and lack of Soviet perspective. Moreover, he found that the book contained "fairly transparent hints about our Soviet reality."[643] (That is to say, the relationship between a writer and an autocratic ruler had not changed since the seventeenth century.) Bulgakov refused to make the major changes demanded of him, such as introducing "a serious Soviet historian" as the narrator. So the project that gave the couple much satisfaction remained unpublished, and Elena put it away with her collection of Bulgakov's manuscripts.

On September 1, 1933, the first anniversary of their reunion, Elena started a diary, recording events that involved Bulgakov. Back in 1926, his writer's diary and the manuscript of his novella *The Heart of a Dog* had been confiscated by the secret police during a search of his apartment. Since then, Bulgakov vowed not to keep a diary: the idea of the police reading his private thoughts was intolerable.

In Stalin's era, few people dared keep diaries or any private records, to avoid incrimination. Elena, however, would chronicle Bulgakov's career, his persecution by the authorities, and arrests of their friends. "I don't know who will ever read these notes of mine. But they mustn't be surprised if I am always writing about practical matters. They won't know of the terrible conditions in which my husband Mikhail Bulgakov had to work."[644] In addition, she collected Bulgakov's archive, determined to preserve every scrap of paper. He contributed manuscripts along with notes, such as "To my only inspirer, my wife Elena Sergeevna."[645] Her love of his work encouraged Bulgakov to continue his novel *The Master and Margarita*, which would become their most important undertaking together.

In October, the couple invited friends for a Bulgakov reading at home. Akhmatova was among the guests, and the couple, anticipating her judgment, were disappointed that she was silent all evening. Refusing to share one's thoughts was only prudent, however. A few days later, Olga told her sister that playwrights Nikolai Erdman and Vladimir Mass[646] had been arrested for writing satirical fables. The news alarmed Bulgakov, and at night he burned part of the novel, deeming it too dangerous to keep.

In the atmosphere of political paranoia and arrests, Bulgakov's psychological condition deteriorated. He developed anxiety, fear of being alone, and dread of open spaces. Now Elena had to escort him not only to the theater but everywhere he went: every trip was a torment for Bulgakov, and he was only able to save himself by telling her funny stories as they walked.

Coming home after the theater, Bulgakov would dictate to her his new chapters from *The Master and Margarita*, work that continued into the night. On January 23, 1934, Elena noted in her diary that Bulgakov was unwell, in bed, and dictated the chapter of a fire in the Berlioz apartment. By coincidence, the fictional event was followed by a real blaze in their home:

> A fire broke out. I yelled: "Misha!!"[647] He came running as he was, in a shirt, barefoot, and found the kitchen already in flames. . . . I woke up Seryozhka,[648] dressed him and took him outside, rather—opened a window, jumped out and took him in my arms. Then I returned to the house. Up to his ankles in water, his hands burned, M.A. was throwing everything into the flames, all he could lay his hands on: blankets, pillows, and washed laundry. Finally, he stopped the fire. . . . We went to sleep at 7 A.M. and at 10 A.M. it was time for M.A. to go to the Theatre.[649]

At other times, when Bulgakov's dark thoughts returned, he called himself a captive and a prisoner. He could not visit his brother's family in France and had been dreaming in vain of museums in Paris and Rome; he would tell Elena how he wanted to see the world. "Do I have that right?" he would ask her, referring to his longstanding wish to travel, and she would reply, "You do."[650] In

May 1934, overcoming fear of refusal, the couple applied for permission to go abroad with the Arts Theater troupe. After they submitted applications, Bulgakov cheered up and, as they walked home, told Elena excitedly, "So, this means I'm not a captive! This means I will see the light!" He imagined a new book he would bring from his travels, dictating it to Elena in Rome; he dreamed of the sun, which would cure him, and of their walks in the evenings. "Am I really not a prisoner?" he kept repeating. Naturally, Elena also dreamed of this trip, which would help her recuperate after her recent pneumonia, contracted in Bulgakov's damp and cold apartment.

By then, both were anxious to move to a newly built apartment house, which belonged to the Writers' Union, the same one where the Mandelstams had settled some six months earlier. When in mid-February they moved to their new flat, Bulgakov described their living arrangement to writer Vikenty Veresaev, "An astonishing apartment-block, I swear! There are writers living above and below and behind and in front and alongside."[651]

In June, the couple went to pick up their passports at the theater. It was a government-subsidized trip and the staff was provided a generous travel allowance, in addition to passports. Olga's allowance was $400, while the two directors received $500. Called in last, the Bulgakovs were given white slips of paper—refusals. As they left the theater, Bulgakov fell ill and Elena took him to the nearest drugstore, from where she called a cab to take them home.

All-knowing Olga foresaw that Bulgakov would be refused, having told Elena they only give travel permission to writers who can be relied on to produce work the Soviet Union needs. "And how did Maka [Bulgakov] prove that he changed his views after Stalin's phone call?" Bulgakov's sister, Nadezhda, also believed he must reform. She conveyed remarks of her husband's relative, a communist, who suggested sending Bulgakov to one of their construction sites, built by prisoners, for three months. To this, Bulgakov replied there was even a better way to reform people—feed them salt herring and deny water, referring to the widely used torture. An editor from the Literary Encyclopedia phoned Olga at the theater, saying they were publishing an article on Bulgakov, which will be "definitely unfavorable." The editor was wondering whether he had reformed his views after *The Turbins*. Bulgakov said it was a pity that the theater's porter did not take the call, for he would have replied, "Yes, he had reformed yesterday at 11 o'clock."

Because of attacks on Bulgakov in the press, theaters were afraid to even mention his name. After director Nemirovich introduced Bulgakov to the audience, he worried whether he had made a political mistake. In 1934, during the 500th performance of *The Turbins*, the author's name was not mentioned in a congratulatory telegram to the theater.

Although Bulgakov was almost taboo, his play *The Turbins* was still universally loved. Stalin and his government continued to see it, applauding after each performance. *The Turbins* was also staged in America, and in September 1934 the Bulgakovs received the American cast at their home. Unaware that Bulgakov had been denied travel, the director told the couple it would be wonderful to see them in New York.

Looking for ways to make money, Bulgakov turned to acting: the theater gave him the role of the judge in *The Pickwick Papers*. Elena remarked in her diary: "I am in despair. Bulgakov—as an actor. . . ." She sat nervously in the audience when Bulgakov appeared in a judge's red mantle and blond wig, visibly enjoying his minuscule part. In fact, he liked acting more than writing adaptations of Gogol and other classics for the theater, projects he only took on to earn a living.

The premiere of *The Pickwick Papers* on December 1 was attended by members of the government, who, however, did not stay to the end. The news spread that Sergei Kirov, a prominent Bolshevik and Leningrad Party chief, had been assassinated, so all Party officials fled the theater. As the country plunged into mourning, few realized the grave consequences of the event. Stalin, who had engineered the murder, would use it as an excuse to conduct his Great Purge, which would claim the lives of millions.

Absorbed with Bulgakov's career, Elena merely wondered whether Kirov had been to the theater lately, in which case it was possible that the last play he saw in life was *The Turbins*. She was busy preparing for Christmas and had made big purchases for their new apartment—a piano for the living room and an antique bureau, which had belonged to Alexander I, for Bulgakov's study. She bought it at a sale of Imperial furniture and was immensely proud of it. Bulgakov, who felt himself a nineteenth-century man, loved working at it.

Christmas had been outlawed by the Bolsheviks, along with other religious holidays, but at the Bulgakovs' apartment it was noisily celebrated: the couple erected a tree, lit candles, and laid presents for the boys. Bulgakov played the march on the piano and the boys strode into the room. "There were wild squeals, clattering and shouts! Then, according to the program, there were performances."[652] They celebrated with music and Elena's wish that the New Year bring no bad news.

In January 1935, Elena still walked Bulgakov to the theater. She had arranged a hypnotherapy treatment for Bulgakov with a Moscow celebrity, Dr. Berg, to ease his phobias and anxiety. The doctor came to their apartment in early February; after a few sessions, he told Elena that he was happy to have cured his favorite writer. Bulgakov proclaimed the treatment a great success and for the first time in half a year walked to the theater alone: hypnosis alleviated his dread of open spaces.

Meantime, he was writing a biographical play about Pushkin for the centennial of his death in 1937. To secure the play's approval, he asked his friend Veresaev to collaborate. The older writer was a renowned Pushkin scholar and had an untarnished political reputation. Enthusiastic about the project, Elena took dictation, helped with research, and even made an independent scholarly contribution, deciphering a note of the poet Vasily Zhukovsky, Pushkin's friend. She delivered her report to a gathering at Veresaev's home, receiving commendation. The play focused on Pushkin's last years, his marriage, and tragic death in a duel. With that, Bulgakov's play offered a rare sympathetic treatment of Pushkin's wife, Natalya. For almost a century, Natalya had been blamed for her lack of interest in the poet's work and for his untimely death, while Bulgakov gave her voice as his muse and the mother of his children. Elena was happy with the play and, although she knew it by heart, continued to be moved by each reading. She also supported Bulgakov through the difficulties of working with a co-author. Upon completing the play, Bulgakov wrote a friend, "Lyusya [Elena] is now tapping energetically at the typewriter. . . . I put my hand on Lyusya's shoulder to restrain her. She has worn herself out and shared all the excitement with me, burrowing into bookshelves with me and turning pale when I was reading it to the actors."[653]

Simultaneously, Elena tried to hasten production of the Molière play, still being rehearsed by the Arts Theater after several years. She had an informal talk with an official, named Egorov, whose job at the theater was to greet government delegations and look after contracts; she mentioned that rehearsals of Bulgakov's play were dragging on, without any end in sight. Alarmed, Egorov began to look for those responsible for the delay and urged the fearful directors to speed things up. In May, Elena received a long-awaited call from her sister, informing her that the theater wanted to perform the play early next year. "Victory!" she wrote in her diary.

In the West, interest in Bulgakov was growing since an American journal called *The Turbins* the first Soviet non-propaganda play and praised him as a comedic playwright. Charles E. Bohlen, a secretary at the American Embassy in Moscow, wanted to translate Bulgakov's comedy *Zoika's Apartment*. (Bohlen, later Roosevelt's interpreter at wartime meetings with Stalin, was an expert on Russian affairs.) The Bulgakovs invited Bohlen to their house for a reading and supper, and he came with a translator, Emmanuil Zhukhovitsky. (He was actually an informer who collected information on foreigners and prominent Russians. An unwelcome guest at the Bulgakovs' apartment, he had been there time and again to snoop on their conversations.) Elena shone as a hostess, treating her guests to caviar, salmon, home-made pâté, vodka, and pies. Before beginning to read the play, Bulgakov showed Bohlen his new application to travel abroad, at which time Zhukhovitsky choked on a pie. "But the Americans said it was wonderful and we must go." The couple was beginning to dream about the United States.

The Bulgakovs were also invited to a ball at the American Embassy; and a note specified that men had to wear tails or dinner jackets. Since Bulgakov had neither, they had to urgently tailor him a black suit at great expense. Elena anticipated the April 23 ball with great curiosity. She was ravishing in her dark-blue dress with pale pink flowers.

> Never in my life have I seen such a ball. The Ambassador stood at the top of the stairs to greet his guests. Everyone was wearing tails, and there were only a few jackets and smoking-jackets. . . . There were people dancing in a hall with columns, floodlights shining down from the gallery, and behind a net which separated off the orchestra there were live pheasants and other birds. We had supper at separate tables in an enormous dining-room with live bear-cubs in one corner, kid goats, and cockerels in cages. There were accordion players during supper.[654]

Among prominent people they met were the famous director Vsevolod Meyerhold and his wife, actress Zinaida Reich; politician and editor of *Izvestiya* Nikolai Bukharin, and Soviet Marshal and Commander-in-Chief Mikhail Tukhachevsky. All would soon be destroyed in the purges, along with the rest of the artistic, military, and government elite. In *The Master and Margarita*, Bulgakov would depict the ball as a grand Satan's ball, attended by corpses; the Devil's arrival in contemporary Moscow reflects the prison-like hell into which the country was descending.

Early in the morning, the couple was returning home in an Embassy car, Elena with a bouquet of tulips from Bohlen. They were accompanied by Baron Boris Shteiger, known around Moscow as "our home GPU" (State Political Department), as Elena describes him in her diary. Shteiger was in charge of foreign relations at the Commissariat for Education; he was also a secret police agent whose duties included spying on foreign diplomats and the artistic elite. He listened to the couple's conversation about people they had met at the embassy. Shteiger would surface in Bulgakov's novel as Baron Maigel, "in charge of acquainting foreigners with places of interest in the capital." The spy was liquidated in 1937 along with the Commissar for Education, Andrei Bubnov.

During one evening in November, to lift their spirits, the Bulgakovs went to the National Hotel, the best in the city, for supper and a dance. Upon arriving, they discovered the restaurant almost empty, no musicians, and only a group of foreigners eating at a table in the corner. Soon after, the couple found they were being watched: a young man took a table nearby and whispered with the waiter but did not order a meal. As he sat there staring at them, Bulgakov remarked, "That's for my soul." The couple would never return to this hotel, frequented by foreigners and by secret police, and would remember how the young man unashamedly followed them outside.

Bulgakov and Elena yearned for a vacation beyond the Soviet borders. They applied to go abroad for three months and as a pledge of their return were leaving the boys behind. But the authorities again denied Bulgakov permission to travel and see his plays in Paris and New York. He now realized it was not destined for him to "see the world." His father had died at forty-eight from nephrosclerosis, a kidney disease caused by hypertension, which Bulgakov believed he had inherited. He told Elena, shortly after they married, that he would die of the same disease and that he did not expect to outlive his father. She was alarmed, but, since doctors did not find anything wrong with Bulgakov, dismissed her fears. Bulgakov, however, did not allow her to forget: they would be sitting with guests and in the middle of their merriment, he would suddenly say, "'You are lucky to enjoy life, while I'll be dead soon.' And he would go on to describe his imminent death, but in such a comic way that it was impossible for all of us not to laugh. And I was first to burst out laughing."[655] In May of 1935, Bulgakov turned forty-four and his stories of how he would die became more recurrent.

On October 30, Akhmatova visited the couple: looking shaken and confused, she said her son Lev and her husband, the art historian Nikolai Punin,[656] had been arrested on the same night. Lev was arrested for the second time, and his only "crime" was being Akhmatova's son. Elena had never seen Akhmatova in such a pitiful state. She had come to consult Bulgakov, whom many considered an expert on writing letters to Stalin, about how to compose her petition. Bulgakov offered suggestions, such as to keep her letter short and make it hand-written. Two days later, again at their door, Akhmatova showed them a telegram telling of her family's release. Pasternak had also helped, having written Stalin on Akhmatova's behalf. Her son Lev, however, would be re-arrested three years later.

That year, the Bulgakovs met Pasternak at a birthday party where he recited his translations of Georgian poems. With pressure on writers to conform, Pasternak had stopped creating original work and earned his living as a translator. Elena thought Pasternak was unlike anyone else she had met and admired his dreamy-like style of rendering poetry. But most of all she liked the fact that he valued Bulgakov. Ignoring other writers, Pasternak made the first toast to Bulgakov, explaining that while others were officially recognized, Bulgakov was "an unlawful phenomenon."

That fall, Elena printed Bulgakov's new comedy, *Ivan Vasilievich*, about an engineer who built a time machine and transported his contemporaries to the epoch of Ivan the Terrible. Ironically, the theme was popular during Stalin's reign, despite the obvious analogy between two reigns of terror. The initial reception of his play was warm, and the reading at the Satire Theater followed "with huge success." In the Repertoire Committee, the play was examined by several censors. Unable to find anything suspicious, they made a marvelous suggestion: "Is it possible for Ivan the Terrible to say that things are better now than they were then?"[657] (Bulgakov did not heed this advice.) When the play was licensed, Elena felt Bulgakov's career was finally gaining momentum since, a month earlier, his Pushkin play had also been approved for performance. In addition, Sergey Prokofiev wanted to write an opera about Pushkin based on the play. Within a few months, Dmitry Shostakovich also considered it for an opera. He joined the couple for lunch at their house. After Bulgakov read from the play, Shostakovich performed his waltz and polka from *The Bright Stream*.

After more than four years of rehearsals, *Molière* premiered on February 16, 1936. It was a stunning success, with twenty-two curtain calls. Elena, victorious, reported events in her diary, "And so, the official premiere of *Molière* has taken place. How many years we have waited for it! The auditorium was, as Molière puts it, larded with distinguished persons . . . there were lots of academics, doctors, actors and writers."[658]

The Americans in the audience "were entranced" with the play, and their ambassador, William Bullitt, called Bulgakov "a master." A young fan approached Elena upon learning she was the author's wife, kissed her hand, and told her that "we students are tremendously happy that Bulgakov's work is again on stage. . . ." Throughout that month, *Molière* was performed to full houses, with a "resounding triumph." Simultaneously, a harassment campaign began in the press, led by the same critics and dramatists who previously had attacked Bulgakov. Motivated by political opportunism and personal envy, they demanded that the play be closed because it was "extraneous to the Soviet stage." On March 9, *Pravda* published an unsigned article, "Superficial Glitter and False Content," which spelled out the end of *Molière* and the end of Bulgakov's career as a playwright. That same day, the theater directors canceled the play, without even attempting to defend Bulgakov. "Here I will enter a large black cross," wrote Elena in her diary, referring to the final lines of her husband's play where Molière, out of favor with the king and hunted down by the Cabal, dies after performing his own play at the theater. "Misha's [Bulgakov's] fate is clear to me," she continued; "he will be alone and persecuted until the end of his days."[659]

The comedy about Ivan the Terrible, *Ivan Vasilievich*, was banned next. In the middle of the dress rehearsal at the Satire Theater, an official from the Moscow Party Committee arrived and, without taking off his coat, passed on the stock phrase to the director, "I don't advise you to produce it." In mid-March, attacks on *Pushkin* were launched, which meant this play would be also banished. Meantime, *The Turbins* was being produced in London and about to be staged in Norway, but the news from abroad did little to alleviate the doom the couple felt. "A difficult time for us," wrote Elena in her diary in March. "It's quiet, sad, and hopeless here after the death of *Molière*," Bulgakov told a friend.[660]

The staff at the Arts Theater pressed Bulgakov to write a repentant letter to the government, admitting his mistakes. Elena shielded Bulgakov from a flurry of phone calls from actors and her own sister proposing that he do just that. Elena retorted Bulgakov had nothing to repent. Theater administration demanded the return of an advance for the banned play *Flight*. Undaunted, Elena replied, "Show me the ban." Although there was no paper trail, the theater continued to insist that they return the money. By then, the couple was seventeen thousand rubles in debt, having lived for months on these advances and on the money they borrowed from friends.

To escape his gloomy thoughts, Bulgakov told Elena satirical tales in the evenings: Stalin and his Politburo come for Shostakovich's new opera at the Bolshoi. Stalin does not clap after the overture, which throws the conductor into despair. After the first act, the conductor and musicians crane their necks to see reaction from the government box: still no applause from Stalin. By the end of the opera, Shostakovich trembles with fear; the musicians and the cast only hope to stay alive. Stalin then holds a meeting with his retinue. "I don't like to impose my opinions on others, so I won't say that I believe the opera is a cacophony and muddle of music; now, I'm asking you comrades to offer your independent opinions." Asked to speak first, Voroshilov calls the opera a "musical muddle." Molotov, stammering from fear, says it's a "cacophony," and Kaganovich, whom Stalin addresses as a "Zionist," proposes it's a "musical muddle coupled with cacophony." Elena could not believe her eyes when next day, *Pravda* ran an unsigned editorial, titled "Muddle Instead of Music." The article was directed against Shostakovich's opera *Lady Macbeth of Mtsensk*, and the word "cacophony" was repeated several times. His ballet *The Bright Stream* was attacked next in an article headlined "False Notes at the Ballet." Shostakovich was out of tune with Party policy, and so was Bulgakov. Immersed in the newspapers, Elena read daily reports about the closure of theaters, exiles, and executions. There was also an avalanche of attacks on people from the literary and artistic spheres; Bulgakov's main tormentor Litovsky, the head of the Repertoire Committee, was not spared, losing his post, which partly satisfied Elena's thirst for retribution. "Litovsky is one of the vilest monsters I have encountered through Misha's literary career."[661]

In summer 1936, Bulgakov completed the first redaction of *The Master and Margarita*. His hero, the Master, who lives in their contemporary Moscow, writes a novel about Christ and Pontius Pilate, and is harassed for his mere attempt to publish it. Margarita, an ultimate literary wife, joins with supernatural forces to rescue the Master and secure eternal life for his novel. Bulgakov, who wrote this under an atheistic dictatorship, was reasserting his belief in freedom of expression. But unlike his hero, Bulgakov and Elena kept his novel secret, only holding occasional readings for trusted friends.

In the fall, Bulgakov resigned his job at the Arts Theater, which was now a painful reminder of *Molière*. As he told Elena, the theater had become "a graveyard of his plays." In October, he signed a contract with the Bolshoi to write opera libretti. His obsessive thoughts about his ruined literary career brought back his agoraphobia, and again he could not walk outside without Elena or little Sergei holding his hand.

Early in 1937, Bulgakov resumed his autobiographical novel about his experiences at the theater. Back in 1929, he had given Elena a first draft of this work, written as a series of letters to a "secret friend," saying it was his "present" to her. Having unearthed this notebook, he was now eagerly writing *A Theatrical Novel,* or *The Notes of a Dead Man,* as he renamed it. The new title reflected his mood: he told Elena that he pictured himself as a drowned man lying on shore with waves rolling over him. But despite this morbid mood and nervous exhaustion, he succeeded in writing one of his funniest works. He composed it with surprising ease, Elena recalls, and completed it without rewrites: "He would return from work at the Bolshoi, proceed to his study and while I was preparing the table, would settle at his bureau and write several pages. Then, he would emerge, rub his hands, and say, 'After dinner I will read you what I've got there.'"[662]

In winter and spring, Bulgakov read chapters from this novel to friends and former theater colleagues, who found it hilarious, recognizing themselves and their two famous directors, Stanislavski and Nemirovich. Elena's sister, who came with her husband Evgeny Kaluzhsky, an actor at the theater, also praised the novel despite her loyalty to Nemirovich. This merriment helped dispel the hopelessness the Bulgakovs felt about the future. Elena was "wildly enthusiastic" about this new novel and described it as the "most important" event in their lives.

Bulgakov's time and creative energy were now consumed with his day job as a librettist. Describing how his talents did not fit his work, he compared himself to a large factory contracted to produce cigarette lighters. His employment at the Bolshoi became a source of additional frustration when he could not escape political pressure even by writing historical libretti. In April, Bulgakov was summoned to the Central Committee and abused for his interpretation of the seventeenth-century Polish invasion of Russia. Bulgakov had failed to show the Russian people's role as sufficiently victorious, so the Party boss was guiding him onto the correct paths. Later in the year, Bulgakov received written instructions on how to rewrite his libretto about Peter the Great: "You should base yourself on comrade Stalin's formulation." The libretto's finale was found to be too idyllic, while it "must have some sort of song by the oppressed people."[663]

Describing developments in her diary, Elena quoted Bulgakov as saying that they had crushed him and now "they want to make him write in a way he refuses to write." His libretti were rejected like his plays. In fact, his native land did not need his writing: over the past seven years, he had created sixteen works in different genres, and all had been banned for political reasons, except his adaptation of Gogol's play *The Inspector*. He and Elena discussed his situation, regurgitating the same accursed question: what should he do? Should he quit the Bolshoi? Should he try to pursue publication of his novel about the Devil? She replied in her diary, "What can I say? To me, when he is not . . . writing his own work, life loses all meaning." Several friends, trying to console Bulgakov, told him that his works would be published posthumously, a "strange way" of cheering him up.

Expecting to live only a few more years, he felt his time was being wasted on unnecessary projects. The centenary of Pushkin's death that year revived their dashed hopes for this play. Bulgakov admitted that he could not hear the word "Pushkin" without a shudder and cursed himself for ever writing a play about him. Elena remembered her anticipation of seeing this play staged, but now "*Pushkin* is knifed and we are back to where we started." In March, the Kharkov Drama Theater initiated a lawsuit demanding the return of the advance for *Pushkin* on the grounds that the work had been banned. The theater was exploiting the situation and Bulgakov had to mount a defense. Elena managed to obtain the crucial piece of evidence, a written confirmation that the Repertoire Committee had licensed the play before issuing the ban. On April 2, Bulgakov presented the evidence in court, and a woman judge dismissed the case. The couple walked away with "moral satisfaction," but the affair had stolen time and energy.

Later that month, while Elena was not home, Nadezhda Mandelstam came to see Bulgakov. The Mandelstams' exile to Voronezh was ending, both were destitute, and neither Nadezhda nor Osip could obtain work. The Bulgakovs' situation seemed not as desperate by comparison. But Elena had her own sorrow: she was troubled by

Bulgakov's dejection when they learned that the Arts Theater was going to Paris and taking his play *The Turbins*: "I'm a prisoner . . . they'll never let me out . . . I'll never see the light."

June 1937 brought reports of more show trials: eight outstanding military commanders, many of whom Elena knew personally from her marriage with Shilovsky, were arrested and charged with treason. All were shot on June 11, when she read the dreadful announcement in *Pravda*. That same day, Bulgakov had to attend a meeting at the Bolshoi, one of many such meetings across the country where people were demanding death to traitors. Elena was particularly close with the family of General Uborevich, who was "tried" and shot on the same day as Marshal Tukhachevsky. Only two years before the start of the Second World War, Stalin destroyed all of the country's military elite. (Elena's first husband, officer Neelov, had been destroyed earlier, in 1936.[664])

In July, Elena persuaded Bulgakov to get away from Moscow, with its horrific atmosphere of trials and sweltering heat, and spend a month in the Ukrainian countryside, without newspapers and telephone calls. Since they did not have a kopeck in the house, Elena borrowed money from friends and they headed to Zhitomir, a small picturesque city in the western Ukraine. During the restful month in a village outside Zhitomir, Bulgakov wrote *A Theatrical Novel* and the Peter the Great libretto for the Bolshoi.

When they returned to Moscow, Elena made a clean copy of Bulgakov's libretto, only to be faced with a new crisis. This work was also rejected, and Bulgakov considered quitting the Bolshoi, but could not because they were desperately short of money. On top of his regular duties, he assisted staging productions and edited others' libretti, returning home exhausted and suffering migraines. Later at night, he would light candles in his study and start revising *The Master and Margarita*.

One night in November, as Bulgakov was working on the novel, they had a visitor from the Arts Theater, actor Grisha Konsky. Bulgakov had befriended this young and talented actor when playing the judge in *The Pickwick Papers*: they shared a dressing room.

Konsky had also come to their apartment for Bulgakov's readings of *A Theatrical Novel* but, more recently, behaved strangely. He interrogated Elena with questions about Bulgakov's work and was obviously spying on him. Elena caught him going through papers on Bulgakov's desk and scrutinizing his library. Their talented friend had become an informer.

That fall, the literary community was shaken by the arrest of the writer Boris Pilnyak. Bulgakov had known him for years, although they had never been friends. In the 1920s, Pilnyak had written a novella, *The Tale of the Unextinguished Moon*, wherein he implied that Stalin was responsible for the death of the military commander Mikhail Frunze. Despite that, Stalin permitted Pilnyak and his wife to travel abroad. The reckoning came a decade later. In late October 1937, Pilnyak was accused of spying, terrorism, and conspiring with writer André Gide, whom he allegedly supplied with negative facts about the Soviet Union. Elena recorded the news of his arrest with obvious trepidation. The following spring, Pilnyak was condemned to death during proceedings that lasted fifteen minutes.

In early 1938, their artistic community discussed two major events. One was the closure of Meyerhold's Theater and its director's imminent fate; the other—Shostakovich's comeback with the success of his Symphony No. 5 in D minor. The premiere in Leningrad the previous fall was an absolute triumph, with ovations lasting half an hour. The Bulgakovs attended the performance at the Moscow Conservatory on January 29. Elena remembers excited crowds in front of the Conservatory, throngs of people going up the marble staircase, ignoring Shostakovich while trying to get through. "After the symphony, the public made a standing ovation, calling for the composer. He came out—excited and pale as death." Shostakovich's return to public life, after extensive harassment in 1936, was a sensation in itself. The Bulgakovs, feeling hopeful and energized, stayed up all night, celebrating with friends in the bar of the Hotel Metropol. The occasion gave some hope to the Bulgakovs that a comeback was possible.

That year, the couple became particularly close with the Erdman brothers. Nikolai Erdman, a dramatist who had worked with director Meyerhold, had been deported to Siberia for his satirical fables in 1933. After serving a three-year sentence, he settled in the town of Kalinin, beyond the hundred-kilometer Moscow zone, where the Mandelstams also had to reside. In February 1938, Bulgakov wrote Stalin on Erdman's behalf, asking him to ease his punishment and to allow him to return to Moscow; Elena delivered the letter to the Central Committee. (While Bulgakov's petition was ignored, Erdman made a comeback in 1941 after writing a script for the major Soviet propaganda comedy *Volga-Volga*.) In 1938, however, Erdman secretly traveled to Moscow and visited the Bulgakovs with his brother Boris, a stage designer, and Elena relished their nightly conversations.

That winter and spring, Bulgakov was editing *The Master and Margarita* and reading chapters to friends. Nikolai Erdman was present during an April 7 reading, one which made "a tremendous impression" on the audience, Elena wrote. "Everyone was particularly impressed with the ancient chapters, which I also adore." Erdman spent the night at their apartment and had literary discussions with Bulgakov. "I'd kill myself for not knowing stenography; I wish I could record all their conversations."[665]

The ancient chapters, depicting Jerusalem two thousand years ago, were unlike anything in their contemporary literature. Elena wrote, after one of the readings: "The audience was wonderful, M.A. read very well. The interest in the novel is tremendous. Misha said at supper: soon I will send it in, it will be published. Everyone was tittering shyly." The novel's ancient chapters majestically portray the events leading to the crucifixion of Jesus under the rule of Pontius Pilate, the fifth Prefect of the Roman province of Judea from 26 to 36 CE. A philosopher preaching the Kingdom of Truth without state violence over individuals and with "no rule by Caesar" was revelatory in Soviet Russia. The story of Christ and Pilate and their conversation about good and evil took on greater meaning during the Terror, when all morality was abandoned.

The desire to see his novel published prevailed over the couple's bitter experience, and in May 1938 Bulgakov approached his old editor, Nikolai Angarsky, with whom he had worked in the 1920s. Elena recalls how the editor came to a reading at their house and, even before he heard Bulgakov's chapters from *The Master and Margarita*, proposed a different project:

> "Can you write a Soviet detective novel? You would have mass circulation, be translated into every world language; lots of money, hard currency. Should I give you an advance now?" Bulgakov refused the offer, saying, "No, I can't write this." When he read the first three chapters Angarsky said, "Well, we can't publish that." "Why not?" "Because we can't."

Bulgakov called *The Master and Margarita* his "sunset novel," marking the end of his literary career.[666] That spring, Elena frequently mentioned "the novel" in her diary. There was no hope of getting it published, but Bulgakov was revising it and driving himself hard. At the end of May, asking Olga to take over the final typing of the novel, Elena left for the town of Lebedyan on the Don River, with Sergei in tow. They settled in a rented cottage shared with relatives. From their scorching apartment, Bulgakov wrote letters daily; it was their second time apart in six years. His days were taken with rehearsals of Glinka's opera *Ivan Susanin*, a Soviet version of what had been known as *A Life for the Czar*. At night, he revised the chapter about Pontius Pilate. "Ah, what difficult, confusing material!"[667] Beginning to dictate to Olga, an expert typist who could withstand long hours without making slips, Bulgakov was afraid to interrupt for a single day. "The novel must be finished! Now! Now!"[668] Working at a furious pace, they succeeded in typing the new version, minus the final chapters, by mid-June.

> "And what will come out of it?" you ask. I don't know. Perhaps, you will put it away in the bureau or in the cupboard where the corpses of my plays lie, and at times you will

remember it. However, we cannot know our future. . . . I have already made my judgment of this work and if I manage to improve the ending I will think that it deserves proofreading and storing it in the darkness of the desk drawer. For the moment I am interested in your opinion, and nobody can tell whether I will ever know my readers' verdict.[669]

Olga, Bulgakov's "estimable typist," was a harsh judge, he wrote Elena, having smiled only once during the entire work, to the words "the lovely seaside." Even satirical scenes of their contemporary Moscow left her unmoved. Realizing that it was unpublishable, Olga uttered an "enigmatic" phrase: "This novel—is your private business." Bulgakov's "only joyous dream" was meeting Elena at the cottage, but lately he had begun to feel unwell, suffering from excruciating headaches and exhaustion. "I'm buried underneath this novel. . . . I've become completely withdrawn, and would be able to open myself up only to one person, but she isn't here! She is growing sunflowers!"[670] In a photograph she sent Bulgakov, Elena stands in the doorway of their country cottage, in a kerchief, looking at Sergei, who is behind the rock fence of their small garden.

After completing the novel in June and spending a month with Elena, Bulgakov was back in Moscow, writing an adaptation of *Don Quixote* for the Vakhtangov Theater. He was practicing Spanish and reading Cervantes in the original, and, to amuse Elena, was sending Spanish missives to her along with his Russian translation. He wrote in July that he imagined her "particularly vividly. If only I could sit and talk to you now!"[671] He hadn't read the Quixote play to anybody and would not read it until they made a clean copy together. In mid-August, they reunited in Moscow where a basket of flowers awaited Elena.

In the fall, the Repertoire Committee passed the Quixote play. But soon after, the play and its author were attacked in an abusive article. The critic's name, like the names of his other tormentors, would only be remembered in literary history in connection with Bulgakov; he pasted their scornful articles on the walls of their apartment. His critics continued to harass him because of his refusal to conform and because many were envious of his talent. The couple was in a "murderous" mood: even though Bulgakov had written twelve plays and was working without letup, they were still hard up.

In October, when the Arts Theater celebrated its fortieth anniversary, there was not a single mention of *The Turbins* and Bulgakov in the newspapers; by then, the play had been performed eight hundred times. "This is persecution by silence," Elena remarked.[672] The theater director Nemirovich and actors valued Bulgakov and wanted him back, but were afraid to mention him in the interviews. That fall, the theater directors and staff were showered with awards and money.

Stalin's sixtieth birthday was to be celebrated in December 1939, and theaters across the country competed for good plays about the leader. Envoys from the Arts Theater came to persuade Bulgakov to write a play about Stalin. "And since the plays of the other authors are extremely weak," observed Elena with glee, "they are hoping that Misha will bail them out."[673] Back in 1936, after the ban of *Molière*, Bulgakov had told his theater colleagues that Stalin was the only topic that interested him at present. But he needed archival materials for this play and realized that they could not be obtained. Shortly after this comment, Elena was at the Bolshoi and saw Stalin in his the government box: "I kept thinking about Stalin and dreaming that he would think of Misha, and our fate would be transformed."[674]

This was also the message of the Arts Theater envoys, who repeatedly told Bulgakov that the Stalin play would change his life and career. Visiting the couple in December 1938 and early in the New Year, they would sit all night, urging him to write the play. In addition, Nikolai Erdman advised him to do it, speaking so persuasively that Bulgakov compared him to a "sermonizing local archpriest."

In December, when Bulgakov was at home with flu, the couple was sorting out his archive. The spectacle of his banned plays so depressed Bulgakov that he told Elena he did not want to live.

She agreed that it was impossible to live and work without seeing the results. By then, he had a plan for the play about Stalin and described the first scenes to Elena. The play would be about Stalin's revolutionary youth in Georgia. Bulgakov had a premonition, however, that writing this play and getting into the spotlight was "too risky" for him and that it would all end badly.[675] Yet he was soon drafting the play.

Elena assumed her usual role, cheering Bulgakov onward: she loved the opening scenes, found that his play was artistically superior to existing ones on the subject, and felt that his characters sounded genuine. She believed their luck was about to turn; but for the first time, they were not together on this. Bulgakov remained cheerless, saying it was his last play, as earlier he had said *The Master and Margarita* was his last novel. In mid-July, Elena recorded chilling news: actress Zinaida Reich had been brutally murdered at her house, weeks after the arrest of her husband, director Meyerhold. After Meyerhold's Theater was shut down, Zinaida had written a critical letter to Stalin for his interference in the arts; this letter was believed to have sealed the couple's fate.

In summer 1939, Bulgakov was completing the play, which he named *Batum*, and Elena was energetically typing it. Even before it was licensed, requests began to pour in from many theaters. Directors vowed to challenge the exclusive right of the Arts Theater to produce *Batum*: "The entire country has to perform it!" Olga phoned to say that Nemirovich called Bulgakov "a marvelous playwright," and loved the main character. "I don't know how much of it is true and how much is false," Elena wondered on August 8, referring to the praise. The very newspapers that had harassed Bulgakov now wanted preliminary information about *Batum*, but Elena said they would have to wait.

Bulgakov's play was being read by Stalin, and the theater people expected his approval. The Arts Theater decided to rehearse the play in Batumi, a Georgian resort and the place where young Stalin had organized strikes before the Revolution. The Bulgakovs were to travel with the theater, and Elena was looking forward to their vacation by the Black Sea. Bulgakov asked her to postpone the trip, a request she dismissed, writing in her diary on August 14 that she could barely wait to go, "Is it possible we're leaving tomorrow! I can't believe my happiness."

On the train, the theater company had a banquet to prematurely celebrate Bulgakov's success: Elena served pies, pineapples in cognac, and other dainties. At the first station, a postwoman handed a telegram to Bulgakov. He turned white. The telegram said there was no need for the theater to travel further. When later that day they returned home, Bulgakov was in "a dreadful state." Pacing the dim rooms (he could not bear light), he was nervously rubbing his hands and saying the place smelled of a corpse, "maybe, that's the dead play?" Elena learned on the phone that the play had met with disapproval at the very top: it was unacceptable to turn Stalin into a fictional character. In addition, Bulgakov was accused of insincerity for having obviously written the play to revive his career. Later, the theater people told Elena that Stalin liked the play but still did not want it produced. Bulgakov's prophecy that *Batum* would be his last play came to pass. On August 27, inundated with phone calls from theaters and film studios asking about the play, Elena had to tell everyone it had been banned. She was even more troubled with Bulgakov's condition: "Misha feels crushed. . . . It's never been like this before." It was a double blow for Bulgakov, whose attempt at political compromise ended in humiliating defeat.

In early September, newspapers were full of reports about Hitler's invasion of Poland, but world events reached Elena through a haze. She was struck with Bulgakov's grave illness. She took him to Leningrad for a change of air, but they had to return immediately because he was losing his sight. In Moscow, specialists diagnosed him with nephrosclerosis, the kidney disease related to hypertension that had killed his father. The doctors' prognosis was that he had only days to live. Bulgakov, who had trained as a doctor and had studied this illness, disagreed and told Elena he would live another six months.

During these final months, suffering severe headaches and nearly blind, Bulgakov rarely left the house. On their few outings together he wore dark glasses and a black skullcap, which Elena had made for him, the same as the one on his literary hero, the Master. She spent days by his bedside, reading to him from the manuscript of *The Master and Margarita* and taking down his final revisions. Acquaintances visiting the Bulgakovs described Elena as completely altered, with deep sadness in her eyes. Olga wrote their mother in Riga that Elena continued to believe Bulgakov would recover and was determined to fight for his life. "'I won't give him up,' she says, 'I won't let him die.' Her love for him is so deep that it doesn't seem like a normal feeling between spouses who have already lived many years together."[676]

In the ending of *The Master and Margarita*, which Bulgakov then dictated to her, the writer and his wife retire to a symbolic refuge where they are granted eternity and peace. When Bulgakov bade farewell to Elena, he told her, "You were everything to me, you replaced the whole planet. In my dream we were together on the planet. . . . My . . . star, that always beaconed to me in my earthly life! You loved all of my works, I wrote them for you. . . ." Twenty years later, in a letter to his brother Nikolai, she recalled:

> My place was on a cushion on the floor next to his bed. He held my hand all the time. . . . On March 9 at about three in the afternoon the doctor said that he wouldn't live more than another two hours. . . . The night passed. On the morning of the 10th he was sleeping or slipping in and out of consciousness, and his breathing became faster, warmer and more even. And I suddenly thought, like a madwoman, that the miracle I had kept promising myself had come to pass. . . .

Bulgakov was lying on a mattress with only a towel around his hips: the mere touch of clothing on his skin gave him excruciating pain. During his final days he could barely speak, and she alone could guess the endings of his words.

"The Master and Margarita?" I asked, thinking that he was referring to the novel. "I promise you that I will submit it, I will get it published!" He listened attentively and said, "So that they would learn. . . ."[677]

Bulgakov was forty-eight when he died on March 10. The following morning, there was a call from Stalin's secretariat: "Is it true that comrade Bulgakov has died?" Bulgakov's friend, scriptwriter Sergei Ermolinsky, who took the call, replied that it was true, and the caller hung up.[678] Before the funeral, prominent sculptor Sergei Merkurov came to take Bulgakov's death mask. (Merkurov had made death masks of prominent writers and politicians, including Leo Tolstoy and Lenin.)

In June, Elena wrote to her mother, in Riga, "I lived with Misha's life and creative work. I've suddenly lost everything."[679] During his final months, Bulgakov told Elena, "When I die, they'll soon start to print me, theaters will snatch my plays from each other, and everywhere they'll start to invite you to give talks about your recollections of me."[680] He would go on describing how she would appear on stage in a black dress with a deep décolleté and begin reminiscing. Although he was saying this half-seriously, his words would discourage Elena from giving talks about Bulgakov.

Five days after his death, she received a letter from the influential writer Alexander Fadeev, future head of the Writers' Union. Having visited Bulgakov when he was ill, impressed with his talent and character, Fadeev had written a tribute to him: "Both political people and literary people know that he was a man who did not burden himself, in his art or in his life, with political lies, that his path was sincere. . . ."[681] The letter was the first official endorsement of Bulgakov's career. Shortly after, when the Writers' Union set up a committee to oversee Bulgakov's literary heritage, Elena asked Fadeev to chair it. She prepared Bulgakov's collection of plays for publication, but even Fadeev, despite his contacts in the Party, could not push it through censorship. Literary encyclopedias of the time described Bulgakov as a class enemy whose writings had ridiculed and discredited Soviet reality; they quoted Stalin's criticism of his play *Flight*.

Fadeev also became Elena's close friend. In October 1941, when Germans were approaching Moscow and panic began, he put Elena and teenaged Sergei on a train to Tashkent with a group of evacuated writers. Describing her farewell to Fadeev, Elena wrote in her diary, "At home . . . Sasha. Supper with him at eleven thirty. White wine."[682] Before leaving for Tashkent, she deposited Bulgakov's archive in the Lenin Library, taking with her only a cache of his manuscripts, including *The Master and Margarita*.

At forty-eight, still attractive and charismatic, Elena was never alone in the Tashkent writers' community. Those who read *The Master and Margarita* associated her with Bulgakov's enigmatic heroine. Akhmatova, also in Tashkent, called Elena "a sorceress" in a poem she dedicated to her. For Vladimira Uborevich, the daughter of the executed military commander, Elena's home replaced her own, which she had lost when her parents perished. Her mother, Elena's close friend, was shot in 1941 as the wife of "the enemy of the people." The girl had a tragic life, being raised in an orphanage and abused, as were all children whose parents had been purged. Elena took Vladimira home while in Tashkent, but the authorities would not leave the girl alone. In 1944, upon reaching eighteen, Vladimira was sentenced to five years in the Gulag for being Uborevich's daughter. In the 1960s, she would find Elena in Moscow and, at her advice, would begin to unburden herself of her horrific experiences by writing letters to her.

In Tashkent, Elena had extraordinary dreams or hallucinations about Bulgakov, which she recorded. It was her way of communicating with her husband beyond the grave: "His face feels warm, just as in life. . . . He subtly winks and smiles at me. Only the two of us know what that means—he will be coming back."

> Today I saw you in my dream. Your eyes, as always when you dictated to me, were enormous, blue, radiant, looking through me to something perceptible to you alone. They

were even bigger and brighter than in life.... I want to ask Misha all those things I did not ask in life. He is trying to make me laugh, recites funny poems. I want to remember them, to write them down.... I come up to him and tell him, "If you only knew how much I miss you...." He looks at me... with tears of joy. He asks, "So then the other man ... does not satisfy you?" He is pleased.

In June 1943, Elena returned to Moscow and was reunited with her sister and with Bulgakov's archive. She wrote poet Vladimir Lugovskoy, with whom she had become intimate in Tashkent, "Now I am fully immersed in the past, spending hours over the notebooks, letters, picture albums...."[683] During the war, when publishing and staging Russian classics was encouraged as a way to boost the morale, the Arts Theater staged Bulgakov's play about Pushkin. Upon returning to Moscow, Elena attended every performance. For the first time, finding herself almost without means, she worked in an artisan cooperative, making hats, and later in the Arts Theater museum. It was also for money that she wrote a play, with a co-author taking it to the Arts Theater. Although the theater apparently approved and held a reading, the play was never licensed for performance. In 1946, Elena wrote a script and signed a contract with a film studio, but, like her play, this work was not destined see light.[684] Bulgakov's name continued to inspire vigilance and closed opportunities for Elena as well.

Immediately after the war, Elena made six attempts to publish *The Master and Margarita*. In 1946, she passed a letter, through a seamstress who worked in a government parlor, to Stalin's personal secretary Alexander Poskrebyshev. In a while, Poskrebyshev phoned to say that the reply would be positive and suggested the person she could approach in the State Publishing House. Elena was elated, but her hopes were dashed that summer with the start of an ideological campaign against Akhmatova and Zoshchenko, a satirical writer.

In the early 1950s, she herself printed Bulgakov's collected works on her typewriter and bound the volumes. Elena would give this samizdat collection to people who could help publish Bulgakov. In 1954, the liberal writer Veniamin Kaverin, first to resurrect Bulgakov's name, favorably mentioned him at a Writers' Congress. The next day, Elena sent him a basket of flowers and a copy of Bulgakov's samizdat collection.[685] In 1955, Kaverin became instrumental in helping her publish a volume containing two of Bulgakov's plays. Although it was mutilated by censors, Elena felt it would pave the way for other books. Sensing the advent of Bulgakov's posthumous fame, she even bought a splendid journal to record the progress of his publication. In 1956, she documented in it the publication of Molière's biography, which appeared more than two decades after it had been written, but in abridged form, like his plays. Elena agreed to the cuts just to get the book published. By then she had secured the support of the prominent writer Konstantin Simonov, editor-in-chief of the *Literary Gazette* and the head of the Writers' Union. But even with the help of famous people, progress in the 1950s was slow, and it was only possible to make one publication at a time.

Bulgakov's major play, *Flight*, made its way to audiences in 1957. A theater in Stalingrad was the first to stage it, and Elena, thrilled, planned to attend the premiere. Her trip was postponed when she slipped on the ice and broke her arm. That year, the play was also staged in Leningrad and Moscow to full houses. Interviewed by Moscow radio for airing abroad, Elena said that this work's production held great emotional importance to her because *Flight* was the play Bulgakov valued most: "He loved it as a mother would love her child."[686] That year, she suffered personal tragedy when her older son Evgeny, who coincidentally also suffered from hypertension, died at thirty-five.

In the early 1960s, Elena again attempted to publish *The Master and Margarita*. She took the manuscript to poet Alexander Tvardovsky, editor in chief of *Novy Mir*, which published Solzhenitsyn's novella *One Day in the Life of Ivan Denisovich* in 1962. Tvardovsky visited Elena at home, and she recorded his words in her diary: "He said he was stunned to realize the scale of Bulgakov's talent. 'His contemporary writers cannot measure up to him.' He spoke at length about his impressions from the novel, but ended by saying—'I have to be honest with you, it's now impossible to raise a question of its publication. I hope we will return to this when there will be a real opportunity.'"[687] Their conversation took place during the Thaw, but Tvardovsky felt that times were not ripe to publish the novel, which the premier, Khrushchev, would clearly not understand or support.

After a two-decade struggle for publication, Elena wrote Bulgakov's brother, Nikolai, in Paris that hers was Sisyphean toil. Many times she was about to succeed with *The Master and Margarita*, when events interfered at the last moment, ruining her efforts. Yet nothing could shake her faith in Bulgakov's genius: "I believe, I firmly believe, that the entire world will soon know his name...." Achieving recognition for Bulgakov became her crusade, "the goal and the meaning of my life."[688]

In the 1960s, journalists and Bulgakov's biographers came to interview Elena, finding that she knew his texts by memory and was eager to talk about him for hours. She was an excellent storyteller, but instead of writing her own memoir, as she had wanted, she gave the material to others. She wrote Bulgakov's family in Paris in 1962, "I am doing all I can to publicize his every line and unveil his extraordinary personality.... I had promised him many things before he died and I believe that I'll fulfill all my promises."[689]

Vladimir Lakshin, deputy editor of *Novy Mir* and Elena's good acquaintance, describes her visit to the magazine. At her request, Lakshin phoned her to say it was an opportune moment to meet Tvardovsky. Thinking it would take her at least an hour to get to the magazine, Lakshin was surprised when she appeared within minutes. "Elena Sergeevna stood in the doorway, wearing a spring black coat, a hat with a fine veil; graceful, beautiful, smiling.... 'How?!' I yelled. 'How did you get here....?' 'On a broom,' she replied, laughing...."[690] Dressed like Margarita, Elena was living her role as a witch while promoting Bulgakov's work. "She was young and beautiful, her laughter was resonant and exciting. And the low, coarse notes of Margarita no one would fail to recognize."[691]

But again it was impossible for the magazine to take it on: Khrushchev's demise in the fall of 1964 ended the short Thaw. Now, *The Master and Margarita* could not appear in *Novy Mir*: censors held the magazine by the throat after it published Solzhenitsyn's novella. When, in 1965, *Novy Mir* brought out Bulgakov's politically less charged *Theatrical Novel*, Elena was seventy-two and still waiting to see Bulgakov's major novel printed. Simonov, experienced and well connected to the Party, suggested taking the novel to an obscure journal, *Moscow*, where censors were not as watchful.

In winter 1966–67, with Simonov's help, *The Master and Margarita* at last appeared, abridged and without the ancient chapters about Christ and Pilate, in the journal. When it was published, word spread quickly and subscriptions to the journal soared. In libraries, there were waiting lists to read it. Eager to keep a copy of the novel, readers ripped out the pages with *The Master and Margarita* from the journal and substituted them with trashy works of socialist realism. In 1967, as she was holding the journal with the novel, Elena told Lakshin that her greatest fear was to die before keeping her word to Bulgakov. Her dream came true when that same year the full text of *The Master and Margarita* was published by Harper & Row in New York and, the following year, was released in Paris in French translation. Bulgakov's name was becoming known around the world.

In 1967, Elena published her translation of a biography by André Maurois, *Lélia, the Life of George Sand*. She had published her translations from the French before, but this would be her most successful book, which ran to several reprints. However, it was only Bulgakov's success that interested her. By then, she had already achieved publication for his plays and his first novel, *The White Guard*. Bulgakov's books and productions were becoming instantly popular; his quotations were repeated in every house. A writer of great versatility, an ingenious storyteller who was comfortable with almost every genre and style, Bulgakov became a champion for generations of Russian readers. Elena's story of how she had preserved his archive and pursued publication became a powerful legend, adding to his reputation.

Bulgakov's fame transformed Elena's life: publishers were inviting her to France and Eastern Europe. In April 1967, she wrote Bulgakov's family in Paris, "Misha is now recognized as a remarkable writer, he is translated in dozens of countries, in France, England, Italy, Spain, Hungary, Czechoslovakia, Poland, Finland etc., etc."[692] But traveling abroad remained complicated: when applying for exit visas, she had to write elaborate explanations of her trip. In September 1967, when Nikolai Bulgakov's widow, Ksenia, invited her to Paris, Elena explained to the authorities that the goal of her trip was to bring Bulgakov's archive to their homeland. Nikolai Bulgakov, a renowned bacteriologist, had corresponded with his brother for decades, and so she had to sort these letters and other materials. In addition, she had to explain how many of her relatives lived abroad. Aside from Bulgakov's family, there was also her own. Her brother Alexander Nurenberg had died, but his family was in Hamburg, Germany; her niece, Henrietta Book, lived in London; and there was also some family in Czechoslovakia, all those people whom both she and Bulgakov had been denied a chance to visit.[693]

Arriving in Paris after Bulgakov's novel was published there, Elena received bunches of flowers from his fans. She walked through the streets that Bulgakov had longed to see and stood by the monument to Molière he had described in the biography. The monument disappointed her: the original appeared inferior to her husband's imagination. She visited Germany, Poland, Czechoslovakia, and Hungary, places where Bulgakov's novel had become wildly popular.

In July 1970, on a hot summer evening in Moscow, Lakshin drove Elena to see raw footage for the film *Flight*, the first work by Bulgakov to make it to the large screen. Elena had been involved in its production as a consultant and now finally saw this powerful film with prominent actors in major roles. The studio screening room was packed and the heat suffocating. The day after seeing Bulgakov's major work, Elena died of a heart attack, at seventy-six. She was not to witness Bulgakov's unmatched popularity in their country, an avalanche of his publications and productions in the decades that followed, and the genuine public outpouring of love for him.

Her ashes were buried in Novodevichy Cemetery, in the same grave as Bulgakov's, under a granite headstone. For some time after Bulgakov's death, she had looked for a suitable monument to install on his grave and spotted a black porous stone lying in the cemetery's debris. The stone-cutters told her that the rock, weighing several tons, came from Gogol's grave and was called "Golgotha." The symbolic stone recalling the place of Christ's execution had been erected on Gogol's grave at the Danilovsky Monastery. During an anti-religious campaign in 1931, when Gogol's remains were moved to Novodevichy Cemetery, "Golgotha" with a cross atop it was discarded. *The Master and Margarita* describes the crucifixion on Mount Golgotha and makes references to Gogol, Bulgakov's esteemed writer. Elena had found a fitting monument for Bulgakov, his creation, and for herself—and produced a memorable legend.

Chapter Six

Natalya Solzhenitsyn: Sister of My Work

Although twenty years separate Natalya's beginnings from Solzhenitsyn's, the couple had major things in common: the gulag and the Second World War, which afflicted his life, had also scarred her childhood. She was born on July 22, 1939, months after her grandfather, Ferdinand Svetlov, a prominent Bolshevik publicist, was purged. Sentenced to eight years in the concentration camps of the Komi Republic, the harsh climate had killed him before his term ended.

Natalya does not remember her father, Dmitry Velikorodny. She was an infant when in 1941, during the Nazis' advance on Moscow, he volunteered for the ill-equipped people's militia and perished. What Natalya remembers from early childhood was her family's dire need and hunger (they lived with her widowed grandmother). Her mother, Ekaterina Ferdinandovna, a student at the Moscow Aviation Institute where she also worked, alone supported the family. They also had to send food parcels to Natalya's grandfather in the gulag until his death in 1943. Natalya's humble beginnings were familiar to Solzhenitsyn, also raised by a single mother whom authorities harassed as "a social alien." Natalya's mother, however, managed to circumvent Soviet questionnaires designed to detect suspect political backgrounds. She became an aeronautical engineer and worked in defense, the most guarded sector of all.

Natalya remembers wartime Moscow, getting up in the dark, as the city was under blackout, and taking long rides on a double-decker trolley to the kindergarten at the Aviation Institute. Her mother told stories to distract her from the cold and hunger. In the evenings, Natalya was always last to be picked up because her mother worked overtime. The Aviation Institute employed test pilots who came to fetch their children from the kindergarten. "I watched them come for their boys and girls, watched with envy and hope: what if my father was alive? What if some man . . . would come and ask for me, 'And where is Natasha Svetlova?'"[694]

But she did not feel miserable in childhood: in fact, her first memory was waking up with joy. Hardship made her stronger and taught her to appreciate being alive in a country plagued by war and genocide. She possessed the same vitality that enabled Solzhenitsyn to survive the war, prison camp, and a cancer clinic. His past mattered to Natalya a great deal: he was a living link to the father and grandfather she never knew. Two decades into her marriage, Natalya would say, "I am grateful to God for keeping Alexander Isaevich alive . . . that we have healthy and wonderful sons. . . ."[695]

Her mother was often away on business trips and Natalya, left on her own, made good use of her grandfather's exquisite library. It had rare volumes of literary and historical works published before Stalin's era and no longer available. When, in high school, she studied Stalin's course on Communist Party history, she compared it against these original works. Her interest in Bolshevik history and knowledge of undistorted facts would impress Solzhenitsyn.

Learning to type at twelve on a German Torpedo typewriter her mother owned, Natalya produced samizdat poems by Mandelstam and Marina Tsvetaeva, bound the copies herself, and gave them to friends. Coincidentally, Tsvetaeva was also esteemed by Solzhenitsyn, who particularly liked her prose.

Natalya was ambitious in school, graduating with a gold medal. She also engaged in sports, winning the Soviet Union's rowing championship twice, and pursued mountain climbing, skiing, and shooting rapids. As a university student, she went hiking and skiing in the Urals, the Caucasus, and the Altai Mountains and also traveled to Tyan Shan and Pamir. (In winter 1959, her group was caught in a blizzard in the Caucasus and spent the night in a mountain valley. By morning, their skis were irretrievably buried in snow, requiring them to walk back to base. All survived, but with serious frostbite.)

Natalya wanted to be a journalist, like her grandfather, but during an orientation day at Moscow University realized that hardliners were still in control and her training would consist of ideological drills. Her generation was steeped in Khrushchev's Thaw and believed in freedom of expression. To maintain it, Natalya chose mathematics, which she had liked in school, and continued her literary pursuits on her own. She entered the Faculty of Mechanics and Mathematics, known for its open-mindedness (in 1965, Mandelstam's first poetry evening would be held there). Solzhenitsyn had made a similar choice before the war, which he called his "mathematical rescue." He studied mathematics and physics at Rostov University because Soviet literature was so infected by politics that just discussing it could land one in trouble.

At twenty-one, Natalya married Andrei Tiurin, a gifted mathematician, who had joined her skiing expeditions and shared her interests in samizdat. Their son Dmitry was born a year later, but the marriage would not last. In 1962, the year Dmitry was born, Natalya read Solzhenitsyn's novella *One Day in the Life of Ivan Denisovich*. She "immediately sensed it was a great event."[696]

It was a feeling many across the country shared. When Alexander Tvardovsky, the editor of *Novy Mir*, first read Solzhenitsyn's manuscript, he sensed the emergence of a powerful new literature. Having read the novella at night, the editor could barely wait to share his impressions. In the morning, he burst into his friends' apartment shouting that a new great writer was born, that he had never read anything like this before. Realizing that Khrushchev alone could sanction publication of the gulag writer, Tvardovsky gave him the manuscript. This was before the XXII Party Congress dismantling Stalin's personality cult. Khrushchev gave his personal permission to publish the novella, and it came out on time for the congress. Delegates received a red book with Khrushchev's speech and a blue volume of the magazine with Solzhenitsyn's novella.

Ivan Denisovich became the first published account about the gulag in the Soviet Union. The novella was not only a work of literature: it was a political event, which rocked the country after decades of dictatorship and made the author an instant celebrity. The magazine's total circulation of one hundred thousand copies was sold out in a single day. But the demand was much greater: there were waiting lists to read it. Playing on the novella's title, a reader sent a telegram to the magazine: "I congratulate you with one day that has changed the world."[697] Solzhenitsyn received hundreds of letters, many from former gulag inmates. Famous writers and intellectuals sought his acquaintance. Akhmatova, then living in Moscow, invited Solzhenitsyn and told him that she was happy to have lived to see his novella and that everyone in the Soviet Union should read it. Akhmatova also introduced Solzhenitsyn to Elena Bulgakov, to whom he gave a signed copy of the magazine with his novella. (Over the years, Solzhenitsyn would stay in touch with Elena, sending her postcards and photographs.) The novella soon became an international event: translated into many languages, it was published in Europe and in America.

Natalya did not seek acquaintance with Solzhenitsyn when he became a celebrity. Actually, she could have met him through her dissident circle if she had wanted to, but her time was consumed with her motherly duties and the graduate school where she studied under the world-famous mathematician Andrei Kolmogorov. Their meeting was predestined, however. In 1968, Solzhenitsyn's major ally Natalya Stolyarova, who had arranged to smuggle the microfilm of *The Gulag Archipelago* abroad, told the writer he needed to broaden his network of allies and meet energetic young people. She suggested Natalya, whom she had met at Nadezhda Mandelstam's house.

Solzhenitsyn's encounter with Natalya took place at her apartment on August 28, 1968. A week earlier, Soviet tanks had rolled into Prague to crush Czechoslovakia's attempt to liberalize its Communist regime. In Moscow, a group of seven young dissidents went to Red Square to express solidarity with the Prague Spring. Just as the protesters unfolded their banner, they were beaten by the KGB and rushed away in police cars. Solzhenitsyn had learned about this from a BBC broadcast, while Natalya offered her insider view. She had ties to the emerging human-rights movement: two members of the group were her friends, and she had considered joining them in Red Square.

> And now this intense young woman with her dark hair swept forward above her hazel eyes and without a trace of affectation in her manner and her dress was telling me not just how the demonstration had gone but even how it had been planned. . . . I was very taken with her fervent social concern—this was my kind of temperament. I could not wait to involve her in our work![698]

This conversation established immediate trust between them and Solzhenitsyn asked Natalya whether she could type *The First Circle*. He gave her a long version of the novel containing ninety-six chapters. She willingly accepted, but told him that she was working on her doctorate and teaching undergraduate classes, so she could only work for two hours each evening. Natalya and her six-year-old son shared a small apartment with her mother, stepfather, and grandmother, and the only room where she could type was their small kitchen.

The work took Natalya four months to complete, and during this period Solzhenitsyn visited many times. Natalya proved to be a capable and interested editor and, aside from typing, suggested changes, verified facts, and presented Solzhenitsyn with meticulous queries. "She even put me right on details of Communist Party history, not an area in which I had expected her to have any expertise. . . ." Natalya was typing his chapters without a single error and "with an excellent eye for presentation," an aspect Solzhenitsyn had not considered before. His manuscripts were dense, double-sided pages, typed without margins and paragraphs. He was an underground writer perennially fearing a search, and his only concern was condensing text to save space. Solzhenitsyn's official life in Soviet letters ended soon after Khruschchev's ouster in 1964. By the time he met Natalya, his several publications had been removed from library shelves and he was under close KGB watch.

On one of his visits, he asked Natalya whether she could keep his illicit archive, to which she replied that "she would take care of it." She organized an efficient system of storing his papers. First of all, she read everything he wrote, then sorted his manuscripts and catalogued them, specifying what was in each bundle.

Because Solzhenitsyn was under surveillance, Natalya could not store his archive at her apartment: the KGB knew all his comings and goings. It had to be smuggled out by her regular visitors. Her ex-husband Tiurin, who often came to visit their son, would not raise suspicion, so Natalya approached him first. Tiurin agreed to take the risk and arranged for his sister Galina, a professor of algebra, to store the archive at her place. She kept the manuscripts in her attic with her skiing equipment, and even her family did not know.

Natalya's major concern was not for her own safety or even that of her friends: the arrangement had to suit Solzhenitsyn first. Her system, resembling interlibrary loans, allowed him to quickly retrieve any paper from his archive. "She would keep track of everything herself—who was storing what and how it was to be collected and returned—leaving my head clear for other things. I just had to deliver what I had finished and order what I needed." For a writer who treasured his time, the arrangement was perfect. Natalya numbered a duplicate set of postage stamps, creating a catalogue to identify the bundles. She kept one set at home, along with a coded list, and another on the packages. When Solzhenitsyn placed an order, Natalya checked her catalogue and passed the proper stamp to Tiurin, who gave it to Galina. Her conspiratorial system worked flawlessly: "To describe her as businesslike would be an understatement; she worked with an alacrity, meticulousness, and lack of fuss that were the equal of any man."

In Natalya he found a trusted friend who was also of the same mind, and helpful on various fronts. He discussed with her everything from his writing to conspiratorial work and response to the authorities, including how and when to act. "Hitherto, I had faced all my crucial strategic decisions alone, but now I had gained an extra pair of critical eyes, someone I could argue things out with and who, at the same time, was a dependable counselor, whose spirit and manner were as unyielding as my own." He became smitten by the much-younger woman, perspicacious and dedicated to his cause, and wanted to see her more often.

Nearing fifty, he was married to Natalya Reshetovskaya, his high school sweetheart.[699] She had recently helped Solzhenitsyn with correspondence and had worked secretly to microfilm his novel *The Gulag Archipelago*. But the relationship was strained by many things: his arrest, imprisonment, and divorce (Reshetovskaya had married another man while Solzhenitsyn was in the gulag). The couple remarried after Solzhenitsyn's return, but had continual disagreements. Solzhenitsyn maintained that his work came first and, while quarreling with her, would say, "I don't need a wife, I don't need a family, I need to write my novel."[700] His second Natalya, Alya, as he called her affectionately, knew instinctively what he needed and requested nothing for herself.

> The fourth or fifth time we met, I put my hands on her shoulders as one does when expressing gratitude and confidence to a friend. And this gesture instantly turned our lives upside down: from now on she was Alya, my second wife, and two years later our first son was born.

Months into their acquaintance, Natalya told a friend, "I was very fond of my husband but until now I never knew what love was."[701] They became "firmly united" in November 1968 when both discovered they wanted a child. Although Solzhenitsyn thought radiation treatment for his cancer had left him infertile, he was hoping for a miracle.

In the fall of 1968, Solzhenitsyn's novels *Cancer Ward* and *First Circle* appeared in the West and became bestsellers. The following year, the American Academy of Arts and Letters made him an honorary member. But recognition in the West only intensified harassment at home. Having received threats and realizing that the KGB could kill him, Solzhenitsyn decided to designate a literary heir. All of his manuscripts were in Natalya's hands, including *The Gulag Archipelago*, the novel that contained more than two hundred testimonies of former inmates. It was only logical to turn over his literary estate to her: Solzhenitsyn wrote a will and was relieved that his work was placed in "the firm and faithful hands of my heir."

The situation with Pasternak's *Doctor Zhivago* repeated itself when, in November 1969, Solzhenitsyn was expelled from the Writers' Union for publishing his works abroad. He rushed to share the news of his purge with Natalya, but she was away on a skiing trip. When she returned from the Caucasus, he came to consult her about tactics. Her advice was laconic: "We've got to hit back!" It matched his determination to launch a counter-battle. In fact, Solzhenitsyn had already written an open letter to the Party and the Writers' Union; he wanted to show it to Natalya before releasing it. Unintimidated by the expulsion, Solzhenitsyn attacked the government head-on. Alluding to Pasternak's harassment a decade earlier, he told Soviet rulers to reset their clocks and open their heavy curtains to see the world outside. In addition, he demanded abolition of censorship, a major societal ill, and "full *glasnost*."[702] Solzhenitsyn's letter stunned his opponents in the Party and the Writers' Union. But it also made the liberal magazine *Novy Mir*, which had published and defended him, a convenient target. Tvardovsky was appalled when he received a copy of the letter and angry that Solzhenitsyn had not even warned him. From then on, the authorities waited for a suitable moment to take revenge on the magazine. Within a year, *Novy Mir*'s senior staff was dismissed on Party orders and Tvardovsky was forced to resign; having lost his magazine, the editor had a stroke and died in 1971.

Solzhenitsyn was burning his bridges. He considered emigrating and had discussed it with Natalya, which generated their first argument. "Alya thought that everyone should live and die in his homeland whatever turn things took, and I thought, camp fashion, let those who are stupid enough die; I'd sooner live to see my work published."[703] Fighting "a Goliath," or the Communist state, was better from abroad, where his works would appear uncensored.[704]

Soviet authorities believed Solzhenitsyn's exile would diminish his harm, so calls to expel him became more frequent. Attempts to intimidate him produced an outpouring of sympathy from abroad: Western writers, such as Arthur Miller, Alberto Moravia, Jean-Paul Sartre, Louis Aragon, and Elsa Triolet sent letters in his support to the Soviet government.

In the fall of 1969, cellist Mstislav Rostropovich sheltered Solzhenitsyn at his dacha in Zhukovka, where authorities would not dare touch him. Ironically, at the height of the campaign against him, Solzhenitsyn found himself in a privileged settlement with government dachas. From there he would travel to Moscow to see Natalya and drop off subversive chapters of his new revolutionary sequence *The Red Wheel*.

Around this time, Solzhenitsyn visited her to deliver the Lenin chapters from this work, which were as "incriminating" as *The Gulag Archipelago*. He left the manuscript with her despite knowing he was being trailed: he spotted several KGB agents from the window of Natalya's apartment. As he would later explain, his desire to return to work at the dacha without wasting time was responsible for this failure of conspiratorial tactics. Back at the dacha, he realized his mistake and lived through "the torments" of having his archive confiscated. "Consumed with apprehension," and envisioning the worst, he rushed back to Moscow, but the would-be "disaster" did not strike this time. (In 1965, the KGB seized Solzhenitsyn's archive from his friend, Veniamin Teush.) Despite his and Natalya's desire to have a child, both were more concerned about his archive than their own safety.

In summer 1970, Natalya gave Solzhenitsyn the news he was waiting for: she was pregnant. Although Natalya said she was prepared to raise their child alone, he immediately wrote Reshetovskaya, revealing the seriousness of their relationship. "I truly *wanted* a child for my old age, *wanted* to have my extension on earth."[705] The admission embittered Reshetovskaya. She would not grant Solzhenitsyn a divorce at a time when he had risen to the top, she told her family. In early October, after the announcement of Solzhenitsyn's Nobel Prize, Reshetovskaya arrived at Rostropovich's dacha, where days later she took an overdose of sleeping pills. But her attempted suicide was discovered, and she was taken to the hospital and saved.

When Solzhenitsyn was awarded the Nobel Prize, Natalya felt "absolute elation, triumph, joy for him and for all of us." There was also her despair because both realized that if Solzhenitsyn were to collect the Prize in Stockholm, Soviet authorities could refuse his re-entry. Nonetheless, when he discussed it with Natalya, she said he ought to go. Later recalling her difficult choice, she would remark, "Our marriage was not registered; I was pregnant with Ermolai, our firstborn. . . . He clearly had to go, but they would definitely refuse to let him back. This would mean separation forever."[706] The Soviet authorities had already considered revoking Solzhenitsyn's citizenship and even drafted such a resolution. In November, the writer decided against traveling to Stockholm and proposed that the Academy give him his diploma and medal in Moscow.

On December 10, Natalya was invited to Rostropovich's dacha to celebrate two events—the Prize and Solzhenitsyn's fifty-second birthday. Despite her capacity for stress, the tension of the past year was beginning to show. On December 30, she gave birth to Ermolai six weeks prematurely. Solzhenitsyn sent her an ecstatic letter to the hospital, calling the birth "a great event." He wrote in his diary that while he had several novels, this was his first son![707] Friends heard him say he had never been so happy, a significant admission for an obsessive writer.

Rostropovich's wife, opera soprano Galina Vishnevskaya, who had observed Solzhenitsyn at her dacha, remarked that he "lived only to write." Getting up before everyone else, he would work at a wooden table outside, so the first thing she would see "was Solzhenitsyn pacing off the kilometers like a tiger—walking alongside the fence, back and forth. Then he would go to the table quickly and write. . . . One felt that his ideas obsessed him, and pulsed feverishly within. . . ."[708]

Rostropovich was asked to be Ermolai's godfather. During a lunch after the christening, Vishnevskaya had a good look at Natalya, "a strong woman and the personification of a good wife and mother. . . . I realized that such a woman would follow him [Solzhenitsyn] into the fire without thinking twice."[709] The christening was celebrated at Natalya's new downtown apartment on central Gorky Street.[710] (Three years later, Solzhenitsyn would be led away by the KGB from this apartment.) Natalya had acquired the flat through a clever exchange in the fall of 1970. Soon after, the house manager received a call from the Politburo, requiring him to find adjoining quarters for the KGB so they could conduct surveillance over the inhabitants. Natalya and Solzhenitsyn knew that their conversations were being recorded around the clock.

Her flat became headquarters of the Solzhenitsyn conspiracy: here his manuscripts were photographed for smuggling abroad. In 1971, the couple decided to make another copy of *The Gulag Archipelago* with his latest revisions and Natalya asked her friend Valery Kurdyumov, a physicist, to microfilm the updated version. Kurdyumov, whose father was a former gulag prisoner, did not refuse to come to her apartment, despite knowing the risk. Microfilming could have been performed elsewhere, but Natalya wanted him to photograph all versions of this extensive novel and even raw drafts. Kurdyumov brought his equipment to her apartment, where for three days and nights he photographed the manuscripts and developed the film. It was to be deposited in Zurich with

Solzhenitsyn's lawyer, Dr. Fritz Heeb, retained through Natalya's efforts. Kurdyumov would pay a high price with his career. Upon Solzhenitsyn's deportation in 1974, he was interrogated by the KGB in the Lubyanka headquarters and threatened with dismissal from the high-security Radio-Technical Institute of the USSR Academy of Sciences. (Other people who had helped Solzhenitsyn also would later be interrogated, threatened with arrest, and beaten, and would lose their jobs. Rostropovich and Vishnevskaya were restricted from performing and had to leave the Soviet Union in 1974.)

Natalya was instrumental in arranging a steady circle of allies with channels to the West, through which Solzhenitsyn would also send his novel *August 1914*. It was delivered to his Paris publisher, Nikita Struve, with a traveler, an unsuspecting French policeman, who thought he was taking "a big box of candy for a sick nun."

In August 1971, while collecting material for *The Red Wheel* in Novocherkassk, southern Russia, Solzhenitsyn was trailed closely by the KGB and injected with a poisonous substance. Although he had not been exposed to the sun, he developed enormous blisters, typical of a second-degree burn, that spread over the entire left side of his body. Within hours he was incapacitated. Back at Rostropovich's dacha, doctors diagnosed him with a massive allergy caused by a highly toxic substance. Still, the cause of his illness remained a mystery until 1992, when a retired KGB colonel, Boris Ivanov, published his account of their failed attempt to assassinate Solzhenitsyn. He described how they tracked Solzhenitsyn in Novocherkassk: one agent followed him on foot through the city, communicating with the rest through a radio transmitter. When Solzhenitsyn entered a crowded grocery store, several agents followed him there. They almost pressed against him while he stood in line and, apparently, it was then that the poisonous substance was injected. Their entire "operation" lasted three minutes. When the KGB agents left the store, Ivanov, who was waiting outside, heard them say, "Now he is done for. It won't take long." In 1994, Ivanov gave Solzhenitsyn a note with names of the other participants.[711] While Solzhenitsyn was bedridden, Natalya came to the dacha to care for him. He was only able to resume writing five months later, the only such interruption in his career.

There was also a setback with Solzhenitsyn's divorce that year: the court granted his wife a six-month adjournment. The authorities supported Reshetovskaya, making the divorce a political affair that would drag on for another year; however, Solzhenitsyn became only more determined to end his marriage. Without being legally married, Natalya would have no visiting rights in the event of his arrest; and if he were deported, she and their son could not follow. In winter 1972, Solzhenitsyn was alerted to a new assassination plan; surprisingly, the information came from a government source, the daughter of the minister of Internal Affairs. Rostropovich's neighbor at the dacha, she told Solzhenitsyn that the KGB was planning to kill him in a car crash. The Internal Affairs minister wanted to prevent this from happening, having advised his government colleagues that Solzhenitsyn's harassment was undermining the country's international prestige. Instead, he suggested treating Solzhenitsyn kindly—"Don't kill the enemy, smother him with a hug"—but his shrewd letter was ignored.[712]

In February, German writer Heinrich Böll, dedicated to human-rights activism, came to Moscow with the goal of meeting Solzhenitsyn. The authorities were unable to prevent the meeting, and it took place on February 20 at Natalya's apartment. Solzhenitsyn's friend, writer Lev Kopelev, fluent in German, translated. Because conversations were bugged, they discussed serious matters in writing, immediately destroying the notes. Solzhenitsyn asked Böll to witness his will, which made Natalya his literary heir and executor, and to deliver the document to his lawyer in Zurich. This was important to Solzhenitsyn, because Natalya was still not legally his wife and he wanted her to manage his literary inheritance. In his turn, Böll advised Solzhenitsyn not to respond to every hostile article in the Soviet press: his books were read around the world, and history would put things right.[713]

On March 30, Natalya welcomed journalists Robert Kaiser from *The Washington Post* and Hedrick Smith from *The New York Times*.[714]

They had come to interview Solzhenitsyn before President Nixon's arrival in Moscow in May. The president would sign the Strategic Arms Limitation Treaty, but Solzhenitsyn's interview would be at odds with Nixon's conciliatory mission. The interview turned into a stressful four-hour ordeal for everyone involved. As the KGB reported, "Solzhenitsyn's mistress warned the correspondents that someone might well be eavesdropping on them, in view of which the rest of the exchange was largely carried out by writing notes."[715] In addition, Solzhenitsyn produced a 25-page typescript, containing questions and answers he had composed in advance. He insisted that it be published in full, to which the journalists, of course, could not agree. Natalya eased the tension with humor and helped achieve a compromise. Solzhenitsyn agreed to take a few live questions, Kaiser remembers, but discussed his answers with Natalya first: "She offered extensive advice, some of which he accepted. The sport of it seemed to please him, though he was obviously nervous about a situation he could not fully control."[716]

Soon the KGB reported another major development: Natalya was preparing to host a reception for the Nobel Prize ceremony in Moscow. However, on April 9, the authorities denied an entry visa to Nobel Foundation Secretary Karl Gierow. After the plan for the ceremony was dropped, Solzhenitsyn wanted to pass a microfilm with his Nobel speech to Sweden. The couple expected that a Swedish journalist, Stig Fredrikson, would agree to take it through the border. Natalya accompanied Solzhenitsyn to the meeting with Fredrikson, who arrived with his wife Ingrid. Both women were pregnant, which, Solzhenitsyn believed, was a good omen for the fruition of his plans. Fredrikson received the roll of film in a dark courtyard and smuggled it inside his transistor radio.

In June 1972, Natalya was in her final months of carrying their second child when she learned of yet another postponement in Solzhenitsyn's divorce. Vishnevskaya recalls that despite her difficult pregnancy, Natalya was handling the situation coolly: "With circles under her eyes and pains in her belly, she said, 'But why all this fuss? I've told him [Solzhenitsyn] already that we can just go on the way we are. I don't need anything. . . .'"⁷¹⁷

On September 23, 1972, the couple's second son, Ignat, was born. The doctor who helped Natalya with her delivery was promptly purged from the Party and lost his teaching position at the Medical Institute. As he was told, this was for "bringing into the world the child of the enemy of the people."⁷¹⁸ Natalya was still recovering from the birth when on October 18 Solzhenitsyn's wife, Reshetovskaya, unexpectedly came to see her. She asked whether the younger woman ever thought about her; Natalya replied that she had and that she was sorry for the grief she had caused. "Forgive me!" Natalya added with emotion.⁷¹⁹ After this meeting, Reshetovskaya withdrew her objections from the Supreme Court, which was then deciding the divorce. In addition, she wrote Natalya that had they met earlier, the divorce would not have lasted two agonizing years. What persuaded her was their personal meeting. The divorce was finalized on March 15, 1973, and on May 11, Natalya and Solzhenitsyn were married. In addition to the church wedding, the couple registered their marriage in a civil ceremony, which gave Solzhenitsyn the legal right to reside with his family in Moscow. But the authorities still refused to permit him to live in the capital. He could be arrested if he stayed with Natalya and the children longer than seventy-two hours.

That year, Solzhenitsyn's struggle with the Soviet state entered a critical phase. In May, the family rented a country cottage in Firsanovka, southeast of Moscow, but their vacation turned into a living hell. The couple received a flurry of threatening mail until Solzhenitsyn sent several samples to KGB headquarters, warning he would make the affair public. In addition, their village was near the airport, and the roar was overwhelming day and night. Solzhenitsyn, needing to write, retreated to a country cottage he had shared with his first wife. Natalya stayed with her mother and the children in the countryside, where they were utterly defenseless against the KGB. She was also coping with another difficult pregnancy and afraid of miscarriage; however, she wrote to cheer Solzhenitsyn and tell him that she was ready to tackle any situation.

That summer, the couple made a superhuman decision: they would not be intimidated by any threats and were ready to die at any moment. When, in 1992, a Russian reporter asked Natalya whether she had qualms about the choice Solzhenitsyn had made for the entire family, Natalya replied that she knew what was at stake and did not hesitate. "But I would be lying to you if I said I had no fear. I was afraid. Mainly for the children. . . ."[720]

On September 2, the couple learned that the KGB had seized the manuscript of *The Gulag Archipelago*. Solzhenitsyn's former helper and typist, Elizaveta Voronyanskaya, was hunted down in Leningrad. The KGB confiscated her memoir in which she told about the existence of *The Gulag Archipelago*. After she was interrogated for five days and nights, the KGB learned where the manuscript could be found. Believing she had betrayed Solzhenitsyn and other people, she committed suicide at sixty-seven.

The Gulag Archipelago was Solzhenitsyn's deepest-kept secret and another "crippling blow to Communism." The novel had been deposited with his Paris publisher long ago, but Solzhenitsyn waited for the right moment to release it. Such a moment came when the KGB seized a copy of the novel. On September 3, Solzhenitsyn arrived in Moscow to consult Natalya about whether they should launch the novel in the West, which would mean a new round of harassment at home. "'We'll have to detonate it, don't you think?' I ask her. 'Let's do it!' is her fearless reply." Solzhenitsyn informed his Western supporters about the seizure of *The Gulag Archipelago* and gave his Paris publisher, Struve, the go-ahead. He pressed him to produce the novel as fast as possible, before the KGB acted. In the middle of these events, on September 8, 1973, Natalya gave birth to their third son, Stepan.

Beginning in November, Solzhenitsyn lived and worked at the writers' settlement, Peredelkino. He stayed at the dacha of writer and long-time helper Lydia Chukovskaya, traveling to see his family in Moscow once a week. Occasionally he made surprise visits. After a regular goodnight call to Natalya, for KGB ears, he would leave the light on and slip out of the house unnoticed. On the way to

Moscow he would change trains, taking circuitous routes, confident he had outsmarted the agents.

Struve's YMCA-Press released *The Gulag Archipelago* on December 28, 1973, ten days ahead of time. He and his wife had been preparing the novel together with only few of their staff aware, to ensure secrecy. Upon its release in France and later in England, the novel would be promptly translated in many countries, with the American edition published by Harper & Row in 1974. "This was a bomb," Struve later remarked contentedly, "that would explode around the world . . . a literary event of the twentieth century."[721]

When Solzhenitsyn heard the announcement about the novel's publication on the BBC, he felt as though "an enormous burden had been lifted" from his shoulders and rushed to Moscow to share the news with Natalya. "That evening Alya and I were in a festive mood—everything was collapsing around us, but we were holding our own." Solzhenitsyn made a list of possibilities for the New Year: the Soviet authorities could respond to the novel's publication with murder, imprisonment, or deportation. Natalya was more optimistic, predicting another newspaper campaign against him.

On January 14, 1974, *Pravda* published an editorial entitled "The Path of Betrayal," and the following day the article was reprinted across the country. Threatening mail and telephone calls began to pour in. For two weeks in a row, the telephone in Natalya's apartment rang non-stop as the KGB tried to break the family's spirit with a campaign of "public anger." The callers demanded to speak with Solzhenitsyn and shouted obscenities. Solzhenitsyn admired Natalya for weathering it calmly:

> She would listen patiently to all the abuse, then say quietly: "Tell me, do you get paid fortnightly in the KGB, or monthly, like in the army?" . . . Sometimes she would even interpolate a few encouraging remarks, let the man speak his lines, and then say, "Is that all? Right—tell Yuri Vladimirovich [chairman of the KGB Andropov] from me that he's heading for trouble with dunces like you on his staff."[722]

As before, the Soviet newspaper campaign against Solzhenitsyn helped promote his book in the West. In the ironic remark of writer Veniamin Kaverin, the authorities were punishing Solzhenitsyn "with world-wide fame."[723] Prior to his novel, some forty books had been published on the gulag topic in the West, all unnoticed.

When Natalya's telephone stopped ringing the first week of February, she said it was the calm before the storm. While the couple was wondering what the authorities would undertake next, the KGB was conducting secret negotiations to deport Solzhenitsyn. On February 2, West German Chancellor Willy Brandt, highly respected for his efforts to improve East-West relations, said Solzhenitsyn was welcome to live and work in Germany. Andropov (he would succeed Brezhnev as Soviet leader), seized the opportunity to divest himself of a troublesome dissident. He sent a memo to Brezhnev that KGB General Kevorkov was negotiating with the Germans. The KGB worried, perhaps unreasonably, that Solzhenitsyn would discover this and disrupt their plan, so Andropov wanted the matter to be urgently resolved.

Solzhenitsyn was working at the dacha in Peredelkino when, on February 8, Natalya phoned to say that he was being summonsed to the Office of Public Procurator of the USSR. When the summons was brought to her apartment Natalya found an excuse not to sign the receipt, which gave Solzhenitsyn a postponement. But a second summons arrived on February 11. That day, he returned to Moscow and wrote a letter refusing to accept the legality of the government order.

In the evening, the couple went for a stroll, discussing their strategies in case of Solzhenitsyn's arrest. Believing that he would be sent to the gulag, he even told Natalya what he would write there—a history of Russia for children. During their walk, the police agents followed at a close distance, which the couple ignored. At home, they went about their usual business and microfilmed Solzhenitsyn's most recent manuscript; they also packed his prison kit.

On February 12, the government signed a decree for Solzhenitsyn's deportation; unaware, the couple spent the morning working in their shared study. In the afternoon there was a ring at the door. When Solzhenitsyn opened, eight towering men rushed in. Natalya demanded their search warrant and, learning there was none, shouted, "Out you go, then."[724] Minutes later, Solzhenitsyn was taken away, but two agents remained in the apartment. Natalya locked herself in the study where, working "at lightning speed," she collected the papers and microfilms, deciding which ones to destroy and which to hide inside books and on her body. It took her twenty-two minutes to prepare for the search and burn the most incriminating materials. Emerging from the study, she was surprised to see that the agents had left.

The police had damaged the lock, leaving the entrance door opened, and her eighteen-month-old Ignat crawled onto the landing. Three-year-old Ermolai had to be picked up from kindergarten and the two other children, Dmitry, eleven, and Stepan, five months, were in the yard with her mother. Natalya could not attend to their needs, but when later that day a friend offered to take her three-year-old for the night, she replied frostily: "No—let him get used to it. He is a Solzhenitsyn."[725]

She phoned friends to tell about the arrest, and human-rights activists began to gather at her apartment, among them Andrei Sakharov, the father of the Soviet H-bomb. He made a statement in a phone interview with a Canadian news agency, denouncing the arrest, and called it a retribution for Solzhenitsyn's book, which advocated for millions of victims. (A founder of the Committee on Human Rights in the USSR, Sakharov was awarded the Nobel Peace Prize in 1975. Like Solzhenitsyn, he was not allowed to collect it and his wife, human-rights activist Elena Bonner, delivered his speech in Oslo. Sakharov was sent into internal exile after his protest against the Soviet invasion of Afghanistan.)

All that day and next, Natalya did not know where her husband was being detained or even if he was still alive. To keep the pressure on the KGB, she decided to release his remaining works in the West, so when Solzhenitsyn's lawyer, Dr. Heeb, phoned from Zurich upon learning of the arrest, Natalya instructed him to do just that.

At night, she sorted the papers more thoroughly, with her mother and friends helping. They burned unwanted letters, copies, and microfilms in a basin on the kitchen floor, where it remained for the next six weeks. Remembering that Solzhenitsyn had written a letter, to be issued in the event of his arrest, she recovered the document, typed copies on onionskin, and summoned Robert Lacontre from *Le Figaro*. He arrived after midnight and promised to distribute the letter, which he smuggled from the apartment, to all news agencies.

On February 14, Natalya received reports from foreign correspondents that Solzhenitsyn had been deported, but refused comment: "I shan't believe it until I hear his voice."[726] Only when he himself phoned from Böll's residence in Germany did she acknowledge the fact, saying she would eventually join him with the children. Some forty people who had assembled in her apartment were present during the call. When they began to congratulate her, Natalya described her husband's deportation as "a misfortune, an act no less brutally arbitrary than imprisonment in a camp."[727]

When deporting Solzhenitsyn, the KGB realized he would be photographed upon arrival to the West. Expecting imprisonment, Solzhenitsyn had donned a sheepskin and old fur cap from his gulag days, so the KGB provided new clothes and a muskrat hat and forced him to change. While on the phone with Natalya, Solzhenitsyn asked her to retrieve his prison garb, which had become part of his image. Natalya rushed to Lefortovo prison and demanded his things, only to learn that they had been burned.

Ahead of her was the arduous task of transferring his papers to the West. By then, most of his completed works had been stored in Switzerland, but there was also an enormous archive, research notes, and printed materials, which Solzhenitsyn had collected over the years for his revolutionary epic *The Red Wheel*. Knowing that his work in exile would depend on it, she packed all he might need, an elaborate task since he treasured every single paper.

To succeed with her mission, she needed the help of many people, from Western scholars to journalists and diplomats, who could smuggle Solzhenitsyn's archive in multiple installments. She established a network of allies through the Norwegian journalist Nils Udgaard, who put her in touch with his friends in the diplomatic corps. Visits by foreign correspondents, whom she pressed into service, allowed freedom of action. Packages marked for shipment were delivered to the apartment of Swedish journalist Fredrikson, who had been Solzhenitsyn's principal link to the West. Eventually, the archive would be smuggled in forty-five installments, bypassing Soviet customs, through various routes and diplomatic pouches.

Though Natalya planned to depart in six weeks, Solzhenitsyn phoned her every day and urged her to come sooner. To ease the pressure, she sent him a letter through Fredrikson, explaining what was keeping her at home. When the coded letter was seized at the border, her entire operation was jeopardized. During the ensuing turmoil, baby Stepan fell ill with pneumonia and she spent nights at his bedside.

Days before leaving, Natalya held a farewell reception, attended by fellow dissidents and foreign correspondents. Sakharov would describe the occasion: "Many good people came to this party, and many a fine Russian song was sung."[728] Most memorable was the mood of the day and Natalya's emotional address made on her own and Solzhenitsyn's behalf:

> They can separate a Russian writer from his native land, but no one has the power and strength to sever his spiritual link with it. . . . And even if his books are now set ablaze on bonfires, their existence in his homeland is indestructible, just as Solzhenitsyn's love for Russia is indestructible. . . . My place is beside him, but leaving Russia is excruciatingly painful.[729]

Natalya felt the pain of deportation more acutely than Solzhenitsyn, who had already moved to Zurich to collect material for his novel about Lenin. (The Bolshevik leader had lived and worked there for several years before the 1917 Revolution.) On March 29,

Natalya with their four children and her mother arrived in Zurich, met by a crowd of reporters and Solzhenitsyn on the tarmac. Allowed to meet her onboard in private, he dived into the plane, where she promptly told him that his archives had been dispatched separately; he emerged, smiling, carrying his two sons.

That spring and summer, when suitcases with Solzhenitsyn's archive were delivered to their house in Zurich, the couple was jubilant: "It was all here—everything that really mattered, the most priceless things of all! We had saved it all!" The three-story house near downtown where Solzhenitsyn was staying "felt empty and unlived in," Natalya recalls. "Rooms snowed under with thousands of letters. . . ."[730] They were swamped by mail from around the world, and bags of unopened letters accumulated in the attic. Solzhenitsyn would not hire a secretary and issued a statement, apologizing that he was unable to reply to his numerous correspondents.

Days after Natalya's arrival, the couple decided to establish the Russian Social Fund to help political prisoners and their families and to support writers and publishers as well. Solzhenitsyn donated his worldwide royalties from *The Gulag Archipelago* to this cause. Natalya became the fund's president, acquiring a score of new responsibilities of which the most troublesome was transferring aid to the Soviet Union. (This fund could not be registered in their homeland until after the Soviet Union was dismantled. Before 1992, it functioned clandestinely and aid could not reach the victims of Stalin's gulag.[731] The Solzhenitsyns mainly helped dissidents and their families who suffered under Brezhnev. In 1976, when the fund's political agenda was discovered, the Soviet authorities revoked Natalya's citizenship.)

Also, within weeks of her arrival, the couple discussed moving to America, where Solzhenitsyn wanted to buy property. There were distractions in Zurich, where fans, reporters, and photographers followed him everywhere. Solzhenitsyn had already quarreled with the press: pursued by reporters while walking in the hills, he bellowed, "Go away! You're worse than the KGB!"[732] The remark was published by many newspapers and a good relationship with the press was lost, which Solzhenitsyn would later regret.

When Zurich's mayor, Sigmund Widmer, offered Solzhenitsyn his farmhouse in Sternenberg to work in, he resumed his solitary writing habits. He would spend most of the week in the picturesque village, traveling to Zurich on weekends, in effect maintaining the same schedule as before his deportation. Meantime, Frau Widmer, solicitous of Natalya, took her on hikes in the mountains.

In October, Solzhenitsyn took time from writing to drive with Natalya through Switzerland, visiting Bern, Geneva, Chillon Castle, and Montreux. Upon arrival in the West, he had received a welcoming letter from Vladimir Nabokov, who extended an open invitation to visit him. Solzhenitsyn had admired Nabokov's talent, having nominated him for the Nobel Prize in 1971. (Nabokov joined the league of prominent writers, including Tolstoy and Chekhov, who did not receive the award.) Proposing a certain day and hour for their meeting, Solzhenitsyn expected Nabokov to confirm, but received no reply. The Nabokovs assumed the date had been settled. At the appointed hour, they waited for their guests in a private dining room at the Montreux Palace Hotel, while the Solzhenitsyns, in the car, argued whether they should go in. Because of the miscommunication, the two famous literary couples never met.

Four years after he had been awarded the Nobel Prize, Solzhenitsyn finally collected it in December 1974. (The festivities that followed coincided with his birthday on December 11.) He was the second Russian writer to receive the Prize, after Ivan Bunin. Natalya, who accompanied Solzhenitsyn to Stockholm, would later say in an interview that she felt "it was our victory, victory of Russia, victory of *Ivan Denisovich*."

The New Year found them in Paris, where the couple visited the publishing house, YMCA Press, that had produced the works they had been sending from Moscow on microfilm, most notably *The Gulag Archipelago*. They had imagined it as a more conspiratorial place, not a house just anyone could enter. In April, Natalya prevailed on Solzhenitsyn to take another driving trip to France for the release of his memoir, *The Oak and the Calf.* Afterwards, they spent several days in Italy. At the end of April, Solzhenitsyn took off to Canada, alone. The airplane ticket was purchased under an assumed name, to conceal his intentions to settle in Canada; however, within days of his arrival, Canadian newspapers wrote that Solzhenitsyn was looking to buy land. Solzhenitsyn traveled through Ontario and Quebec to buy a place that looked "Russian." Father Alexander Shmemann drove him to see places with Russian Orthodox communities and churches. In May, he summoned Natalya from Zurich, and she rejected the shortlisted options. Solzhenitsyn wanted to live near a Russian community in Canada or in America, while Natalya preferred to remain in Europe where they would be less isolated.

For lack of time (Natalya was returning to Zurich and Solzhenitsyn had speaking engagements in America), the issue had to be solved by a third party. In October 1975, a Russian émigré architect, Alexei Vinogradov, to whom Solzhenitsyn gave power of attorney, bought a house and fifty acres of land in Cavendish, Vermont. It was a former farm, with the house buried in the woods and concealed from the road. Solzhenitsyn liked the forested property for its remote location, its two ponds and brooks that looked Russian. It resembled Yasnaya Polyana with its ponds and woods. The place was called "Twinbrook," but Solzhenitsyn renamed it "Five Brooks," the actual number on the property. He only regretted that there were no meadows or clearings (which would have made it more like Tolstoy's estate).

The family's move to America was to be handled clandestinely: when, in March 1976, Natalya applied for U.S. visas, nobody in Zurich or elsewhere knew. On April 2, Solzhenitsyn left Europe for New York, telling his confidant, Father Shmemann, that he had left for good. Shmemann commented in his diary, "Today (of course, secretly from all the rest) Solzhenitsyn moved to America! This country does not leave anybody unchanged. . . . But will he see America . . . beyond the trees?"[733] In early July, Natalya joined Solzhenitsyn to watch construction of their new house. He lived in a small cottage by the pond where the noise of construction disturbed him until year's end. The new three-story house had spacious storage for his library and archive, a private chapel, and a top-floor study with a glass ceiling and numerous windows where he would work in winter. (Solzhenitsyn needed light and quiet to write, Natalya remarked, adding that otherwise he was unpretentious.) A twenty-meter underground tunnel connected the main house with the small cottage where Solzhenitsyn worked in other seasons. At the end of July, the rest of the family arrived in Cavendish.

The Solzhenitsyns' escape from Zurich came as a shock to the mayor who had welcomed the exiles. They left without saying thanks, and all of Switzerland was offended. Only Svetlana Allilueva, Stalin's daughter, could understand their conspiracy: "That's Russian," she commented.[734] But in fact, Solzhenitsyn broke with a tradition of Russian writers, who stood for openness, and with Tolstoy's and Dostoevsky's practice of receiving visitors indiscriminately. Visitors to Solzhenitsyn would face a chain-link fence, eight feet high, topped with barbed wire, and a sign on the gate, "No Trespassing."

Solzhenitsyn shut himself from the Western world with which he was now in conflict. In public appearances he criticized the West's embrace of socialism, the pleasures of its consumer society, and the lack of spiritual values. He disparaged Roosevelt, compared Britain's position in the world to that of Uganda, and so on. The West was discovering that the famous dissident was not a democrat: newspapers described him as a "bearded prophet" and anti-capitalist. Solzhenitsyn's audiences found his heated political rhetoric overwhelming and out of touch. The writer discovered himself isolated and ridiculed by the press, so his decision to live as a recluse was logical. In addition, he wanted to protect his family from American culture.

Writer Lydia Chukovskaya, who had sheltered Solzhenitsyn in the Moscow countryside, had observed him back in 1973–74 working sixteen hours a day, six days a week. His self-imposed "strictest possible regime" resembled that of a corrective labor camp. "The lesson was intended for heroic shoulders, for a lifetime's labor with no days off. ...."[735] His mission in the past was to tell the world about the gulag; after his arrival in the West, Solzhenitsyn was determined to write the true history of the 1917 Revolution and reestablish the facts distorted by the Bolsheviks. Comprising ten volumes, his saga *The Red Wheel* would consume him and Natalya for two decades.

At thirty-eight, Natalya, a city woman, settled on their secluded estate, in "a zone of quiet" where she would remain for eighteen years. Solzhenitsyn could not afford interruptions, so there were few visitors. Getting used to isolation was hard: she had never lived in a place so remote, having to drive ten miles to pick up necessities. Her life was ruled by Solzhenitsyn's inflexible schedule, which she would try to present to a Russian reporter as satisfying: "It's very simple. Alexander Isaevich gets up early, at about seven o'clock. . . . Coffee—and back to work. . . . We live in a forest . . . work fourteen hours a day; people might say, it's a convict's life, but we are happy."[736]

In 1977, Natalya began to produce Solzhenitsyn's collected works in twenty volumes on an IBM computer, creating what they called a *"samizdat* in exile." She indexed the works, edited, typeset, and proofread the volumes. In a foreword to his Vermont edition, Solzhenitsyn wrote that she worked with a meticulousness impossible for a regular publishing house.

Natalya, who matched Solzhenitsyn's tremendous capacity for work, handled another major project. After deciding to create the All-Russian Memoir Library, Solzhenitsyn appealed to émigrés who had fled Russia after the Revolution and during or after the Second World War to send memoirs, photographs, and letters. The couple received thousands of manuscripts, which included testimonies by former inmates of the German concentration camps. Natalya handled this flood of contributions, corresponded with the authors, catalogued the materials, and eventually, in the 1990s, transferred it all to Russia for storage and publication.

In addition, she helped Solzhenitsyn with his research for *The Red Wheel*. The amount of her groundwork for just this sequence could have occupied a research institute. "Entire archives, libraries" cooperated with the author, inundating the couple with mountains of material, which Natalya processed and organized. Solzhenitsyn said her contribution was so great that it was impossible to describe it. Natalya was his editor, and she had replaced his entire audience. Her attention to detail and grammar helped improve his style. She participated in every stage of his writing: "I dare not say which other Russian writer had beside him such a collaborator, such a fine and keen critic and adviser. I have never met in my life a person with such a brilliant editor's talent as my wife, sent to me indispensably in my seclusion. . . ."[737] In fact, Natalya was the only editor Solzhenitsyn had known, aside from his brief association with *Novy Mir*. He anticipated her suggestions, which she made in the margins of his first proofs; as with a real publishing house, the pages were then brought to Solzhenitsyn. Stepan recalls carrying proofs "from the editor's station" to the author's: his mother's revisions were penciled in red, while Solzhenitsyn's changes were entered in blue.[738] When the printer broke down, Solzhenitsyn missed their scheduled collaboration and was visibly nervous without it.

Such responsibilities consumed most of her day, leaving no time even to read for pleasure. To her Moscow friends, Evgeny Pasternak (Boris Pasternak's son) and his wife Elena, Natalya wrote that Solzhenitsyn is "of course, the bright center of our life and its purpose."[739] (Evgeny Pasternak was among those who came to see Natalya off at the Moscow airport when she was leaving to join Solzhenitsyn in exile. For this alone, he was dismissed from his teaching position at the Moscow Power Engineering Institute.)

In her diaries, comprising thirty thick notebooks, Natalya recorded Solzhenitsyn's work progress and his moods. Her style bears the influence of Solzhenitsyn, unsurprising because she was occupied with his works almost exclusively while living in isolation. Her husband never stopped writing: Natalya could not remember him experiencing a single creative crisis. Even with Solzhenitsyn working outside the house in his cabin, the family had a sense of unremitting deadline. Biographer Michael Scammell, who visited the place in 1977, describes an atmosphere of "purposefulness and order to the entire household, which had the cohesiveness of a kind of informal monastery, each individual working away for the common good—a situation that Solzhenitsyn emphatically approved of and encouraged."[740]

By their own example, the couple taught their children how to work. At ten, Ermolai helped his mother typeset a volume of the All-Russian Memoir Library. Preserving their sons' native tongue was important, and so the couple supplemented private schooling with instruction at home. Solzhenitsyn taught math, physics, and astronomy, while Natalya gave lessons in Russian language and literature (the same division as in the Tolstoy family). The children met their father at a regular time to receive his instruction: "It did not even occur to them that they could knock on his door 30 seconds later...."[741]

Father Andrew Tregubov, a local Orthodox priest of Russian descent, taught them divine law; in addition, Natalya read the Gospels with the boys. Every morning, the children came to their father's cottage to pray in the pine forest. They would kneel down to recite their prayers, including one Solzhenitsyn had himself composed, that God would let them return to Russia. He told the boys that a rock on their estate was a bewitched Pegasus and that one day it would carry them all to their homeland.

Natalya's mother, an important household member, was the family's driver, photographer, and expert cook. Ignat, whom she drove to private music lessons, recalls her as their good genius: she was a uniting force in the family, and their childhood and youth were unthinkable without her. (The sons were educated at Harvard and in private schools in London; Ermolai became a Sinologist, Ignat—the music director of the Chamber Orchestra of Philadelphia. Rostropovich once visited the family in Cavendish and was the first to discover Ignat's musical talent. Stepan, the youngest, became a civil engineer and architect as well as Solzhenitsyn's translator and editor.)

In 1981, five years into their stay in America, the couple qualified for US citizenship, but decided against it, even though they had no citizenship at all. Natalya applied only in 1985, to simplify travel. On June 24, she wrote in her diary that she was heading to the citizenship ceremony "with a heavy heart, utterly miserable." Afterwards, she switched off the phone for several days so as not to receive congratualtions: having to swear allegiance to the American government was a necessary sacrifice.[742]

The year 1985 marked the beginning of Mikhail Gorbachev's perestroika reforms, which the Solzhenitsyns, paradoxically, did not welcome. In December of 1986, Gorbachev telephoned Sakharov, terminating his internal exile; he was soon reinstated in the Academy of Sciences. Unlike Sakharov, who considered the defense of civil rights and openness to be the bases of society, Solzhenitsyn assigned them "only a secondary importance," believing religion should play the key role. In his memoir, Sakharov outlines Solzhenitsyn's views, strikingly different from his own, which became more apparent during glasnost:

> Solzhenitsyn's mistrust of the West, of progress in general, of science and democracy, inclines him to romanticize a patriarchal way of life . . . to expect too much from the Russian Orthodox Church. He regards the unspoiled northeast region of our country as a reservoir for the Russian people where they can cleanse themselves of the moral and physical ravages caused by communism, a diabolic force, imported from the West.[743]

It would be later written that if Solzhenitsyn had returned during perestroika, when hardliners opposed the reforms and the support of influential people like him was needed, the country would have given him a hero's welcome. Instead, he chose to wait until the time for his homecoming was ripe and his conditions were met. His major condition was publication of *The Gulag Archipelago* in the Soviet Union, which at the start of perestroika was almost unthinkable.

In 1986, in Cavendish, the couple celebrated an anniversary of *The Red Wheel*: fifty years had passed from the day Solzhenitsyn first decided to produce a comprehensive account of the 1917 Revolution. The couple had worked indefatigably on this project, but recently Natalya had been feeling crushed by its weight. Her tremendous resilience began to wane, and she complained it was difficult to go on working sixteen hours a day on Russia's catastrophe and the Bolsheviks' intrigue and betrayal.[744] Solzhenitsyn, unwilling to terminate the saga, was yet to discover that the public would ignore his ten-volume Bolshevik history. Living in cultural isolation, he may not have realized that his readers, on both sides of the Atlantic, had little interest in the topic.

Solzhenitsyn described Gorbachev's perestroika as a "murky" phenomenon and remarked in his diary that "the temperature" of the change remained low.[745] Meantime, Soviet literary magazines were publishing revelatory works which could not come out during seventy years of political censorship, each publication advancing glasnost one step further. In 1988, *Novy Mir* approached Solzhenitsyn for permission to produce *Cancer Ward*, an event in itself since the novel was only published abroad, but he insisted that *The Gulag Archipelago*, his major work about the repressions, must go first. However, the old guard fought furiously against it, and Gorbachev was afraid that the novel would tip the delicate balance. When despite Gorbachev's refusal the editor of *Novy Mir* decided to take it on, Natalya wrote in her diary that even an attempt at publication was a victory.[746] Despite their misgivings, *The Gulag* appeared in this popular magazine in 1989, at the height of glasnost, when circulation of *Novy Mir* exceeded one million copies. *The Gulag* was printed in one million six hundred thousand copies.[747]

At the end of the year, Soviet authorities indicated that Solzhenitsyn's citizenship would be restored if he applied. Natalya described this offer as "shameful" in an interview with *The New York Times*, explaining that Solzhenitsyn had been kicked out and now would not "ask permission to enter.... We've waited a long time. We will wait until they become wise."[748] In 1990, still under Gorbachev, citizenship to Solzhenitsyn and to Natalya was restored. But the couple remained unconvinced. While refusing to support Gorbachev, calling his reforms "a myth," they met the fall of the Soviet Union with joy. In August 1991, the Solzhenitsyns were watching on the news the removal of Dzerzhinsky's statue on Lubyanka Square. The fifteen-ton monument to the founder of the Bolshevik secret police was dismantled to cheers from the crowd. Natalya wrote in her diary that Solzhenitsyn felt proud and happy for the Russians but also wondered whether the change was permanent. The writer, in his diary, called the event the greatest day in his life.[749] The following month, Solzhenitsyn received official rehabilitation and an apology from the Russian government, along with President Yeltsin's assurance that the country was taking a new path.

In spring 1992, Natalya went to Moscow to arrange for their return. She met with President Yeltsin and the Moscow mayor, Yuri Luzhkov, obtaining their welcome and support. The Moscow government promised to return Natalya's former downtown apartment for headquarters of the Russian Social Fund, which at last could be registered. She acquired a city apartment where the family would reside temporarily and, because Solzhenitsyn needed his solitude to go on writing, also sought country properties. Eventually, with the mayor's special permission, Natalya purchased 10.7 acres of land to build a house in Troitse-Lykovo, a historical area of Moscow. Before the Revolution, this place belonged to a number of prominent aristocratic families, beginning with Peter the Great's uncle. In the twentieth century, it accommodated a sanatorium for the Soviet government where Lenin convalesced in 1922. Solzhenitsyn's fascination with Lenin, whom he had portrayed in *The Red Wheel*, apparently did not end with the epic.

In 1993, Mike Wallace interviewed the couple, still in Cavendish, for CBS. He found Solzhenitsyn self-absorbed: "Everything in life was business, everything was hard work. His days were numbered, and he had very important work to do." In contrast, Natalya was "extremely attractive, interesting, indeed fascinating; a woman of immense intelligence; the ultimate protector and keeper of the flame; his handmaiden."[750] Aside from her other responsibilities, Natalya handled Solzhenitsyn's public affairs. That year, while preparing for their return to Russia, she had to keep the media in the dark about their itinerary; the exclusive rights to film Solzhenitsyn's homecoming would be sold to the BBC.

Their departure was scheduled for May 25, 1994. Two months earlier, Natalya's son from her first marriage, Dmitry, died of a heart attack at thirty-two. The pain of having to bury her son was overwhelming and would not be assuaged over the years. Dmitry's father, Tiurin, flew in from Moscow for the funeral in the Orthodox Church near Cavendish. All this took place in the middle of daunting preparations for the move. Natalya had to oversee shipping Solzhenitsyn's enormous archive and library, for which she needed four hundred packing cases. The move was so well organized that Solzhenitsyn was able to work almost to the day of their departure. He was traveling to Moscow through the Far East, landing in Magadan (a symbolic center of Stalin's gulag). From there, he would make a two-month journey on a special train, which the BBC had hired and in which the family had two private coaches. The Russian media were often sarcastic in their depiction of Solzhenitsyn's journey. One newspaper wrote, "Solzhenitsyn is returning to the country, which he does not know and where he is practically forgotten."[751] The Solzhenitsyns' dislike of the press was well-known. When an army of Russian journalists and cameramen closely followed the couple in Vladivostok, Natalya snapped at them, "You press people are the world's second oldest profession."[752] (The remark was reminiscent of Solzhenitsyn's, upon his arrival to the West, when he shouted at the paparazzi that they were worse than the KGB). Unhappy with the coverage of Solzhenitsyn's journey by the Russian media, Natalya deemed it disrespectful.[753] She left the tour after a few weeks and flew to Moscow, leaving Solzhenitsyn with one of their sons.

Natalya had told *Izvestiya* that Solzhenitsyn intended to become a unifying force upon his return.[754] But he clearly failed in this goal. While still in Cavendish, he wrote an article, "How to Revitalize Russia," discussing Russia's future after the dissolution of the Soviet Union. In 1990, the article was published in millions of copies by two national newspapers, but it was deemed offensive by other nationalities. Solzhenitsyn referred to Ukraine as "little Russia," the term used in the 19th century, and described Kazakhstan as "Russia's underbelly." With ethnic tensions running high, one of the newspapers containing his article was publicly burned in Kazakhstan and in Ukraine.

In the fall of 1994, invited as a special guest to the Duma, Solzhenitsyn attacked Yeltsin's privatization program and market reforms. His speech was broadcast on television and later published in full, but his ideas had little impact: none of the factions would want to make Solzhenitsyn their own. Later, his book, *Russia in the Abyss*, became widely seen as "apocalyptic." The book appeared during Russia's fiscal default in 1998, and some readers misinterpreted the title as Solzhenitsyn's prediction of Russia's economic collapse. In fact, the book was discussing the country's spiritual decline. Solzhenitsyn's deliberate use of archaic words in this book and during his public performances created ambiguity, becoming partly responsible for his disconnect with the audiences. After their return, when the press attacked him, Natalya served as a buffer between her husband and the outside world.

In spring 1995, the couple moved to their new country residence where Solzhenitsyn resumed his secluded life, with regular hours for writing. Natalya guarded his peace and handled his extensive correspondence. She was also engaged in public life. That same year, the Russian Social Fund, of which she was president, along with YMCA-Press in Paris and the Moscow government, opened the Russian Abroad Foundation Library. The numerous émigré manuscripts the Solzhenitsyns had shipped from Vermont formed the heart of the collection.

After their return to Russia, Natalya told an interviewer why she had wanted to marry Solzhenitsyn: "It was very clear to me . . . what I wanted to do for him. . . . To share—struggle. To share—work. To bear and raise worthy descendants."[755] She kept all her promises, but believed their struggle was ongoing and their work lifelong: Solzhenitsyn's mission as a national writer carried a heavy load, which they pulled together over the years.

Her new task was helping Solzhenitsyn recapture his readership. In the 1990s, subscription to his works had plummeted, reflecting Russia's default, general impoverishment, and decrease of interest in classical literature and history. Solzhenitsyn's books were no longer banned and, as someone remarked, reading them was more interesting when one could be arrested for this. During perestroika, numerous works about Stalin's repressions were published and the market was saturated. In addition, intellectuals, who had supported him in the past, turned away from Solzhenitsyn, disappointed with his anti-Western stance. During this time, Natalya looked for alternative ways to promote his works, even describing *The First Circle* as a political detective story.

When Solzhenitsyn began his last monumental work, *Two Hundred Years Together*, a two-volume study of Russian-Jewish relations, Natalya was once again assisting him with research. True to her remark that "every book needs to be nurtured,"[756] she sifted through piles of material, edited, and annotated the volumes. But the work would not add to Solzhenitsyn's glory. The topic of Jewish influence on Russian history was sensitive and Solzhenitsyn, a staunch defender of Orthodoxy, could not avoid bias. Upon its publication in 2001–2002, Natalya shielded the work from charges of anti-Semitism, brushing them off as ludicrous.

In 2000, the Solzhenitsyns acquired an unlikely ally in the new Russian president, Vladimir Putin. In September, Putin and his wife Lyudmila met the couple at the Solzhenitsyns' country residence behind closed doors. After the visit, Solzhenitsyn told "Vesti" television that Putin impressed him as a man concerned primarily "with Russia's destiny, not his personal power."[757] In turn, Natalya described Putin as a dynamic, well-functioning leader, working to solve the country's problems.[758] A photograph of her accepting a bouquet from Putin appeared on the Internet. No longer dissidents, the Solzhenitsyns had emerged as a politically powerful couple. Sakharov's widow, Elena Bonner, told *The Evening Moscow* that the alliance between the former KGB officer and Solzhenitsyn was fascinating to her and worthy of Dostoevsky's pen.[759] Although Putin would reveal himself as a corrupt leader, would endorse the KGB, and would crush political freedoms and democratic institutions, the couple did not criticize his presidency.

In 2007, Putin awarded Solzhenitsyn the State Prize of the Russian Federation for his humanitarian work. The only previous recipient of this award was the head of the Russian Orthodox Church, Patriarch Alexy II. Solzhenitsyn was unwell and stayed home, so Natalya received the award for him at the Kremlin.

On August 3, 2008, just months before his ninetieth birthday, Solzhenitsyn died of heart failure. He was buried in the cemetery of Donskoy Monastery in Moscow, as personally consented to by Patriarch Alexy II five years earlier. Around the world he was remembered as a literary giant who had exposed Stalin's atrocities and had made a powerful indictment of the communist regime. This achievement will not be overshadowed by his contradictory views and actions of the later years.

In 2009, Putin received Natalya in the Kremlin to discuss teaching *The Gulag Archipelago* in school. Although Putin has made every effort to rehabilitate Stalin, he also surprisingly endorsed this major anti-Stalinist work. Today, Solzhenitsyn's volumes are available in bookstores, alongside works promoting a positive view of Stalin and his henchmen. How the two views can be reconciled or simultaneously taught in schools defies analysis.

THE WIVES

In April 2002, I came to the headquarters of the Russian Social Fund, the very downtown apartment from where Solzhenitsyn was led away by the KGB. I had asked Natalya for an informal talk: I wanted to understand her as a person, not Solzhenitsyn's spokeswoman. Short in stature, energetic, and attractive, Natalya was wearing a black pantsuit, a white shirt, and a gray necktie. She took me to her study, sat at her desk, and, as she spoke, kept stroking its shiny surface with small confident hands. Natalya is charismatic but likes to speak uninterrupted.

She believes that in Russia women are more dedicated to their families than in the West. They also tend to be more involved in their husbands' affairs. But truly dedicated writers' wives are rare, even in Russia. Her predecessors did not influence her decision to abandon her career as a mathematician and partake in Solzhenitsyn's work. She has never regretted her choice and believes her assistance to Solzhenitsyn more important than obtaining a doctorate in mathematics. She then turned to Tolstoy's marriage, which she knew intimately. She disapproved of Sophia for not following Tolstoy on his spiritual path and for her disagreements with him when he renounced property: "She should have followed him and lived in a hut, as he had asked." If Sophia loved Tolstoy, she had to go along; if she stopped loving him, "she had to step aside." It was unreasonable to expect Tolstoy to participate in their children's upbringing. Solzhenitsyn, for example, was able to give one hour a day to the children. Natalya continued her argument with Sophia, drawing a parallel between Tolstoy's renunciation of copyright and Solzhenitsyn's decision to give up profits from *The Gulag Archipelago*, which she supported.

She dislikes the word "sacrifice" and substitutes "love" for it. Nadezhda Mandelstam did not make a sacrifice: she loved the poet. "They were together and she [Nadezhda] believed they should die together." (Natalya, of course, was also prepared to die for Solzhenitsyn's cause.)

As I was leaving, Natalya said Russia was going through difficult times, and the role of the writer in society had changed. The question that concerned her was whether the new generation would read Solzhenitsyn. She gave me a three-volume collection of his non-fiction, published in Russia for the first time and which she had annotated and edited.[760]

Natalya's portrait remains unfinished because she continues to work. In recent years, she was occupied with a project she had started with Solzhenitsyn, issuing his thirty-volume edition of collected works. Today, Natalya wields considerable influence and has become Russia's most powerful literary widow. Over time, the complete picture of her literary marriage will emerge.

Epilogue

Despite investing themselves in greater talents, the six wives in this book made their own mark as publishers, translators, and editors. Their collaboration with writers made them prominent in their day. But their roles beside the geniuses were extraordinarily difficult. The problems they handled—shielding writers from practical concerns, balancing their moods, and dealing with their oversized egos—made them stronger and more resilient.

Such writers as F. Scott Fitzgerald, James Joyce, and D. H. Lawrence used their marriages for literary inspiration and material. William Wordsworth relied on his family—his sister, his wife, and his sister-in-law—to copy out his manuscripts. Thomas Carlyle also wanted his wife to assist him, but according to Rosemary Ashton, the author of *Thomas and Jane Carlyle,* Jane "became increasingly bitter and resentful of this role, though obviously it hugely helped her husband." In Russian literary marriages, the women did not resent taking a secondary position and, in fact, viewed their collaboration as rewarding.

These women played important and powerful roles as the writers' intellectual companions, confidantes, and creative partners. In their widowhood, they carried on as before, translating and promoting their husbands' works, establishing their museums, and helping biographers. This book should change a popular perception of such lives as miserable, lonely, and unfulfilled.

While Russia's most celebrated literary couples are portrayed in this book, readers should know about other literary wives who made contributions to Russian letters. I want to mention at least two of them here.

Klavdia Bugaev was a muse and collaborator of the prominent twentieth-century writer and poet Andrei Bely. (In 1933, the couple met the Mandelstams in the Crimea, but never became friends.) Much like Elena Bulgakov, Klavdia left her comfortable first marriage (her husband was a medical doctor) to join a writer who was barely published after the Revolution. In 1931, Klavdia was arrested as a prominent member of the Anthroposophical Society, which promoted spiritual philosophy and was banned under Stalin. Bely wrote in desperation to theater director Vsevolod Meyerhold: "Klavdia Nikolaevna is more than my life—but 1,000 lives."[761] Later that year, Klavdia was released from Lubyanka prison due to Meyerhold's efforts. Soon after, she and Bely officially married, which was only a few years before his death in 1934. A professional librarian, Klavdia spent the following three decades cataloguing Bely's archive and writing a memoir, which essentially was a survey of the writer's life and works. She analyzed Bely's innovative vocabulary, conducting this selfless work without financial help: Bely was an apolitical writer and of no value to the Soviet state. Bely's diary and letters, of which she made a copy, survive because of her efforts. Paralyzed and bedridden during her last seventeen years, she remained the only reliable source for Bely scholars across the world. Her reminiscences were published posthumously in America in 1981; two decades later, they appeared in Russia.

The wife of Ivan Bunin, Vera Muromtseva, had studied chemistry at the Moscow University. She was also passionately interested in literature and met Bunin at a literary evening in 1906. Vera left university to join the writer on his travels to Palestine, Egypt, and Europe. After the 1917 Revolution, the couple emigrated to France, where Vera kept a diary chronicling Bunin's life. His companion of forty-six years, she also collected Bunin's archive and wrote his biography. Fluent in four European languages, she published her translations, but to the émigré community she was memorable for her dedication to the writer. Prominent twentieth-century poet Marina Tsvetaeva, who had met the couple in France and corresponded with Vera, remarked that Bunin was indebted to her for his literary achievement. "Her unconditional love, dedication, and selflessness gave the world another classic of Russian literature. I'm confident that Ivan Bunin would not have achieved what he had without his Vera."[762]

Throughout its history, Russia's writers were the main opposition to repressive regimes. Their struggle for freedom was important and inspiring; some were prepared to die for their work, which put greater value on genuine literature. Russian literary wives had helped these works emerge and had ensured their survival and, by doing so, made lasting cultural contributions to the world.

Endnotes

1. Grigory Baklanov, Russian writer. His novels include *The Moment Between the Past and the Future* (London: Faber and Faber, 1994) and *Forever Nineteen* (New York: J.B. Lippincott, 1989).
2. Stacy Schiff, *Véra (Mrs. Vladimir Nabokov)* (New York: Random House, 1999), 52.
3. Ibid., xiv.
4. Anna Dostoevsky, *Dostoevsky: Reminiscences*, trans. Beatrice Stillman (New York: Liveright, 1975), 364.
5. Boris Pasternak, *I Remember: Sketch for an Autobiography* (Cambridge: Harvard University Press, 1983), 66.
6. *The Diaries of Sophia Tolstoy*, trans. Cathy Porter (New York: Random House, 1985), 42.
7. Ibid., 41.
8. Dostoevsky's name and patronymic.
9. Anna Dostoevsky, *Dostoevsky: Reminiscences*, 90.
10. Ibid., 5-6.
11. In the 1960s, Russian stenographer Poshemanskaia managed to crack her code. It took another three decades before the complete diaries appeared in a scholarly edition in Russia.
12. Joseph Brodsky, "Nadezhda Mandelstam: An Obituary" *in* Nadezhda Mandelstam, *Hope Against Hope*, trans. Max Hayward (New York: The Modern Library, 1999), viii.
13. Nadezhda Mandelstam, *Hope Abandoned* (New York: Atheneum, 1974), 264.
14. In another conversation, Natalya told me that she would never allow writing her biography as long as Solzhenitsyn was alive.

15. Stacy Schiff, *Véra*, 73.
16. Anna Dostoevsky, *Dostoevsky: Reminiscences*, 1.
17. *Osip i Nadezhda Mandelshtamy v rasskazah sovremennikov*, ed. O.S. Figurnova (Moskva: Natalis, 2002), 453.
18. The thirteenth-century Russian hero, patron saint of Russian warriors, and symbol of Russian nationalism.
19. Anna Dostoevsky, *Dostoevsky: Reminiscences*, 5–6. Unless otherwise specified, all citations referring to Anna's childhood and betrothal come from *Reminiscences*.
20. Turku Cathedral (Åbo domkyrkha in Swedish), built in the thirteenth century, was the main Evangelical Lutheran Church of Finland and the national shrine.
21. Anna's ancestors on her father's side were landowners from Poltava province in the Ukraine. When they settled in Petersburg, their surname Snitko was altered to the Russian-sounding Snitkin.
22. Aimee Dostoevsky, *Fyodor Dostoevsky* (New Haven: Yale University Press, 1922), 127.
23. At the end of the 1850s, a number of secondary schools for girls were opened. Mariinskaya Gymnasium opened in 1858, the year Anna became enrolled; she graduated it with a silver medal.
24. The magazine was published by Dostoevsky and his brother.
25. Petrashevsky, a follower of the French utopian socialist Charles Fourier, started a literary discussion group, participated in by writers, students, government officials, and army officers who opposed autocracy.
26. http://art.thelib.ru/science/unusual/misc/kak_rodilsya_vokrug_sveta.html
27. A.G. Dostoevskaia, *Dnevnik 1867 goda*, ed. Zhitomirskaia (Moskva: Nauka, 1993). April (17?), 1867. This edition can be found on http://az.lib.ru/d/dostoewskij_f_m/text_0630.shtml. Zhitomirskaia was the first to point out that Anna had made significant changes to her original diaries. Unless otherwise specified, translation is by the author.
28. Anna Dostoevsky, *Dostoevsky: Reminiscences*, 17.
29. Nihilism, a new social phenomenon in Russia, emerged in the 1860s and became reflected in Turgenev's *Fathers and Sons* and Chernyshevsky's *What is to be Done?* Dostoevsky portrayed Nihilists in *Crime and Punishment* and *The Devils*.
30. Aimee Dostoevsky, *Fyodor Dostoevsky*, 139.
31. Leonid Grossman, *Dostoevsky* (Moskva: Molodaya Gvardiya, 1965), 381. Translation is by the author.
32. As Dostoevsky told Anna, he himself freed Korvin-Krukovskaya from her pledge. But according to Joseph Frank, it is uncertain whether she even accepted Dostoevsky's proposal. Joseph Frank, *The Miraculous Years*, (1865–1871) (Princeton: Princeton University Press, 1995), 23.

33. Quoted in Joseph Frank, *The Miraculous Years*, 161–62.
34. Apollinaria's famous sister, Nadezhda Suslova, was Russia's first woman to become a medical doctor in 1867.
35. Suslova's second and last novella is entitled *Chuzhaya i Svoi* (*Estranged and Own*).
36. A.G. Dostoevskaia, *Dnevnik 1867 goda*, October 12 (31), 1867.
37. Quoted in Joseph Frank, *The Miraculous Years*, 23.
38. *Fyodor Dostoevsky: Complete Letters*, ed. and trans. David A. Lowe (Ardis: Ann Arbor, 1990), vol. 2, 211.
39. Ibid.
40. Ibid., 217.
41. Ibid., 219.
42. Ibid., 235.
43. Anna Dostoevsky, *Dostoevsky: Reminiscences*, 121
44. *The Diary of Dostoevsky's Wife*, trans. Madge Pamberton (New York: Macmillan, 1928), p. 7. This chapter employs two editions of Anna's diaries—the complete one, available in Russian online, and the translated version.
45. Now Vilnus, the capital of Lithuania.
46. A.G. Dostoevskaia, *Dnevnik 1867 goda*, April (17?), 1867.
47. *The Diary of Dostoevsky's Wife*, 29.
48. Ibid.
49. A.G. Dostoevskaia, *Dnevnik 1867 goda*, September 21/9, 1867.
50. Anna Dostoevsky, *Dostoevsky: Reminiscences*, 118.
51. A.G. Dostoevskaia, *Dnevnik 1867 goda*, August 18 (6), 1867.
52. Ibid., April (19?), 1867.
53. Ibid., June 26, 1867.
54. Anna Dostoevsky, *Dostoevsky: Reminiscences*, 117.
55. *The Diary of Dostoevsky's Wife*, 56.
56. A.G. Dostoevskaia, *Dnevnik 1867 goda*, June 6 (May 25), 1867.
57. Ibid., April 21 (May 3), 1867.
58. Ibid., April 29 (May 11), 1867.
59. Anna Dostoevsky, *Dostoevsky: Reminiscences*, 125.
60. *The Diary of Dostoevsky's Wife*, 64.
61. A.G. Dostoevskaia, *Dnevnik 1867 goda*, April 27 (May 9), 1867.
62. *Fyodor Dostoevsky: Complete Letters*, vol. 2, 227.
63. Ibid., 235.
64. Ibid., 232.
65. Ibid., 236.
66. Ibid., 241.
67. Ibid., 237.
68. A.G. Dostoevskaia, *Dnevnik 1867 goda*, May 8 (20), 1867.
69. *Fyodor Dostoevsky: Complete Letters*, vol. 2, 239–40.

70. A.G. Dostoevskaia, *Dnevnik 1867 goda*, May 11 (23), 1867.
71. *Fyodor Dostoevsky: Complete Letters*, vol. 2, 243.
72. Anna Dostoevsky, *Dostoevsky: Reminiscences*, 130.
73. Ibid., 131-32.
74. *The Diary of Dostoevsky's Wife*, 227.
75. Ibid., 264.
76. Ibid., 306.
77. A.G. Dostoevskaia, *Dnevnik 1867 goda*, August 8 (July 27), 1867.
78. *Fyodor Dostoevsky: Complete Letters*, vol. 2, 252.
79. A.G. Dostoevskaia, *Dnevnik 1867 goda*, August 23 (11), 1867.
80. Fyodor Dostoevsky, *Sobranie sochinenij v pyatnadtsati tomah* (Peterburg: Nauka, 1996), vol. 15, 319.
81. Anna Dostoevsky, *Dostoevsky: Reminiscences*, 137.
82. Nikolai Strakhov's expression quoted in Joseph Frank, *The Miraculous Years*, 305.
83. Dostoevsky's notebooks for *The Idiot*. Joseph Frank, *The Miraculous Years*, 274-75.
84. *Fyodor Dostoevsky: Complete Letters*, vol. 2, 297.
85. A.G. Dostoevskaia, *Dnevnik 1867 goda*, October 11 (September 29), 1867.
86. Ibid., September 18 (6), 1867.
87. Anna Dostoevsky, *Dostoevsky: Reminiscences*, 137-38.
88. Ibid., 140.
89. Joseph Frank, *Dostoevsky: The Miraculous Years (1865-71)*, 277.
90. A.G. Dostoevskaia, *Dnevnik 1867 goda*, October 1 (September 19), 1867.
91. Dostoevsky's letter to Dr. Stepan Yanovsky, Dec. 31, 1867 (January 12, 1868). Joseph Frank, *The Miraculous Years*, 244.
92. Anna Dostoevsky, *Dostoevsky: Reminiscences*, 141.
93. Ibid, 142.
94. *Fyodor Dostoevsky: Complete Letters*, vol. 3, 36.
95. Ibid., 53.
96. Ibid., 63.
97. Ibid., 67.
98. Anna Dostoevsky, *Dostoevsky: Reminiscences*, 147.
99. *Fyodor Dostoevsky: Complete Letters*, vol. 3, 88.
100. Ibid., 104.
101. Ibid., 99.
102. Anna Dostoevsky, *Dostoevsky: Reminiscences*, 153.
103. Ibid.
104. Dostoevsky's letter to Nikolai Strakhov. Anna Dostoevsky, *Dostoevsky: Reminiscences*, 153.
105. *Fyodor Dostoevsky: Complete Letters*, vol. 3, 174.
106. Ibid., 185.
107. Anna Dostoevsky, *Dostoevsky: Reminiscences*, 182.

108. *Fyodor Dostoevsky: Complete Letters*, vol. 3, 193.
109. Anna Dostoevsky, *Dostoevsky: Reminiscences*, 162.
110. Nechaev escaped to Switzerland, where he continued subversive activities. In 1872, he was arrested in Zurich and handed over to the Russian police.
111. Anna Dostoevsky, *Dostoevsky: Reminiscences*, 165.
112. Dostoevsky's father was killed on his estate by serfs.
113. *Fyodor Dostoevsky: Complete Letters*, vol. 3, 341.
114. Anna Dostoevsky, *Dostoevsky: Reminiscences*, 170-71.
115. Ibid.
116. Ibid., 184.
117. The first chloroform narcosis in Russia was tested by Nikolai Pirogov in 1847. The anesthetic was first applied during surgeries in 1848.
118. Anna Dostoevsky, *Dostoevsky: Reminiscences*, 199.
119. Ibid., 183.
120. Ibid., 216.
121. Ibid., 218.
122. Quoted in Joseph Frank, *The Mantle of the Prophet: 1871-1881*, 202.
123. *Fyodor Dostoevsky: Complete Letters*, Vol. 4, 39-40.
124. Ibid., 148.
125. Ibid., 84-85.
126. Ibid., 86.
127. Anna Dostoevsky, *Dostoevsky: Reminiscences*, 238.
128. AD letter to FD, July 26, 1873. F.M. Dostoevsky, A.G. Dostoevskaia, *Perepiska* (Leningrad: Nauka, 1976), 110-11. Unless otherwise indicated, Anna's letters to Dostoevsky come from this source. Translation is by the author.
129. AD letter to FD, August 16, 1873.
130. *Fyodor Dostoevsky: Complete Letters*, Vol. 4, 317.
131. Anna Dostoevsky, *Dostoevsky: Reminiscences*, 191.
132. Ibid., 238-39.
133. *Fyodor Dostoevsky: Complete Letters*, Vol. 4, 199.
134. AD letter to FD, February 12, 1875.
135. AD letter to FD, June 22, 1874.
136. Anna Dostoevsky, *Dostoevsky: Reminiscences*, 258.
137. AD letter to FD, June 21, 1875.
138. AD letter to FD, June 22, 1874.
139. FD letter to AD, July 9 (June 27), 1876. F.M. Dostoevsky, A.G. Dostoevskaia, *Perepiska*, 208.
140. AD letter to FD, July 18, 1876.
141. *Fyodor Dostoevsky: Complete Letters*, vol. 4, 303.
142. Alyosha Dostoevsky, their younger son, who was eleven months at the time.
143. *Fyodor Dostoevsky: Complete Letters*, vol. 4, 316.

144. Anna Dostoevsky, *Dostoevsky: Reminiscences*, 264.
145. Anna began to collect stamps at 21, in Dresden. According to her *Reminiscences*, she did not buy a single stamp for her extensive collection, but simply took them off envelopes. The fate of her collection is unknown.
146. Anna Dostoevsky, *Dostoevsky: Reminiscences*, 270. Unless otherwise specified, all citations referring to Dostoevsky's final years and his death come from this source.
147. *Fyodor Dostoevsky: Complete Letters*, Vol. 5, 233.
148. Joseph Frank, *The Mantle of the Prophet: 1871–1881*, 525.
149. *Fyodor Dostoevsky: Complete Letters*, Vol. 5, 236.
150. Anna Dostoevsky, *Dostoevsky: Reminiscences*, 337.
151. Anna tells this story in her *Reminiscences*; however, what exactly triggered Dostoevsky's hemorrhage is unknown.
152. Anna Dostoevsky, *Dostoevsky: Reminiscences*, 349.
153. As Dostoevsky had written Maikov, he had become "an uncompromising monarchist when it comes to Russia." Joseph Frank, *Dostoevsky: The Miraculous Years (1865–71)*, 279.
154. Sergey Belov, *Zhena pisatelya* (Moskva: Sovetskaya Rossiaya, 1986), 157.
155. Anna Dostoevsky, *Dostoevsky: Reminiscences*, 384.
156. Leonid Grossman's words.
157. This house perished during World War II.
158. Sergey Belov, *Zhena pisatelya*, 171.
159. Ibid.
160. Leonid Grossman, "A.G. Dostoevskaya i ee vospominaniya." In *Vospominaniya A.G. Dostoevskoy* (Moskva: Gosudarstvennoe izdatel'stvo, 1925), 12–14.
161. Anna Dostoevsky, *Dostoevsky: Reminiscences*, xii.
162. Sergey Belov, *Zhena pisatelya*, 176.
163. Leonid Mironovich Leonidov, actor and stage director (1871–1941).
164. Sergey Belov, *Zhena pisatelya*, 193.
165. Ibid., 194.
166. Ibid., 199.
167. In five days, from March 8 to 12, 1917, a mass movement in Petrograd overturned the tsarist government.
168. *Vospominaniya A.G. Dostoevskoy*, 16.
169. Ibid., 14.
170. Sergey Belov, *Zhena pisatelya*, 200.
171. Andrei Dostoevsky, "Anna Dostoevskaya," Journal *Zhenshchiny mira (Women of the World)*, No. 10, 1963.
172. Russian State Library, Manuscript Department, F. 93, 3, 59 a. Translation is by the author.
173. AD letter to F.F. Dostoevsky, February 6, 1918, F. 93, 3, 59 a.
174. *The Diaries of Sophia Tolstoy*, 27.

175. Tatyana Tolstoy, *Tolstoy Remembered*, trans. Derek Coltman (New York: McGraw-Hill, 1977), 275.
176. Sophia's mother and uncles were technically illegitimate and could not inherit the family name, Islenev. Instead, they received an improvised name Islavin.
177. O. Yu. Safonova, *Rod Bersov v Rossii* (Moskva: Entsiklopedia syol i dereven, 1999), 19–20.
178. Nikolai Rubinstein, founder of the Moscow Conservatory and pianist, conductor, and composer; he was a younger brother of Anton Rubinstein, who founded the Petersburg Conservatory.
179. Sophia Tolstoy, *My Life*, Part 1. This memoir will be quoted from the original manuscript kept at the Tolstoy State Museum in Moscow. (GMT, f. 47, parts 1–8). Translation is by the author.
180. Tatyana Kuzminskaia, *Tolstoy As I Knew Him: My Life At Home and At Yasnaya Polyana*, trans. Nora Sigerist (New York: Macmillan, 1948), 5.
181. Sophia Tolstoy, *My Life*, Part 1.
182. *The Diaries of Sophia Tolstoy*, 835.
183. Sophia Tolstoy, *My Life*, part 1.
184. *Tolstoy's Diaries*, ed. and trans. R. F. Christian (London: Anthlone, 1985), vol. 1, 164.
185. Sophia Tolstoy, *My Life*, Part 1.
186. Leo Tolstoy, *Anna Karenina*, trans. Richard Pevear and Larissa Volokhonsky (New York: Penguin, 2002), 21.
187. *Tolstoy's Diaries*, vol. 1, 166.
188. Sophia Tolstoy, *My Life*, Part 1.
189. *The Diaries of Sophia Tolstoy*, 832.
190. Ibid.
191. Ibid., 835.
192. Sophia Tolstoy, *My Life*, part 1.
193. *The Diaries of Sophia Tolstoy*, 838.
194. Ibid., 839.
195. Tatyana Kuzminskaia, *Tolstoy As I Knew Him*, 81–82.
196. Sophia Tolstoy, *My Life*, Part 1.
197. Sophia Tolstoy, *Who Is To Blame? Oktyabr'*, No. 10, 1994. Translation is by the author.
198. *The Diaries of Sophia Tolstoy*, 3.
199. Sophia's (SA) letter to her sister Tatyana Kuzminskaia (TA), February 13, 1863. Sophia Tolstoy's correspondence with her sister is held at GMT and is quoted here from this source. Translation is by the author.
200. *The Diaries of Sophia Tolstoy*, 17.
201. Sophia Tolstoy, *The Autobiography* in *Dve zheny: Tolstaia i Dostoevskaia* (Berlin, 1925), 15–16.

202. Leo Tolstoy, *War and Peace*, trans. Richard Pevear and Larissa Volokhonsky (New York: Alfred A. Knopf, 2007), 1157.
203. *The Diaries of Sophia Tolstoy*, 22–23.
204. Tatyana Kuzminskaia, *Tolstoy As I Knew Him*, 233.
205. Sophia Tolstoy, *The Autobiography*, 17.
206. *Tolstoy's Letters*, ed. and trans. R. F. Christian (London: Anthlone, 1978), vol. 1, 182.
207. LN letter to *Alexandrine*, July 5, 1865. Translation is by the author.
208. *The Diaries of Sophia Tolstoy*, 41.
209. SA letter to Tolstoy (LN), November 26, 1864. Sophia's letters to Tolstoy are quoted from *Pis'ma k Tolstomu: 1862–1910*, ed. P. Popov (Moskva-Leningrad: Academia, 1936). Translation is by the author.
210. LN letter to SA, December 6, 1864. Unless otherwise specified, Tolstoy's letters to Sophia are quoted from vols. 83–84 of Tolstoy's *Complete Collected Works in 90 volumes*, ed. V.G. Chertkov (Moscow-Leningrad, 1928–58). Later Jubilee Edition.
211. LN letter to SA, December 4, 1864.
212. Ibid.
213. *Tolstoy's Letters*, vol. 1, 190.
214. An old oak grove on the Yasnaya Polyana estate.
215. SA letter to LN, December 9, 1864.
216. *Tolstoy's letters*, vol. 1, 190.
217. Sophia Tolstoy, *My Life*, Part 2.
218. Sophia Tolstoy, *The Autobiography*, 14-15.
219. LN letter to SA, November 14, 1866.
220. SA letter to LN, November 14, 1866.
221. *The Diaries of Sophia Tolstoy*, 42.
222. Sophia Tolstoy, *The Autobiography*, 15.
223. *Tolstoy's Letters*, vol. 1, 220.
224. *The Diaries of Sophia Tolstoy*, 846.
225. *Tolstoy's Letters*, vol. 1, 222.
226. LN letter to Fet, October 21, 1869.
227. Sophia Tolstoy, *My Life*, part 2.
228. *Tolstoy's Letters*, vol.1, 240–41.
229. Tatyana Tolstoy, *Tolstoy Remembered*, 110.
230. *The Diaries of Sophia Tolstoy*, 845.
231. Sophia Tolstoy, *My Life*, Part 2.
232. *Tolstoy's Letters*, vol. 1, 235.
233. SA letter to TA, July 8, 1873.
234. Ibid.
235. Sophia Tolstoy, *My Life*, part 2.
236. SA letter to TA, August 25, 1873.
237. Sophia Tolstoy, *My Life*, part 2.

238. Ibid.
239. SA letter to LN, July 27, 1871.
240. *The Diaries of Sophia Tolstoy*, 50.
241. Sophia Tolstoy, *My Life*, part 2.
242. Leo Tolstoy, *Anna Karenina*, 607.
243. Sophia Tolstoy, *My Life*, part 2.
244. Ibid.
245. SA letter to TA, December 19, 1873.
246. SA letter to TA, February 6, 1874.
247. SA letter to TA, December 10, 1874.
248. Ibid.
249. SA letter to TA, February 23, 1874.
250. Tatyana Tolstoy, *Tolstoy Remembered*, 49.
251. Ilya Tolstoy, *Tolstoy, My Father* (Chicago: Cowles, 1971), 96.
252. *Tolstoy's Letters*, vol. 1, 293.
253. Nikolai Strakhov's letter to LN, February 1877.
254. Nikolai Gusev, *Chronicle of the Life and Works of L.N. Tolstoy* (Moscow: State Literary House, 1958), vol. 1, 490.
255. Sophia Tolstoy, *My Life*, part 3.
256. *The Diaries of Sophia Tolstoy*, 850.
257. Nikolai Gusev, *Chronicle*, vol. 1, 513.
258. Ibid., 516.
259. SA letter to TA, November, 1879.
260. Sophia Tolstoy, *My Life*, part 4.
261. SA letter to TA, November 29, 1879.
262. SA letter to TA, January 9, 1880.
263. LN letter to Vladimir Stasov, May 1, 1881.
264. *Tolstoy's Letters*, vol. 2, 340.
265. LN letter to SA, August 2, 1881.
266. Sophia Tolstoy, *My Life*, part 3.
267. SA letter to TA, February 19, 1880.
268. Sophia Tolstoy, *My Life*, part 3.
269. Ibid., part 4.
270. LN letter to SA, November 10, 1883.
271. See more on this in Aylmer Maude, *The Life of Tolstoy: Later Years* (London: Oxford University Press, 1930), vol. 2, 249–265.
272. SA letter to TA, March 3, 1881.
273. Tatyana Tolstoy, *Tolstoy Remembered*, 193.
274. Pointed out in Leo Tolstoy, *Plays: Volume Three*, trans. Marvin Kantor with Tanya Tulchinsky (Evanston: Northwestern University Press, 1998). Drawn from their conversations, this play is believed to be Tolstoy's most autobiographical work.
275. Sophia Tolstoy, *My Life*, part 3.

276. Leo Tolstoy, *And the Light Shineth in Darkness*, Act 1, scene 19. *Plays: Volume Three*, 39.
277. Tolstoy L.N., *Jubilee Edition*, vol. 83, 579.
278. Sophia Tolstoy, *My Life*, part 4.
279. Ibid.
280. LN letter to Chertkov, June 24, 1884.
281. SA letter to TA, April 12, 1885.
282. SA letter to LN, February 25, 1893.
283. SA letter to LN, October 29, 1884.
284. SA letter to LN, March 5–6, 1882.
285. *Tolstoy's Letters*, vol. 2, 392. Despite writing this, Tolstoy attempted to sell a limited printing of one treatise, *What I Believe*, at 25 rubles. In comparison, the twelve-volume edition Sophia produced cost 18 rubles.
286. SA letter to TA, fall 1885.
287. SA letter to TA, December 20, 1885.
288. Tatyana Tolstoy, *Tolstoy Remembered*, 202.
289. SA letter to LN, December 23, 1885.
290. SA letter to LN, December 24, 1885.
291. SA letter to LN, March 28, 1889.
292. Sophia Tolstoy, *My Life*, part 4.
293. SA letter to TA, January 9, 1885.
294. Strakhov's letter first published in *Yasnaya Polyana Almanach*, Tula, 1978.
295. SA letter to LN, May 5, 1886.
296. *Tolstoy's Letters*, vol. 2, 402.
297. *The Diaries of Sophia Tolstoy*, 79.
298. Aylmer Maude, *The Life of Tolstoy: Later Years*, vol. 2, 478.
299. *The Diaries of Sophia Tolstoy*, 77.
300. Ibid., 78.
301. SA letter to TA, March 13, 1889.
302. *The Diaries of Sophia Tolstoy*, 371.
303. *Tolstoy's Diaries*, vol.1, 271.
304. Sophia Tolstoy, *My Life*, part 5.
305. Ivan Bunin, *The Liberation of Tolstoy* (Evanston: Northwestern University Press, 2001), 55.
306. Nikolai Strakhov's letter to Tolstoy, April 24, 1890.
307. *The Diaries of Sophia Tolstoy*, 141.
308. Sophia Tolstoy, *My Life*, part 5.
309. Aylmer Maude, *The Life of Tolstoy: Later Years*, vol. 2, 400.
310. Ibid., 158.
311. One pood equals about 36 pounds.
312. *The Diaries of Sophia Tolstoy*, 168.
313. Ibid., 169.
314. LN letter to SA, November 23, 1891.

315. SA letter to LN, November 20, 1891.
316. *Tolstoy's Letters*, vol. 2, 489.
317. SA letter to TA, January 8, 1892.
318. SA letter to LN, September 16, 1893.
319. *The Diaries of Sophia Tolstoy*, 73.
320. LN letter to SA, September 26, 1896.
321. *Tolstoy's Letters*, vol. 2, 517.
322. Sophia Tolstoy, *My Life*, part 3.
323. SA letter to Leonila Annenkova, fall 1896.
324. SA letter to LN, October 12, 1895.
325. *Tolstoy's Diaries*, vol. 2, 418.
326. *Tolstoy's Letters*, vol. 2, 557.
327. SA letter to LN, May 14, 1897.
328. SA letter to LN, September 11, 1894.
329. SA letter to LN, October 29, 1895.
330. Sophia Tolstoy, *My Life*, part 7.
331. *The Diaries of Sophia Tolstoy*, 916.
332. Ibid., 374.
333. Ibid., 443.
334. Ibid.
335. Ibid., 420.
336. Ibid., 447.
337. Ibid., 457.
338. Ibid., 442.
339. Ibid.
340. SA letter to TA, March 28, 1904.
341. The memoir *My Life* was published in English. Sophia Andreyevna Tolstaya, *My Life* trans. John Woodsworth and Arkadi Klioutchanski (Ottawa: University of Ottawa Press, 2010). Unfortunately this translation does not accurately render Sophia's style.
342. *Tolstoy's Diaries*, vol. 2, 555–56.
343. SA letter to TA, November 26, 1906.
344. Alexandra Tolstaia, *Doch'* (Moskva: Vagrius, 2000), 271.
345. Alexander Goldenweiser, *Lev Tolstoy: Reminiscences* (Moscow: Zakharov, 2002), 166.
346. Georgy Orekhanov, *V.G. Chertkov v zhizni L.N. Tolstogo* (Moskva: PSTGU, 2009), 152.
347. *Tolstoy's Diaries*, vol. 2, 589.
348. Ibid., 678.
349. *Tolstoy's Letters*, vol. 2, 703.
350. *The Diaries of Sophia Tolstoy*, 536.
351. Ibid., 498.
352. *Tolstoy's Diaries*, vol. 2, 683.

353. Tatyana Komarova, *On the Flight and Death of L. N. Tolstoy* (Yasnaya Polyana Yearbook, 1992).
354. Sergei Belov, *Zhena pisatelya*, 180.
355. Sophia Tolstoy, *Autobiography*, 55.
356. Tikhon Polner, *Tolstoy and His Wife* (Moscow: Nash Dom—L'Age d'Homme, 2000), 195-96. Translation is by the author.
357. *Tolstoy's Letters*, vol. 2, 562.
358. Nadezhda Mandelstam, *Hope Against Hope* (New York: Atheneum, 1970), 211.
359. Nadezhda Mandelstam, *Hope Abandoned* (New York: Atheneum, 1974), 507.
360. *Osip i Nadezhda Mandelshtamy v rasskazah sovremennikov*, 297.
361. Roberta Reeder, *Anna Akhmatova* (New York: Picador USA, 1994), 18.
362. Nadezhda Mandelstam, *Hope Abandoned*, 310.
363. Ibid., 14.
364. Ibid., 13-14.
365. Abbreviation for Artists, Writers, Actors, and Musicians.
366. *Osip i Nadezhda Mandelshtamy v rasskazah sovremennikov*, 476-77.
367. Nadezhda Mandelstam, *Hope Abandoned*, 15.
368. Ibid., 136.
369. Oleg Lekhmanov, *Mandelstam* (Boston: Academic Studies, 2010), 65.
370. Nadezhda Mandelstam, *Hope Abandoned*, 260.
371. Ibid., 135.
372. Donald Rayfield, *Stalin and his Hangmen* (London: Viking, 2004), 77.
373. Nadezhda Mandelstam, *Hope Abandoned*, 20.
374. Ibid., 17.
375. Ibid., 515.
376. Osip Mandelstam, *Critical Prose and Letters* (Ann Arbor: Ardis, 1979), 484.
377. Nadezhda Mandelstam, *Hope Abandoned*, 542.
378. Ibid., 217.
379. Ibid., 65, 71.
380. Ibid. 78.
381. Ibid.,142.
382. Ibid., 260.
383. *Osip i Nadezhda Mandelshtamy v rasskazah sovremennikov*, 481.
384. Nadezhda Mandelstam, *Hope Abandoned*, 196.
385. Ibid.
386. Nadezhda Mandelstam, *Kniga tret'ya* (Paris: YMCA Press, 1987), 81-82.
387. Nadezhda Mandelstam, *Hope Abandoned*, 198.
388. Ibid., 232
389. Nadezhda Mandelstam, *Hope Abandoned*, 117.
390. *Osip i Nadezhda Mandelshtamy v rasskazah sovremennikov*, 150.
391. Clarence Brown, *Mandelstam* (Cambridge, Cambridge University Press, 1973), 101.

392. Nadezhda Mandelstam, *Hope Against Hope*, vii.
393. Nadezhda Mandelstam, *Hope Abandoned*, 203.
394. Ibid., 195-96.
395. Oleg Lekhmanov, *Mandelstam*, 94.
396. Ibid.
397. Nadezhda Mandelstam, *Hope Abandoned*, 206.
398. Ibid.
399. Ibid., 158.
400. *Osip i Nadezhda Mandelshtamy v rasskazah sovremennikov*, 101.
401. Ibid., 297.
402. Anna Akhmatova, *My Half Century: Selected Prose* (Ardis: Ann Arbor, 1992), 96.
403. Oleg Lekhmanov, *Mandelstam*, 91.
404. Nadezhda Mandelstam, *Hope Abandoned*, 212.
405. Carl Proffer, *The Widows of Russia and Other Writings* (Ann Arbor: Ardis, 1987), 23.
406. Emma Gershtein, *Memuary* (Moskva: Zakharov, 2002), 596-97.
407. Nadezhda Mandelstam, *Hope Abandoned*, 208-09.
408. Ibid., 212.
409. Osip Mandelstam, *Critical Prose and Letters*, 495.
410. Nadezhda Mandelstam, *Hope Abandoned*, 261.
411. Osip Mandelstam, *Critical Prose and Letters*, 512.
412. Anna Akhmatova, *My Half Century: Selected Prose*, 97.
413. Nadezhda Mandelstam, *Hope Abandoned*, 262.
414. Ibid., 135.
415. Ibid., 236-37.
416. Ibid., 397.
417. Ibid., 528.
418. Ibid., 263.
419. Oleg Lekhmanov, *Mandelstam*, 98.
420. Ibid., 110.
421. Nadezhda Mandelstam, *Hope Against Hope*, 117.
422. Nadezhda Mandelstam, *Hope Abandoned*, 549.
423. Ibid., 134.
424. Nadezhda Mandelstam, *Kniga tret´ya*, 134.
425. Nadezhda Mandelstam, *Hope Abandoned*, 264.
426. Ibid., 264.
427. Ibid.
428. Ibid., 234.
429. Areas afflicted by the famine included Ukraine, Northern Caucasus, Volga Region, Kazakhstan, the South Urals, and West Siberia.
430. Nadezhda Mandelstam, *Hope Against Hope*, 158.
431. Nadezhda Mandelstam, *Hope Abandoned*, 469.

432. Ibid, 347.
433. Nadezhda Mandelstam, *Hope Against Hope*, 158.
434. Quoted in Roberta Reeder, *Anna Akhmatova*, 196.
435. Nadezhda Mandelstam, *Hope Against Hope*, 159.
436. Ibid., 157.
437. Nadezhda Mandelstam, *Hope Abandoned*, 265.
438. The line from the first variant of the poem that fell into the hands of the secret police.
439. *Osip i Nadezhda Mandelshtamy v rasskazah sovremennikov*, 109.
440. Olga Ivinskaya, *A Captive of Time* (New York: Warner Books, 1978), 122.
441. Anna Akhmatova, *My Half Century: Selected Prose*, 99.
442. Nadezhda Mandelstam, *Hope Against Hope*, 11.
443. Isaiah Berlin, *The Soviet Mind: Russian Culture Under Communism* (Washington, D.C.: Brookings Institution Press, 2004), 76.
444. Nadezhda Mandelstam, *Hope Against Hope*, 4.
445. Ibid., 5.
446. Ibid., 15. Unless otherwise specified, all citations referring to Mandelstam's first arrest and the couple's Voronezh exile come from this source.
447. Enukidze was Secretary of the Central Executive Committee.
448. Oleg Lekhmanov, *Mandelstam*, 140.
449. Anna Akhmatova, *My Half Century: Selected Prose*, 106.
450. *Osip i Nadezhda Mandelshtamy v rasskazah sovremennikov*, 152.
451. Anna Akhmatova, *My Half Century: Selected Prose*, 104.
452. *Osip i Nadezhda Mandelshtamy v rasskazah sovremennikov*, 252.
453. Osip Mandelstam, *Critical Prose and Letters*, 564.
454. Ibid., 560.
455. Ibid., 572.
456. Ibid., 562.
457. Ibid., 564.
458. Ibid., 570.
459. Ibid., 562.
460. Anna Akhmatova, *My Half Century: Selected Prose*, 108.
461. Nadezhda Mandelstam, *Hope Abandoned*, 613.
462. Nadezhda Mandelstam, *Hope Against Hope*, 353.
463. Ibid.
464. Ibid., 357.
465. Ibid., 361.
466. Ibid., 362.
467. Nadezhda Mandelstam, *Hope Abandoned*, 609.
468. Anna Akhmatova, *My Half Century: Selected Prose*, 108.
469. Osip Mandelstam, *Critical Prose and Letters*, 573.
470. Oleg Lekhmanov, *Mandelstam*, 162.

471. http://mandelshtam.lit-info.ru/review/mandelshtam/002/141.htm
472. Nadezhda Mandelstam, *Hope Abandoned*, 620.
473. Ibid., 610.
474. Ibid.
475. Ibid., 180.
476. Ibid., 597.
477. Ibid., 509.
478. Nadezhda Mandelstam, *Ob Akhmatovoi* (Moskva: Tri kvadrata, 2008), 284.
479. *Osip i Nadezhda Mandelshtamy v rasskazah sovremennikov*, 368.
480. Nadezhda Mandelstam, *Hope Against Hope*, 276.
481. *Osip i Nadezhda Mandelshtamy v rasskazah sovremennikov*, 378.
482. Nadezhda Mandelstam, *Hope Against Hope*, 283.
483. Nadezhda Mandelstam, *Hope Abandoned*, 558.
484. Ibid., 379-80.
485. Ibid., 381.
486. Ibid., 384.
487. Ibid., 584.
488. *Osip i Nadezhda Mandelshtamy v rasskazah sovremennikov*, 329-30.
489. Nadezhda Mandelstam, *Hope Abandoned*, 386.
490. *Osip i Nadezhda Mandelshtamy v rasskazah sovremennikov*, 344.
491. Ibid., 342.
492. Nadezhda Mandelstam, *Hope Abandoned*, 586.
493. Ibid., 587.
494. Nadezhda Mandelstam, *Hope Against Hope*, 215-16.
495. Ibid., 376.
496. *Osip i Nadezhda Mandelshtamy v rasskazah sovremennikov*, 417.
497. Nadezhda Mandelstam, *Hope Abandoned*, 184.
498. Ibid., 617–18.
499. Ibid., 361.
500. Nadezhda Mandelstam, *Hope Against Hope*, vi.
501. Ibid., v.
502. Carl Proffer, *The Widows of Russia and Other Writings*, 15. Unless otherwise specified, all citations referring to the Proffers' meeting with Nadezhda come from this source.
503. Nadezhda Mandelstam, *Hope Against Hope*, 259.
504. Nadezhda Mandelstam, *Vospominaniya* (Moskva: Soglasie, 1999), xviii.
505. Nadezhda Mandelstam, *Hope Against Hope*, vi.
506. Carl Proffer, *The Widows of Russia and Other Writings*, 38.
507. Nadezhda Mandelstam, *Hope Against Hope*, xi.
508. Osip Mandelstam, *The Complete Critical Prose and Letters*, ed. and trans. Jane Gary Harris (Ann Arbor: Ardis, 1979), 570.

509. *Osip i Nadezhda Mandelshtamy v rasskazah sovremennikov*, 515.
510. Ibid., 395-96.
511. Ibid., 497.
512. Ibid., 504.
513. *Complete Poetry of Osip Emilievich Mandelstam*, trans. Burton Raffel and Alla Burago (Albany: State University of New York Press, 1973), 211.
514. Nadezhda Mandelstam, *Kniga tret'ya*, 310.
515. For general background information on Véra, I am indebted to Brian Boyd, *Vladimir Nabokov: The Russian Years* (Princeton: Princeton University Press, 1990), *Vladimir Nabokov: The American Years* (Princeton: Princeton University Press, 1991) and to Stacy Schiff, *Véra (Mrs. Vladimir Nabokov)* (New York: Random House, 1999).
516. *The Garland Companion to Vladimir Nabokov*, ed. Vladimir Alexandrov (New York: Garland, 1995), xxxiii.
517. Dmitry Volkogonov, *Lenin: A New Biography* (New York: Free Press, 1994), 238.
518. Stacy Schiff, *Véra*, 29.
519. Brian Boyd, *Vladimir Nabokov: The Russian Years*, 214.
520. Andrew Field, *Nabokov: His Life in Part* (New York: Viking, 1977), 178.
521. Ibid., 173.
522. Stacy Schiff, *Véra*, 3.
523. Brenda Maddox, *Nora: The Real Life of Molly Bloom* (Boston: Houghton Mifflin, 1988), 25.
524. Stacy Schiff, *Véra*, 11.
525. Ibid., 10.
526. Alexander Bahrah, *Bunin v halate* (Moskva: Soglasie, 2000), 120-21.
527. Stacy Schiff, *Véra*, 12.
528. Brian Boyd, *Vladimir Nabokov: The Russian Years*, 239.
529. Stacy Schiff, *Véra*, 62.
530. Ibid., 46.
531. Ibid., 42.
532. Ibid., 56.
533. Ibid., 52.
534. Andrew Field, *Nabokov: His Life in Part*, 172.
535. Stacy Schiff, *Véra*, 57.
536. Brian Boyd, *Vladimir Nabokov: The Russian Years*, 291.
537. Ibid., 343.
538. Ibid., 396.
539. Stacy Schiff, *Véra*, 74.
540. Andrew Field, *Nabokov: His Life in Part*, 200.
541. Vladimir Nabokov, *Speak, Memory* (New York: G.P. Putnam's Sons, 1966), 295.
542. Brian Boyd, *Vladimir Nabokov: The Russian Years*, 408.

543. Andrew Field, *Nabokov: His Life in Part*, 198.
544. Ibid., 206.
545. *Vladimir Nabokov: Selected Letters: 1940–1977*, ed. Dmitry Nabokov (New York: Harcourt Brace Jovanovich, 1989), 23–24.
546. Stacy Schiff, *Véra*, 85.
547. *Vladimir Nabokov: Selected Letters*, 19–20.
548. In Germany the Nabokovs and other émigrés from Bolshevik Russia received temporary passports. These had expired.
549. Diminutive from Dmitry.
550. Nina Berberova, *The Italics Are Mine* (New York: Harcourt, Brace & World, 1969), 324.
551. Stacy Schiff, *Véra*, 98.
552. Brian Boyd, *Vladimir Nabokov: The Russian Years*, 421.
553. Vladimir Nabokov, *Speak, Memory*, 302.
554. *Vladimir Nabokov: Selected Letters*, 30.
555. Vladimir Nabokov, *Speak, Memory*, 292.
556. Stacy Schiff, *Véra*, 108.
557. Ibid., 179.
558. Brian Boyd, *Vladimir Nabokov: The American Years*, 83.
559. Stacy Schiff, *Véra*, 120.
560. *The Nabokov–Wilson Letters: Correspondence between Vladimir Nabokov and Edmund Wilson 1940–1971*, ed. Simon Karlinsky (New York: Harper&Row, 1979), 121.
561. Stacy Schiff, *Véra*, 167.
562. Ibid., 131.
563. Ibid., 189.
564. Ibid., 187.
565. Ibid., 151.
566. Ibid., 184.
567. Ibid., 163.
568. Ibid., 171.
569. Brian Boyd, *Vladimir Nabokov: The American Years*, 222.
570. Stacy Schiff, *Véra*, 171.
571. Brian Boyd, *Vladimir Nabokov: The American Years*, 221.
572. Stacy Schiff, *Véra*, 220.
573. Ibid., 221.
574. Ibid., 200.
575. Christopher Hitchens, *Arguably: Essays* (Toronto: McLelland & Stewart, 2011), 73-74.
576. Vladimir Nabokov, *Perepiska s sestroi* (Ann Arbor: Ardis, 1985), 69. Translation is by the author.
577. Vladimir Nabokov, *Poems and Problems* (New York: McGraw-Hill, 1970), 155.

578. Brian Boyd, *Vladimir Nabokov: The American Years*, 201.
579. Vladimir Nabokov, *Poems and Problems*, 175.
580. Stacy Schiff, *Véra*, 214.
581. VN letter to Elena Sikorskaya, September 29, 1953.
582. VN letter to Wilson, July 30, 1954.
583. Wilson's letter to VN, November 30, 1954.
584. Brian Boyd, *Vladimir Nabokov: The American Years*, 264.
585. Ibid., 267.
586. Stacy Schiff, *Véra*, 201.
587. Ibid., 206.
588. Brian Boyd, *Vladimir Nabokov: The American Years*, 269.
589. Stacy Schiff, *Véra*, 213.
590. Brian Boyd, *Vladimir Nabokov: The American Years*, 301.
591. Ibid., 365.
592. VN letter to Elena Sikorsky, May 24, 1959.
593. Stacy Schiff, *Véra*, 243.
594. Brian Boyd, *Vladimir Nabokov: The American Years*, 371.
595. Ibid., 373.
596. Stacy Schiff, *Véra*, 343.
597. Brian Boyd, *Vladimir Nabokov: The American Years*, 501.
598. Stacy Schiff, *Véra*, 269.
599. Martin Amis, *Visiting Mrs. Nabokov and Other Excursions* (London: Jonathan Cape, 1993), 119.
600. Stacy Schiff, *Véra*, 254.
601. Ibid., 255–56.
602. Ibid., 259.
603. Ibid., 271.
604. Brian Boyd, *Vladimir Nabokov: The American Years*, 459.
605. Ibid., 568.
606. Ibid., 570.
607. Stacy Schiff, *Véra*, 297.
608. Brian Boyd, *Vladimir Nabokov: The American Years*, 471.
609. Stacy Schiff, *Véra*, 53.
610. Ibid.
611. Ibid., 277.
612. Ibid., 296.
613. Andrew Field, *Nabokov: His Life in Part*, 180.
614. Ibid., 176.
615. Andrew Field, *The Life and Art of Vladimir Nabokov* (New York: Crown, 1977), 96.
616. Andrew Field, *Nabokov: His Life in Part*, 177.
617. Ibid., 180.
618. Stacy Schiff, *Véra*, 297–98.

619. Ibid., 299.
620. *Vladimir Nabokov: Selected Letters*, 546.
621. Stacy Schiff, *Véra*, 360.
622. Ibid., 365.
623. Martin Amis, *Visiting Mrs. Nabokov and Other Excursions*, 117, 115.
624. *Dnevnik Eleny Bulgakovoi*, eds. L. Yanovskaya, V. Losev (Moskva: Knizhnaya palata, 1990), 16. Unless otherwise specified, all citations in this chapter come from this source. Translation is by the author.
625. Lydia Yanovskaia, *Zapiski o Mikhaile Bulgakove* (Holon, Israel: Publishers "Moria," 1997), 347–49. Translation is by the author.
626. Mikhail Bulgakov, *The Master and Margarita*, trans. Michael Glenny (New York: Harper & Row, 1967), 215.
627. http://moscowia.su/images/ris2/11.htm
628. International relief operation was organized by Fridtjof Nansen, a Norwegian explorer, appointed a commissioner in the League of Nations in 1921. America sent the largest flow of aid: ARA, American Relief Administration, fed 11 million people each day.
629. The church was destroyed during the Soviet anti-religious campaign.
630. J.A.E. Curtis, *Mikhail Bulgakov: A Life in Letters and Diaries* (London: Bloomsbury, 1991), 69.
631. Stalin corresponded with Vladimir Bill-Belotserkovsky, author of propaganda plays.
632. *Mikhail Bulgakov: A Life in Letters and Diaries*, 70.
633. Ibid., 104.
634. Ibid., 108–10.
635. Marietta Chudakova, *Zhizneopisanie Mikhaila Bulgakova* (Moskva: Kniga, 1988), 371.
636. *Vospominaniya o Mikhaile Bulgakove*, ed. E.S. Bulgakova (Moskva: Sovetskij pisatel', 1988), 387.
637. Mikhail Bulgakov, *The Master and Margarita*, 216.
638. Evgeny Shilovsky's letter to Sergei and Alexandra Nurenberg, September 3, 1932. Russian State Library, Manuscript Department, f. 562, 62, 56.
639. Ellendea Proffer, *Bulgakov: Life and Work* (Ann Arbor: Ardis, 1984), 345.
640. Anatoly Shvarts, *Zhizn' i smert' Mikhaila Bulgakova* (Tenafly, N.J.: Ermitazh, 1988), 34.
641. *Mikhail Bulgakov: A Life in Letters and Diaries*, 157.
642. Ibid., 158.
643. Ibid.
644. Ibid., 190.
645. Marietta Chudakova, *Zhizneopisanie Mikhaila Bulgakova*, 388.
646. Nikolai Erdman and Vladimir Mass, Soviet playwrights.
647. Diminutive from Mikhail.

648. Diminutive from Sergei.
649. *Dnevnik Eleny Bulgakovoi*, 53-54.
650. *Mikhail Bulgakov: A Life in Letters and Diaries*, 168.
651. Ibid., 165.
652. Ibid., 189.
653. Ibid., 212.
654. Ibid., 198.
655. *Vospominaniya o Mikhaile Bulgakove*, 389.
656. Punin was Akhmatova's third (common-law) husband.
657. *Mikhail Bulgakov: A Life in Letters and Diaries*, 214.
658. Ibid., 220.
659. Ibid., 221.
660. Marietta Chudakova, *Zhizneopisanie Mikhaila Bulgakova*, 435.
661. *Mikhail Bulgakov: A Life in Letters and Diaries*, 254.
662. Marietta Chudakova, *Zhizneopisanie Mikhaila Bulgakova*, 443.
663. *Mikhail Bulgakov: A Life in Letters and Diaries*, 258.
664. Although in her diary Elena recorded the news about Neelov's death in 1935, this may have been a mistake. On other instances, she wrote that he died in 1936.
665. Marietta Chudakova, *Zhizneopisanie Mikhaila Bulgakova*, 449.
666. MB letter to EB, June 15, 1938. Bulgakov's letters to Elena come from M.A. Bulgakov, *Sobranie sochinenij v pyati tomah* (Moskva: Hudozhestvannaya literatura, 1990), vol. 5. Translation is by the author.
667. MB letter to EB, May 27, 1938.
668. *Mikhail Bulgakov: A Life in Letters and Diaries*, 272.
669. MB letter to EB, June 15, 1938.
670. MB letter to EB, June 14, 1938.
671. MB letter to EB, July 30, 1938.
672. *Mikhail Bulgakov: A Life in Letters and Diaries*, 282.
673. Ibid.
674. Ibid., 234.
675. Marietta Chudakova, *Zhizneopisanie Mikhaila Bulgakova*, 460.
676. Ibid., 477.
677. Ibid., 481.
678. *Vospominaniya o Mikhaile Bulgakove*, 481.
679. Russian State Library, Manuscript Department, f. 562, 33, 22.
680. *Vospominaniya o Mikhaile Bulgakove*, 419.
681. Colin Wright, *Mikhail Bulgakov: Life and Interpretations* (Toronto: University of Toronto Press, 1978), 255.
682. Lydia Yanovskaya, *Zapiski o Mikhaile Bulgakove*, 255.
683. EB letter to Lugovskoy, June 20, 1943. Translation is by the author.
684. Russian State Library, Manuscript Department, f. 562, 33, 22.
685. Sergei Ermolinsky, *Dramaticheskie sochineniya* (Moskva, 1982), 199.

THE WIVES

686. *Vospominaniya o Mikhaile Bulgakove*, 381.
687. Elena recorded Tvardovsky's visit on a separate sheet with a date "October 19." The next entry, dated October 20, tells about Solzhenitsyn's and Natalya Reshetovskaya's visit to her apartment after publication of *Ivan Denisovich*. Russian State Library, Manuscript Department, f. 562, 29. 11.
688. EB letter to Nikolai Bulgakov, September 7, 1962. Translation is by the author.
689. Ibid.
690. Vladimir Lakshin, *Vtoraya vstrecha* (Moskva: Sovetskij pisatel', 1984), 359-60.
691. Ibid., 356.
692. Lydia Yanovskaya, *Zapiski o Mikhaile Bulgakove*, 294.
693. Russian State Library, Manuscript Department, f. 562, 28, 23.
694. *Komsomol'skaya Pravda*, December 31, 1994.
695. Ibid.
696. *Argumenty i Facty*, December 1997, N 50 (895).
697. Lyudmila Saraskina, *Alexander Solzhenitsyn* (Moskva: Molodaya Gvardiya, 2008), 497.
698. Alexander Solzhenitsyn, *Invisible Allies* (Washington: Counterpoint, 1995), 197. Unless otherwise indicated, citations from Solzhenitsyn in this chapter come from this source.
699. Solzhenitsyn married Reshetovskaya in 1940. She divorced him while he was serving his sentence, and they were remarried in 1957.
700. Lyudmila Saraskina, *Alexander Solzhenitsyn*, 611.
701. D.M. Thomas, *Alexander Solzhenitsyn: A Century in His Life* (New York: St. Martin's Press, 1998), 365.
702. Lyudmila Saraskina, *Alexander Solzhenitsyn*, 626.
703. Alexander Solzhenitsyn, *The Oak and the Calf* (London: Collins and Harvill Press, 1980), 294.
704. Lyudmila Saraskina, *Alexander Solzhenitsyn*, 622.
705. Ibid., 642.
706. Russian television documentary *On the Last River Reach* aired on Solzhenitsyn's eighty-fifth birthday, December 11, 2003.
707. Lyudmila Saraskina, *Alexander Solzhenitsyn*, 649.
708. Galina Vishnevskaya, *Galina: A Russian Story* (New York: Harcourt Brace Jovanovich, 1984), 404.
709. Galina Vishnevskaya, *Galina*, 405.
710. Apartment No. 169 in Kozitsky Lane No. 2; for a while, the headquarters of the Russian Social Fund. This apartment is expected to become Solzhenitsyn's museum.
711. Lyudmila Saraskina, *Alexander Solzhenitsyn*, 658-59. Solzhenitsyn tells the entire story in his memoir, *The Grain Fell Between the Two Millstones*.

712. Lyudmila Saraskina, *Alexander Solzhenitsyn*, 662.
713. Ibid., 666.
714. For information on this episode I am indebted to Michael Scammell, *Solzhenitsyn: A Biography* (New York: W.W. Norton, 1984), 758.
715. *Solzhenitsyn Files*, ed. Michael Scammell (Chicago: Edition q, 1995), 213.
716. Michael Scammell, *Solzhenitsyn: A Biography*, 760.
717. Galina Vishnevskaya, *Galina*, 405.
718. Lyudmila Saraskina, *Alexander Solzhenitsyn*, 672.
719. D.M. Thomas, *Alexander Solzhenitsyn: A Century in His Life*, 391.
720. *Komsomol'skaya Pravda*, June 20, 1992.
721. *Aleksandr Solzhenitsyn*, film directed by Françoise Wolff (Montreal, QC: Ciné Fête c1999).
722. Alexander Solzhenitsyn, *The Oak and the Calf*, 390-91.
723. Hans Björkegren, *Alexander Solzhenitsyn: A Biography* (New York: The Third Press, 1972), 117.
724. Alexander Solzhenitsyn, *The Oak and the Calf*, 410.
725. Ibid., 421.
726. Ibid., 450.
727. Ibid., 444.
728. Andrei Sakhakov, *Memoirs* (New York: Alfred Knopf, 1990), 407.
729. Michael Scammell, *Solzhenitsyn: A Biography*, 856.
730. *Literaturnaya gazeta*, September 9, 1998.
731. The Russian Social Fund is now helping more than a thousand former political prisoners.
732. D.M. Thomas, *Alexander Solzhenitsyn: A Century in His Life*, 423.
733. Lyudmila Saraskina, *Alexander Solzhenitsyn*, 729.
734. Ibid., 733.
735. Michael Scammell, *Solzhenitsyn: A Biography*, 821.
736. Interview, *Komsomol'skaya Pravda*, June 20, 1992.
737. Alexander Solzhenitsyn, *The Grain Fell Between the Two Millstones*, *Novy mir*, No. 9, 2000. Translation is by the author.
738. *Literaturnaya gazeta*, April 5, 1995. Solzhenitsyn used colored pencils for different writing tasks.
739. Lyudmila Saraskina, *Alexander Solzhenitsyn*, 742.
740. Michael Scammell, *Solzhenitsyn: A Biography*, 980.
741. *Argumenty i facty*, December 1997, N 50.
742. Lyudmila Saraskina, *Alexander Solzhenitsyn*, 780.
743. Andrei Sakharov, *Memoirs*, 408-09.
744. Lyudmila Saraskina, *Alexander Solzhenitsyn*, 790.
745. Ibid., 787.
746. Ibid., 792.
747. Ibid., 798.

748. Joseph Pearce, *Solzhenitsyn: A Soul in Exile* (London: HarperCollins Publishers, 1999), 258.
749. Lyudmila Saraskina, *Alexander Solzhenitsyn*, 805.
750. D.M. Thomas, *Alexander Solzhenitsyn: A Century in His Life*, 504.
751. Lyudmila Saraskina, *Alexander Solzhenitsyn*, 814.
752. D.M. Thomas, *Alexander Solzhenitsyn: A Century in His Life*, 512.
753. Lyudmila Saraskina, *Alexander Solzhenitsyn*, 821.
754. *Izvestia*, July 23, 1993.
755. *Komsomol'skaya Pravda*, December 31, 1994.
756. Russian Television Channel *Kul'tura*, May 27, 2003.
757. Lyudmila Saraskina, *Alexander Solzhenitsyn*, 869.
758. Newspaper *Utro*, March 1, 2001, N 41.
759. Lyudmila Saraskina, *Alexander Solzhenitsyn*, 869–70.
760. Alexander Solzhenitsyn, *Publitsistika v tryoh tomah* (Yaroslavl: Verhne-Volzhskoe knizhnoe izdatelstvo, 1995.)
761. K.N. Bugaeva, *Vospominaniya ob Andree Belom*, ed. John Malmstad (Sankt-Peterburg: Izdatel'stvo Ivana Limbaha, 2001), 19.
762. http://www.peoples.ru/family/wife/vera_muromtseva-bunina/rss.xml

Select Bibliography

Primary Sources

Akhmatova, Anna. *My Half Century: Selected Prose.* Ed. Ronald Meyer. Ann Arbor: Ardis, 1992.

Bugaeva, Klavdia. *Vospominaniya ob Andree Belom.* Ed. John Malmstad. Sankt-Peterburg: Izdatel`stvo Ivana Limbaha, 2001.

Bulgakov, Mikhail. *The Master and Margarita.* Trans. Michael Glenny. New York: Harper & Row, 1967.

———. *Sobranie sochinenij v pyati tomah.* Moskva: Hudozhestvannaya literatura, 1990.

Complete Poetry of Osip Emilievich Mandelstam. Trans. Burton Raffel and Alla Burago. Albany: State University of New York Press, 1973.

The Diaries of Sophia Tolstoy. Trans. Cathy Porter. New York: Random House, 1985.

The Diary of Dostoevsky's Wife. Trans. Madge Pamberton. New York: Macmillan, 1928.

Dnevnik Eleny Bulgakovoi. Ed. V. Losev and L. Yanovskaya. Moskva: Knizhnaya palata, 1990.

Dostoevsky, Anna. *Dostoevsky: Reminiscences.* Trans. Beatrice Stillman. New York: Liveright, 1975.

Dostoevskaia, A. G. *Dnevnik 1867 goda*. Ed. S.V. Zhitomirskaia. Moskva: Nauka, 1993.

Fyodor Dostoevsky: Complete Letters. Ed. and trans. David A. Lowe. Ann Arbor: Ardis, 1990.

Dostoevsky, F. M. *Sobranie sochinenij v pyatnadtsati tomah*. Peterburg: Nauka, 1996.

Dostoevsky, F. M., and A. G. Dostoevskaia. *Perepiska*. Leningrad: Nauka, 1976.

Kuzminskaia, Tatyana. *Tolstoy As I Knew Him: My Life At Home and At Yasnaya Polyana*. Trans. Nora Sigerist. New York: Macmillan, 1948.

Makovitsky, D. P. 4 vols. *The Yasnaya Polyana Notes*. Moskva: Nauka, 1979.

Mandelstam, Nadezhda. *Hope Abandoned*. Trans. Max Hayward. New York: Atheneum, 1974.

———. *Hope Against Hope*. Trans. Max Hayward. New York: Atheneum, 1970.

———. *Kniga tretya*. Paris: YMCA Press, 1987.

———. *Ob Akhmatovoi*. Moskva: Tri kvadrata, 2008.

———. *Vospominaniya*. Moskva: Soglasie, 1999.

Mandelstam, Osip. *Critical Prose and Letters*. Ed. Jane Gary Harris; trans. Jane Gary Harris and Constance Link. Ann Arbor: Ardis, 1979.

Complete Poetry of Osip Emilievich Mandelstam. Trans. Burton Raffel and Alla Burago. Albany: State University of New York Press, 1973.

Nabokov, Vladimir. *Speak, Memory*. New York: G. P. Putnam's Sons, 1966.

———. *Perepiska s sestroi*. Ann Arbor: Ardis, 1985.

———. *Poems and Problems*. New York: McGraw-Hill, 1970.

The Nabokov–Wilson Letters: Correspondence Between Vladimir Nabokov and Edmund Wilson 1940–1971. Ed. Simon Karlinsky. New York: Harper & Row, 1979.

Pasternak, Boris. *I Remember: Sketch for an Autobiography*. Trans. David Magarshack. Cambridge: Harvard University Press, 1983.

Solzhenitsyn, Alexander. *Invisible Allies*. Trans. Alexis Klimoff and Michael Nicholson. Washington: Counterpoint, 1995.

———. *The Oak and the Calf*. Trans. Harry Willetts. London: Collins and Harvill, 1980.

———. *Publitsistika v treh tomah*. Yaroslavl': Verhne-Volzhskoe knizhnoe izdatelśtvo, 1995.

———. "Ugodilo zernyshko promezh dvuh zhernovov." *Novy mir*, No. 9, 2000.

Tolstoy, Alexandra. *Out of the Past.* Ed. Katharine Strelsky and Catherine Wolkonsky. New York: Columbia University Press, 1981.

———. *Doch'.* Moskva: Vagrius, 2000.

Tolstoy, Ilya. *Tolstoy, My Father. Reminiscences.* Trans. Ann Dunnigan. Chicago: Cowles, 1971.

Tolstoy's Diaries. 2 vols. Ed. and trans. R. F. Christian. London: Anthlone, 1985.

Tolstoy's Letters. 2 vols. Ed. and trans. R. F. Christian. London: Anthlone, 1978.

Tolstoy, Leo. *Anna Karenina.* Trans. Richard Pevear and Larissa Volokhonsky. New York: Penguin, 2002.

———. *Childhood, Boyhood & Youth.* In *The Works of Leo Tolstoy.* Trans. Aylmer and Louise Maude. London: Oxford University Press, 1928–37.

———. *Plays: Volume Three.* Trans. Marvin Kantor with Tanya Tulchinsky. Evanston: Northwestern University Press, 1998.

———. *War and* Peace. Trans. Richard Pevear and Larissa Volokhonsky. New York: Alfred A. Knopf, 2007.

Tolstoy, L. N. *Polnoe sobranie sochinenij v 90 tomah.* Ed. V. G. Chertkov. Moskva–Leningrad: Goslitizdat, 1928–58.

The Tolstoys' Correspondence with N. N. Strakhov. Ed. A. A. Donskov. Ottawa: Slavic Research Group, 2000.

Tolstoy, Sophia. "Avtobiografia." In *Dve zheny: Tolstaia i Dostoevskaia.* Ed. Yu. Aikhenvald. Berlin: Izdatelstvo Pisatelei, 1925.

———. *Ch'ya vina?* Oktyabr'. No. 10, 1994.

———. *Moya zhizn'.* GMT. (L. N. Tolstoy State Museum)

———. *Pesnya bez slov.* GMT.

———. *Pis'ma k Tolstomu: 1862–1910.* Ed. P. Popov. Moskva-Leningrad: Academia, 1936.

Tolstoy, Tatyana. *Tolstoy Remembered.* Trans. Derek Coltman. New York: McGraw-Hill, 1977.

Vladimir Nabokov: Selected Letters, 1940–1977. Ed. Dmitry Nabokov and Matthew J. Bruccoli. New York: *Harcourt Brace Jovanovich*, 1989.

Vospominaniya o Mikhaile Bulgakove. Ed. E. S. Bulgakova. Moskva: Sovetskij pisatel', 1988.

Secondary Sources

Amis, Martin. *Visiting Mrs. Nabokov and Other Excursions*. London: Jonathan Cape, 1993.

Bahrah, Alexander. *Bunin v halate*. Moskva: Soglasie, 2000.

Bartlett, Rosamund. *Tolstoy: A Russian Life*. Boston: Houghton Mifflin Harcourt, 2011.

Belov, Sergey. *Zhena pisatelya*. Moskva: Sovetskaya Rossiya, 1986.

Berberova, Nina. *The Italics Are Mine*. Trans. Philippe Radley. New York: Harcourt, Brace & World, 1969.

Berlin, Isaiah. *The Soviet Mind: Russian Culture Under Communism*. Ed. Henry Hardy. Washington, D.C.: Brookings Institution Press, 2004.

Björkegren, Hans. *Alexander Solzhenitsyn: A Biography*. New York: The Third Press, 1972.

Boyd, Brian. *Vladimir Nabokov: The Russian Years*. Princeton: Princeton University Press, 1990.

———. *Vladimir Nabokov: The American Years*. Princeton: Princeton University Press, 1991.

Brodsky, Joseph. "Nadezhda Mandelstam: An Obituary." In Mandelstam, Nadezhda, *Hope Against Hope*. Trans. Max Hayward. New York: Modern Library, 1999.

Brown, Clarence. *Mandelstam*. Cambridge: Cambridge University Press, 1973.

Bulgakov, Valentin. *The Last Year of Leo Tolstoy*. Trans. Ann Dunnigan. New York: Dial Press, 1971.

Bunin, Ivan. *The Liberation of Tolstoy*. Ed. and trans. Thomas Gaiton Marullo and Vladimir T. Khmelkov. Evanston: Northwestern University Press, 2001.

The Cambridge Companion to Tolstoy. Ed. Donna Tussing Orwin. New York: Cambridge University Press, 2002.

Chudakova, Marietta. *Zhizneopisanie Mikhaila Bulgakova*. Moskva: Kniga, 1988.

Curtis, J. A. E. *Mikhail Bulgakov: A Life in Letters and Diaries*. London: Bloomsbury, 1991.

Dostoevsky, Andrei. "Anna Dostoevskaya." In Zhurnal *Zhenshchiny mira*, No. 10, 1963.

Field, Andrew. *Nabokov: His Life in Part*. New York: Viking, 1977.

———. *The Life and Art of Vladimir Nabokov*. New York: Crown, 1977.

Frank, Joseph. *Dostoevsky. The Miraculous Years, 1865–1871*. Princeton: Princeton University Press, 1995.

———. *Dostoevsky. The Mantle of the Prophet, 1871–1881*. Princeton: Princeton University Press, 2002.

Fyodor Dostoevsky, A Study. By His Daughter Aimee Dostoevsky. New Haven: Yale University Press, 1922.

The Garland Companion to Vladimir Nabokov. Ed. Vladimir Alexandrov. New York: Garland, 1995.

Gershtein, Emma. *Memuary*. Moskva: Zakharov, 2002.

Gorky, Maxim. *Literary Portraits*. Trans. Ivy Litvinov. Moscow: Foreign Languages Publishing House, 1982.

Grossman, Leonid. *Dostoevsky*. Moskva: Molodaya Gvardiya, 1965.

———. "A.G. Dostoevskaya i ee vospominaniya." In *Vospominaniya A.G. Dostoevskoi*. Moskva: Gosudarstvennoe izdatel'stvo, 1925.

Gusev, Nikolai. *Letopis' Zhizni i tvorchestva L'va Nikolaevicha Tolstogo*. 2 vols. Moskva: Goslitizdat, 1958.

Hitchens, Christopher. *Arguably: Essays*. Toronto: McLelland & Stewart, 2011.

Ivinskaya, Olga. *A Captive of Time*. Trans. Max Hayward. New York: Warner Books, 1978.

Lekhmanov, Oleg. *Mandelstam*. Boston: Academic Studies, 2010.

Maddox, Brenda. *Nora: The Real Life of Molly Bloom*. Boston: Houghton Mifflin, 1988.

Maude, Aylmer. *The Life of Tolstoy: Later Years*. London: Oxford University Press, 1930.

Møller, Peter Ulf. *Postlude to the Kreutzer Sonata. Tolstoy and the Debate on Sexual Morality in Russian Literature in the 1890s*. Leiden: E. J. Brill, 1988.

Osip i Nadezhda Mandelshtamy v rasskazah sovremennikov. Ed. O. S. Figurnova. Moskva: Natalis, 2002.

Pearce, Joseph. *Solzhenitsyn: A Soul in Exile*. London: HarperCollins, 1999.

A Pictorial Biography of Mikhail Bulgakov. Ed. Ellendea Proffer. Ann Arbor: Ardis, 1984.

Polner, Tikhon. *Lev Tolstoy i ego zhena*. Moskva: Nash dom–L'Age d'Homme, 2000.

Proffer, Carl. *The Widows of Russia and Other Writings*. Ann Arbor: Ardis, 1987.

Proffer, Ellendea. *Bulgakov: Life and Work*. Ann Arbor: Ardis, 1984.

Rayfield, Donald. *Stalin and his Hangmen*. London: Viking, 2004.

Reeder, Roberta. *Anna Akhmatova*. New York: Picador USA, 1994.

Safonova, O. Yu. *Rod Bersov v Rossii*. Moscow: Village Encyclopedia, 1999.

Sakharov, Andrei. *Memoirs*. Trans. Richard Lourie. New York: Alfred Knopf, 1990.

Saraskina, Lyudmila. *Alexander Solzhenitsyn*. Moskva: Molodaya Gvardiya, 2008.

Scammell, Michael. *Solzhenitsyn: A Biography*. New York: W. W. Norton, 1984.

Schiff, Stacy. *Véra (Mrs. Vladimir Nabokov)*. New York: Random House, 1999.

Shvarts, Anatoly. *Zhizn' i smert' Mikhaila Bulgakova*. Tenafly, N.J.: Ermitazh, 1988.

Solzhenitsyn Files. Ed. Michael Scammell. Chicago: Edition q, 1995.

Thomas, D. M. *Alexander Solzhenitsyn: A Century in His Life*. New York: St. Martin's Press, 1998.

Vishnevskaya, Galina. *Galina: A Russian Story*. Trans. Guy Daniels. New York: Harcourt Brace Jovanovich, 1984.

Volkogonov, Dmitry. *Lenin: A New Biography*. Trans. and ed. Harold Shukman. New York: Free Press, 1994.

Wright, Colin. *Mikhail Bulgakov: Life and Interpretations*. Toronto: University of Toronto Press, 1978.

Yanovskaia, Lydia. *Zapiski o Mikhaile Bulgakove*. Holon, Israel: Publishers "Moria," 1997.

Index

A

Ada, 202, 206
Admoni, Vladimir, 133
Aikhenvald, Yuli, 181–82
Akhmatova, Anna, 115–17, 124–27, 133, 135–40, 143, 146–48, 151–53, 156–57, 163–64, 168, 219, 227, 243, 253
Aldanov, Mark, 189
Alexander I, 103
Alexander II, 4, 33
Alexander III, 93–94
Alexandrov, Mikhail, 38
Alexy II, Patriarch, 284
Allilueva, Svetlana, 274
Amis, Martin, 201, 206
And the Light Shineth in Darkness, 85
Andropov, Yuri, 266–67
Angarsky, Nikolai, 236
Anna Karenina, 65, 67, 75–81, 83, 94, 101, 105, 106, 180
Aragon, Louis, 258
Arens, Elena, 154, 162
Ashton, Rosemary, 287
August 1914, 261

B

Babaev, Eduard, 156
Balzac, Honoré de, 25
Barbusse, Henri, 123
Baryshnikov, Mikhail, 208
Batum, 239
Bazykina, Aksinya, 67
Behrs, Andrei, 62, 63
Behrs, Elizaveta (Liza), 63, 64, 65, 66
Behrs, Sophia, 62–63. *See also* Tolstoy, Sophia
Behrs, Tatyana (Tanya). *See also* Kuzminskaia, Tatyana
Belozerskaya, Lyubov, 212, 215, 217
Bely, Andrei, 127, 288
Berberova, Nina, 180, 187
Beria, Lavrenty, 152, 161
Berlin, Isaiah, 208
Bernstein, Sergei, 157–58
Biryukov, Paul, 102, 109
Bliumkin, Yakov, 118
Bohlen, Charles E., 224
Böll, Heinrich, 262, 269
Bonner, Elena, 268, 270, 284
Boyhood, 62

INDEX

Brandt, Willy, 267
Brezhnev, Leonid, 166, 267, 271
Bright Stream, The, 228, 230
Brodsky, Joseph, xvii, 172
Brothers Karamazov, The, xiv, 32,
　46–48, 50–51, 56–57, 144
Brown, Clarence, 118, 167–68, 170
Bugaev, Klavdia, 288
Bukharin, Nikolai, 128–30, 136–37,
　140, 225
Bulgakov, Elena, 207–49
　birth of, 207, 208
　children of, 210, 217
　death of, 248
　early years of, 207–20
　education of, 209
　family of, 207–9
　later years of, 240–48
　marriage to Bulgakov of, 209–10
　role of, xvi, xviii
Bulgakov, Ksenia, 248
Bulgakov, Mikhail, 207–49
　death of, 242
　early years of, 207–20
　employment denied to, 212–14
　later years of, 236–42
　meeting Elena, 207, 211, 216–17
　publication denied to, xvi, 212,
　　214, 228–29, 232, 236–37
　relationship with Stalin, xvi,
　　212, 214–16, 222, 240
Bulgakov, Nadezhda, 221
Bulgakov, Nikolai, 218, 246, 248
Bullitt, William, 228
Bunin, Ivan, 169, 180, 272, 288–89

C
Cabal of Hypocrites, the, 213
Callier, Jaqueline, 205
Camera Obscura, 185
Cancer Ward, 257, 279
Carlyle, Thomas, 287
Carracci, Annibale, 19

Chagall, Marc, 149, 176
Chekhov, Anton, 194, 272
Chekhov, Maria, 58
Chertkov, Vladimir, 86–87, 96, 98,
　101, 107–11
Childhood, 62, 89
Chopin, Frédéric, 63, 99
Christie, Agatha, 171
Chukovskaya, Lydia, 265, 274
Chukovsky, Korney, 145
Church News, 102
Citizen, The, 38, 40, 48
Confession, A, 83, 90
Conrad, Joseph, 192
Contemporary Annals, 183
Correggio, Antonio da, 19
Crime and Punishment, xiv, 5, 8, 10,
　12, 25, 29

D
Dalsky, Mamont, 209
Dante, 134, 148
Das Kapital, 156
David Copperfield, 62
Dawn, 31
Days of the Turbins, The, xvi, 208, 211,
　212, 214, 216, 218, 222–24, 229,
　233, 238
Dead Souls, The, 218
Death of Ivan Ilyich, The, 88, 95
Defense, The, 183, 194
Despair, 185
Devils, The, 28, 35, 42
Diary for Myself Alone (Tolstoy), 110
Diary of a Writer (Dostoevsky), 38,
　42–43, 45, 50
Dickens, Charles, 4, 25, 62
"Discovery, A," 196
Dobuzhinsky, Mstislav, 176
Doctor Zhivago, 199–200, 257
"Doctors' Plot," 160–61
Dom Juan, 213
Don Giovanni, 65

INDEX

Don Quixote, 237
Dostoevsky, Andrei, 58, 60
Dostoevsky, Anna, 1–60
   betrothal of, 11–13
   birth of, 1
   children of, 28, 32, 34–35, 39–40, 42, 45–46, 59–60
   death of, 59–60
   early years of, 2–5
   education of, 3–4
   family of, 2–3
   later years of, 52–55
   marriage of, 13–16
   meeting Dostoevsky, 5–6
   publishing business of, 36–38, 54–56, 92
   role of, xi–xvi, xviii
   Sophia Tolstoy and, 88, 111
   as stenographer, xiii, xv, 4, 6, 7, 12, 15, 20, 21, 36, 56
Dostoevsky, Fyodor, 5–60
   betrothal of, 11–13
   children of, 28, 32, 34–35, 39–40, 42, 45–46, 59–60
   death of, 51–52
   early years of, 3
   marriage of, 13–16
   meeting Anna, 5–6
Dostoevsky, Fyodor, Jr. (Fedya), 35, 39–40, 53, 58–60
Dostoevsky, Lyubov (Lyuba), 32, 34–35, 44, 49, 52–53, 56, 59–60
Dresdner Nachrichten, 21
"Dreyfus Case" (Mandelstam), 129
Dzerzhinsky, Felix, 118, 128, 280

E

Egyptian Stamp, 128
Eisenstein, Sergei, 208
Encounter, The, 179
Enukidze, Avel, 137
Epoch, 37
Epstein, Jason, 199

Erdman, Boris, 235
Erdman, Nikolai, 220, 235, 238
Erenburg, Ilya, 116, 118, 164, 167
Erenburg, Lyuba, 119
Ergaz, Doussia, 198
Ermolinsky, Sergei, 242
Eugene Onegin, 196–97, 203
Evening Moscow, The, 284
Exter, Alexandra, 116
Ezhov, Nikolai, 149

F

Fadeev, Alexander, 149–50, 242–43
"False Notes at the Ballet," 230
Family Medicine, 84
Fathers and Sons, 6
Faust, 114, 192
Feigin, Slava, 176
Fet, Afanasy, 83
Field, Andrew, 203–4
First Circle, The, xvii, 254, 257, 283
First Love, 67
Fitzgerald, F. Scott, xviii, 287
Fitzgerald, Zelda, xviii
Flight, 212, 214, 216, 229, 243, 245, 248
Fondaminsky, Ilya, 189–90
For a Communist Education, 132
Fourth Prose, 132
Francis of Assisi, Saint, 99, 144
Fredrikson, Ingrid, 263
Fredrikson, Stig, 263, 270
Frost, Robert, 169
Fruits of Enlightenment, The, 98
Frunze, Mikhail, 234

G

Galperina-Osmerkina, Elena, 122
Gambler, The, xiii, 9, 21, 25, 57
Gay, Nikolai, Jr., 93, 97
Gay, Nikolai, Sr., 97
Gellhorn, Martha, xviii–xix
Gelshtein, Gdal, 172

INDEX

Gelshtein, Vita, 172
Gershtein, Emma, 125
Gide, André, 234
Gierow, Karl, 263
Girodias, Maurice, 198, 199
Glory, 182
Godunov, Boris, Tsar, 138
Goethe, Johann Wolfgang von, 114, 192
Gogol, Nikolai, 218, 232, 249
Golitsyn, Alexander, 103
Gone With the Wind, 199
Gorbachev, Mikhail, 155, 278, 280
Gordon, John, 198
Gorky, Maxim, 210, 216
Gorskaya, Alexandra, *See also* Nurenberg, Alexandra 207
Great Purge, 217, 222
Greene, Graham, 198
Grossman, Leonid, 56, 58, 60
Guadanini, Irina, 186
Gulag Archipelago, The, 137, 254, 256–58, 260, 265–66, 271–72, 279, 284–85
Gumilev, Lev, 146, 148, 227
Gumilev, Nikolai, 117, 148

H
Harris, James, 201
Heart of a Dog, The, 219
Heeb, Fritz, 261, 268
Hemingway, Ernest, xviii–xix
Hitchens, Christopher, 195
Hitler, Adolf, 184–86, 240
Homer, 61
Hope Abandoned, 167, 171
Hope Against Hope, 113, 170
"How to Revitalize Russia," 282

I
Idiot, The, 25, 31, 34, 38, 42
Iliad, 61
Inferno, The, 134

Inspector, The, 232
Insulted and Injured, 3, 5, 11
Investigation of Dogmatic Theology, An, 82
Invitation to a Beheading, 185, 187
Isaeva, Marya, 7
Islavin, Konstantin, 63
Islavin, Lyubov, 62
Islenev, Alexander, 62
Ivan IV (The Terrible), Tsar, 51, 148, 227, 229
Ivan Susanin, 236
Ivan Vasilievich, 227, 229
Ivanov, Boris, 261
Ivich-Bernstein, Alexander, 157–58
Ivich-Bernstein, Sophia, 158
Izvestiya, 136, 209, 225, 282

J
Jaclard, Charles, 47
Journal for All, 105
Journey to Armenia, 134
Joyce, James, xvi, 287
Joyce, Nora, xvi, 179
July 1941, x

K
Kafka, Franz, 143
Kaganovich, Lazar, 229
Kaiser, Robert, 262–63
Kaluzhsky, Evgeny, 231
Karpovich, Mikhail, 190
Katkov, Mikhail, 12, 14, 26, 29, 31, 33
Kaverin, Veniamin, 171, 245, 267
Kevorkov, Vyacheslav, 267
KGB, 172–73, 202, 254–55, 257–69, 271, 281, 284–85
Khardzhiev, Nikolai, 159
Khazin, Alexander, 115
Khazin, Evgeny 115, 131, 138
Khazin, Yakov, 114, 116
Khazina, Nadezhda, 113–15. *See also* Mandelstam, Nadezhda

INDEX

Khazina, Vera, 114, 145, 155
Khlebnikov, Velimir, 121
Khodasevich, Vladislav, 180
Khrushchev, Nikita, 157, 247
Khrushchev's Thaw, 157, 159, 170, 246–47, 252
King, Queen, Knave, 182
Kingdom of God Is Within Us, The, 98
Kirov, Sergei, 222–23
Kolyma Tales, 169
Koni, Anatoly, 111
Konsky, Grisha, 233–34
Kopelev, Lev, 262
Korvin-Krukovskaya, Anna, 7, 9, 11, 47
Kovalevskaya, Sofia, 7
Kovrigina, Zinaida, 58
Kramskoy, Ivan, 76–77, 105
Kretova, Olga, 145
Kreutzer Sonata, The, 93–95, 100, 102, 195
Kurdyumov, Valery, 260–61
Kuzminskaia, Tatyana. *See also* Behrs, Tatyana, 63, 68, 70, 71, 78, 79, 82, 89, 90, 91

L

Lacontre, Robert, 269
Lady Macbeth of Mtsensk, 230
Lakshin, Vladimir, 246, 247, 248
Lamont, William, 194
Lashkova, Vera, 173
Lawrence, D. H., 287
Le Figaro, 269
Lélia, the Life of George Sand, 247
Lenin, Vladimir, 114, 124, 159, 177, 280
Leningrad, 156
Leuthold, Dorothy, 190
Lev Tolstoy and His Wife, 112
Life for the Czar, A, 236
"Life of a Great Sinner, The," 32
Literary Gazette, 133, 142, 245

Litovsky, Osaf, 230
Little Dorrit, 25
Lolita, 194–201, 203, 205
Lugovskoy, Vladimir, 244
Luzhkov, Yuri, 280

M

Macdonald, Dwight, 199
Maikov, Apollon, 24–25, 32
Makovitsky, Dushan, 105
Mandelstam, Nadezhda, 113–74
  birth of, 113–14
  death of, 173
  early years of, 114–21
  education of, 115, 156
  family of, 114–15, 120–21
  homelessness of, 120–23, 131, 148–49, 165
  later years of, 152–74
  marriage of, 120–21
  on Nabokov, 195
  preserving archive, 136, 150–51, 154–58, 164–66, 168, 174
Mandelstam, Osip, 116–74
  death of, 152–53
  early years of, 117–21
  exile to Cherdyn of, 138–40
  exile to Voronezh of, 140–46
  family of, 117
  final days of, 152–56
  homelessness of, 120–23, 131, 148–49
  later years of, 150–56
  marriage of, 120–21
Marx, Alfred, 55
Mary, 181
Mass, Vladimir, 220
Master and Margarita, The, xvi, 209, 211–14, 217, 219–20, 225, 230, 233–36, 239, 241–47, 249
Maude, Aylmer, 92, 95
Maupassant, Guy de, 143
Maurois, André, 247

Mayakovsky, Vladimir, 128, 168, 211, 214
Mazzini, Giuseppe, 103
Men, Alexander, 172
Meyerhold, Vsevolod, 225, 239, 288
Midnight in Moscow, 173
Miller, Arthur, 258
Miltopeus, Maria Anna, 2. *See also* Snitkin Anna Nikolaevna
Milyukov, Paul, 180
Misérables, Les, 39
Molière, Jean-Baptiste, 213, 216, 218, 238
Molière, 224, 228, 229, 230
Molotov, Vyacheslav, 130, 214, 229
Moravia, Alberto, 258
Moscow Gazette, The, 76, 247
Moskva, 164
Murillo, Bartolomé, 19
Muromtseva-Bunina, Vera, 288–89

N

Nabokov, Dmitry, 184, 186–87, 193, 196, 202
Nabokov, Véra, 175–206
  birth of, 176
  death of, 206
  early years of, 175–80
  education of, 178
  family of, 175–76
  later years of, 200–206
  Mandelstam and, 124, 171
  marriage of, 180–81
  as mother, 184, 186–87
  role of, x–xi, xvi–xviii
Nabokov, Vladimir, 179–206
  death of, 205
  early years of, 175–80
  fame of, 199–200
  later years of, 200–206
  as lepidopterist, 183–84, 190–91, 195–99, 205

  Mandelstam and, 124, 171
  marriage of, 180–81
  meeting Véra, 179
  Nabokov, Vladimir, Sr., 179–80
Narbut, Vladimir, 116
Naryshkin-Kurakina, Elizabeth, 48
"Natasha," 65
Nechaev, Sergei, 33
Neelov, Yuri, 209, 233
Nekrasov, Nikolai, 40–41, 45
Nemirovich-Danchenko, Vladimir, 56, 208, 222, 231, 238–39
Nevsky, Alexander, Saint, 1–2
New Time, 95
New York Review of Books, The, 171, 188, 199–200
New York Times, The, 206, 262, 279
New Yorker, The, 197, 199
Nicholson, Nigel, 201
Nixon, Richard, 263
Noise of Time, The, 123
Notes from the House of the Dead, 3, 11, 38
Notes of a Dead Man, The (Bulgakov), 231
Notes of the Fatherland, 40
Novy Mir, 164, 246–47, 252, 258, 276, 279
Nurenberg, Alexander, 208, 248
Nurenberg, Alexandra. *See also* Gorskaya, Alexandra
Nurenberg, Elena, 207–8. *See also* Bulgakov, Elena
Nurenberg, Olga, 208, 236–37
Nurenberg, Sergei, 207

O

Oak and the Calf, The, 273
Observer, The, 206
"Ode to Stalin," 146
Olkhin, Pavel, 4–5, 20
On Human Duty, 103
On Life, 99

INDEX

One Day in the Life of Ivan Denisovich, xvii, 245, 252–53, 272
Osmerkina, Tatyana, 172

P

Pale Fire, 205
Panina, Sophia, 103
Pasternak, Boris, xii, 123–24, 127, 137, 140, 143, 157, 169, 199–200, 214, 227, 257, 276
Pasternak, Evgeny, 276
perestroika, 278–79, 283
Peter I (the Great), Tsar, 75, 142, 231, 233, 280
Pickwick Papers, The, 222, 233
Pilnyak, Boris, 234
Pirogova, Anna, 75
Pnin, 197
Pobedonostsev, Konstantin, 48, 90, 103
Poe, Edgar Allan, 180
Poet and Peasant, 20
Polikushka, 68, 112
Polner, Tikhon, 112
Poor Folk, 32
Poskrebyshev, Alexander, 244
Possessed, The, 32, 33, 34, 36
Pravda, 128, 134, 228, 230, 233, 266
Proffer, Carl, 125, 168, 171, 195, 202
Proffer, Ellendea, 168, 171, 202
Prokofiev, Sergei, 57, 228
Punin, Nikolai, 124, 151, 227
Pushkin, 229, 232
Pushkin, Alexander, 196, 223–24, 228–29, 231–32, 244
Pushkin, Natalya, 224
Putin, Vladimir, 283–84

R

Rachmaninov, Sergei, 188
Rafael, 19
Raw Youth, A, 40–42
Real Life of Sebastian Knight, The, 188

Realm of Darkness, The, 93
Red Wheel, The, 258, 261, 269, 275–76, 279
Reich, Zinaida, 225, 239
Rembrandt and His Wife, 19
Rembrandt van Rijn, 19
Repin, Ilya, 105
Requiem, 151
Reshetovskaya, Natalya, 256, 259, 262, 264
Resurrection, 101, 102
Rolf, Filippa, 200, 203
Roosevelt, Franklin D., 224, 274
Rosanov, Vasily, 55–56
Rostropovich, Mstislav, 258–62, 277
Rozanova, Maria, 170
Rubinstein, Nikolai, 63
Rul, 179, 180
Russia in the Abyss, 282
Russian Gazette, 95, 96, 98
Russian Herald, The, 12, 13, 25–26, 28, 31, 46, 50, 71, 79, 80

S

Sabatier, Paul, 99
Sakharov, Andrei, 268, 278, 284
Sartre, Jean-Paul, 258
Saryan, Martiros, 131
Scammell, Michael, 277
Sebastopol Stories, 62
Second Book, The, 121–22
Shakespeare, William, 61, 148
Shalamov, Varlam, 169
Shalyapin, Fyodor, 209
Shileiko, Vladimir, 125
Shilovsky, Evgeny, 209–10, 214–15, 217, 233
Shklovsky, Vasilisa, 124, 134, 148, 161
Shklovsky, Victor, 124, 148
Shmemann, Alexander, 273
Shostakovich, Dmitry, 228, 229, 230
Shteiger, Boris, 225–26

INDEX

Silence, 180
Simonov, Konstantin, 166, 245, 247
Sinyavsky, Andrei, 170
Sistine Madonna, 18
Slezkin, Yuri, 144
Slonim, Evsey, 175–78
Slonim, Véra, 175–80. *See also* Nabokov, Véra
Smith, Hedrick, 262
Snegirev, Vladimir, 106
Snitkin, Anna, 1. *See also* Dostoevsky, Anna
Snitkin, Anna Nikolaevna. *See Also* Miltopeus, Maria Anna
Snitkin, Grigory, 2–3
Snitkin, Ivan, 32–33
Sollogub, Vladimir, 70
Solzhenitsyn, Alexander, 250–86
   in America, 273–74
   arrest of, 268–69
   assassination attempts on, 261–62
   as celebrity, 252–54
   children of, 256, 259–60, 263–65, 268, 271
   death of, 284
   deportation of, 269–70
   divorce of, 264
   early years of, 250–60
   family of, 159
   later years of, 275–86
   marriage of, 256, 264
   meeting Natalya, 253–54
   Nabokov and, 272
   return to Russia, 280–83
   in Zurich, 270–72
Solzhenitsyn, Ermolai, 259–60, 268, 277
Solzhenitsyn, Ignat, 264, 268, 277
Solzhenitsyn, Natalya, 250–86
   in America, 273–74
   children of, 252, 259–60, 263–65, 268, 271
   deportation and, 269–71

   early years of, 250–60
   education of, 252
   family of, 250–51
   interview with, 284–86
   later years of, 275–86
   marriage of, 252, 264
   meeting Solzhenitsyn, 254
   return to Russia, 280–83
   role of, xvii–xviii
   in Zurich, 270–72
Solzhenitsyn, Stepan, 265, 268, 270, 276–78
Son of the Fatherland, 12
Song Without Words, 100
Soul of a People, The, 103
Speak, Memory, 188, 189
Stalin, Joseph, xv–xvii, 130, 135–37, 140, 160–61, 212–19, 222, 227–29, 233–35, 238, 244, 274, 284
Stanislavsky, Konstantin, 208, 231
Stavsky, Vladimir, 149
Steinberg, Saul, xi
Stolyarova, Natalya, 253–54
Stone, 116
Strakhov, Nikolai, 30, 79, 81, 83
Struve, Nikita, 261, 266
Sukhotin, Mikhail, 108
Sukhotin, Tatyana. *See also* Tolstoy, Tatyana, 71, 73, 80, 82, 83, 85, 86, 91, 102, 108
Sunday Express, The, 198
Sunday Time, 198
Surkov, Alexei, 163
Suslova, Apollinaria, 9, 10, 21
Svetlov, Ferdinand, 250
Svetlova, Ekaterina, 250
Svetlova, Natalya, 170. *See also* Solzhenitsyn, Natalya

T

Taboritsky, Sergei, 186
Tale of the Unextinguished Moon, The, 234

INDEX

Taneev, Sergei, 99–100
Tartuffe, 213
Tatlin, Vladimir, 126
"Terrible Question, A," 98
Teush, Vaniamin, 259
Theatrical Novel, A, 231, 233, 234, 247
Thomas and Jane Carlyle, 287
Thornton, Elena, 191
Time, 3, 9, 37
Time & Tide, 201
Times Literary Supplement, 199
Tiurin, Andrei, 252, 255–56, 281
Tiurin, Dmitry, 252, 281
Tiurin, Galina, 255–56
"To a Secret Friend," 213
Tolstoy, Alexandra (Alexandrine, lady-in waiting), 48, 70, 83, 99
Tolstoy, Alexandra (Sasha), 87, 91, 107, 109–12
Tolstoy, Alexei, 135, 218
Tolstoy, Alyosha, 91
Tolstoy, Ilya, 80, 96
Tolstoy, Ivan (Vanechka), 93, 99–100
Tolstoy, Leo, 61–112
  betrothal of, 67
  children of, 61, 69, 71, 75, 77, 79–80, 82–83, 87, 91–93, 96, 99, 106
  death of, 110–11
  early years of, 61–68
  family of, 62–63
  in famine relief, 76, 96–98
  later years of, 107–10
  marriage of, 62, 67–68
  religious views of, 81–83, 99
Tolstoy, Maria (Masha), 106
Tolstoy, Mikhail (Misha), 91
Tolstoy, Nicholas, 62
Tolstoy, Sergei, 69, 82, 96
Tolstoy, Sophia, 61–112
  Anna Dostoevsky and, 88, 111

artistic pursuits of, 63, 77, 104–05
betrothal of, 67
children of, 61, 69, 71, 75, 77, 79–80, 82–83, 87, 91–93, 96, 99, 106
death of, 112
early years of, 61–68
education of, 65
family of, 61–66
in famine relief, 76, 96–98
later years of, 107–12
marriage of, 62, 67–68
medicine practiced by, 84
as photographer, 65, 92, 103, 105
publishing business of, 87–88, 92–97, 105
role of, xi–xiii, xv–xvi, xviii
as writer, 65, 68, 74, 76, 100, 104–05
Tolstoy, Tatyana (Tanya). *See also* Sukhotin Tatyana
Tregubov, Andrew, 277
Trial, The, 143
Tribute Money, The, 19
Triolet, Elsa, 258
Tsvetaeva, Marina, vii, 127, 251–52, 289
Tukhachevsky, Marshal Mikhail, 225, 233
Turgenev, Ivan, 6, 48, 62–64, 67, 83
Tvardovsky, Alexander, 245–46, 252–53, 257–58
Two Hundred Years Together, 283
Two Wives, The, 182
Tyshler, Alexander, 116

U

Uborevich, General Ieronim, 233
Uborevich, Vladimira, 243
Udgaard, Nils, 270
Ulysses, xvi
Updike, John, 205–6

INDEX

V
Vaksel, Olga, 125
Velikorodny, Dmitri, 250
Veresaev, Vikenty, 221, 223
Vigdorova, Frida, 166
Vinogradov, Alexei, 273
Vishnevskaya, Galina, 260–61, 263
Volga-Volga, 235
Volpin, Nadezhda, 124
von Meck, Galina, 153
von Suppé, Franz, 20
Voronezh Notebooks, 144
Voronyanskaya, Elizaveta, 265
Voroshilov, Kliment, 229

W
Wallace, Mike, 280
War and Peace, xii, xvi, 61, 65, 69–70, 72–75, 78–79, 105–7
Washington Post, The, 262
What I Believe, 86, 90
White, Katherine, 197
White Guard, The, 209, 211, 213, 218, 247

Who Is to Blame? 68
Widmer, Sigmund, 272
Wiedenfeld, George, 201
Wilson, Edmund, 191, 197
Winer, Bart, 203
"Wolf, The," 157
"Women and Stenography," 21
Wordsworth, William, 287

Y
Yagoda, Genrikh, 136
Yanovskaya, Lydia, 207
Yasnaya Polyana, 66
Yeltsin, Boris, 280, 282

Z
Zamyatin, Evgeny, 218
Zeibig, Woldemar, 20–21
Zhukhovitsky, Emmanuil, 224
Zhukovsky, Vasily, 223
Zoika's Apartment, 224
Zoshchenko, Mikhail, 156, 244
Zvezda, 156

Acknowledgements

Many people supported me during the research and writing of this book. I want to thank translator and author Antonina Bouis, biographers Robert Calder and Michael Shelden, and writers Dave Carpenter, Myrna Kostash, Dave Margoshes, and Yann Martel, who read portions of my manuscript.

I am also indebted to my husband, Wilfred, for his insightful editing suggestions: these were helpful, as ever. My special thanks go to my parents, from whom I inherited my love of literature.

This book would have been impossible without grants from the Canada Council for the Arts and the Saskatchewan Arts Board. I am grateful to the many librarians and museum curators for helping with my research at the L.N. Tolstoy State Museum in Moscow, the Manuscript Department of the Russian State Library, the Russian State Archive of Literature and Art, the Berg Collection at the New York Public Library, and the University of Saskatchewan Library.

About the Author

ALEXANDRA POPOFF is the author of the 2010 award-winning *Sophia Tolstoy: A Biography*. She wrote for Russian national newspapers and magazines in Moscow and, as an Alfred Friendly Press Fellow, published articles in *The Philadelphia Inquirer* and its Sunday magazine. She also contributed to *Huffington Post* and *The Boston Globe*. Popoff lives in Canada, where she obtained post-graduate degrees in Russian and English literature.

HILLSBORO PUBLIC LIBRARIES
Hillsboro, OR
Member of Washington County
COOPERATIVE LIBRARY SERVICES